D1376519

PEARL

December 7, 1941

DANIEL ALLEN BUTLER

CASEMATE

Philadelphia & Oxford

For Scott Bragg, the best friend anyone could ask for—or ever hope to have…

Published in the United States of America and Great Britain in 2020 by
CASEMATE PUBLISHERS
1950 Lawrence Road, Havertown, PA 19083, USA
and
The Old Music Hall, 106–108 Cowley Road, Oxford OX4 1JE, UK

Hardback Edition: ISBN 978-1-61200-938-4
Digital Edition: ISBN 978-1-61200-443-3

A CIP record for this book is available from the British Library

Printed and bound in the United States of America by Sheridan

Typeset by Versatile PreMedia Service (P) Ltd

For a complete list of Casemate titles, please contact:

CASEMATE PUBLISHERS (US)
Telephone (610) 853-9131
Fax (610) 853-9146
Email: casemate@casematepublishers.com
www.casematepublishers.com

CASEMATE PUBLISHERS (UK)
Telephone (01865) 241249
Email: casemate-uk@casematepublishers.co.uk
www.casematepublishers.co.uk

Contents

Note to the Reader

Please keep in mind that in this narrative, all times and dates given are local; where necessary for purposes of clarity, the corresponding time and/or date in another locality will be included in parenthesis.

As the nomenclature used by the Japanese in identifying aircraft types is often confusing—it made sense to the Japanese, but can seem over-complicated to Western readers—the aircraft used in the Pearl Harbor attack are primarily identified by their Allied code names—Zero, Kate, Val, etc.—except where another designation is used in a direct quotation.

Also, this narrative follows the traditional structure for Japanese personal names, that is, the first name recorded is the family name, the second is the individual's given name.

Finally, in the context of this narrative, the phrase "the Pacific War" is specifically employed in reference to the collective battles and campaigns fought by the armed forces of the United States and Imperial Japan in the Pacific Ocean between December 1941 and August 1945. It should not be construed as including, either chronologically or geographically, the larger war against Japan.

Introduction

What happened at Pearl Harbor?

What *really* happened at Pearl Harbor?

And how did it all come to pass?

"Pearl Harbor" is one of those incidents in history that almost everyone knows *of*, but hardly anyone seems to know *about*. When someone says, "Pearl Harbor is where Japan attacked the United States and brought America into the Second World War," they are essentially correct, but what do those words actually mean? What took place that December morning in 1941, when the sun rose and the bombs fell, as more than 350 dive bombers, high-level bombers, torpedo planes, and fighters of the Imperial Japanese Navy, did their best to cripple the United States Navy's Pacific Fleet, killing 2,403 American servicemen and civilians, and wounding another 1,178 as they did so? Why did the Japanese attack Pearl Harbor? Was the attack even a military necessity, or could it have been avoided if the Japanese or the Americans—or both—had been willing to talk a little longer? And finally, what were the consequences for both America and Japan?

For the past quarter century, the story of Pearl Harbor has been steadily carved apart, dissected, and presented in ever smaller pieces. Those pieces are increasingly narrow, specialized, technical, or academic, often in an apparent attempt to avoid reaching meaningful conclusions, near to the point where the larger story begins to be obscured. Yet it is that larger story of the Pearl Harbor attack that should compel our attention—especially as it is a story that takes place through the agency of human beings, *because* of the actions and motives of human beings.

Pearl: December 7, 1941 steps away from a narrow, technical, or academic focus, to instead present to someone who may be unfamiliar with the larger story as much of that story as can be included between the covers of a single volume. It may be that for some this canvas is insufficiently detailed, or viewed from the wrong perspective, or doesn't place a particular vignette or incident in sufficient prominence. That may be so—to them. But this is not meant to be an exhaustive history of the Japanese attack itself; any work pretending to be such—if it were even possible to produce such a creature—would need to be several times the length.

Still, in these pages will be found accounts of the actions of many people, and for each story told there are thousands more for which there is no room—or no record. Lieutenant John Finn, who was awarded the Medal of Honor for his actions at Kaneohe Naval Air Station that December morning, once observed, "You gotta understand that there's all kinds of heroes, but they never get a chance to be in a hero's position." That is the underlying premise in *Pearl: December 7, 1941*: because of the limitations of time, space, and, all too often anymore, mortality, one individual is asked to be representative of dozens, sometimes hundreds.

The people presented here, then, are those who—through thought, word, or deed—brought about, were witness to, or took part in a single terrible event, which in turn triggered the most far-flung and bitter war the United States or Japan ever fought. In those thoughts, words, and deeds lies the meaning of Pearl Harbor, for its consequences permanently erased whatever paths into the future the two nations might have taken had there been no war, and replaced them with destinies that seemed unimaginable before the first bomb fell. No one would have believed as the sun rose that December morning that four short years later the United States would have become one of the world's two super-powers; no one could have dreamed that in a few decades Japan would evolve into an economic juggernaut, while at the same time turning its back on seven centuries of military—and militarist—tradition; few people even considered the possibility that one of the most stable international friendships would be forged out of the bitter war the two nations were about to fight. History is often an account of unintended consequences of human actions, yet these were the consequences of Japan's attack on Pearl Harbor, and for those consequences to be explicable, why and how that attack came to be planned and executed—the blunders, moments of genius, and strokes of pure luck, good and bad—needs be set forward clearly and concisely.

And finally, it should be understood from the outset that within these pages are no "untold secrets" or "mysteries revealed," no "smoking guns" or "revelations" of conspiracies or cover-ups. Neither conspiracy theorists nor revisionists seeking to rewrite history to further their agendas—whatever they may be—will find comfort here, for Occam's Razor is still as sharp as ever. No nefarious motives are required to explain how the Japanese' success in their attack on Pearl Harbor came about; an acknowledgment of the fact that those who were making decisions were human, and thus fallible, is more than sufficient. No one is omniscient, errors of commission and omission occur every day, they are part and parcel of the human condition, and that human condition was in play in all of the events and incidents, large and small, in the months and years that preceded—and proceeded to—the terrible morning history now knows simply as "Pearl Harbor." Arrogance, ignorance, prejudice, gullibility, wishful thinking, ambition, over-optimism, fear, and good old human error are all that are required to explain why Imperial Japan and the United States of America blundered into war on the 7th day of December, 1941.

How they did so is the story that follows…

Dawn at Pearl

They had done it!

There it was and there they were.

The panorama that greeted the astonished commander's eyes was stunning. Before him lay an imposing display of seapower, an entire battle fleet, an array of naval firepower the like of which was rarely seen in these times, and would never again be seen after this day.

Raising a pair of high-power binoculars to his eyes, Commander Fuchida Mitsuo of the Imperial Japanese Navy, first swept his gaze across the vast American naval base at Pearl Harbor, then settled on the southeast side of Ford Island, which sat in the middle of the harbor. There he saw what was known as "Battleship Row," a string of moorings where the most powerful warships of the United States Navy's Pacific Fleet tied up when in port. It was a Sunday morning, the battleships of the Pacific Fleet routinely spent weekends in the harbor, and this Sunday was no different.

There were seven of them—Japanese spies had reported eight. Where was the eighth? Ah, there it was, lying in drydock, a sitting duck. But it was Battleship Row that kept drawing back Fuchida's gaze. There, stretched out for almost a mile, lay the core of the American battle fleet: *California* at the west end of the line of warships, then a few hundred yards aft of her, the tanker *Neosho*. Astern of the tanker sat *Oklahoma*; inboard of her, *Maryland*; *West Virginia*, fondly known as *WeeVee*, and *Tennessee* sat behind the first pair of battleships, with *West Virginia* in the outer berth. Then came the repair ship *Vestal*, tied up alongside *Arizona*; 75 feet behind them was *Nevada*. Over in the immense 1010 Drydock was *Pennsylvania*. Arrayed throughout the rest of the harbor were eight heavy and light cruisers, twenty-nine destroyers, four submarines, and scores of minelayers, minesweepers, tenders, tugs, and other fleet auxiliaries.

Yet for all of its latent power, the scene before Fuchida's eyes was one of peace and unpreparedness that almost defied comprehension. It was also baffling, inexplicable—almost an affront to his professionalism. In years to come he would write, "I have seen all German ships assembled in Kiel Harbor. I have also seen the

French battleships in Brest. And finally I have often seen our own warships in review before the Emperor, but never, even in deepest peace, have I seen ships anchored less than 500 to a thousand yards from one another... Had these Americans never heard of Port Arthur?"[1]

Fuchida, leading more than 350 bombers, dive bombers, torpedo bombers, and fighters, had come to Pearl Harbor to destroy that fleet.

The strike force wasn't powerful enough to sink or cripple all of the warships in the harbor that morning, but it was the battleships that mattered most. Without them, and even with its aircraft carrier force intact, it would be months, even years before the US Navy would dare challenge the might of its Imperial Japanese counterpart. After eight months of meticulous planning, six weeks of relentless training, six days at sea, and two hours in the air, Fuchida had his aircraft and aircrews in the right place at the right moment to strike a decisive blow that would determine the future of the Japanese Empire. Looking around for American fighter planes and seeing none, noting a complete absence of any anti-aircraft fire coming from the warships below, Fuchida was suddenly certain that the attack force had achieved complete surprise over the Americans. He nodded to his wireless operator, who began tapping out a signal to the Japanese fleet 200 miles to the north.

"*To-ra! To-ra! To-ra!*"

CHAPTER I

The Rising Sun

"We interrupt this broadcast to bring you this important bulletin from the United Press. Flash! Washington. The White House announces Japanese attack on Pearl Harbor."[1]

On December 7, 1941, the sun rose and the bombs fell, as the Empire of the Rising Sun and the great sleeping giant, the United States of America, collided at the junction of the roads to war each had been traveling for the past five years. For one, the path had been short and direct, bestrode with determination and self-assurance; for the other, the journey was meandering, full of false starts and misdirections. When the first bomb exploded at Pearl Harbor at 7:55 AM, the war that began would, for both Japan and the United States, be the defining event of their histories. The conflict would remake the destinies of both nations, and, by its end, reshape the world into something of which neither nation, nor their governments, nor their people, could have conceived that December morning.

* * *

Though no historical event is truly inevitable, even the most astute observer of the early 1940s, watching the drama unfolding in China and the western Pacific Ocean, could have been excused for concluding that Japan and America must find themselves in a confrontation that could only end in blood and thunder. It would be a war born more out of a handful of misunderstandings, some willful, others not, than from deliberate acts of malice, but history is replete with examples of wars spawned in such a manner. The attack on Pearl Harbor was the misbegotten child of arrogance, American as well as Japanese, the arrogance of the leaders of two peoples who were unshakably convinced of the rightness—and righteousness—of the policies they conceived and carried out in the name of the nations for which they were responsible. It was the arrogance of men who on one hand were prepared, even eager, to go to war, and on the other were willing to accept war, however reluctantly, if it came, both all the while utterly convinced that their opponents were bluffing and would ultimately back away from the abyss of conflict if confronted with sufficient threats and bluster.

Japan and America had much in common. They were relatively young nations, in the sense that the United States came into existence little more than 150 years before the Pearl Harbor attack, while Japan had finally thrown off its feudal trappings only in the mid-19th century, ending two millennia of willful isolation. Likewise both had emerged onto the global stage as world powers fairly recently, and within a few years of each other, the United States in 1898, Japan in 1905. They were nations of intelligent and hard-working, proud and determined people, industrious and ingenious, yet also gifted artistically. Both peoples believed, albeit for differing reasons, that they held a special place in human affairs, in some way set apart from and above the rest of the community of nations.

Yet, despite such superficial similarities, there were deep and profound differences, political, social, economic, and military, between the Empire of Japan and the United States of America. To most Americans, Winston Churchill's characterization of the Soviet Union as "a riddle wrapped in a mystery inside an enigma" would have been equally apt if it were applied to *Dai Nippon*. Which meant, of course, that when the Japanese struck Pearl Harbor, the attack came as an even greater surprise, if that were possible, to the American people than it was to the United States Navy and Army. Knowing little to nothing of Imperial Japan and its people, most Americans never imagined that the Japanese possessed in full measure the means, audacity, and will to undertake such a bold action. Worse, though, was the blunt fact that, in the years before the attack, America's politicians and diplomats never had a real grasp of how Japan's history and the character of its people had, in a sense, conspired to convince the Imperial Government, along with the Imperial Army and Navy, that as the Japanese Empire grew, it was edging toward economic strangulation, to the point where by 1940 Japan stood at the brink of national catastrophe. Forcible expansion came to be seen as the only way to ensure that the Empire and its people would survive—even at the risk of provoking a war with the United States.[2]

Ironically, it had been the United States Navy, in the form of the famous "black ships" commanded by Commodore Matthew Perry, that in 1854 essentially dragged Japan kicking and screaming out of 16th-century feudalism and into the modern world. The unannounced, unexpected appearance of Perry's squadron in Edo Bay shook Japan to its core, as the social, political, and military hierarchies all recognized how the Empire's two and one-half centuries of isolation had left it backward and weak, ripe for the sort of exploitation the Western powers were then carrying out in China.

That isolation had seemed like a good idea at the time. Europeans and Japanese first became aware of each other at the end of the 15th century, as Dutch and Portuguese explorers pushed further and further east out of the Indian Ocean and into the Pacific. The Dutch came to trade, the Portuguese to trade and proselytize; both would encounter only limited success, as linguistic barriers and profound cultural differences interfered with efficient trading, and the Japanese had no patience for strange new religions.

In the end, the Europeans found the Japanese—and Japan—near-incomprehensible, so radically different were they from the peoples and lands with whom the Dutch and Portuguese were accustomed to trading. For their part, the Japanese decided that the Europeans were vulgar and boorish: with their outlandish clothing, crude manners, vulgar customs, and odd religious practices, they did indeed warrant description as *gaijin*, that uniquely Japanese noun that consigns all foreigners to the status of barbarians. An informal prohibition came into being, barring any contact between Japanese and Europeans anywhere save on Dejima Island, in Nagasaki Bay, where a single Dutch trading mission was allowed to reside.

This closure of Japan to foreigners—most especially Europeans—was formalized by an edict issued by the *shōgun* Tokugawa Iemitsu in 1633. The policy was known as *Sakoku* or the "Closed Country," but in reality was an act of total seclusion: not only were non-Japanese banned from entering Japan save for the trading missions in Satsuma and Tsushima, but the Japanese themselves were forbidden to leave their homeland, under penalty of death if they were caught. Should they succeed and attempt to return, the penalty was also death. *Sakoku* would remain in force until the dissolution of the shogunate in 1867.[3]

The shogunate closely paralleled a phenomenon that had frequently arisen in feudal Europe, that of "the power behind the throne," where a lesser noble held the true authority in the realm while the reigning monarch was little more than a puppet or figurehead, but unlike the Europeans, for whom the careers of such people were transitory and opportunistic, the Japanese had institutionalized and formalized the arrangement. Imperial authority and prerogatives had long since been eroded by generations of ambitious *daimyō*—semi-autonomous regional warlords—until the emperor's active role in the affairs of the Empire was reduced to little more than a ceremonial fiction. In his stead, the *shōgun*, or supreme warlord, whose power stopped just short of that of a military dictator, ruled Japan while the emperor reigned, a situation which had obtained for nearly 400 years when the first Europeans arrived in Japan. The title of *shōgun* was nominally hereditary, but he exercised his authority more through *force majeure* than by legitimacy, and maintaining a hold on the shogunate depended as much on the strength of the *shōgun*'s personal powerbase as on a line of succession. The strength of the Tokugawa clan was such that, when Commodore Perry's quartet of "black ships" appeared in Edo Bay (as Tokyo Bay was then known) on the afternoon of July 8, 1853, the office of *shōgun* had passed through 13 heirs in direct descent from the first Tokugawa *shōgun*, Tokugawa Ieyasu, to its current holder, Tokugawa Ieoshi. Yet the arrival of those ships sounded the death knell for the shogunate, and marked the beginning of 13 years of political and military upheaval the like of which Japan had never before known.

The Dutch trading mission in Nagasaki Bay had served as Japan's "window on the West," but the Japanese failed to comprehend exactly what they had been seeing through it. They watched as the Western powers, particularly Great Britain, France, and the United States, imposed a succession of inequitable treaties on China, carving out spheres of influence, trade enclaves, and demanding extralegal status for their citizens who would come to reside in China, steadily chipping away at China's sovereignty. The Chinese, in a fit of smug, self-righteous superiority, had imposed their own state of isolation 200 years before the Japanese *Sakoku,* but rather than protect China from the encroachments of the "foreign devils," it ultimately left the country technologically backward, militarily weak, and ripe for exploitation against which it could not defend itself.

Now, apparently, it was Japan's turn, as within days of his arrival in Edo, Perry presented to the *shōgun* a formal demand from the United States' government for just such a treaty. A trade agreement would eventually be concluded with the Americans (1857) quickly followed by similar treaties with the British, French, Dutch, and Russians, but in the meantime, the emperor, the *shōgun*, their advisors, and the more powerful of the *daimyō* disagreed ferociously about how best to contain and control these *gaijin* encroachments. The emperor's advisors saw the bickering among the *daimyo* and their resultant impotence, along with that of the *shōgun*, as an opportunity to restore the imperial power and prerogatives so long eroded by the warlords; acting in the emperor's name, they began to methodically undermine the ancient feudal order to the point of collapse. By the time the dust had settled, Japan had been riven socially and politically from top to bottom, as the Tokugawa shogunate fell in 1867, and the Meiji Restoration, which returned supreme political power to the emperor and his advisors, was imposed a few months later; the offices and authority of the *daimyō* were abolished, and the *Boshin* Civil War of 1868–69 ensured the permanence of the restoration.

The Meiji Restoration took its name from Emperor Meiji, who, as Crown Prince Mutsohito, took the imperial throne upon the death of Emperor Komeio in 1867. "Meiji," meaning "enlightened rule," was the name Mutsohito gave to his reign, and the name by which he would be known after his death: in Japan it became synonymous with the transformation that swept across Japan in the space of barely more than a generation. Ironically, he took little interest in the "restoration" of imperial power being carried out in his name—the blunt truth was that his role was almost entirely passive, doing little more than giving tacit approval to the transformation of Japan being accomplished in his name. Nonetheless, Mutsohito, as Emperor Meiji, became the symbol to both East and West of the emergence of "modern Japan."

Before the 1880s had drawn to a close, *Dai Nippon*—literally "Great Japan"—had acquired a written constitution and a bicameral legislature (where the House of Representatives, or Diet, was elected through limited male suffrage, while the House of Peers was appointed by the emperor), giving the Empire the superficial appearance of a modern parliamentary democracy, though the Diet possessed little real power. With the *daimyōs'* domains reorganized as prefectures, after a handful of rebellions and a civil war, most of the warlords passively accepted posts as imperial governors, their *samurai* retainers transforming themselves into a class of hereditary bureaucrats.

That bureaucracy, which was surprisingly efficient, a steadily expanding railroad network—and with the latter a burgeoning industrial base—along with the adoption of European clothing, manners, and architecture, completed Japan's accumulation of the physical trappings of 19th-century Western culture and technology. Given the speed and apparent ease with which Japan adopted and adapted to the ways of the West, coupled with the Japanese willingness to draw more-or-less equally on British, French, German, Russian, and American advice and experience when and as needed, the Western world soon developed a measure of admiration and respect for Japan that they had never accorded China.

Just as significant as any political or social changes it undertook, the Imperial Government, now centered in Tokyo, as Edo was renamed, set about creating a standing army and a vastly enlarged, modern navy, closely following European examples for organizing, training, and equipping both. Styled as the Imperial Army and Imperial Navy, they were directly subordinate to the emperor, through the Army and Navy Ministers: military policies and strategies were not subject to restriction or restraint by the Japanese Diet; the official national policy became *"Fukoku Musen"*—"Rich country, strong army." Much as had happened in Germany a quarter-century earlier, the material demands of Japan's railroads created an expanding steel industry that was readily turned to munitions production and so a robust arms industry came into being. By 1890, the transformation was complete, and *Dai Nippon* was to all appearances very much a true imperial—and potentially imperialist—power. The question now was whether or not Japan would choose to act like one.

The answer came in 1894, when China and Japan went to war for dominion over the kingdom of Korea. The Hermit Kingdom, as it was known, had long been a client state of China, and for centuries was the traditional staging point for Chinese invasions of the Home Islands of *Dai Nippon*: this gave the Japanese a strategic incentive for wresting the peninsula away from the Chinese. Equally important, Japan, lacking almost all the raw materials required by modern industry, save for coal alone, coveted Korea's iron deposits. After a decade of political maneuvering, agitation, and provocation in Korea, including assassinations and attempted coups in Seoul by both Chinese and Japanese puppets, on August 1, 1894, China declared war on Japan.

European military experts were near-unanimous in their belief that the war would end swiftly in a crushing Chinese victory. Much as had Japan, China spent most of the 1880s modernizing her army and navy: on paper, at least, the Chinese navy was the most powerful fleet in the Far East, while China's army boasted a massive superiority in manpower. But the Japanese swiftly moved into Korea, where the

Imperial Army, better organized, trained, and equipped than its Chinese counterpart, won a string of victories that drove the Chinese out of the peninsula. Meanwhile, the Chinese navy, which had been crippled by the corruption and inefficiency that riddled the Chinese bureaucracy, was decisively defeated by the theoretically less-powerful Japanese fleet. This allowed the Japanese to invade Manchuria and occupy the islands and headlands in the western reaches of the Yellow Sea that commanded the approaches to Beijing. By March 1895, the Chinese had no choice but to sue for peace.

The Treaty of Shimonoseki established beyond question that Japan had become an imperialist power. China agreed to pay an indemnity of over 16 million pounds (in weight!) of silver, renounced any claims to future influence in Korea, essentially leaving the peninsula kingdom to the future tender mercies of the Japanese, and ceded the island of Formosa, several smaller but strategic islands, and the Liaodong Peninsula to Japan. By the time the dust settled and the ink was dry, Japan had become the dominant military and political power in the Far East.

Ten years later, Japan served notice that she was not merely an Asian power, but a world power. Barely had the ink dried on the Treaty of Shimonoseki than the Germans, French, and Russians began bullying the Japanese to withdraw from the Liaodong Peninsula, fearing the possibility of all access by sea to Beijing, where they had large national legations, being closed by the Japanese navy. The Russians were especially heavy-handed, having designs of their own on the peninsula, along with the rest of Manchuria. The Japanese eventually acquiesced and abandoned Liaodong, as they felt that, should push come to shove, Japan lacked the strength to stave off the combined naval and military forces the Europeans could bring to bear. Within months of the Japanese withdrawal, the Russians struck a deal with the Chinese and occupied the Liaodong Peninsula, and in 1897 began constructing the fortress of Port Arthur, which became the naval base for Russia's Pacific Fleet.

But if the foothold in mainland China was lost, Japan's grip on Korea grew even tighter—and increasingly repressive. Anti-Japanese uprisings were ruthlessly crushed, and assassinations—including members of the Korean ruling family—continued to be commonplace. The Tsar's government saw an opportunity and, working vigorously to draw Korea into the Russian sphere of influence, did their best to stir the pot when- and wherever possible, encouraging the Korean people's resentment of the Japanese presence in their land. In 1901, at the height of China's Boxer Rebellion, 100,000 Russian troops moved in to occupy Manchuria, which became a Russian province in all but name, and the Japanese government feared that an outright annexation of Korea would be next. Efforts made in 1903 to negotiate an accommodation between Tokyo and Moscow failed, and by the end of the year both the tsar and the emperor had decided that the issue would only be settled by war.

Japan moved first and struck first. A declaration of war was presented to the Russians in Moscow on February 8, 1904, but three hours prior to the document landing on the desk of Vladimir Lamsdorf, Russia's foreign minister, the Japanese navy launched a surprise attack that crippled the Russian fleet at Port Arthur. To the consternation of the European powers, the Japanese proved to be unstoppable, winning every confrontation with the Russians on land and sea. Beginning with the siege of Port Arthur, then followed by fearsome pitched battles at Sandepu, the Yalu River, and Mukden, the Japanese army methodically drove the Russians out of Korea and southern Manchuria by March 1905.

But it would be two naval battles that essentially decided the outcome of the war. The first was the Battle of the Yellow Sea, on August 19, 1904, when the Russian Far East Fleet attempted to break out into open water, only to be badly battered and forced to retreat back into Port Arthur; it would never sail again. The second, which sealed the fate of Russian ambition in the Far East, was the Battle of Tsushima. Named for the Tsushima Strait, the waters that separate Japan and Korea where the battle was fought, it was the defining event of the Imperial Japanese Navy, not only for its traditions, but also for its tactical thinking and strategic philosophies.

Hoping to achieve an overwhelming numerical superiority against the Japanese navy, the tsar ordered the bulk of Russia's Baltic Fleet—eight battleships, three coast-defense ships, eight cruisers, and eleven destroyers—on an 18,000-mile odyssey through European waters, down the coast of Africa, around Cape Horn and across the Indian Ocean to the Yellow Sea, where it was to join the Far East Fleet in destroying the Japanese navy. It was a forlorn hope, for the fleet based at Port Arthur had already ceased to be an effective fighting force, and Port Arthur itself would fall to the Japanese on January 2, 1905, fully three months before the Baltic Fleet would arrive.

With Port Arthur denied to it, the Russian Baltic squadron, now styled the Second Pacific Squadron, had no place to go but Vladivostok, Russia's only remaining Pacific port. The long journey from the Baltic Sea had left Russian ships worn out, their officers and men demoralized—none more so than the fleet's commanding officer, Admiral Zinovy Rozhestvensky. By nature hot-tempered and disinclined to take his subordinates into his confidence, Rozhestvensky had little faith in the initial plan to send the Baltic Fleet to Port Arthur. As the voyage to the Far East progressed, he grew increasingly pessimistic, and try as he might to conceal his misgivings, his doubts soon spread through his fleet.

The Japanese, on the other hand, were, after their run of victories over the Russians, supremely confident, even in the face of the enemy's numerical superiority. Their fleet commander, Admiral Togo Heihachiro, drilled his crews relentlessly in gunnery and ship-handling, and was confident of their ability to outshoot and outmaneuver their enemy. Moreover, Togo was supplied with excellent intelligence by his scouting forces—torpedo boats, destroyers, and auxiliary cruisers that were shadowing the Second Pacific Squadron. Through the use of the newfangled wireless, these units were able to advise Togo that Rozhestvensky was steering a course for the Tsushima Strait, where the Japanese duly met the Russians on May 27, 1905.

Togo's skillful deployment of his fleet negated the enemy's numerical advantage as the Japanese were able to position their fleet so that they would "cross the T" of the Russian fleet, that is, steam directly across the course of the Second Pacific Squadron, which had the effect of halving the number of guns the Russian ships could bring to bear. In the seven-hour gunnery duel which ensued, the Russian fleet was for all practical purposes annihilated: all eight battleships and the three coast-defense ships were sunk or scuttled, while seven of the eight cruisers and nine of the eleven destroyers were either sunk, scuttled, or interned in neutral ports; with the sunken ships went over 5,000 crewmen. Japanese losses totaled three torpedo boats and 116 men. The tsar's government had no choice but to sue for peace.

The Treaty of Portsmouth, signed on September 5, 1905, brought the war to an end. The President of the United States, Theodore Roosevelt, acted as the primary mediator in the negotiations between Japan and Russia, and was presented with a Nobel Peace Prize for his efforts, the first of only two American presidents to legitimately earn the award. The treaty was hailed as a model of moderation, lacking as it did any of the sort of punitive provisions which at the time were typical of such settlements. Russia conceded Korea and Manchuria to be within Japan's sphere of influence, giving Tokyo effective control of both, and ceded Port Arthur to the Japanese as well—Japan would immediately occupy Korea and formally annex the country in 1910. Yet no Russian territory was lost, however, and Roosevelt was able to persuade the Japanese to accept Russia's refusal to pay reparations, a point on which the tsar was adamant in order to preserve as much Russian prestige as possible. (That it was a European power which was "saving face" was a bit of irony not lost on the peoples and governments of Asia.)

Though the emperor's delegation agreed to it, conceding the question of reparations was profoundly unpopular with the Japanese, for the price of victory in human terms had been high. While the naval battles had been relatively bloodless—the Imperial Navy suffered fewer than 500 fatalities—almost 86,000 of the emperor's soldiers had been killed in battle, died of wounds, or succumbed to disease in the 18 month-long war—one out of every six Japanese soldiers sent out to fight the Russians. That there would be no recompense for the loss of husbands, fathers, brothers, sons, was both painful and humiliating for the Japanese; it was not long before the suspicion began to grow, in the corridors of government as well as among the people of Japan's cities, villages, and countryside, that Roosevelt had deliberately favored Russia at Japan's expense, sparing the European power from having to formally capitulate to an Asian—and by implication, inferior—people. The usual note of wariness, even suspicion, that typified any dealings with the *gaijin* became more marked in Japan's diplomatic relations with the Western powers.

At the same time that Japan's victory over Russia startled the Great Powers of Europe, as well as the United States, it worked a subtle change in the perception of the Japanese as to their place in the world order, especially in that Japan was now unquestionably the dominant military and naval power in the Far East. Inherent in the Japanese belief that they, as a people, were descendants of a goddess was the assumption that they were superior to all other peoples and races. While they could not pretend that the victories over the Russians had come easily, or without high cost, that they had not lost a single battle seemed proof that the Japanese naturally possessed superior fighting skills, a race, as it were, of natural warriors.

This idea quickly became an article of faith with the Japanese, psychologically, morally, and spiritually: they had defeated the Russians not merely through superior training, discipline, and organization, but because the Japanese soldier or sailor was an inherently superior fighting man. They were encouraged in this belief by the Imperial Government itself, which was, of course, dominated by the military. Exploiting a seemingly minor flaw in the Meiji Constitution, the senior officers of the Imperial Army and Navy discovered that they could block the formation of a new government in the Diet—or bring down a sitting government—simply by refusing to accept the office of Minister of War: the constitution required the prime minister to resign should he be unable to fill *all* open posts in his cabinet. By effectively giving the army and navy the power to determine who would hold office, this placed the creation and execution of Japan's national policies, foreign and domestic, in the hands of those senior officers, and put paid to any notions that Japanese parliamentarians may have entertained in regard to civilian control of the military. By the turn of the century the army and navy had formed their own general staffs; both chiefs of staff, subordinate only to the emperor, were not accountable in any way to the Ministry of War.

Rarely in the last few centuries, then, have there been nations as rampantly militaristic as was the Empire of Japan from the end of the 19th century to the middle of the 20th, as every aspect of Japanese society became in some way subordinated to the demands and expectations of the army and navy. It was a national mindset that did not exist prior to 1868, but was instead one of the unexpected social consequences that followed the political upheaval of the Meiji Restoration. Officers of all ranks in the newly created Imperial Army and Navy were, understandably, among those most fervent in their support of the new imperial order, and vigorously promoted the "Rich country, strong army" ideal by appealing to the innate patriotism of the Japanese commoners.

Indoctrination began while children were still in elementary school: the standard reading primer opened with the words "Advance, advance, soldiers advance!" Military service was extolled with a jingoism that would have made Rudyard Kipling blush: duty, especially military duty, to the emperor and the Empire was the highest calling to which any Japanese could aspire, while congratulations rather than condolences would be offered by their neighbors to families of soldiers and sailors killed in battle. An 8th-century poem frequently invoked to imbue young men with the proper sense of self-sacrifice became the militarists' catechism:

> We shall die in the sea
> We shall die in the mountains
> In whatever way
> We shall die beside the Emperor
> We shall never look back.

Given that most of the senior officers of the new army and navy had once been *samurai* or the descendants of *samurai*, the imperial government chose to co-opt—or, more precisely, hijack—an icon of the Tokugawa shogunate in order to give weight and authority to their patriotic appeals: their own *samurai* warrior class. In doing so, they romanticized—and distorted—the *samurai* as liberally as centuries of Western chroniclers and myth-makers have done to the medieval European knights and their supposed code of chivalry. They presented the *samurai* as noble, self-effacing, righteous warriors charged with defending their liege-lords with their lives while protecting defenseless peasants from predatory bandits and rogue warlords, yet the truth was they had served those very warlords, enforcing their masters' law and will with the edge of a sword. The *samurai* had been the only class in Japanese society permitted to carry weapons, but with the abolition of the *daimyōs* and their private armies of *samurai*, that distinction vanished. Now service in the imperial armed forces was being touted as admission into a new incarnation of the warrior caste.

It was heady medicine indeed, particularly in the light of the succession of defeats the Japanese army and navy inflicted on their Russian counterparts and the affirmation of the natural superiority of Japanese soldiers and sailors over not only their Asian counterparts, but those of the Western powers also. It was a dangerous delusion, for it encouraged military adventurism, and if it were to prove false, the consequences for *Dai Nippon* could prove disastrous. British naval historian Geoffrey Regan, analyzing the consequences of Japan's victory, summed up the situation succinctly when he said that Tsushima "… created a legend that was to haunt Japan's leaders for forty years… It had all been too easy. Looking at Togo's victory over one of the world's great powers convinced some Japanese military men that with more ships, and bigger and better ones, similar victories could be won throughout the Pacific." In short, the Japanese victory in 1905 set the stage for the confrontation with the United States almost four decades hence.[4]

Tsushima also had the effect of giving an immutable shape to the strategic thinking of the Imperial Navy. As often happens in military history, what had proven to be *a* successful strategy became *the* successful strategy: Tsushima, and the events leading up to the battle, had been the decisive confrontation of the war, as the near-annihilation of the Second Pacific Squadron had compelled the Russians to seek peace. Thus the strategic doctrine of the Decisive Battle became the strategic dogma of the Imperial Navy. In any future war an enemy's strength would be whittled down in a succession of small-scale actions until such time as the enemy battle fleet could be lured into a false position, where it would be crushed in the Decisive Battle by superior Japanese ships manned by superior Japanese sailors. Not recognizing that its very inflexibility rendered the concept of the Decisive Battle a strategic dead end, the institutional intellect of the Imperial Navy came to be solely devoted to formulating the means and methods by which a Decisive Battle could be brought about.

Japan would go to war again in 1914, though the Great War would offer no opportunities for a Decisive Battle in the Far East. Actually in this instance the Japanese had no interest in a confrontation of that sort, as their intent was focused on other objectives. Ostensibly Japan joined the Allies in response to the Anglo-Japanese Treaty of 1902, where Japan pledged to guard Great Britain's colonial interests in the Far East in the event of Britain going to war with Imperial Germany. In practice, this presented the Japanese military with an unprecedented opportunity to significantly expand the empire with minimal risk. Germany's High Seas Fleet was bottled up in the European waters of the North Sea by the Royal Navy, unable to support the German East Asia Squadron based at the fortress of Tsingtao (now styled Qingdao) in China; the squadron itself was scattered across the western Pacific when the war erupted and soon fled eastward to the coast of South America, reducing Germany's naval presence in the Far East to a few cruisers and the occasional commerce raider.

This weakness allowed the Japanese to seize virtually unopposed the German colonial territories in the Marianas, Marshall, Caroline, and Palau Islands; territories in Shandong Province, leased from China by Germany in 1897, were occupied less than a month after the war began. In November 1914, Tsingtao fell to a combined Anglo-Japanese land and naval force after a three-month siege; the city was immediately occupied by the Japanese army. Abruptly Japan found itself once again in the position created by the Treaty of Shimonoseki two decades earlier: possession of Shandong Province and the Liaodong Peninsula, together with the annexation of Korea, in essence turned the Yellow Sea into a Japanese lake and gave Japan the power to deny access by sea to and from Beijing.

Feeling their oats, the Japanese saw an opportunity to exercise an economic domination of the Chinese that would reduce China to little more than a glorified puppet state. On January 18, 1915, an ultimatum that became known as "The Twenty-one Demands" was presented to the government of the new—and still somewhat shaky—Republic of China. (Two thousand years of imperial rule in China had been ended by the Wuchang Uprising in October 1911, which overthrew the monarchy and established a nominal republic.) In short, the Demands required China to accept in perpetuity all of Japan's territorial acquisitions and expansions in mainland Asia, cede the whole of Manchuria to Tokyo, severely curtail trade with any of the Western powers, and hand control of China's financial institutions and police forces to Japanese officials.

Despite Japanese insistence that the Demands be kept secret until such time as China responded to them, the Chinese quickly informed the British and American governments of their contents, with the result that both London and Washington DC brought heavy diplomatic pressure to bear on Tokyo in an effort to persuade the Japanese to withdraw—or at least moderate—the most intrusive provisions of the ultimatum. The threat of economic retaliation by the United States, via embargoes, as well as boycotts of and punitive tariffs on imports of Japanese-manufactured goods, compelled Tokyo to back down: already Japan's industries were so dependent on American imports of raw materials that having them curtailed or even cut off would have a devastating effect on the island nation's economy. So a modified set of "demands," now numbering just 13, was submitted to Beijing instead. The Chinese accepted them, as they amounted to little more than minor adjustments to the status quo, but the consequences for future relations between Japan and America were far from trivial. A lingering resentment of the United States among the Japanese people and government alike that had emerged in the aftermath of the Treaty of Portsmouth now began to turn into antagonism and the belief that the Americans, who possessed their own colonial "empire" in the western Pacific, had adopted a deliberate policy of keeping Japan permanently consigned to the status of a second-rank power.

That such a policy existed was given further credence by the Washington Naval Conference, held in Washington DC in late 1921 and early 1922. Ostensibly it was a joint diplomatic effort on the part of Great Britain and the United States to avoid a post-Great War repeat of an economically crippling naval race of the sort that had plagued Britain and Germany in the decade prior to 1914. The stated purpose of the conference was to produce a treaty that would initiate a 10-year "naval holiday" during which no new capital ships—battleships and battlecruisers—would be built, while limiting the size, armament, and numbers of other classes of warships. Along with Britain and America, Japan, France, and Italy would take part.

Problems arose when specific ratios of ship types were suggested for the various navies, specifically a ratio of 5:5:3 for battleships—still the ultimate arbiter of naval power—for the US Navy, the Royal Navy, and the Imperial Navy. For every five battleships the Americans and British each possessed under the proposed treaty, the Japanese would be allowed to have three. Those supporting this proposal—namely the Americans and the British—argued that the US Navy and the Royal Navy needed more battleships because both fleets had simultaneous strategic commitments in the Atlantic and Pacific Oceans, while the Japanese had only one ocean to defend, the Pacific. To the Imperial Navy, though, this seemed to be nothing short of a deliberate attempt to institutionalize the numerical inferiority of the Imperial Navy. Given that any further Japanese expansion in the Pacific would run headlong into American or British possessions—or both, under the wrong circumstances—it seemed highly plausible to the Imperial Navy's negotiators in Washington and the government in Tokyo that the US Navy and the Royal Navy could—and would—readily make common cause against Japan, and bring a decisive numerical superiority to bear against the Imperial Navy.

Added fuel for the flames of speculation came when Tokyo learned that officials in Washington had informed their counterparts in London that the United States would be signatory to no treaty whatsoever unless the Anglo-Japanese Alliance was dissolved. While in many ways doing so was little more than a symbolic gesture on the part of Great Britain, the alliance having served its purpose but then been rendered obsolete by the end of the Great War, its formal renunciation was still perceived as further proof of Anglo-American collusion in opposing Japanese ambitions in the Pacific. Ultimately, Japan signed the Washington Naval Treaty, but no sooner was it ratified than the Imperial Navy began a massive modernization program, intended to make Japanese warships ton-for-ton more effective fighting units than their American or British counterparts, while at the same time exploring ways of circumventing the more restrictive provisions of the treaty.

Not every Japanese naval officer believed the Washington Treaty to be a bad idea, though. Yamamoto Isoroku, who at the time of the conference was a mere commander, but who had already spent two years as a student at Harvard University and had come to know America and Americans well, later opined that the treaty had actually worked in Japan's favor: Japanese industry could never match the production capabilities of American factories and shipyards, so that, as he saw it, the real limitations imposed by the treaty were borne by the British and Americans. "Anyone who has seen the auto factories in Detroit and the oil-fields in Texas," he asserted, "knows that Japan lacks the power for a naval race with America... The ratio works very well for Japan—it is a treaty to restrict the other parties."[5]

Despite the apparent blow to national prestige, the treaty, particularly the "Naval Holiday," was in fact a blessing in disguise for Japan: it was ratified just in time to save the national economy from total collapse. During the Great War, the Japanese economy hummed right along, as Japan's industries added their weight to the Allied war effort by supplying munitions as well as civilian goods that the other Allies weren't producing. When the war ended, however, factories and foundries in America and Britain went back to their pre-war production lines and the demand for Japanese output plummeted. Being a resource-poor island nation, Japan was utterly dependent on foreign trade to be able to purchase the raw materials her industries needed; to keep their doors open and their own production lines moving, business and industries turned to securing increasingly large loans from banks both domestic and foreign. There was little economic growth and the banking system wasn't particularly stable; some observers characterized the nation as being in a state of "chronic depression."

Then Mother Nature sucker-punched Japan with the Great Kanto Earthquake on September 1, 1923. The most powerful recorded seismic event in Japan up to that time, the quake shook the entire main island of Honshu. Its epicenter was 25 miles southwest of Tokyo and it devastated the capital city. The quake and its aftershocks, together with tsunami and widespread fires, took the lives of nearly 143,000 Japanese and at the same time laid waste to vast swaths of the Kanto Plain, the economic heart of Japan. The total cost of the destruction was estimated to be four times greater than Japan's national budget in 1923. Drastic emergency action by the government made a fairly swift recovery possible, but four years later, when the bill for that emergency aid came due, the resulting financial crisis, triggered by rumors of a government default on bonds issued following the Great Kanto Earthquake, led to the collapse of most of Japan's smaller banks and the subordination of the remaining large national banks to the four great *zaibatsu*.

The *zaibatsu* were family-controlled vertical monopolies, and as such were neither new nor uniquely Japanese. What set them apart from, say, the Krupp or the du Pont families, however, was that they each included a wholly owned banking subsidiary. In 1927 this gave the four largest *zaibatsu*, Mitsubishi, Sumitomo, Yasuda and Mitsui, an ascendency over the rest of the banking industry, allowing them unprecedented influence over the nation's economic policies, which they would, of course, manipulate to their advantage whenever possible. But it was not the economic clout of the *zaibatsu* that further drove Japan down the road to war. That was accomplished by the interlocking political and military interests they advanced as well. Mitsubishi was the perfect example: not only was the Mitsubishi Bank a wholly-owned subsidiary, the parent company's heavy industries division supplied warships for the Imperial Navy, while the *Rikken Minseito*, or Constitutional Democratic Party, one of the two largest political parties in the Japanese legislature, was universally regarded as Mitsubishi's political arm, advancing the navy's policies and programs in the Diet. Mitsui was similarly tied to the Imperial Army and the *Rikken Seiyukai* (Constitutional Association of Political Friendship), Japan's other major political party in the 1920s and 1930s. Sumitomo and Yasuda followed suit, though without being so blatantly aligned politically; the sum of the situation was that what was good for the army or navy was good for the *zaibatsu* and vice-versa—and supposedly it was all good for Japan. Naturally, this arrangement only accelerated the pace at which Japanese society was being militarized.

It was economics that finally forced Japan into—or provided the pretext for, depending on the perspective taken—the international adventurism which was the prologue for the War in the Pacific. By 1931 the Japanese Empire proper was the home islands, the Kurile and Ryukyu islands, and the Nanpo Shoto chain (which included Iwo Jima); Formosa was a dependency, an Imperial possession not formally integrated into the Empire; the southern half of the disputed island of Sakhalin, which the Japanese called Karafuto, annexed after the Russo-Japanese

War in 1905; Korea, forcibly annexed in 1910; and the former German Pacific possessions, collectively known as the Mandates, awarded to Japan in the general peace settlement at Versailles. In China, Japan held leases which granted outright ownership in all but name of Tsingtao and the Kwantung Peninsula. It was a sphere of influence and power far larger than Japan had ever before possessed, but it was not enough for a nation whose population had doubled in the last 50 years, that found it necessary to import almost a fifth of the food needed to feed its people, and had to import all but the tiniest fraction of the oil, iron ore, rubber, copper, phosphate, lead, aluminum, and other modern raw materials necessary to sustain the industries which kept those people employed. All of those materials lay geographically near at hand but nonetheless outside Japanese control; the solution was obvious—it was also potentially explosive.

It was in the resource-rich Chinese province of Manchuria, where Japan's interests had supplanted Russia's after the Russo-Japanese War, that the Japanese made their first openly aggressive acquisition, without even the fig leaf of a genuine diplomatic pretext. On September 20, 1931, the Kwantung Army—which had a strength of barely 30,000 men despite its rather grandiose title—swiftly moved up the length of the South Manchurian Railway, effectively occupying the southern half of the province in six days. (China's Kuomintang government, locked in a death-struggle with the Chinese Communists and quasi-independent local warlords, lacked the strength to defend the province.) The invasion was actually an act of massive insubordination engineered by a pair of overly ambitious ultra-nationalistic colonels, carried out against the express orders of both the government and Imperial General Headquarters, which had heard rumors that just such an escapade was being planned.

Once the invasion was an accomplished fact, however, the Imperial General Headquarters could endorse the action or else suffer a massive loss of face, not only in Japan but throughout Asia: the decision was made to reinforce the Kwantung Army to complete the occupation of the rest of Manchuria. The civilian government of Prime Minister Reijiro Wakatsuki was unable to bring the Army to heel, and so fell on December 13, 1931. In the long view, that would prove to be a pivotal date in Japan's progress down the road to war, as it marked the beginning of the end of genuine civilian government in Japan: despite adhering to the parliamentary forms required by the Meiji Constitution, from this day forward more and more of the governance of the Empire would be in the hands of the army and navy militarists.

Perhaps not surprisingly, the invasion of Manchuria and the subsequent creation of the puppet state of Manchuko (the ancient Chinese name for the province) didn't provoke the sort of international condemnation that might have been expected. The industrialized nations of the West were being wracked socially and economically by the Great Depression, now in its third year, and domestic problems rather than foreign issues dominated their governments' attention and agendas; they had little interest in vigorous—and expensive—reactions to events on what was figuratively and literally the other side of the world. The League of Nations did form a commission to investigate and ultimately assign blame for the invasion of Manchuria, but when the commission's report led to a motion in the League's General Assembly to condemn Japan as an aggressor, the Empire promptly withdrew from the League on March 27, 1933. That the League was powerless to do more than engage in debates and pass resolutions convinced the militarists that Japan would be able to expand at will at the expense of neighboring nations, without any serious opposition.

This was not the first time the Japanese had defied the League, of course; it was merely the first—and only—time the defiance was so openly blatant. The conditions under which the Pacific islands that were once German possessions had been mandated to Japan after the First World War had given the Japanese the authority to administer the islands more or less as they saw fit, but specifically forbade the construction of naval or military installations on any of them. The ink was hardly dry on the documents handing over the islands than the Japanese set about doing precisely that: Imperial Army engineers spent most of the 1920s fortifying the islands against seaborne invasion, constructing harbors and fleet anchorages where possible, and with the rise of airpower in the 1930s, building airfields.

All the while, of course, the Japanese were solemnly declaring to the League that nothing of the sort was being done. For years the League's member nations couldn't be bothered to independently verify the reports, and so took these assurances at face value—until January 1935, when the League passed a resolution to deprive Japan of the mandates. Japan's response was to ignore the resolution, supremely confident that the League would do nothing to enforce it—which is exactly what the League did: nothing. A further demonstration of Japan's increasing disdain for the Western powers came in January 1936, when the Japanese delegation withdrew from the Second London Naval Disarmament Conference—the latest follow-on to the 1922 Washington Conference—because the United States and Great Britain continued to refuse the Japanese Navy parity with their own fleets.

Meanwhile, domestic politics in Japan had turned openly bloody. As happens with almost any political idea or ideal, the growing swell of patriotism and nationalism among the Japanese people was soon the breeding ground for extremists, most of whom had little understanding of—or regard for—the pragmatic workings of both business and politics. Instead they imagined themselves as the true loyal subjects of the emperor and the keepers of the spirit of *Dai Nippon*: it was the politicians and businessmen who were betraying Japan with their endless compromises and deal-making. March 1932 saw the "League of Blood" plot, where 20 senior government officials and members of the *zaibatsu* were targeted for assassination as a prelude to an ultra-nationalist *coup d'état* that would effect a "Showa Restoration," a faint echo of the Meiji Restoration, where the institutions of representative government would be completely abolished and the emperor would rule absolutely. Two months later a handful of navy officers shot and killed Prime Minister Tsuyoshi Inukai, in yet another attempted coup. What was perhaps most ominous about these incidents was not the relative leniency with which the guilty were punished but rather the wide-spread public sympathy for them.

The domestic political violence came to a head at the end of February 1936. In what became known as the February 26 Incident, a handful of reckless but naive young army officers led 1,500 soldiers in an attempted revolt that would purge the army, navy, and government of their ideological opponents, many of whom were to be assassinated, including Prime Minister Okada Keisuke—the would-be victims' alleged crime was being perceived as threats to the *kokutai*, the national identity. Like earlier conspirators, the young officers also sought to impose a "Showa Restoration." Several of the targeted individuals were killed, but Okada survived and the revolt's main objective, seizing the Imperial Palace, was never accomplished. Sympathizers within the army tried to move in support of the radicals, but were prevented at first by the army's senior officers vacillating over how to respond, and then by the openly expressed fury of the Emperor who ordered the *coup* suppressed by any means necessary. By February 29 the conspirators recognized that they had failed: apart from a handful of assassinations they had achieved none of their objectives, most of the soldiers under their command had deserted them, and two of their number committed suicide; the rest surrendered to the military police.

The aftermath of the February 26 Incident was far different than that of the earlier abortive coups. There would be no opportunity for the February 26 conspirators to do as the defendants in the previous coup attempts had done, and turn their trails into political platforms to whip up public support for themselves and their cause. A series of closed prosecutions were held over a period of 18 months, and when they were concluded, 59 of the uprising's leaders were found guilty of mutiny. Seventeen were executed, the remainder were given prison sentences ranging from three years to life.

The February 26 Incident brought to a close the most violent period of modern Japanese politics, but it did nothing to strengthen the position of the civilian government. An imperial command issued on May 18 required that the Minister of War and Minister of the Navy both be active-duty army and navy officers respectively—reserve or retired officers were now ineligible. This effectively reduced the government to little more than a rubber stamp for whatever policies the army or navy wished to pursue: the resignation of the Minister of War or the Minister of the Navy could bring down a government if no active duty officer were willing to take their place.

The idea of the "Showa Restoration" extolled as the goal of the attempted and planned coups in the early 1930s brings to the fore Emperor Hirohito, and the role that he played in creating and executing Japan's domestic and foreign policies during the first years of his reign. Born in 1901, Hirohito inherited the throne in 1926 from his father, Yoshihito, known posthumously as Taisho, who in turn had succeeded the Emperor Meiji in 1912. "Showa," meaning "enlightened peace," was the name Hirohito gave to his reign—it would become, by tradition, his name after his death. It was also, for the first 20 years of his reign, a carefully constructed and maintained farce.

In post-Second World War Japan it was politically expedient, domestically and internationally, to portray Hirohito as an emperor who had reigned but really did not rule—not quite a figurehead but a monarch who, nonetheless, was essentially detached from the real workings of his government and Empire. Eventually, though, a far different picture gradually emerged, one where the emperor was not only aware and informed of Japan's affairs, domestic and international, but took an active, if not always highly visible, part in them. The idea of a "Showa Restoration"—stripping the Diet, prime minister, and Cabinet of any effective power, reducing them to mere functionaries, in the process making the emperor an absolute monarch—reveals the presence of a more forceful personality willing to actually exercise his imperial power than would be expected of a detached, isolated monarch. Hirohito was a far cry from the indifferent Emperor Meiji.

That this would be so was due to a peculiar set of personal and political circumstances surrounding Hirohito. When the Meiji Restoration became an accomplished fact, the emperor was counseled and guided by a collection of nine advisors who became known as the *genro*—the "principal elders." They guided Japan through her westernization and modernization, her first foreign adventures and her wars against China and Russia. They served Meiji throughout his reign, and those still alive when Taishō ascended to the throne served him as well. Rather weak-willed and only of average intelligence, Taisho, whose health was always fragile, preferred to live a semi-reclusive life, and for the most part left affairs of the Empire to the *genrō* and the cabinet, rarely acting against their advice. By the time Hirohito succeeded his father, however, only one of the *genro* remained alive, with no one of sufficient moral and political stature and prestige to take their places. Hirohito, then, when making imperial decisions, felt far less constrained by temperament or tradition to defer to the counsel of his advisors. Hirohito possessed, by all accounts, a first-class intellect, and as he had subtly demonstrated during the first six years of his reign, then openly displayed, during the February 26 Incident, a will of iron and a measure of ruthless determination.

This ruthlessness manifested itself not just in domestic politics but in Japan foreign affairs as well. Like many a young man, he'd had his dreams of martial prowess and heroic battlefield deeds. As he grew older those dreams evolved from fantasies of personal glory into imagined imperial military adventures, and upon becoming Emperor, the possibility offered itself of those adventures becoming reality. Hirohito had heard the same rumors in 1931 as did the Imperial General Headquarters that an unauthorized invasion of southern Manchuria was being planned; his silence on the subject gave it his tacit approval. He openly endorsed the occupation of northern

Manchuria in early 1932 and China's Jehol province the following year. Hirohito's reign was proving itself to be every bit as expansionist as that of his grandfather, Emperor Meiji's, had been.

Any doubts about this were laid to rest in the summer of 1937 when Japan and China openly went to war in the wake of the Marco Polo Bridge incident—itself a Keystone Kops-like bit of foolishness where a Japanese soldier supposedly went missing and a Chinese soldier was shot in retaliation—that two nations truly intent on maintaining the peace would have quickly settled. Instead, the incident, which was a deliberate Japanese provocation, triggered a Japanese invasion of Hebie Province and the capture of Beijing and its port city of Tianjin in August 1937. Staff work at the Imperial General Headquarters for these operations had actually begun six weeks earlier, with Hirohito being fully briefed as planning progressed. This was to be an all-out effort by the Japanese, who were determined to not only seize Hebie Province but all of northeast China's major railheads and seaports, in an effort to accomplish the economic subjugation of China that had been denied Japan in 1915 when the Twenty-one Demands were rejected.

By the end of 1937 the capital city of Nanjing (or Nanking as it was then known) had been captured by the advancing Japanese forces, forcing the Chinese government to relocate to Chongqing (Chunking), in the Chinese interior. Given the mutual belligerence that had existed between China and Japan after the invasion of Manchuria, the rest of the world was hardly surprised when war broke out again, and initially a "pox on both your houses" attitude prevailed internationally, but what happened in Nanjing during the first six weeks of Japanese occupation turned world opinion bitterly against Japan, where it would remain until September 1945. Hirohito's image suffered as well: on August 5, 1937 he had ratified a proposal from the Japanese army to remove the constraints of international law on the treatment of Chinese prisoners; this would be interpreted as the legal justification for the Nanjing massacre.

It is doubtful that there has ever been a greater or more complete catalog of atrocities, in both number and kind, committed by an occupying army against a civilian population than were done in Nanjing during those six weeks. In stark figures, between December 13, 1937 and late January 1938 Japanese soldiers tortured and murdered up to 300,000 Chinese civilians and prisoners of war, and raped tens of thousands of women during the Nanjing Massacre—indeed, the butchery would quickly become known world-wide as the "Rape of Nanking."

Nanjing was a sort of Japanese Rubicon: afterward there would rarely be any sort of prior restraint in the actions of the Imperial Army—or the Imperial Navy, for that matter, in the form of the Imperial Marines. Incidents would occur, as when the USS *Panay*, an American gunboat stationed on the Yangze River, was bombed and sunk by the Imperial Navy Air Service, the Japanese would apologize—or not—and pay damages and reparations—or not. But from the end of 1937, Japan relentlessly pursued a ruthless grand strategy of expansion which would assure the Empire access to all the resources it required, regardless of the consequences.

That same year also saw the opening of negotiations between Japan and Nazi Germany to create a military alliance; the talks would culminate in Japan's ambassador to Berlin, Kurusu Saburo, signing the Tripartite Pact on September 27, 1940, creating the Rome–Tokyo–Berlin Axis. It was no more than a marriage of convenience (Japanese belief in their own racial supremacy and Nazi "Master Race" theories, while superficially similar, should never be conflated—philosophically they were worlds apart), but the pact created the impression of the three great militarist powers—Germany, Japan, and Italy—acting in concert, and the idea of a unified Axis strategy would bedevil the Allies throughout the Second World War. What it accomplished at the time was to distract the Western powers in their defense planning—the German threat to Europe would force Britain, France, and the Netherlands to consider drawing down the strength of their garrisons in the Far East, while the Japanese threat to those possessions demanded those same garrisons be reinforced. The result was that both Britain and the Netherlands especially would be badly overstretched when the shooting actually started.

Japan's grand strategy eventually coalesced into an idea that was deemed the "Greater East Asian Co-Prosperity Sphere," whereby all the peoples of Asia would benefit from the expulsion of the European colonial governments and then prosper under the benevolent rule of a new set of overlords, the Japanese. It had a certain "Asia for the Asians" appeal to it, but in reality the plan's objective was for the Dutch East Indies, the Philippines, China, and the nations of Indochina, as well as the Pacific islands, to supply the needs and demands of Japan's economy, regardless of the consequences for their own. There would, however, be little benevolence to the Japanese rule—indeed, it would be a thinly disguised military occupation carried on in perpetuity, the local populace treated as conquered peoples.

If Nanjing was the Imperial Army and Navy's Rubicon, then autumn 1940 must be regarded as the point of no return for the Empire as a whole. On September 22, an agreement was concluded with the Vichy government officials in Hanoi allowing free passage through French Indochina of limited numbers of Japanese troops—a few hours later the Imperial Army openly invaded the French colony. Over the next few days, Tokyo apologized profusely and made a great show of disciplining the commanding general, who, it was claimed, had acted without orders, but the result was the same regardless of whatever legal niceties were involved: French Indochina was now occupied by the Japanese army. Hard on the heels of that particular bit of military farce came the news that Ambassador Kurusu had signed the Tripartite Pact, formalizing the alliance between Nazi Germany, Fascist Italy, and Imperial Japan.

The Emperor's final approval of the pact had been given on September 19 in a Conference in the Imperial Presence with representatives of the Cabinet, the Army, and the Navy. The pretext for signing the pact was securing oil from the Dutch East

Indies. It was believed that, as the Germans had occupied the Netherlands, Berlin would be more amenable to acquiescing to the annexation of the oilfields by an ally, rather than a mere friendly power. One of the subtexts of the conference was the pending war with the United States—the Imperial government already took for granted that there would be such a war, the question was how to best manipulate the circumstances to Japan's advantage. The chief of staff of the Imperial Navy, Admiral Prince Fushimi, the emperor's second cousin, was blunt, stating that, "It is quite likely that a Japanese–American war will be a protracted one," although he also asserted that given the choice of how to acquire oil from the Dutch East Indies, through peaceful means or the use of force, "the Navy very much prefers peaceful means," the better not to provoke the Americans.

Privy Councilor Hara Yoshimichi, at this point speaking for himself and not the Emperor remarked that, "I think it will be impossible to obtain oil from the Dutch East Indies by peaceful means," meaning that any move by the Japanese into the archipelago, with or without Dutch consent, would be regarded as an act of aggression in Washington DC. He then asked what the government's position was.

Rather than the prime minister, Prince Konoye Fuminaro, it was Foreign Minister Matsuoka Yosuke who replied: "If Japan were to abandon all, or at least half, of China, it might be possible to at least shake hands with the United States, but still pressure on Japan would not cease—not in the foreseeable future... The object of this pact is to prevent the United States from encircling us." The Emperor as was customary, said nothing, instead making his views known through Privy Counselor Hara. As much of the debate was merely *pro forma*, Hirohito had already decided whether or not Japan would sign the Tripartite Pact. Once the discussion had run its course, he nodded to Hara, who pronounced the Emperor's will: "Even though a Japanese–American clash may be unavoidable in the end, We hope that sufficient care will be exercised to make sure that it will not come in the near future, and that there will be no miscalculations. We give Our approval on this basis." And with that, the pact became a reality: the signing in Berlin a week later was merely a formality.[6]

Finally, on October 12, Prime Minister Prince Konoye announced to the Imperial Diet the creation of the Imperial Aid Association, its purpose being to promote the goals of the *Shintaisei* ("New Order") movement. Political parties were abolished, there was now only the Empire. The whole of Japan's national fabric was to be mobilized, ostensibly to bring the war in China to a successful conclusion. In reality, Japan was gearing up for total war against the United States. The stage was now set for an open confrontation with America, albeit one that was, for the time being, diplomatic and not military, throughout 1941.

As it was, the President of the United States, Franklin Roosevelt, had already decided that Japan needed to be brought up on a short leash, and on July 2, 1940, signed an Export Control Act that banned the shipment to Japan of those materials the Japanese needed most to continue with their conquests: aircraft and aircraft parts, including engines, along with machine tools, and aviation gasoline. Some members of his cabinet as well as his unofficial advisors urged him to halt the export of all oil, crude and refined, to Japan, which was almost completely dependent on American supplies of petroleum products. Roosevelt demurred—he was intent on halting Japanese aggression and expansion, not bringing about the collapse of Japan's national economy: the consequences of a complete embargo on oil were so drastic that such an act would be little short of a declaration of war, and might actually be interpreted as such by the Japanese. Roosevelt did not need a war in the Pacific with Japan when there was every possibility that America might find itself in open conflict with Nazi Germany in the Atlantic.

Still, Roosevelt wasn't blind to the growing Japanese threat, and even before the Export Control Act was passed, he moved the US Navy's Pacific Fleet from its base in San Diego, California, to Pearl Harbor in Hawaii in what was meant to be a show of force that, he hoped, would deter the Japanese from attempting any further conquests. Here Roosevelt unwittingly played into the hands of the generals and admirals in Tokyo who were planning Japan's next military and naval moves. They were convinced that an attack on British possessions in Southeast Asia—most particularly oil-rich Burma (modern Myanmar)—would draw the United States into the war at Great Britain's side. It was an erroneous assumption, but Roosevelt's decision to move the Pacific Fleet to Hawaii—3,000 miles closer to Japan than America's West Coast and the perfect springboard for offensive action in the Central Pacific—seemed to confirm that assumption. If that were so, it might be necessary to launch a preemptive strike against the American fleet in the Pacific that would cripple it sufficiently to buy Japan the time to secure her defensive perimeter in the islands of the Central Pacific. In the spring of 1940, Yamamoto Isoroku, now a full admiral and Commander-in-Chief of the Combined Fleet, began studying where and how this strike could be carried out. On January 7, 1941, Yamamoto wrote a letter to Admiral Oikawa Koshiro, the Navy Minister, positing the idea of an attack on the American fleet at Pearl Harbor, and within days the preliminary planning for the operation was underway.

The need to strike at the Americans seemed to grow with every passing week. Barely a month after Yamamoto sent off his letter to Oikawa, the American secretary of state, Cordell Hull, informed the Japanese ambassador to Washington DC, Nomura Kichisaburo, that exports to Japan of zinc, nickel, bronze and brass, copper, and potash, the latter vital not only to Japan's farmers as fertilizer but also as an essential compound in the manufacture of explosives, were now banned under the Export Control Act—scrap iron and steel had been cut off in September 1940—followed shortly by an embargo on materials used in the petroleum industry: refining equipment, piping, storage tanks, and more. The intent was clear: depriving Japanese industry of those metals and materials would make further weapons manufacturing impossible, and when the machinery in Japan's refineries wore out, there would be no replacements, which meant that the Japanese army and navy would run out of refined fuel, no matter how much crude Japan imported. Worse, Japanese industry wouldn't be able to manufacture replacement equipment in time to prevent it from happening.

The willingness among the most stridently warlike admirals and generals (Yamamoto was not among them) to go to war with the United States grew with each announcement of new American restrictions. Yet at this point, Hirohito, of all people, balked at the idea. He had learned something from Japan's war with China: at an Imperial Conference where his Minister of War, General Sugiyama Gen, and Minister of the Navy, Fleet Admiral Nagano Osami, assured him that the operations neutralizing American power in the Pacific would require no more than three months to complete, he rounded on them, snapping, "At the outbreak of the China Incident, you asked me to approve sending Army troops there, saying that the Incident would be settled in a short time. But has it yet been ended after more than four years? Are you trying to tell me the same thing again? With what confidence do you say 'three months'?" However expansionist and imperialistic he might be, Hirohito was hardly delusional, and he had no desire to willingly add the United States to the list of enemies Japan would face when her forces began moving south into Indochina and the Dutch East Indies. He insisted that diplomacy be given a chance—it might yet be that a solution could be found where the Americans could be pacified while the Japanese retained possession of the most vital—if not all—of their conquests. Let the planning for the attack on Pearl Harbor proceed, but Ambassador Nomura would continue to talk peace with Secretary Hull.[7]

The iron dice were finally cast on July 26, 1941, when President Roosevelt issued an executive order which froze *all* Japanese assets in the United States after the Japanese occupied French Indochina with the permission of the Vichy government. The consequences of the order were harsh and immediate: all financial transactions by Japanese businesses with American businesses were immediately suspended; funds in any account, private or commercial, held by a Japanese national in any American bank were seized; Japanese merchant shipping was barred from entering any port in the United States, and ships currently in American ports were denied permission to sail. Most critically for Japan's war effort and equally for the Empire's domestic economy, shipments of machine tools of any description, scrap metal of any kind, and *all* oil, crude or refined, were banned.

While all of these measures would have serious consequences for Japan, the embargo on oil, especially crude oil, had the potential to prove devastating. The Imperial Navy was left with an 18-month supply of fuel oil—less if it undertook any offensive operations—and the army faced almost identical limits, while the effect on the domestic economy was unthinkable. Japan now had no choice but to seize the oil fields in the Dutch East Indies and Burma; Roosevelt, anticipating this, issued a warning on August 17, declaring that the United States would act against Japan if the Japanese were to invade any further "neighboring countries."

Diplomacy was now a farce, at least in the opinion of most of the Japanese leadership. Prime Minister Prince Konoye was the near-lone exception. Still searching for the elusive compromise he believed was possible, he proposed a withdrawal of Japanese forces from most of China and Indochina once peace was made with the Chinese Nationalists, after which the "Open Door" trade agreement would be restored; he also suggested that Japan would effectively renounce the Tripartite Pact if the Roosevelt Administration would lift the embargoes on Japan. When these proposals were rejected—Washington was demanding a complete withdrawal of Japanese troops from *all* of China and Indochina and would accept nothing less—Konoye then offered to personally meet with Roosevelt and negotiate face-to-face. Roosevelt in turn insisted that the Japanese agree to his terms before any such meeting took place—which, of course, would have negated the need or purpose of such a meeting. The loss of face Konoye suffered at this rebuff from Roosevelt resulted in his government collapsing in October, and with it went the last voice of moderation among Japan's leadership, as Konoye's successor was Major General Tojo Hideki.

On November 2, 1941, Hirohito informed Tojo and the chiefs of staff that he gave his assent to war with the United States. On November 3 Admiral Nagano explained in detail the plan for the Pearl Harbor attack, though Hirohito withheld his approval of the operation until November 5. The Emperor added one stipulation to the operation: should negotiations with the Americans succeed, the strike force must be prepared to return to Japan immediately—there must be no "incidents" involving the American navy. Ten days later aircraft carriers, battleships, cruisers, destroyers, and submarines began getting under way, the submarines bound directly for Hawaii, the surface ships to a rendezvous in windswept, fog-shrouded Hitokappu Bay in the Kurile Islands, where they would form the *Kido Butai*, or Strike Force, that would carry out the attack on Pearl Harbor.

On December 1, at a formal Imperial Council, Hirohito announced to his assembled advisors that he formally sanctioned war against the United States, Great Britain, and the Netherlands. By then the *Kido Butai* had already set sail for Hawaii.

CHAPTER 2

The Sleeping Giant

A tale is sometimes told that, when he learned the Imperial Navy's attack on Pearl Harbor had begun before Japan formally declared war on America, Admiral Yamamoto was overheard to mutter in despair, "I fear all we have done is to awaken a sleeping giant, and fill him with a terrible resolve." While the story is almost certainly apocryphal—no record of such a statement by the commanding officer of the Combined Fleet has ever been found—its characterization of the United States of America in the waning days of 1941 was certainly accurate enough.

* * *

Much as did Japan, the United States came late onto the world stage. Formed in 1789 with the ratification of its Constitution, the American republic remained essentially self-absorbed for the next 110 years, and understandably so. It had a whole continent almost entirely to itself to explore, where it could grow and develop a national character with none of the periodic interruptions by intrusive neighbors that were endemic to Europe in the 19th century. As the young nation began to expand westward out of the confines of its original 13 states, huddled as they were along the Atlantic coastline, settlers soon found that there was not only apparently near-limitless farmland, but also an embarrassment of riches in natural resources. Timber from the upper Great Lakes region and the Pacific Northwest, iron ore from northern Minnesota, Wisconsin, and Michigan's Upper Peninsula, coal from the Appalachian and Rocky Mountains, and, eventually, oil from the Southwest, provided the building blocks for the world's most dynamic industrial economy from the mid-19th century to the mid-20th.

This surfeit of resources left the United States free of any dependence on the rest of the world for raw materials to feed its industries; the Americans would require markets instead. Which is what brought about the United States' first encounter—and confrontation—with the Empire of Japan, Commodore Matthew Perry's expedition to Edo in 1853. An earlier attempt at establishing a trade relationship between America and Japan had been turned away by the Japanese in 1846, but Perry was determined to be neither put off nor thwarted. He would achieve the two objectives set for him by the American government—the establishment of a coaling station in Japan's Home Islands for the use of American warships and merchantmen, and the opening of Japan as a market for American businesses—even if it were necessary, as he threatened to do, to bombard the city of Edo to compel the Japanese to agree.

The Japanese chose not to call Perry's bluff—wisely, in the event, as he wasn't bluffing at all—and indicated a willingness to at least talk, if not actually negotiate. Having successfully brandished the stick, Perry now held out the carrot, and described what he saw as the ways Japan could benefit from such an agreement. The evidence before the *shogun* and *daimyo* alike that the ways and means of Japan's 16th-century society stood no chance of resisting those of the 19th-century West was irrefutable. The Empire needed to buy time to modernize, so that it could eventually deal with the Western powers as an equal; for that, agreements had to be made with those nations which would offer Japan some protection from being reduced to glorified vassalage, as had happened with China.

The Treaty of Kanagawa between the United States and the Empire of Japan was signed on March 31, 1854. In it, the Americans were granted everything they sought when Commodore Perry's "black ships" steamed into Edo Bay—a coaling station, a consulate, which would eventually become a full-fledged embassy, and open trade, ending Japan's 200 years of self-imposed isolation. It also served as the model for the "unequal treaties" Japan would reluctantly conclude with Great Britain, Russia, France and the Netherlands, all of which encroached to some greater or lesser degrees on Japan's sovereignty, and were regarded by the Japanese as calculated insults to the Empire's national honor. The determination to redress those insults would spur Japanese militarism, which would, in turn propel Japan into her aggressive wars with China and Russia and raise the Empire to the status of the dominant naval and military power in the Far East.

Once the treaty was concluded, the United States' government essentially ignored Japan for the next 50 years, preoccupied as it was, first with its Civil War, then Reconstruction and the westward expansion across the North American continent. This was no deliberate snub of the Japanese, but a continuation of what had been one of the two cornerstones of American foreign policy for most of the nation's history, the deliberate avoidance of "entangling alliances." The idea was first articulated in 1798 in the Farewell Address of President George Washington at the end of his second term, when he declared that "It is our true policy to steer clear of permanent alliance with any portion of the foreign world." Thomas Jefferson, the republic's third president, reiterated this idea in his inaugural address, affirming America's dedication to "Peace, commerce, and honest friendship with all nations—entangling alliances with none."[1]

Throughout the 19th century, then, successive administrations heeded the guidance of Washington and Jefferson: treaties were carefully drafted to avoid standing military or political obligations that might be called upon outside the specific terms of the agreement. Hand in hand with this practice went a level of interest in the affairs of other nations just sufficient to prevent as far as possible the United States from being taken by surprise diplomatically or militarily. Americans were interested in detachment, not isolation: they simply wanted to keep the rest of the world at arm's length while they exploited the North American continent, a desire which coalesced into a policy known as non-interventionism.

The other cornerstone of American foreign relations was the Monroe Doctrine, articulated in 1823 by President James Monroe, who declared "The occasion has been judged proper for asserting, as a principle in which the rights and interests of the United States are involved, that the American continents, by the free and independent condition which they have assumed and maintain, are henceforth not to be considered as subjects for future colonization by any European powers." Monroe went on to say that "[The United States] should consider any attempt on [Europe's] part to extend their system to any portion of this hemisphere as dangerous to our peace and safety." Stripped of its diplomatic curlicues, the doctrine was a warning that any European state attempting to interfere in the affairs of independent nations in North and South America would risk war with America. At the time the United States possessed neither an army nor a navy strong enough to put teeth into the declaration—80 years would have to pass before that capability became a reality. However, the doctrine's intent neatly coincided with Great Britain's determination to suppress any remaining colonial ambitions in the Americas among Europe's Continental powers, primarily France and later Germany, so that it was the Royal Navy which tacitly enforced it for the time being.[2]

In practice the Monroe Doctrine proved to be somewhat malleable, most frequently in regard to the United States' right to intervene or interfere in the internal politics of Central and South American nations. Monroe explicitly stated that his policy applied only to nations in North and South America which had attained sovereignty: the United States presumed no right to interfere in the established colonial affairs of other nations. Over the years that limitation, too, became somewhat flexible, no more so than in 1898, when a long-running insurrection among the people of the island of Cuba, who were seeking independence from their Spanish masters, became a *casus belli* for the United States to go to war with the Kingdom of Spain.

The Spanish–American War was a pivotal point in American history. Not because, as Japan would do in her war with Russia seven years later, the United States won an unexpected victory over Spain; bluntly put, the war was America's to lose, so negligible had Spain become as a naval and military power. What gave a 10-week, *opéra bouffe* war its disproportionate significance was that when peace was concluded with the 1898 Treaty of Paris, the United States was left filling an unaccustomed and not entirely comfortable role, that of a colonial overlord. In the treaty Spain ceded all of its overseas colonies and possessions to America; in the Pacific Ocean, these included the Philippine Islands, along with the smaller island of Guam. As Japan at the time was still a power only in her home waters and the Yellow Sea, it seemed most unlikely that the United States' presence in the western Pacific might evolve into a point of friction between the two nations.

Even after the Spanish–American War, the premise of America's foreign policy was a determination to remain apart, though not exactly aloof, from the international machinations of the other Great Powers, while at the same time prepared to deter other nations from meddling American affairs, an idea summed up in President Theodore Roosevelt's well-known aphorism, "Speak softly and carry a big stick." It was this position that allowed the United States to avoid becoming entangled in the Great War when it erupted in the summer of 1914, and it served well until Imperial Germany directly threatened America with war via the Zimmerman Telegram in February 1917. Even then, though Americans would fight alongside the French and British to bring about a German defeat, the United States declared war on Imperial Germany as a co-belligerent, and not a full ally of Great Britain and France. It was no small distinction, as it allowed the American government, in the form of the Wilson Administration, a freedom of choice and action not otherwise possible if a formal alliance had committed America to helping the Allies achieve their specific war aims.

It was after the Great War that non-interventionism began to fray at the edges, unraveling through the 1920s into actual isolationism. The first evidence this was happening appeared in 1920, when the United States Senate soundly rejected ratification of the Treaty of Versailles, and with it, membership in the League of Nations, choosing instead to conclude separate peace treaties with Germany, Austria, and Hungary in August 1921. The central argument for refusing ratification was made by Senator William Borah, a Nebraska Republican, who famously declared that the treated would "have forfeited and surrendered, once and for all, the great policy of 'no entangling alliances' upon which the strength of this Republic has been founded for 150 years." This decision did not in itself doom the League, as, in truth, nothing could have saved the League from its own pusillanimity in the mid- to late 1930s, but it did signal an already strong reluctance on the part of Washington DC to continue playing an active role in world affairs.[3]

The Naval Conference of 1922 was further confirmation of the direction toward which American foreign policy was shifting. Convened as it was for reasons that were in equal parts self-interested and altruistic, the public face of the conference was an effort to avert the sort of naval arms race that had plagued Great Britain and Imperial Germany before 1914, which was the source of so much misunderstanding and ultimately grief for those two empires, through imposing strict limits on sizes and numbers of warships the world's major naval powers were allowed to possess. Privately, for the American government at least, it was first and foremost an opportunity to cut naval appropriations. In 1919, Congress had drastically reduced the Army in size from a wartime peak of over 2 million soldiers of all ranks to just 286,000 officers and enlisted men, as there was no longer a need for a huge army. Further strength reductions followed annually until, by 1924, the US Army numbered just 110,000 officers and men, smaller than it had been in 1916, before America entered the war. It was now the Navy's turn to go under the axe; it was no coincidence that the initial limitation proposals presented by the American delegation to the Naval Conference tallied exactly with the types of ships and numbers Congress determined were the minimum necessary to maintain a fleet large enough to defend America's coastline.

While the Washington Conference succeeded in preventing another naval arms race, it did nothing to stave off a three-way naval rivalry which would, not quite two decades hence, have devastating consequences for Great Britain, Japan, and the United States. France and Italy, the other two naval powers invited to the conference, were little more than also-rans: hobbled by geography and limited industrial bases, they were never significant factors in the shifting equations of post-Great War naval power. Their presence at the conference was more of a sop to their continued pretensions of Great Power status than a reflection of strategic realities—a reality which was acknowledged in the tonnage allotments and capital ship ratios that were negotiated at the conference.

In practical terms, those ratios meant that for every five battleships possessed by the Royal Navy—it was still the world's largest battle fleet, and so served as the benchmark for every other navy—the US Navy was allowed five, and Japan's Imperial Navy three; constraints on cruisers and destroyers were similar. The Japanese immediately protested, insisting that such an arrangement would relegate the Imperial Navy to permanent second-rank status, and impose on it a crippling numerical inferiority should Japan ever find itself at war with Great Britain or the United States. The arguments put forward by the British and Americans justifying their larger fleets were that Britain was required to defend a world-wide empire, while the United States had to protect coasts on both the Atlantic and Pacific Oceans; Japan's only strategic concern, it was argued, was the western Pacific; therefore the Imperial Navy had no need for numerical parity with its British and American counterparts.

The Japanese, not entirely unreasonably, thought the argument was specious. In the event of a war between Japan and the United States, the only navy against which the US fleet might have to defend America's Atlantic coast in strength was the Royal Navy—the French and Italian fleets were too small to pose any sort of plausible threat there, and the Germans for all practical purposes no longer had a navy. Yet the possibility of America going to war with Britain, let alone Britain and Japan acting in concert against America, was so remote as to be unthinkable. Far more likely was a scenario where the Americans and British made common cause against the Japanese, in which case, should the proposed capital ship ratios be adopted and implemented, the Imperial Navy would find itself at a hopeless disadvantage from the outset. The Japanese delegation to the conference protested as sharply as they could short of withdrawing altogether, but when the Five Power Treaty, otherwise known as the Washington Naval Treaty, was concluded, the sealed and attested signature of Admiral Kato Tomosaburo was appended to it.

As is the case with most watersheds, it was not immediately evident that a fundamental change had taken place in Japan's relationship with Britain and the United States as a consequence of the Washington Naval Conference—but one had indeed occurred. The militarists in Tokyo loudly declared the treaty a national insult, and played heavily on the suggestion that the British and Americans were quietly conspiring to confine the Japanese fleet solely to the waters around the Home Islands. Where Japan's relations with Great Britain and the United States had been cautious but cordial, they quickly shifted to formally correct and suspicious: it was taken as given that should the Japanese attempt to expand into Asia and the Pacific, the British and Americans would be the Empire's future enemies.

The Japanese felt further provoked two years later when the 1924 Immigration Act was passed by Congress and signed into law, albeit reluctantly, by then-President Calvin Coolidge. Quotas in one form or another on immigration to the United States were hardly new to the landscape of American politics, but this new act set even more-restrictive limits than had ever before been in place, quotas based on the national and ethnic origins of people already resident in the United States. In one carefully worded paragraph of Section 13, all immigration from Japan was barred, with very few exceptions allowed. By incorporating a phrase lifted from certain state laws already on the books in California and Washington—"aliens ineligible for citizenship"—the act endorsed those laws and restrictions and gave them Federal authority. The states along America's Pacific Coast had long histories of "Yellow Peril" hysteria associated with hypothetical threats resulting from Chinese and Japanese immigration and had produced laws as far back as 1870 specifically written to exclude Asian immigrants from owning property or becoming naturalized citizens. For Japanese wanting to emigrate to states that previously had no such restrictions, the 1924 Act meant that they were now barred from entering the country entirely. The Japanese Government protested long and loudly, but to no avail. The new law was viewed by Americans as a measure of self-protection, and as such enjoyed an astonishingly wide range of approval.[4]

More to the point, and more telling of the times, the American people just didn't care what Japan and the Japanese thought of the 1924 Immigration Act. Americans have always been somewhat self-centered, and in the 1920s that self-centeredness was morphing into self-absorption: to Americans, no one else in the world was as interesting, as intriguing, as fascinating, as Americans. As seen from Main Street, USA, in the years following the Great War most of the nations of Europe engaged in some degree of introspection—not all of it honest—while Japan brooded, and China teetered on the brink of a three-way civil war between the Kuomintang, the

Communists, and a motley gaggle of warlords in the north. The American people, meanwhile, were returning to their pre-war attitude of "a pox on all their houses," convinced that little, if anything, had been accomplished for all the blood and treasure the world spilled and spent between 1914 and 1918; the rest of the world had no need of America's help in weaving a new handbasket for yet another trip to hell.

In the wake of the stock market collapse in October 1929 that ushered in the Great Depression, what remaining incentive there was for a proactive American foreign policy quickly vanished: with the economic crisis at home growing more desperate with each passing month, engaging in international politics quickly became one more luxury that America could not afford. Non-interventionism finally gave way to outright isolationism. Decisions made and policies put forward by President Herbert Hoover, who succeeded Coolidge in 1929 and who was, ironically, a convinced internationalist, would define the role America would—or would not, depending on perspective—play in world affairs for most of the 1930s. Though the Smoot-Hawley Tariff Act of 1930 has often been cited as the tipping point for the United States' slide into isolationism, the truly defining moment came in 1931 when the Japanese invaded Manchuria.

Hoover was furious, as Japan had flagrantly, almost defiantly, violated the letter and the spirit of the Nine Power Treaty of 1922, which guaranteed the territorial integrity of China, and to which Japan was a signatory. Hoover was convinced that when a multinational agreement was violated, only a multinational response would have any effect on the offending nation: a unilateral reaction could—and by the Japanese would—be ignored. This was a natural extension of Hoover's overall concept of foreign policy: by nature international problems and crises required international cooperation to resolve. He had a point: the Great Depression itself was the bastard child of a perfect storm of international financial disasters, any one of which individually the world economy could have endured, not without suffering, but without collapse. When the American stock market crashed in October 1929, followed by a series of bank failures in Europe two years later, and just months after that the French and British governments defaulted on their war loan payments to the Americans, the strain was more than the international financial structure of the day could bear. Worldwide, industries were left without investors, surviving banks teetered on the brink of insolvency, and the money supply dwindled until it nearly vanished. Hoover hoped that international cooperation would be able to solve the problem and put the financial Humpty Dumpty back together; he would be voted out of office before he ever had a chance to find out if it were so.[5]

As for the Japanese and their Manchurian adventure, Great Britain, France, and the Netherlands, the only other signatories to the Nine Power Treaty which had any significant military or naval strength in the Far East, all looked to the United States to take the lead in responding to Japan's aggression. Hoover knew, though, that there would be little to no support in Congress for any sort of active intervention against the Japanese, even if the US Army and Navy were in a position to pose a realistic threat to Japan—which, of course, they were not. Instead, on January 7, 1932, the American secretary of state, Henry Stimson, sent identical notes to China and Japan which announced that

> …the American Government deems it to be its duty to notify both the Imperial Japanese Government and the Government of the Chinese Republic that it cannot admit the legality of any situation *de facto* nor does it intend to recognize any treaty or agreement entered into between those Governments, or agents thereof, which may impair the treaty rights of the United States or its citizens in China, including those that relate to the sovereignty, the independence, or the territorial and administrative integrity of the Republic of China, or to the international policy relative to China, commonly known as the open door policy.[6]

This became known as the "Stimson Doctrine," a refusal on the part of the United States to recognize the legitimacy of any foreign power's expansion by force. Both Hoover and Stimson knew it was a hollow gesture: the United States was too weak to do anything more than express moral outrage as its response to international treaties being flaunted and violated; the secretary of state in particular felt deeply embarrassed by such a tacit admission of American impotence.

The 64-year-old Stimson was one of the last of a dying breed, a senior civil servant who regarded his tenure in office as the fulfilment of a patriotic duty rather than an opportunity to accrue personal power or build a private empire within the government; by the time a Republican was returned to the White House in 1952, they would all be gone. Stimson was born into a wealthy New York family on September 21, 1867, took his undergraduate degree from Yale, and graduated from Harvard Law School in 1890. For two decades he worked as a corporate lawyer in New York City, becoming a partner in the law firm of Elihu Root, who served as something of a role model for Stimson. In 1899 Root was unexpectedly asked by President William McKinley to serve as secretary of war; he subsequently spent the next quarter-century moving between his law practice and government service, serving variously as secretary of war, secretary of state, and senator from the State of New York. He would also serve as Stimson's mentor when the younger man entered public life.

Stimson made a brief foray into elective politics, never to venture there again, when he ran—unsuccessfully—for governor of New York in 1910; his introduction to Washington DC came the following year when President William Taft asked him to take the post of secretary of war, in no small part due to Root's recommendation. He held the appointment until March 1913 when Woodrow Wilson succeeded Taft and replaced Stimson with Lindley Garrison; when the United States declared war on Imperial Germany in 1917, Stimson went to France with the American Army, as an artillery officer—for the rest of his life he would be extremely fond of being addressed as "Colonel," the rank he attained by the time of the Armistice in November 1918. After the war he returned to his law practice in New York, not coming back into government service until 1927, when President Calvin Coolidge asked him to mediate a settlement of the Nicaraguan Civil War; a two-year stint as Governor General of the Philippines followed. Stimson finally returned to Washington in March 1929 to become Herbert Hoover's secretary of state.

In the spring of 1933 Stimson once more resumed his law practice, having been replaced by Cordell Hull after Hoover lost his bid for re-election to Franklin Roosevelt. He wasn't finished with Washington, however, as he would return to the capital seven years later, in July 1940, where at the behest of Roosevelt he resumed his one-time mantle of secretary of war, replacing Harry Woodring. Events between 1933 and 1940 had convinced the president that Woodring, a strict non-interventionist, was no longer suited to that office, and the hawkish tendencies of Stimson were better suited to the new direction in which Roosevelt was about to take American foreign policy, in a world become far more perilous than it had been in 1933.

Japan's aggressive expansion into Manchuria was followed in 1935 by the Italian invasion of Ethiopia; in 1936, the Nazis re-occupied the Rhineland, which had been demilitarized under the Treaty of Versailles and administered by the Allies separately from the rest of Germany. Versailles, its provisions and restrictions, had become a dead letter. Next came the forcible annexation of Austria by Nazi Germany, followed by the systematic dismemberment of Czechoslovakia—in which Britain and France colluded—in 1938 and 1939. Abruptly, unexpectedly, what was essentially a reconstituted German Empire, once again militarily strong and economically dynamic, had emerged in the heart of Europe, led by a man more openly aggressive than Kaiser Wilhelm II, even at his most bellicose, had ever dreamed of being. It was little wonder, then, that Stimson felt compelled to confide to his diary that "the situation in the world seemed to me like the unfolding of a great Greek tragedy, where we could see the march of events and know what ought to be done, but seemed to be powerless to prevent its marching to its grim conclusion."[7]

Unlike Roosevelt, who remained intently focused on a rearming and expanding Germany, Stimson saw as equally threatening a Japan where the domestic policies and politics were systematically conditioning the Japanese people to not merely accept but embrace the militarists' adventurism in southern Asia and the western Pacific. He did what he could to keep the president aware of the rising danger of the Rising Sun, even as Roosevelt persisted in seeing Nazi Germany as the greater threat to America and American interests. And truth be told, even had the president shifted his focus westward, there was little he could have done about it. Roosevelt was sharply constrained by the expectations of the American public, who demanded that the lion's share of the federal government's energies and attention be focused on solving the nation's economic debacle. This time it was not self-absorption that in the 1920s had turned America's attention from international affairs, but sheer economic survival and self-preservation: when Roosevelt took office in March 1933, 15 million Americans were unemployed—nearly a quarter of the United

States' labor force. It wasn't that Americans were ignorant of or indifferent to the events, incidents, and crises rending Europe nd the Far East, rather the case was that, insulated by the broad expanses of the Atlantic and Pacific Oceans, the threat which had the most immediacy for nearly every American was whether or not the household's breadwinner would still have employment tomorrow, and if he lost his job, how would the family keep food on the table and a roof over its head.

* * *

The American people's disillusionment with world affairs grew even deeper when in September 1934, the Special Committee on Investigation of the Munitions Industry initiated hearings in the Senate. Better known at the time and to posterity as the Nye Committee, after its chairman, Senator Gerald Nye, a North Dakota Republican, the committee was spurred on by two books, *Merchants of Death* by H. C. Engelbrecht and F. C. Hanighen, and *War Is a Racket* written by Smedley D. Butler, a retired Marine Corps major general. Both books presented strongly worded allegations of large-scale profiteering by American arms manufacturers and bankers during the Great War; American businessmen, it was claimed, had been making money—a lot of it—from Allied casualty lists.[8]

In time, *Merchants of Death* came to seen for what it was, a sensationalist pseudo-exposé, the quintessential "tale told by an idiot, full of sound and fury, signifying nothing"; Butler and his work, on the other hand, were not so easily dismissed. By nature Butler resembled no one so much as George S. Patton, Jr, then merely a "colorful" lieutenant colonel in the US Army, though the comparison would have appalled both men equally. He was seen as a mercurial individual, courageous and brilliant as a combat officer, but at times regarded by his superiors as a bit "erratic." Butler was one of only a handful of men in the entire history of the United States to have been awarded the Medal of Honor twice, a circumstance which imparted a special credibility to his opinions. Moreover, he was articulate and persuasive, and struck a chord that resonated with middle- and working-class Americans, as well as much of the rural United States, where suspicion of "evil bankers" was a tradition of long standing: military spending and preparations were regarded as necessary evils at best. Between them, Butler, Englebrecht, and Hanighen—along with Senator Nye himself—were able to generate a lot of smoke, and the American public, seeing the smoke, naturally assumed there was a fire under it. Nye declared that the committee would reveal that "war and preparation for war is not a matter of national honor and national defense, but a matter of profit for the few."

From September 1934 to February 1936, the committee called a total of 205 witnesses over the course of 93 hearings, In the end it found little evidence to support, let alone confirm the allegations of collusion and price fixing, as well as manipulation of government policy, that had been put forward. The committee's activities came to a crashing halt, however, when Nye began a highly partisan attack on the late

President Woodrow Wilson, a blunder of the first water in a Senate controlled by the Democratic Party during a Democratic administration. Nye's colleagues finally saw the committee for what it truly was—political theater staged for Nye's political self-promotion—and voted to dissolve the proceedings. In its final report, rather than revealing some vast international multi-corporation conspiracy to perpetuate the war and accrue vast profits, it was the committee which was exposed, shown to have produced staggering volumes of smoke, but with no corresponding fire to be found anywhere. After 18 months of investigative work, it could only express a vague moral outrage at how long-standing practices and existing regulations had permitted American banks and munitions makers to do business with the belligerent powers during the Great War without breaking any federal laws.

Nye's once ascendant political star went into an irreversible decline, but the damage had been done: as they watched totalitarian regimes sweep into power in Europe and Asia, most Americans came to believe that the war which the United States had funded, supplied, and ultimately joined, in order to "make the world safe for democracy" had in fact done nothing of the sort, but been fought for the bottom line on the balance sheets of international corporations and banking houses. A succession of increasingly restrictive Neutrality Acts passed through Congress between 1935 and 1939, sharply delimiting the actions allowed to the United States government, as well as American businesses and private citizens, in diplomatic affairs or commercial dealings with any belligerents in any war, anywhere. Isolationism had finally triumphed.

The first Neutrality Act, which went into effect on August 31, 1935, was straightforward enough, barring American businesses, whether manufacturers or trading companies, from selling or supplying arms and munitions of any description to any nation involved in a war. The Act was meant to be pre-emptive: at the time a crisis was growing in Africa between Fascist Italy and the Kingdom of Ethiopia, one that would erupt in open warfare six weeks later. The act also explicitly established that Americans traveling on passenger ships of a belligerent nation did so at their own risk: American citizenship gave them no special protection nor rendered those ships immune from attack; there would be no repeat of the embarrassing 1915 diplomatic *contretemps* that followed the *Lusitania* disaster.

As written, the 1935 legislation was to be a temporary measure, expiring six months after its passage, but in February 1936, a second Neutrality Act was passed just in time to extend the first act for an additional fourteen months. It also added a provision making it illegal for American bankers and financiers to make loans or advance credit to warring nations. This was a singular victory for Senator Nye, who continued to insist, despite the lack of any evidence produced by his committee, that the Wall Street-based banks and brokerage houses had somehow deliberately prolonged the Great War and maneuvered the United States into fighting alongside the Allies.

Roosevelt signed these two acts into law readily enough, but not because he concurred with their purpose—far from it: he was certain that attempts to isolate the United States from world affairs was the sort of high-minded but naive folly which would in a few years' time exact a very high price in American blood and treasure. Politically, though, he could not risk a veto of either of the Neutrality Acts: Roosevelt wasn't quite certain that, even with his own party holding control of both the House of Representatives and the Senate, his vetoes would not be overridden. An open rift between Congress and the White House could have given the impression that his was a weak presidency, just at the time when his administration was trying any and every means possible to reverse America's economic debacle.

After Roosevelt's death in 1945 and the subsequent near-apotheosis of the man and his reputation, the measures put in hand during his first term in office would be presented as a coherent, well-thought-out program for economic recovery, when in truth they were anything but. Instead, they were a haphazard, almost ramshackle succession of ideas—mostly of the "let's try this and see if it works" variety—which failed as often as they succeeded. The blunt truth was that Roosevelt, like Hoover before him, was facing not an economic crisis but a catastrophe without precedent in history. None of Hoover's corrective measures had worked, Roosevelt knew that much, but knowing what *hadn't* worked was not the same as knowing what *would*, hence the desperation of those first four years, along with the near-exclusive focus on domestic affairs. Once America's economic house had been restored to something resembling order, then could the question of what role would the United States play in world affairs be addressed.

Some aspects of that role were clear from the day Franklin Roosevelt became president in March 1933. He did not particularly like nor respect the Japanese, seeing them, as did most Americans of the day, as a race of squinty-eyed, buck-toothed, bandy-legged little men, obsequious and untrustworthy, who aped Western mannerisms but lack the intelligence, competence, and courage of Westerners. Of course, Roosevelt's prejudices didn't end with the Japanese: he thoroughly despised Adolf Hitler, and by extension distrusted the German people as a whole, while like most of the Eastern social elite he thoroughly detested all Italians. At the same time, he was a pronounced Anglophile, a character trait which would exert a distinct influence on how he shaped America's foreign policy, when he finally got around to doing so.

That happened in the summer of 1937; fresh off his crushing defeat of Alf Landon in the 1936 presidential election, and with even larger majorities in the House and Senate, Roosevelt now felt confident enough to begin to undermine some of the restrictions put in place by the 1935 and 1936 Neutrality Acts. He knew that it was unlikely to the point of near-impossibility that a repeal of the second act—which would also naturally void the first—could make it through the House and Senate, so instead he began to look for the inevitable loopholes in their language. It would require the sort of executive sleight-of-hand at which Roosevelt had already proven himself a master, whereby all but the most strident isolationists would be reassured that the Neutrality Acts were still in place and being enforced, and that any apparent "irregularities" were a consequence of circumstances the acts didn't cover or hadn't anticipated.

It was classically ironic that the Neutrality Act of 1937 provided Roosevelt with the opportunities he needed. It first extended indefinitely the terms and restrictions of the previous two acts, and expanded their scope to include civil wars as well as conflicts between nations. This new restriction was understandable: the Spanish Civil War was devastating that unfortunate country, the most zealous interventionists were urging the United States to side with the Spanish Republicans against the openly fascist Falangists, and hundreds of idealistic American men and women were making their way to Spain, volunteering to fight. The act also prohibited merchant ships registered in the United States from carrying trade to belligerents, and American citizens were now banned entirely from traveling on ships owned by nations at war.

It was the restriction on American ships that provided Roosevelt with the narrow crack he was seeking for the thin edge of the wedge he wanted to drive into the Neutrality Acts. He was able to persuade Congress to include a provision in the 1937 Act which allowed, at the president's discretion, the sale of oil, rubber, steel, copper, brass, specialized ores such as nickel, tungsten, and manganese, as well as machine tools and other manufacturing equipment, to certain belligerent powers, so long as the buyers paid for the materials on the spot and transported them in their own ships. By prohibiting the use of American-flagged merchant vessels, the legal fiction could be maintained that there was no involvement by the United States government in what were deemed private business transactions. An added fig leaf was a reiteration of the moratorium on the extension of credits or loans to any belligerent government. The sale of finished munitions and armaments was still prohibited, of course, but Roosevelt reasoned that while Britain and France would likely not be able to retool their own industries and stockpile enough raw materials out of their own resources in time to adequately face the German onslaught he already believed to be inevitable, allowing the British and French to acquire tools and materials from the United States would go far toward closing the gap in their own production capacities. It was a shrewd move, as even the most ardent isolationist could agree that if Europe were plunged into another war, it was best to let the Europeans settle it among themselves, and keep the war on the far side of the Atlantic.

However, it was the Japanese, when they invaded China in July 1937, who gave Roosevelt the chance to run his first open end-run around the Neutrality Acts. Naturally, the president favored China in its struggle against Japan, a favoritism that was shared by many Americans who, because of the work of American Christian missionaries in China, had developed a somewhat avuncular attitude toward the Chinese—provided they stayed in China, of course. Roosevelt's secretary of state,

Cordell Hull, carefully noted that a formal state of war had not been declared between China and Japan, nor was the conflict a civil war; Roosevelt, in turn, announced that, because of this technicality, the Neutrality Acts did not apply to the situation in China.

Isolationists in Congress loudly proclaimed to anyone who would listen that the president was bandying semantics while his decision undermined the intent of the neutrality legislation, but they were hoist on their own petard: their carefully crafted bills had never anticipated such a situation. As a gesture of conciliation, Roosevelt ruled that American ships could not deliver any war materials to China; British shipping companies were happy to transport the cargoes, and China, which had almost no arms industry of its own, was able to continue its fight against Japan. Almost as an afterthought, Roosevelt then issued an executive order prohibiting the export of all aircraft to Japan, in what he called a "moral embargo." Tokyo barely took note of it.

Yet there was more to American foreign policy in the 1930s than just the issue of how the United States would react and then respond to the rising tensions in Europe and the Pacific. From the first day of Roosevelt's administration—he spoke of it in his inaugural address—he was determined to broadly reshape the relationships between the United States and the nations of South and Central America, an undertaking he christened "The Good Neighbor Policy." At first intended to mitigate America's reputation in Latin America for "*Yanqui* imperialism" acquired following the Spanish–American War, by the end of the decade the policy evolved into a major diplomatic effort to blunt attempts by the Axis powers—Germany in particular—to subvert the governments of several South American nations through domestic fascist movements, particularly those of Argentina, Brazil, and Uruguay. The responsibility for carrying out the Good Neighbor Policy was given to the secretary of state, Cordell Hull.

When asked in 1933 by the newly elected president to become the United States' senior diplomat, Cordell Hull had already spent 40 of his 62 years in public service. Born in a log cabin in Pickett County, Tennessee, Hull, whose father was a farmer, was determined, even as a child, to become a lawyer, a goal he achieved at the age of 19 when he graduated from the Cumberland University School of Law in 1891. Two years later he was elected to the Tennessee House of Representatives; after two terms, he went back into legal practice before sitting as a local judge in his home county. In 1907 he moved to Washington DC, having been elected to the first of 11 terms he would spend in Congress, where he established a reputation as an expert in financial and commercial policies. Tennessee voters sent him to the Senate in the 1930 election, but he resigned his seat when Roosevelt offered to him the post of secretary of state in 1933. Hull was not a typical politician—his was a shy, retiring personality, he was not a compelling public speaker, nor was he known for his personal charm. He was, however, respected for his integrity and pragmatism, as well as having the courage of his convictions: he was not given to trimming his political sails to the changing winds of popular opinion.

This personal integrity stood him well in a series of conferences with his counterparts from South and Central American between 1933 and 1940, where his earnest and unassuming nature went far in giving credibility to the pledge made by Roosevelt at his inauguration, that as president he would "dedicate this nation to the policy of the good neighbor...who resolutely respects himself and...the rights of others, the neighbor who respects his obligations and respects the sanctity of his agreements..." Yet, however much a political asset Hull might be to him, Roosevelt didn't like the man: despite his egalitarian posturings, at heart Roosevelt remained very much the East Coast elitist, and he regarded Hull as little more than an over-educated backwoods bumpkin, much preferring the company and counsel of fellow Harvard graduate Sumner Welles, whom he appointed undersecretary of state in 1936. Underestimating Hull was a mistake, as Hull was certainly Roosevelt's intellectual equal, if not his better, and a far more accomplished, if less ambitious, politician. Certainly he was far more pragmatic in his approach to foreign policy than Roosevelt, who frequently imagined that he could daunt foreign powers and dictate policy to them through what he believed was the sheer power of his personality and position.

Hull also did not fall prey to the sort of diplomatic tunnel vision to which Roosevelt was becoming increasingly susceptible. As the succession of diplomatic crises and confrontations in Europe progressed in the late 1930s, the president became increasingly focused on them, so that all other questions of foreign policy became secondary. Hull remained well aware that there existed a threat to world peace other than Nazi Germany, namely Imperial Japan; here he found a natural ally in the Cabinet in Henry Stimson. When Japan invaded China in 1937, Roosevelt, Hull, and Stimson were all equally outraged, due in no small part to their shared belief that international treaties were meant to be observed, not openly broken or simply ignored. But Hull, with his congressional experience in finance and commerce, soon sensed something about Japan's actions which Roosevelt, so intent on thwarting the rise of Nazi Germany, overlooked. In Europe, every aggressive move by Adolf Hitler was undertaken for the purpose of increasing Germany's political power—only minor consideration, if any, was given to economic factors. But as Hull saw it, Japan's invasion of China was driven by economics: the militarists in Tokyo had decided that they would take by force what they otherwise would have to obtain through trade.

Initially, Hull expected that, if the Chinese could hold out long enough, the Japanese economy would begin to falter under the strain of trying to support the war effort, forcing an end to the adventurism of the militarists in Tokyo. This was why he urged Roosevelt to exempt the Chinese from the Neutrality Acts and extend the "cash and carry" policy to China. Hull miscalculated, however, as Japan's economy proved to be more robust than he'd expected, and the militarists, rather than drawing in their horns, began to openly advocate for Japan to become a signatory to the Pact of Steel and join the Axis. Such an eventuality was, of course, Roosevelt and Hull's worst nightmare, as distant and unrelated incidents involving any of the Axis powers could trigger a worldwide war. Meanwhile, the offhand manner in which Japan disposed of the *Panay* incident was an unmistakable demonstration of what little regard Japan held for the United States or any possible threat America could pose to the Empire.

It was an attitude produced by Japanese arrogance combined with a perception of American timorousness, but in truth it was hardly realistic. The truth was that, even though he had overestimated the strain the war in China would place on Japan's economy, Cordell Hull had been fundamentally correct: the reach of Japanese belligerence exceeded Japan's economic grasp. A quick, dispassionate survey of the war making potential of each nation should have convinced the Japanese of the folly of provoking the Americans to the point where they lashed back, either out of rage or because they'd come to believe they had no other choice. At the beginning of 1939, when the country was still trudging through its recovery from the worst depths of the Depression—there were still 15 million unemployed workers—the United States' economy nonetheless dwarfed that of Japan by every meaningful measure. With more than twice Japan's population, America was producing five times as much steel and eight times as much coal as the Empire, and was supplying 80 percent of the oil, crude and refined, needed by Japan's industries and armed forces; America's gross national product was over eleven times that of Japan's, the per capita income six times greater.

The generals and admirals of the Imperial Army and Navy General Staffs knew all of this, and simply didn't care, confident as they were of the superiority of a Japanese soldier or sailor's innate fighting skills, and convinced that by the time the United States mustered the resolve to fight, the Empire's defensive perimeter in the islands of the Pacific would be impenetrable. America would never be willing to pay the price necessary to defeat Japan. In short, the Japanese were as dismissive of the Americans as Americans were of the Japanese. It would prove to be the most costly miscalculation in the history of the Empire, for it would not only trigger the war both nations believed they could avoid, it would ultimately bring the Japanese Empire to a place it had never before been—to its knees.

* * *

As it was for much of the world, 1939 was the turning point for the United States—or more precisely, for the American people. In March, when the Nazis occupied what was left of Czechoslovakia after that nation's betrayal at Munich the previous September, the pretense that Adolf Hitler had merely been gathering back into Germany's fold her people who had been sundered from the Reich by the

Treaty of Versailles could no longer be sustained. His ambitions were now seen for what they were—unambiguously aggressive. As much in Chicago, Detroit, Denver, Los Angeles, New York, or Washington DC as in London, Paris, Berlin, Warsaw, Rome, or Moscow, another continent-wide war in Europe was now seen as all but inevitable. Italy's dictator, Benito Mussolini, once seen as the senior partner in the Pact of Steel, as absurd as the idea may have become, would unquestionably follow wherever Hitler led, and the Japanese ambassador in Berlin, Kurusu Saburo, was actively negotiating the terms under which the Empire would soon become the third major power among the Axis nations.

Even before the German panzers rolled into Prague, the American people had begun to face the grim possibility that yet another war in Europe was looming; to Roosevelt, that war was all but inevitable, given how France and Great Britain seemed resolved to remain irresolute in their opposition to Hitler and the Nazis. As he saw it, his duty as president was to persuade a majority of American voters that when the war erupted, the threat it would present to the safety and security of the United States would be real and immediate: Hitler's hunger for territory and aggressive expansion seemed insatiable, and if France and Great Britain fell to the Nazis, the front line in any confrontation between the United States and Germany would suddenly be at the limit of America's territorial waters.

Roosevelt had to move carefully, though, as, perversely enough, the isolationists in America were approaching the peak of their political influence even as events in Europe were accelerating toward a violent and bloody climax. He was rather forcibly reminded of this truth in the days following a closed-door meeting with the members of the Senate Military Affairs Committee, held at the White House on January 31, 1939. There, Roosevelt tried to explain what he saw as the present strategic realities, an attempt to foster support in the full Senate for his proposals to ease those provisions of the Neutrality Acts which, he was convinced, were hindering—even crippling—the rearmament programs of France and Great Britain. At one point, hoping to drive home the point that it was in America's best interests to enable the French and British to confront and defeat the Germans in Europe rather than risk having Hitler's *Wehrmacht* overrun the Continent and leave the United States to face the Nazis alone, he asserted that "the frontier of the United States is the Rhine." Roosevelt always had a gift for turning a memorable phrase; in this case he turned one that was a bit too memorable: within 24 hours, one of the senators present at the meeting—who has never been determined—leaked those words to the press.[9]

The remark created an uproar among American isolationists that approached hysteria. Deliberately taken out of context, it was cited as proof that the president was secretly planning to send American soldiers to fight in Europe, and editorials immediately appeared in isolationist-leaning newspapers from coast to coast, denouncing Roosevelt's alleged duplicity. Some of the sharpest criticism originated in the president's own party, where isolationist sentiment ran long and deep: while the

Democrats had retained control of both Houses of Congress in the 1938 election, the 75th Congress, which was seated just days before the controversial meeting at the White House, would prove to be a fractious bunch, not at all willing to simply rubber-stamp White House policies, foreign or domestic. Within days, in an effort to keep the peace within his own party, Roosevelt felt compelled to formally deny that he'd ever made such a statement.

The incident was notable for what it revealed about Roosevelt and the American people. Perceptive observers would have noted that the entire White House conference had been given over to the growing crisis in Europe and what practical options were available to the United States in response—it was evident that the Pacific was the farthest thing from Roosevelt's mind. Equally pointed was how starkly it demonstrated that isolationism—or at least non-interventionism—was still the prevailing attitude among most of the American public.

For all of the remarkable volume of fact and opinion that is readily accessible in the so-called "Information Age," it's difficult to dispute the assertion that the average American of the 1930s was, as a rule, more genuinely informed than his or her counterpart would be a half-century and more later. Some of history's best, most conscientious newspaper reporting, ranging all across the political spectrum, together with brilliant, minute-by-minute live radio coverage of the succession of crises in 1938 and 1939, gave the American public to recognize just how real the likelihood of another world war was, and how that conflict was looming larger day by day. The understanding was also growing that the decision to go to war might not be left up the United States government—the Axis could very well choose to bring the war to America. Whether or not the United States should be prepared to defend herself was never questioned: just how and where that defense would—and should—be carried out was the contentious issue.

Should the United States openly, actively stand with the Allies before war became a reality, in the hope of deterring further Nazi aggression, or failing that, should the United States once more become embroiled in a European war, sending her Army and Navy across the Atlantic to fight as she had done little more than 20 years earlier? Was America's best course of action simply to be what Roosevelt would come to call "the great arsenal of democracy," providing arms, aircraft, munitions, equipment, and other support to the British and French without committing the US Army and Navy to combat operations? Or should the Americans simply leave the Europeans alone altogether, to settle their problems in their own time and out of their own resources? Naturally, to the most ardent interventionists there could be no acceptable course of action other than for the United States to stand shoulder-to-shoulder with Great Britain and France, prepared to defend Europe in any and every possible way; the most determined isolationists would have none of it, preferring to reaffirm the "pox on all your houses" refrain and leave Europe utterly alone. As is usually the case when such questions arise, the opinion of the great majority of Americans lay between those two views, but on the whole they could see no good reason to jump into a war which was in no way one of America's making.

Germany finally answered the question of where and when the war would begin in Europe by invading Poland in the early morning hours of September 1, 1939. Two days later, Great Britain and France, honoring their alliances with Poland, declared war on Germany. Nazi U-boats began sinking merchant ships without warning almost immediately, and Admiral Harold Stark, the US Navy's Chief of Naval Operations (CNO) wasted no time in responding: within 24 hours he initiated patrols along the Atlantic coast and in the Caribbean by naval ships and aircraft; their orders were to escort the warships of any of the belligerent power out of America's territorial waters. On September 5, President Roosevelt issued Executive Proclamation 2348 "in order to preserve the neutrality of the United States and of its citizens and of persons within its territory and jurisdiction, and to enforce its laws and treaties…" The United States was now formally and officially a neutral power, and under the terms of the proclamation, would undertake every legal action and responsibility to maintain that neutrality. Roosevelt then proceeded to christen Admiral Stark's naval patrols the Neutrality Patrol.[10]

That evening, in one of his famous "Fireside Chat" radio broadcasts, Roosevelt explained to the American people what he had done and what he intended to do, saying that "When peace has been broken anywhere, the peace of all countries everywhere is in danger." It was vitally important for Americans to understand that neutrality did not mean immunity from danger, and that staying totally aloof from Europe's new war could someday evolve into a threat to the United States should the Nazis and Fascists win that war. The greatest danger to America now, Roosevelt said, was allowing the desire to avoid war at all costs become more important than the security of the nation.[11]

Its name notwithstanding, the "Neutrality Patrol" was anything but neutral. Within a month Roosevelt unexpectedly announced an exclusion zone off the Atlantic seaboard that extended up to 1,000 miles from shore, calling it the Pan-American Security Zone. Within it, any hostile action by any belligerent warship was forbidden, under penalty of being sunk courtesy of the US Navy.

That was the theory, at least: in practice, the threat applied only to German and Italian ships and submarines. Allied convoys sailing to Europe were routinely escorted by American destroyers and cruisers that were ostensibly part of the Neutrality Patrol, while the positions of surfaced German U-boats detected by American warships were invariably broadcast "in the clear"—that is, unencrypted—which allowed British, Canadian, and French escorts to hunt them down. This was the first step in a series of steadily escalating provocations carried out over the next two years whereby Roosevelt hoped to provoke Hitler into ordering a violent retaliation, giving the president a *casus belli* to present to Congress; by April 1941, the Pan-American Security Zone had been extended nearly halfway across the Atlantic.

Hitler, though, refused to be drawn, however furious he might have been—and was—at Roosevelt's manipulation of international law and American neutrality legislation. What Roosevelt did next made *der Führer* even angrier: on November 4, at the president's urging, the Neutrality Act of 1939 was passed, repealing the most restrictive provisions of the 1935 and 1937 Neutrality Acts, effectively scrapping what remained of the arms embargo put in place almost five years earlier. Great Britain and France were now allowed to purchase aircraft, tanks, guns, ammunition, whatever they wished, from whomever they wished as long as they paid for them on the spot. Roosevelt argued that a total embargo on arms sales penalized nations that were trying to defend themselves against aggression, and thus indirectly aided the aggressors; that Congress accepted his reasoning was a clear signal of how support for strict isolation and non-intervention had eroded in American popular opinion since January of that year.

The president made no effort to disguise his belief that Adolf Hitler and the Nazis represented a mortal threat to Western civilization, but his narrow focus on Europe left him little time to do more than apply bandages to serious problems elsewhere in the world. In the spring of 1940, the Imperial Navy began fortifying the Marshal Islands, which sat almost astride the shortest, most direct sea route between Hawaii and the Philippines; rather than take the time to assess the strategic reasons why the Japanese were doing so, Roosevelt ordered Battle Force, as the US Navy's Pacific Fleet was then designated, to move its main Pacific base from San Diego, California, to Pearl Harbor in Hawaii. This "show of strength" would, he fancied, be sufficient to intimidate the Japanese from carrying out any expansionist plans they might have for the Central Pacific, and by repositioning the fleet 2,600 miles to the west, would add to the security of the Philippines and Guam.

It was not a wise decision, nor was it popular within the ranks of the Navy's senior officers. The commander of Battle Force, Admiral James Richardson, protested it respectfully but vigorously. In his opinion, Pearl Harbor was a strategic trap for the fleet—while its shallow bottom was, theoretically at least, protection against torpedo attack, the single channel which served as Pearl's entrance and exit was a key vulnerability. Arguably, sinking a single large ship could create a choke point in the channel that would make it passable by only one ship at a time; conceivably, under the right circumstances, the channel could be blocked entirely, rendering the harbor useless and trapping any ships at anchor inside it. Roosevelt, however, did not ask for the advice of his admirals before making the decision to move the fleet, he simply presented it to the Navy as a *fait accompli*. When Admiral Richardson pressed his case to the president personally, Roosevelt relieved him of command of Battle Force; he would be replaced by Admiral Husband Kimmel.

While Battle Force was moving to Pearl Harbor, all hell was breaking loose in Europe, as the long-awaited German attack on France and the Low Countries began on May 10, 1941. Within a matter of days Belgium and the Netherlands were overrun, France was fighting for her life, and the British were retreating to the English Channel coast at Dunkirk and Calais. At the same time, rumors reached Secretary of State Hull that the Tripartite Pact negotiations between Tokyo, Berlin, and Rome were entering their final stages; in a matter of months, Japan would formally join the Axis. Hull was certain that, once the pact became a reality, the Japanese would only feel encouraged to continue their aggressive expansion, casting covetous eyes on the Dutch colonies of Java and Borneo and their priceless oilfields. The Dutch government-in-exile, now seated in London, would have few if any reinforcements available to bolster the defenses of its Far East colonies, so Hull, in the forlorn hope of exercising some form of restraint on the Japanese, sent a carefully worded reminder to the Imperial Foreign Ministry that the United States would not tolerate the imposition of any sort of "protectorate" over the Dutch East Indies. Implicit in the note was the understanding that the same consideration applied to French Indochina. In reply, Foreign Minister Togo assured Hull that Japan desired no changes in the political and economic status quo in the Southwest Pacific. For his part, Roosevelt, utterly absorbed in the growing debacle in France, merely approved Hull's communications *pro forma*.

When he could be persuaded to devote a significant degree of attention to the Pacific, Roosevelt continued to cling, limpet-like, to the idea that strongly worded diplomatic correspondence like Hull's, coupled with vague threats of some sort of retaliatory response by the US Navy, should Tokyo prove less than tractable, would be sufficient to "overawe" the Japanese and hold them in check. Here his prejudices played him false, as he overestimated American military and naval strength while underestimating that of the Japanese; at the same time he was quite sure—and to be fair, he was misled by the paucity of accurate intelligence available to him—that the Japanese lacked the technical capability and operational competence to pose a genuine threat to the United States. Within weeks of the Nazi invasion of France and the Low Countries, he ordered the largest peace-time expansion of the US Army and Navy in the nation's history, one that would dwarf any similar mobilization by the Japanese, yet, while Japan's economy was already fully mobilized for war, it would be months or even years before the American expansion was complete and the full war-making potential of the nation's industrial might could be brought to bear against any enemy, real or potential.

In the meantime, the United States' land and air forces remained quantitatively and qualitatively inferior to Japan's, and while the US Navy was numerically superior to its Imperial counterpart, the need to defend both the Atlantic and Pacific coasts eroded that superiority to the vanishing point. In fact, the growing demands of the Neutrality Patrol, which Roosevelt would continually reinforce throughout 1940 and 1941, despite the fact that the Germans had no surface navy to speak of, would leave Battle Force—later the Pacific Fleet—numerically inferior to the Japanese Navy. Roosevelt knew this full well—he confessed as much to his secretary of the interior,

Harold Ickes, even as he demonstrated that he still had his priorities wrong, saying, "It is terribly important for the control of the Atlantic for us to keep peace in the Pacific. I simply have not got enough Navy to go round—and every little episode in the Pacific means fewer ships in the Atlantic."[12]

The upshot of Roosevelt giving the priority to Atlantic Fleet was that, far from being intimidated by American bluster, the Emperor and his admirals and generals would come to feel confident enough of victory as to make a deliberate decision to go to war with America—and Roosevelt lacked the military might to dissuade them from that decision. Economic arguments would never be sufficient; forbearance only encouraged further aggression. It was only when he came to understand that the men in Tokyo regarded him as ineffectual, and therefore irrelevant, did the president attempt to move decisively in the Pacific, but by then it would be too late to deflect Japan from its path to war with America. He would become aware of this truth very late in the game, as it were: America's military potential was incredibly vast, but Japan was ready for war *now*.

The return of Henry Stimson to the Cabinet on July 10, 1940, less than two weeks before the French signed an armistice with the Germans, was the first indication of any shift in Roosevelt's perception of the Japanese threat. Stimson had never been a friend of Japan, and while he had once advocated the sort of economic sanctions against Japan that the president had so far undertaken, he long since recognized that they had become hollow gestures. He thoroughly approved, then, of Roosevelt's Executive Order banning the sale and export of aircraft parts and engines, machine tools, and aviation gasoline to the Japanese, knowing that it would at least hurt—though not cripple—Japan's ability to continue the war in China while trying to expand into the Central and Southwest Pacific. When scrap steel—absolutely vital to Japan's steelmaking industry—was added to the list of banned commodities, Roosevelt and Stimson, along with Cordell Hull, who also heartily endorsed the decision, could assure themselves that the Japanese were finally aware that the United States was serious.

All three men agreed that the point of no return for the Japanese came on September 27, 1940, when Japan finally signed the Tripartite Pact; to them this was little short of a deal made with the Devil. By becoming full partners in the Axis, the Emperor along with his generals and admirals, left no doubt that military expansion was now the cornerstone of Japan's foreign policy—nothing would "inhibit" Japan's plans for acquisition through conquest. The president began to shift diplomatic gears, now determined to buy as much time as possible for America's rearmament programs to take hold and produce results while doing what he could to cripple Japan's capacity to make war.

This determination was expressed in the succession of embargoes imposed between January and July 1941; these were no mere slaps on the Japanese wrist: cutting off access to specialized ores and metals, scrap iron and steel, and refinery equipment were blows aimed directly at Japan's national economy, not merely her war effort. When all Japanese economic and financial assets in the United States were frozen and the sale and export of oil to Japan was suspended by Executive Order, Roosevelt was confident that the tables had been effectively turned: if the Japanese truly wanted war, they could have it—but it would be a war that they already knew they must lose. The door to a diplomatic solution, a peaceful resolution of the disputes between the United States and the Empire of Japan, was still open, but for it to remain open, the Japanese would now have to negotiate in good faith. Whether or not they would choose to do so would remain to be seen.

CHAPTER 3

Men, Ships, Planes, and Plans

While the executive order signed by President Roosevelt on July 26, 1940, was the tipping point for the Japanese in their decision as to whether or not Japan would have to go to war with the United States, the likelihood that such a confrontation would come to pass had already been growing for months. Hand in hand with recognizing that war was becoming nigh-on inevitable went the question of how to win that war if it did. Admiral Yamamoto's remark about "the auto factories in Detroit and the oil-fields in Texas" was a succinct summation of the immense problem Japan as a whole, not just the Army and Navy, would face if war came to pass: Japan did not then and would never possess the resources, material or industrial, to defeat the United States in a prolonged war.

Hirohito's admirals, generals, government ministers and advisors—indeed, the Emperor himself—weren't ignorant of this reality, nor did they pretend to be. On July 21, 1940, Navy Chief of Staff Admiral Nagano reminded the Cabinet of Prime Minister Prince Konoye's freshly seated Government that "By the latter half of next year it will be difficult for us to cope with the United States. After that, the situation will become progressively worse… Time is not on our side."[1]

Unspoken but inherent in Nagano's statement was the demand that if there was to be war with the United States, it was best if it came sooner rather than later, when Japan's disadvantages could be minimized and her advantages—especially seizing and holding the initiative—would be maximized. It was self-evident that any war with the Americans would be first and foremost a naval war, and while in absolute terms—total tonnage, number of ships and naval aircraft, manpower—the US Navy's margin of superiority over the Imperial Navy was insurmountable, the fact that the Americans were compelled by events east and west to divide their naval strength between the Atlantic and Pacific Oceans offered the Japanese a small but real window of opportunity for decisive action against the US Navy, one that could—and would, if properly exploited—compel the Americans to come to the negotiating table and cede to *Dai Nippon* the territories the Japanese coveted.

The sixty-four-dollar question, in the American idiom of the day, was how could this be accomplished? When Admiral Nagano presented his strategic assessment to the new Cabinet, perceptive naval officers were already asking this, as the fall of France in June gave the U-boats of the Nazi *Kriegsmarine* almost unlimited access to the Atlantic, raising the tension between the United States and Germany even further. This could be turned to Japan's advantage, as Roosevelt would almost certainly further strengthen the Neutrality Patrols at the expense of the US Navy forces deployed in the Pacific.

The strategic challenge was not to simply provoke a confrontation with the Americans—any fool could do that, and even the most militant of Japan's senior officers understood that allowing the US Navy to try conclusions with the Imperial Navy on anything approaching an equal footing would ultimately be a fatal mistake, regardless of the outcome of the battle. Every ship sunk, aircraft shot down, or sailor drowned would be far more damaging to the Japanese than corresponding losses would be to the Americans, simply because replacing them would demand proportionally far more of Japan's limited resources than making good such losses would require of America's vastly greater pool of material and men.

The solution then would be found in contriving a way to bring about qualitative and quantitative superiority for the Imperial Navy at a precise point and in such a way where the damage inflicted on the US Navy would be heavily out of proportion to the size of the Japanese forces involved. Strategic and tactical surprise would be vital, as surprise itself was always a considerable force multiplier—often decisively so. Did such a point exist, and if so, how was it to be attacked?

It was here that the man whom history would inseparably link with the Japanese attack on Pearl Harbor stepped onto the stage: Admiral Yamamoto Isoroku. An intriguing, even fascinating individual, Yamamoto stood distinct from most of his contemporaries, never having ossified into one of those stale, stolid, unimaginative martinets routinely produced by the Imperial Naval Academy at Eta Jima, more timid bureaucrats than fighting sailors, no matter how much they imagined themselves to be molded in the fearsome *samurai* tradition. Nor was he a wild-eyed maverick to be marginalized, packed off and rendered harmless in some dead-end posting: Yamamoto was talented, competent, and possessed of the intelligence and imagination to be able to look beyond mere tradition in order to examine the reasons why traditions came to be. While never questioning the absolute necessity of discipline among the Navy's officers and men, he understood that blind obedience to orders issued simply because "the Book" declared it should be so could be crippling in wartime, and stifled original thinking in strategy and tactics during times of peace.

Most anyone who knew Yamamoto Isoroku early in his naval career would have predicted that the young man had an outstanding future ahead of him; few if any would have had the slightest inkling that he would one day, in the span of less than two years, turn the fundamental premises of the Imperial Navy's strategic doctrine on their collective ear. Born Takano Isoroku on April 4, 1884, in the small village of Kushigun Sonshomura in Niigata Prefecture, he was the sixth son of Takano Sadayoshi and his second wife, Mineko. The name "Isoroku" was a small joke on the part of his father, as it was a testament to Sadayoshi's virility—it means "fifty-six" in Japanese, Sadayoshi's age when his sixth son was born.

Exactly when and how Isoroku decided on a career in the Imperial Navy remains uncertain, but it was a firm decision, for when he turned 16, he took the highly competitive entrance examinations for admission to the Naval Academy. Specializing in naval gunnery, he graduated in the spring of 1904, and was assigned to the shiny new armored cruiser *Nisshin*, which almost immediately went into action against the Russian Navy's Far East Squadron, as Japan and Russia had gone to war in February of that year. *Nisshin* fought in the Battle of the Yellow Sea and at Tsushima, both times as part of the screening force for Admiral Togo's battleships. The ship suffered heavy damage at Tsushima, taking 13 hits, and the young ensign was twice wounded. "When the shells began to fly above me I found I was not afraid," he wrote to his parents while convalescing. "The ship was damaged by shells and many were killed. At 6:15 in the evening a shell hit the Nisshin and knocked me unconscious. When I recovered I found I was wounded in the right leg and two fingers of my left hand were missing."[2]

For the next nine years Isoroku's career mirrored that of tens of thousands of junior officers in navies all around the world: a succession of postings to different ships, always training, while broadening and deepening his practical knowledge and familiarity with the workings of the navy. Ordered to the Naval Staff College in 1913, he graduated in 1916, was promoted to lieutenant commander, and posted to the staff of the Second Battle Squadron. For him, as for most of the officers of the Imperial Navy, the years of the Great War were singularly uneventful; the Second Battle Squadron never left home waters during the entire conflict.

That was also the year he changed his name from "Takano Isoroku" to "Yamamoto Isoroku". He was adopted into the powerful Yamamoto family, a circumstance that would present him with social opportunities that would never have been available to the son of a humble schoolmaster. Such adoptions were common among wealthy and influential families in Japan, a practical solution to the problem of ensuring a family's name did not die out when there were no male heirs born into the current generation. As the youngest of six Takano sons, he had no obligation to maintain the continuity of his birth family—his brothers could see to that—and the offer of adoption was a great honor, which he accepted with alacrity.

In 1918, Yamamoto married Mihashi Reiko, a woman from his home prefecture of Niigata, with whom he had two sons and two daughters; eventually it would emerge that theirs was not a particularly close marriage. As a bachelor, Yamamoto had been a frequent patron at certain select *geisha* houses, an indulgence he continued after his marriage and a practice which carried no stigma in Japanese society. (It should be remembered that the *geisha* were not common prostitutes, being educated and skilled in arts that were not carnal—music, dance, poetry—and valued for their intelligent conversation. For sex, Yamamoto would turn to a succession of mistresses.) He was highly amused by the nickname some of his favorite *geisha* gave him: "eighty sen." It seems that in pre-war Japan, the standard fee for a manicure was one yen, but as Yamamoto had lost the index and middle fingers on his left hand at Tsushima, he was charged for only eight digits.

To relax, Yamamoto practiced calligraphy, an art at which he became quite accomplished, and gambled, his favorite games being *Shogi* (a Japanese game very similar to chess), *mah jong*, billiards, bridge, and especially poker. It's impossible to say when gambling became one of Yamamoto's favored pastimes, or when he came to realize that he had a distinct talent for "games of chance," but immediately following the end of the First World War he was given an unexpected opportunity to develop and exploit that talent.

In June 1919 he found himself in Cambridge, Massachusetts, walking across Harvard Yard; he would spend two years at the university, courtesy of the Imperial Navy, studying English and economics, as well as attending to certain other duties. He became rather popular in some student circles, as he was invariably polite, amiable without being ingratiating, and had a quick wit, which only rarely edged over into the biting sarcasm that he often directed at his countrymen; he felt most comfortable among underclassmen who, like himself, had a fondness for gambling. Yamamoto's keen intellect, along with his social and political connections—he was already cultivating friendships with members of the Imperial family—had marked him as an officer who was almost certainly destined for flag rank. This posting to the United States was further evidence of high expectations, as it was understood that he would learn all that he could about Americans as a people and America as a nation, the better to understand them both, in preparation against the day when Japan and America would go to war with each other.

No vast, dark conspiracy had suddenly coalesced in Tokyo, dedicated to driving the two nations into conflict, but there had been a shift in strategic perception at the highest levels of Japan's armed forces. That shift began even before the Great War came to an end: the Japanese saw that the European colonial powers would no longer possess the strength or the will to check Japanese ambitions at the Empire's boundaries. The Dutch would certainly have the will but not the strength, France would lack both. The British would have the strength, barely, but not the will: while hardly a spent force in the affairs of the Far East, Great Britain was unlikely to soon come into conflict with *Dai Nippon*. The two empires' spheres of influences rarely overlapped, and should the mood of the Japanese government once again turn expansionist, their territories were for the time being too widely separated to be a source of friction. China had been carved up by rival warlords and was a threat to no one. That left only the United States as a possible adversary.

It was a situation brought about first of all by Far Eastern geography: with the Philippines sitting squarely in the way should the Empire want to expand southward, the likelihood of a collision between the two nations was very real. More than just geography was responsible, though. Resentment still lingered over President Theodore Roosevelt's perceived favoritism toward Russia in arbitrating the Treaty of Portsmouth, and tainted the apparent cordiality between the two nations. That resentment and the steadily growing belief at all levels of Japanese society that they were a people superior to all others strengthened the position of the militarists in the government, for whom war was the preferred solution to international disputes.

The Japanese weren't alone in anticipating a war in the Pacific: in Washington DC, the War and Navy Departments were jointly developing "War Plan Orange," a detailed strategic and operational blueprint for a war against Japan. Of course, the Americans were also creating War Plan Red, for operations against Great Britain; War Plan Yellow, should the United States and China find themselves fighting each other; War Plan Indigo, the invasion of Iceland; War Plan Crimson, in case the United States went to war with Canada—in other words, a whole range of contingency plans were created, some realistic, others clearly fanciful, all given a colored code-name. For the most part, these plans were just theoretical exercises used by Army and Navy command staffs to hone their skills at writing efficient troop or fleet movement orders, calculating supply requirements, and solving other logistical challenges. Where the Americans and Japanese differed in their methods of war-planning was that the Americans were drawing up plans to be used *if* they were needed, while the Japanese were creating theirs for *when* they would be needed.

By the time young Lieutenant Commander Yamamoto was dispatched to the United States, Admiral Togo's victory at Tsushima had achieved near-mythic status within the Imperial Navy—and ossified strategic thinking in the fleet's highest ranks. Tsushima had been a near-perfect example of the "decisive battle" as defined by Captain Alfred Thayer Mahan, an American naval theorist whose writings in the last decade of the 19th century profoundly influenced the strategic thinking and development of the world's largest navies. Mahan defined "sea power" as a nation's ability to control, in peace and war, the sea lanes on which that nation's commercial shipping traveled; navies existed to protect their own sea lanes and disrupt those of the enemy. Arguing in essence that "the best defense is a good offense," Mahan asserted that the most effective way for a nation to defend its own sea lanes and shipping was to aggressively seek out the enemy's fleet and destroy it, preferably in one great, thundering, decisive battle. The purpose of all naval strategy and planning then should be to bring about that battle.

To the Japanese, who zealously embraced Mahan's ideas and concepts and soon turned them into a doctrine that approached dogma—a sin which admittedly beset most of the world's navies at the time—the doctrine of *Kantai Kessen*, the Decisive Battle, another Tsushima, became the Holy Grail of Japanese naval planning. The trick was bringing it about: ideally the *Kido Butai*, the main striking force, would wait for the American battleship fleet to advance westward toward the Japanese Home Islands, constantly harassed by the Imperial Navy's cruisers, destroyers, and submarines. In this they would be emulating Togo, who had patiently waited for the Russians, overextended and demoralized, to move into a position where his own, smaller fleet had the advantage, and then struck decisively. Exhausted, its numbers depleted, the American battle fleet would arrive at the point Japanese planners had chosen for the Decisive Battle, and there be annihilated. *Banzai!*[3]

At least, that was how it was supposed to work in theory. In practice, the Americans would have plans of their own which might not include having their battleships willingly steam westward, harried by enemy cruisers and submarines, to do battle at a time and place of the Imperial Navy's own choosing; it could also be expected that the Japanese fleet would suffer harassment of its own at the hands of American light forces and submersibles. The likely outcome of such a national strategy would have been the two fleets meeting at something like near-parity, which the Japanese could not afford to have happen. The Imperial Navy would spend the next two decades trying to find a way to bring about the Decisive Battle on terms heavily in Japan's favor.

Meanwhile, having acquired a considerable fluency in English, newly promoted Commander Yamamoto returned to Tokyo in July 1921, where an instructor's post at the naval war college awaited him. Three years later he changed his specialty from gunnery to naval aviation, having concluded that battleships and battleship doctrine were rapidly approaching a tactical and strategic dead end, and was named the executive officer of Kasumigaura Naval Air Station, 40 miles northeast of Tokyo, the cradle of Japanese naval aviation.

Advancement for Yamamoto remained steady and rapid. In 1926, after being promoted to captain, he went back to the United States, this time as the senior naval attaché at the Japanese Embassy in Washington DC, a posting he would hold for two years. Able to move about the country more readily and more extensively than he did as a student, Yamamoto was able to see first-hand the scale and extent of American industry, from steel mills in Pittsburgh, Pennsylvania and Gary, Indiana, automobile factories in Detroit, to the oilfields of Texas and southern California, and the growing aircraft industry in and around Los Angeles and Seattle. The experience affected him profoundly, as he realized that the difference in industrial capacity, actual and potential, between Japan and the United States was no mere gap, it was a yawning chasm. After spending two years at the Washington embassy, he returned to Japan more firmly convinced than ever that war with the United States would be disastrous.

At the age of 40 he went through pilot training, received his naval aviator's wings, and in December 1928 he was given command of the aircraft carrier *Akagi*. It was a prestigious command, and the ideal posting for Yamamoto: *Akagi* was one of only two fleet carriers in the Imperial Navy at the time (*Kaga* was the other), and one of the largest aircraft carriers in the world. She was also the "floating laboratory" where the doctrine and tactics of Japanese naval aviation were being developed. Converted from the incomplete hull of a battlecruiser (*Kaga*, her half-sister, was built on an unfinished battleship hull), *Akagi* was launched on April 22, 1925, and commissioned on March 25, 1927. Her air group included 28 torpedo bombers, 16 fighters and 16 reconnaissance aircraft; together with *Kaga*, which carried an identical air group, they formed the First Carrier Division. During fleet maneuvers the carriers acted as a combined scouting force and strike force, tasked with wearing down enemy strength; during these exercises Yamamoto was able to note how a small number of massed air attacks did far more cumulative damage to an enemy fleet than did more numerous but smaller air strikes.

His command of *Akagi* lasted slightly less than a year, as November 1929 found Yamamoto in Great Britain, a delegate at the London Naval Conference, a follow-on to the Washington conference of 1922. These negotiations focused on restricting the numbers, sizes, and capabilities of cruisers, destroyers, and submarines, while confirming the limitations on battleships and aircraft carriers set in 1922. After the new treaty was signed on April 22, 1930, Yamamoto, who had been promoted to rear admiral, took command of the First Air Fleet at the Naval Air Corps headquarters, the Imperial Navy once again neatly slipping a round peg into a round hole, as he was becoming a steadily more vocal proponent of naval aviation, convinced that it was only a matter of time before aircraft carriers supplanted battleships among the world's navies as they surpassed them in striking power.

It was a radical idea, not well-received within the flag ranks of the Imperial Navy, dominated as they were by traditional "big gun" admirals, for whom the battleship was the *ne plus ultra* of warship evolution. As Yamamoto gained experience with naval air operations and their potential, he became more outspoken, sometimes overstating his case to make his point: he once remarked that, "[Battleships] are like elaborate religious scrolls which old people hang in their homes, a matter of faith, not reality... In modern warfare, battleships will be as useful to Japan as a *samurai* sword."[4]

Yet, Yamamoto hadn't completely abandoned the battleship; there was still a place in modern naval warfare for the traditional line-of-battle engagement, if only because the Imperial Navy still lacked sufficient numbers of aircraft carriers—and aircraft—to mount truly decisive air operations; this he well understood. He made this understanding quite clear at the London Naval Conference in 1934, where he led the Japanese delegation. It was Yamamoto who informed the other delegations that Japan found unacceptable the current restrictions on the number of battleships she was allowed to possess—if the Imperial Navy was not granted parity in numbers with the British and American navies, the Japanese would withdraw from the conference and all of the existing naval treaties. When the British and Americans demurred, the Japanese delegates walked out. Thinking that this was a bluff merely to preserve Japan's national honor, Ramsay McDonald, the British prime minister, tried to cajole Yamamoto and his officers into returning, asking, "If the other powers agree to paper parity, will Japan promise not to build to it?" Yamamoto was blunt: "Very sorry, but no. If we have parity, we build." The delegation formally withdrew from the Conference and renounced both earlier treaties, at a stroke removing all restraints on the Imperial Navy's shipbuilding programs. When the Second London Naval Treaty was concluded on March 25, 1936, it was already a dead letter.[5]

Yamamoto was now a vice admiral and the vice minister of the Imperial Navy. Once in office he began to press for the construction of additional carriers as well as the development of a new generation of faster, more powerful, longer-ranged airplanes: if the aircraft that could achieve decisive results had yet to be designed and built, then he would force the pace to make them a reality. The designs for the three aircraft types that would be used in the strike on Pearl Harbor, the Nakajima Type 97 bomber (which could carry torpedoes or bombs, and which the Allied would call the "Kate"), the Aichi Type 99 dive bomber (the "Val"), and Mitsubishi Type 0 fighter (the "Zero"), were the results of Yamamoto's impetus.

Despite the intensity with which Yamamoto sometimes voiced his thoughts on naval air power and the future of battleships, he was able for the most part to keep such expressions impersonal and professional, directing them at ideas rather than individuals. This allowed him, while he was serving with the fleet, to avoid the political intrigues and factionalism that were growing within the Imperial Navy, factions that included not only the battleship admirals and airpower advocates, but also varying shades of militarists and moderates. As Vice Minister of the Navy, though, such detachment was no longer possible.

His disdain for the cult of the battleship made him unpopular among the battleship admirals, of course; when he learned that plans were in hand for a pair of 65,000-ton battleships (they would become *Yamato* and *Musashi*, the largest such warships ever built), he acidly dismissed them with an old Asian proverb: "The fiercest serpent may be overcome by a swarm of ants." Likewise he found himself at odds with those zealots in the airpower camp for not joining in when they proclaimed the omnipotence of the airplane. They, like True Believers of any ilk, were so enamored of their own dogma—a mirror image of the battleship admirals—that they were unable or unwilling to recognize that as of yet their reach exceeded their grasp: the aircraft currently available to them lacked the power and range to carry out the sort of decisive strikes they envisioned and predicted.

More ominously for Yamamoto, his open endorsement of the naval limitation treaties made bitter enemies among those ultra-nationalist admirals and captains who saw the building of as many ships—especially battleships—as possible, regardless of need or consequences, as the only true means of expressing and projecting Japanese power. This despite the fact that he had effectively scuttled the Second

London Naval Agreement by refusing to accept what he saw as arbitrary limitations being imposed on the Imperial Navy. His reasoned and rational justification of the treaties was given short shrift by those officers for whom war was becoming an end in and of itself, rather than a means to attaining national objectives, and who saw any restriction of Japanese armaments as an affront to Japan's honor. Likewise, in December 1937, when Yamamoto, in his official capacity as Deputy Navy Minister, met with American Ambassador Joseph Grew to offer Japan's formal apology for the USS *Panay* incident, the militarists took this as yet another instance of Yamamoto compromising national honor; it was shortly thereafter that he received his first threat of assassination.

As for the Imperial Army, he had nothing but contempt for the majority of its senior officers, who, as he saw it, were methodically subverting the civilian government for their own short-sighted ends—to Yamamoto, martial glory and military adventurism made for a poor foundation for national policy. Beneath contempt were those Army radicals who chose to impose their will on the nation by assassination and violence; not only were their actions dishonorable, such deeds could only lead to chaos and anarchy as they drove governance into descending to a realm where the rule of law was superseded by the rule of the gun, bomb, or sword—a return to the days of the *samurai* and the shogunate, but without a *shōgun* to restore order.

Worst of all to Yamamoto was the increasing likelihood of Japan forming a military alliance with Nazi Germany. The Germans and Japanese had already signed the Anti-Comintern Pact in November 1936; ostensibly meant as a show of solidarity in opposing the influence of the Communist International—the Comintern—it contained secret clauses that pledged either nation to benevolent neutrality should the other signatory go to war with the Soviet Union. This was all to Japan's good as far as it went, but events in the years to follow—Japan's invasion of Manchuria and war with China, Germany's *Anschluss* with Austria, the Munich Crisis, and the annexation of the rump of Czechoslovakia—would turn the two nations into pariahs in the international community, compelling them in their isolation to draw closer together diplomatically.

Yamamoto's opposition to an alliance with Germany was not due to any sense of revulsion for the Nazis or their ideology, but rather was the product of a typically level-headed, almost detached analysis of strategic realities. He repeatedly pointed out to a succession of Navy Ministers that Japan imported four-fifths of the iron ore and scrap metal her industries needed, along with all her rubber and almost all her oil, from the United States or one of the colonies of those European powers which were aligning against Germany. Alliance with the Germans could well result in Japan being cut off from the raw materials she needed to survive. In that event, Japan, facing economic collapse, would have to go to war to seize those raw materials, a war that would not be of the Empire's choosing, as it would almost certainly involve the United States. Given that Germany and Japan were on opposite sides of the globe, the Germans could offer little real support to the Japanese in such a war. Courting such a possibility, then, was foolishness, especially given that, as Yamamoto wrote to Vice Admiral Shimada Shigetaro in September 1939, "there is no chance of winning a war with the United States for some time to come."[6]

* * *

On the other side of the Pacific Ocean, the United States Navy was experiencing its own share of political infighting, and though it was not as lethal as was the feuding in the Imperial Navy, it was no less bitter for all that. The 1920s and most of the 1930s had been lean times for the Navy—and the Army as well—as overly parsimonious congresscritters saw the most expedient way to trim the federal government's budget was to carve away at military and naval appropriations. And while those same politicians might protest that they were merely trimming fat, they were cutting away a lot of muscle at the same time.

Even the true purpose behind the Washington Naval Conference in 1922 had been reducing naval budgets, no matter how publicly the politicians might proclaim that they were trying to avert another World War. And it succeeded: once ratified, the Washington Naval Treaty saved American taxpayers over $1 billion (at 1922 values) in construction costs for ships proscribed by the treaty. This was equal to the combined expenditures saved by all of the other signatories to the Washington Treaty.

Those other naval powers—Great Britain, France, Italy, and Japan—promptly diverted the funding they had earmarked for battleships to the construction of cruisers, destroyers, submarines, and other types of auxiliary vessels not limited by the treaty, a course the United States didn't follow. By 1926 the US Navy's budget for new construction was actually smaller than it had been ten years earlier, when the United States hadn't yet become a belligerent in the Great War. While it could have been—and was—argued that, already possessing the world's largest fleet, there was no reason for the American navy to further expand, the penny-pinchers in Washington DC were also handicapping the ability of the existing navy to effectively defend the United States, as they either delayed or outright denied the navy the funds to build replacements for worn-out support vessels and fleet auxiliaries, the colliers, tankers, repair ships, and munitions ships vital to keeping the fleet moving and fighting.

By contrast, in the six years that followed the signing of the Washington Treaty, the other naval powers were busy constructing cruisers, destroyers, and auxiliaries of all kinds—Japan built 125 new ships; France, 119; Italy, 82; and Great Britain, 74. In that same span, the United States built exactly 11. The secretary of the navy, Curtis Wilbur, trying to reverse, or at least halt, the navy's slow death by atrophy and starvation, submitted a proposal to Congress in 1927 that asked for 74 new ships to be laid down within five years and completed within eight. The plan included 25 cruisers, five aircraft carriers, nine destroyers, and 35 submarines. There was no mention of new battleships, even though the navy would begin retiring the oldest ones in the fleet in 1931, four years hence. As battleships required, on average, four years to build, it was clear that there would be no replacements.

In the event it wouldn't have mattered, as Congress rejected Secretary Wilbur's proposal, instead substituting its own plan for a three-year construction program of 15 heavy cruisers and one aircraft carrier. As for new battleships, the navy was authorized instead to begin modernizing its existing ships, mainly through rebuilding their superstructures, upgrading their armor and torpedo protection, and adding more powerful anti-aircraft guns and secondary batteries. It was a short-sighted solution, as it meant that, just to keep the fleet at its current strength, the Navy's oldest battleships, some of which were almost worn out, would have to remain in service indefinitely. If the Japanese, realistically the only potential enemy for the US Navy—no one on either side of the Atlantic could conceive of a war between the United States and Great Britain—chose to retire their oldest battleships and replace them with new construction, the American fleet would have no modern ships of its own to counter them.

Just as they did in the Imperial Navy, battleships still had pride of place in the US Navy. At the end of the 1920s, the US Navy had only two aircraft carriers—*Lexington* and *Saratoga*—though they were the largest and most advanced carriers afloat at the time. (A third ship, *Langley*, had been converted from a collier into a carrier, but was never regarded as anything more than a glorified training ship which was never intended to actually go into action.) But while the American naval aviators were rapidly developing an effective doctrine for naval airpower, they found themselves hampered by the same problem that Yamamoto Isoroku would face a few years later—they lacked the numbers to mount truly decisive air strikes on an enemy fleet. Until that day came, if it ever did, the long reign of the battleship would continue.

The Americans had followed the lead of the British and Germans in the years before the Great War—as did the Japanese—in making the battleship their primary naval weapon: this was not a case of "monkey see—monkey do," but the product of careful observation of other navies' experiences. There had been a handful of times when some "new school" of naval warfare had sprung up, usually involving the French, whose navy was always inferior in numbers and quality to that of the British, and usually revolving around some form of commerce raiding or using swarms of light units—cruisers, destroyers, or torpedo boats—to inflict unacceptable losses on the enemy's battleship strength. These efforts were notable only for their lack of success—even Imperial Germany's U-boats, while proving to be fearsome commerce raiders in the Great War, never seriously threatened the battleship's primacy. The battleship fleet had become the arbiter of naval warfare simply because for the time being the only thing that could decisively defeat it was another battleship fleet. Airpower would not change that unless and until carrier aircraft became much longer ranged and carried far larger payloads: in 1930, the longest-ranged planes had a radius of action—that is, the distance they could fly to a target and return to their carriers—of little more than 200 miles, while carrying a single 1,000-pound torpedo or a pair of 500-pound bombs, weapons far too light to inflict serious damage on a battleship.

When the Great Depression overwhelmed the economies of the industrialized nations, the situation became even worse for the American armed forces as the lean years of the 1920s descended into something akin to famine. By 1933, the combined budgets for the Army and Navy were being arbitrarily reduced by 10 percent annually, with even deeper cuts to come: at one point in 1934, President Roosevelt informed his army chief of staff, General Douglas MacArthur, that the Army's funding for 1935 would be slashed by half. MacArthur was appalled: at the time, the Army was equipped almost entirely with weapons left over from the Great War—aging French artillery pieces, worn-out machine guns, 20-year-old rifles that were loaded with 20-year-old ammunition; there was a total of 12 tanks in running condition in the entire army. The Navy's circumstances were no better, as all new construction was halted, replacement equipment was procured in dribs and drabs, funds for maintaining the existing fleet were pared down to the absolute minimum; an order for a dozen new aircraft to replace 1918-vintage torpedo bombers was considered an extravagance.

Naturally, Congress was no ally to either service, and as they desperately flailed about to stem the flow of red ink in the nation's books, members of the House and Senate sometimes overstepped the bounds of propriety; the adversarial tone that would become a fixture in future relations between Congress and the armed forces found its origins in these years. In one celebrated incident, General MacArthur, responding to congressional questions about the army's proposed budget, was asked, when a member of the committee noted that some of the funds were to be used to purchase toilet paper, if the army was expecting a serious epidemic of dysentery. MacArthur stalked out of the hearing in disgust.

Actually, such a *faux pas* was as much the product of hysteria as it was antagonism: Congress and Roosevelt together were facing a collection of challenges that were sufficient to make weak men quail and strong men hesitant. Theirs was the responsibility for guiding America toward an economic recovery from the worst depression in all of industrialized history at the same time as they were charged to defend the nation against foreign aggression, which had been given a new lease on life courtesy of the militant regimes now in power in Berlin, Rome, and Tokyo. At the time success in either task couldn't be considered as given and they often seemed mutually exclusive. Within weeks of President Roosevelt taking office, the new secretary of the navy, Claude Swanson, informed the White House that all but five of the fleet's 72 destroyers would be reaching the end of their service lives in 1936, and there were no replacements authorized or building; a similar, but not yet as drastic, situation existed with the Navy's cruisers as well. This was a problem which could be neither ignored nor deferred; the sticking point wasn't whether new ships should be built, but how the government would pay for them.

It was Congress that unexpectedly—and inadvertently—came to the rescue. In June 1933, the National Industrial Recovery Act was passed; in it was an allocation of $3.3 billion for public works. Interpreting "public works" as broadly as possible, the administration decided that $237 million would be used to build new warships: two aircraft carriers, 10 cruisers—six heavy and four light—and 20 destroyers. More were to follow in short order, as the Vinson Act, named for it primary sponsor, Senator Carl Vinson, was passed on March 27, 1934; it authorized further expanding the fleet with an additional carrier, 65 more destroyers, 30 submarines, and nearly 1,200 aircraft. Just as important as the numbers was the sense of urgency embedded within the Act: all of the new construction was to be started within three years (it took time to design new ships) and the entire program was to be completed by the end of 1942. The Act also included a requirement, in addition to the new construction authorized, for ships and airplanes currently in service which reached the end of their service lives or were declared obsolescent to be replaced on a one-for-one basis with newly built airframes or hulls, in order to maintain the Navy at a firmly established strength.

Four years after the Vinson Act, Roosevelt signed into law the first of two additional Naval Expansion Acts. It authorized a 20 percent increase in the overall strength of the Navy, along with enlarging existing naval bases and building new airfields, dry docks, and training stations. The second, the Two-Ocean Navy Act, followed in the summer of 1940, and went even further: it increased the size of the Navy by 70 percent, its largest peacetime expansion in the nation's history, and specified by type and class the numbers of ships to be built. These included seven new battleships, 18 aircraft carriers, 29 heavy and light cruisers, 115 destroyers, and 42 submarines; all were to be completed and commissioned by 1945; it also authorized expanding naval aviation to the unheard-of strength of 15,000 aircraft.

Both acts were passed in reaction to events overseas: on one hand, there were Germany's bloodless conquests of Austria and Czechoslovakia, her invasion and swift defeat of Poland (which she immediately partitioned with the Soviet Union), and the stunning triumph over the Western Allies in May and June 1940; on the other were Japan's open war with China and her aggressive moves toward Indochina and the Dutch East Indies. Even the most ardent isolationist could no longer pretend that war could not be brought to America if the Axis powers chose to do so, or that the United States might find itself fighting the Axis alone. Just the needs of self-defense, then, required the nation to draw on the immense reserves of labor and industry that most Americans never realized the country possessed.

This was the realization of Admiral Yamamoto's worst fears: the United States had begun to flex the industrial muscles that Japan could never equal, building the United States Navy to a size and at a rate that Japan could never match. If the militarists in Tokyo succeeded in starting the war which they seemed to so fervently desire, Japan would have to strike the first blow, and soon, otherwise Yamamoto's prediction of inevitable defeat would become a fact.

* * *

On the morning of February 1, 1941, at the United States Naval Base Pearl Harbor, Hawaii, a man who usually wore the two-star shoulder boards of a rear admiral (upper half) in the United States Navy put on the four-star shoulder boards of a full admiral, a temporary rank that went with his new assignment as Commander-in-Chief, Pacific Fleet (CINCPAC), and Commander-in-Chief, United States Fleet (CINCUS). His name was Husband Edward Kimmel. Slightly stocky in build, average in height, with an honest, open face that accurately represented the man's character, the 59-year-old Kimmel had already spent 40 years in the US Navy. An Annapolis graduate, Class of '04, he was the son of Marius Manning Kimmel, a retired United States Army officer and West Point graduate who had the unusual distinction of having served in both the Union and Confederate armies during the Civil War. Born in Henderson, Kentucky on February 26, 1882, young Husband Kimmel, who graduated as valedictorian of his high school class, hoped to follow in his father's footsteps as a cadet at West Point.

There was to be no appointment to West Point for Husband Kimmel, but he was offered one to Annapolis, which he quickly accepted. Graduating 16th out of 62 in his class in February 1904, he spent two years on sea duty before being commissioned an ensign, the standard procedure in those days, as it was a way to weed out those cadets who weren't up to the physical and mental challenges of life aboard a warship. Now that he was officially a naval officer, his career echoed that of Yamamoto Isoroku, a steady climb through the ranks, with ever greater responsibility: promoted to lieutenant (both grades) in 1909; lieutenant commander in August 1916; commander in February 1918; and captain in July 1926. Along the way, he found the time to court Dorothy Kinkaid, who was the daughter of an admiral, marrying her on January 31, 1912. Unlike Yamamoto, Kimmel's marriage was a happy one, and he and Dorothy would have three sons—Manning, Thomas, and Edward—two of whom, Manning and Thomas, would become naval officers, Annapolis graduates like their father. Manning, the commanding officer of the submarine USS *Robalo*, would die while a prisoner of war, reportedly brutally murdered by his Japanese captors.

Like Yamamoto, Kimmel specialized in gunnery early in his career, and several of his postings as a junior officer reflected this. He went aboard the battleship USS *Georgia* when she circumnavigated the globe as part of the Great White Fleet, then in 1907 reported to his first assignment in Washington DC, taking a course in Ordnance Engineering in the Navy Department's Bureau of Ordnance; later he would return to the Ordnance Bureau as the Assistant to the Director of Target Practice and Engineering Performances. He spent a total of five years in the Atlantic Fleet before being transferred to the West Coast; he served as an aide to the commander of the Atlantic Fleet's Fourth Battleship, later filling the same role for the commander of the Third Division, and in between worked in every shipboard department, as well as in minor staff positions, simultaneously learning the "nuts and bolts" of a warship's internal operations while closely watching senior officers as they managed the problems of division, squadron, and fleet command. After his transfer west he was assigned to be the ordnance officer on the USS *California*, then later was the aide and fleet gunnery officer on the staff of the Commander-in-Chief of the US Pacific Fleet, Admiral Cameron Winslow—all postings of the sort that were typical for a bright young officer who was seen to have flag potential.

Kimmel went back to Washington DC in early 1917, once again as the Assistant Director of Target Practice, but his tenure there was cut short when the United States declared war on Imperial Germany on April 6. October found him in London, on the staff of Rear Admiral Hugh Rodman, the commanding officer of the US Navy's Battleship Division Nine, which had been attached to the Royal Navy's Grand Fleet. He saw action in the North Sea while on detached duty aboard a British cruiser, in the Second Battle of Heligoland Bight. In October 1918 he went aboard the USS *Arkansas*, where he would remain for the next 18 months as her executive officer.

Kimmel was acknowledged to be a highly intelligent officer, thoroughly competent with a lively imagination. He was recognized for his seamanship and navigation skills, as well as his ability to handily manage the day-to-day details of shipboard command. He racked up a string of outstanding fitness reports, where praise for his professional skills was accompanied by comments such as "a splendid officer of high character," "good common sense and initiative," and "an all-around officer of great promise." Kimmel came close to being the ideal naval officer, the product of the Annapolis tradition of those times, which was dedicated as much to producing gentlemen as it was fighting sailors. If there was any defect to be found in Husband Kimmel, it was an almost excessive attention to detail, which some critics later saw as evidence of a lack of self-confidence: delegation of responsibility didn't come easily to him, and he was known to needlessly fuss over the details of tasks that should have been left to subordinates.

Any officer who ever hoped to attain flag rank in the United States Navy first had to command a battleship—this was more than tradition, it was a rite of passage, for it was universally understood throughout the fleet that only a man who knew battleships could someday lead them into action. Promoted to captain in July 1926, Kimmel's chance at such a command didn't come until 1933, when he spent a year on the bridge of the USS *New York* as her captain; four years later, in November 1937, he was promoted to rear admiral.

He first hoisted his flag as the commander of Cruiser Division 7 (CruDiv 7 in Navy parlance) in July 1938, then shifted his flag to the USS *Honolulu* a year later as

Commander Cruisers, Battle Force, and simultaneously commanding officer, Cruiser Division 9. CruDiv 9 was at that time based in San Pedro, California; it was part of the scouting screen for Battle Force, the designation given to the battle fleet stationed on the West Coast of the United States since 1930, a tacit and somewhat unsubtle admission of just who the Navy expected to be its next opponent. In February 1941, the same day Kimmel took command, Battle Force was re-designated as the Pacific Fleet, with a strength of four aircraft carriers, 12 battleships, 14 light cruisers, and 68 destroyers, a formidable array of seapower by any standard, powerful enough to stand as the nemesis of Japanese plans for expansion in the Pacific.

It wasn't long, though, before that strength was being whittled away: in the spring of 1941, the Neutrality Patrol drew off what was effectively a quarter of the Pacific Fleet's strength—one carrier, three battleships, six cruisers, and 28 destroyers. While it could be, and was, argued that the situation in the North Atlantic justified the transfers—after all, there was a real, live shooting war going on there between the Royal Navy and the *Kriegsmarine*—the Pacific Ocean was half again as large as the Atlantic, with the prospect of its own real, live shooting war growing more likely every day. Leaving the Pacific Fleet numerically inferior to the Imperial Japanese Navy was hardly the counsel of prudence.

Admiral Richardson, Kimmel's predecessor at Pearl, may have lost his command because he had so strongly disagreed with Roosevelt over the wisdom of moving the fleet to Pearl, but that didn't mean he was wrong. Kimmel came to understand this very quickly after he replaced Richardson: he soon realized that as fleet anchorages went, Pearl was something of a mixed bag. The logistical advantages of being 3,000 miles closer to where any engagement with the Japanese was likely to occur than if the fleet were still based on the West Coast weren't inconsiderable; the dockyard facilities were second only to the very largest naval bases like San Diego, San Francisco, and Bremerton; and, with an average depth of only 40 feet, the harbor was shallow enough to prevent torpedo attacks, at least in theory. On the debit side of the ledger, though, there was only one way in or out of Pearl Harbor, a single narrow channel, and the harbor itself was rather small—unlike, say, the Royal Navy's immense base at Scapa Flow, where the distance between anchored ships could be measured in hundreds, even thousands of yards, the mooring berths on Battleship Row in Pearl allowed for only 75 feet between the bow of one ship and the stern of the next, creating a concentrated target for an enemy attack. That Kimmel recognized these vulnerabilities was made clear in a memo he sent off on February 18, 1941, to the chief of naval operations in Washington DC, which concluded with the statement "I feel that a surprise attack (submarine, air, or combined) on Pearl Harbor is a possibility, and we are taking immediate practical steps to minimize the damage inflicted and to ensure that the attacking force will pay."[7]

The chief of naval operations—"CNO" in the Navy's verbal shorthand—in 1941 was Admiral Harold Stark, known throughout the Navy by his fellow flag officers and behind his back by junior officers and enlisted men as "Betty" Stark. The nickname was hung on him at the Naval Academy, when upperclassmen hazed him for being a descendant of a Revolutionary War general whose wife was supposedly named Elizabeth "Betty" Stark (her name—she was a real person—was actually Molly Stark). Born on November 12, 1880, Stark grew up in Wilkes-Barre, Pennsylvania, the scion of a well-to-do local family. He was a student at Harry Hillman Academy, a highly exclusive private school, an experience which brought forward some of the character traits which later made him a successful naval officer: he was intelligent, disciplined, and amiable.

Appointed to the United States Naval Academy in 1899, Stark "passed out"—graduated—in 1903, 30th in his class of midshipmen. In 1907, when his training cruises were behind him, he was assigned to the USS *Minnesota*, one of the last pre-dreadnought battleships built for the US Navy. Two years later, already recognized as an outstanding ship handler and navigator, he began an eight-year stint in a succession of torpedo boats and destroyers, rising to command of the Asiatic Fleet's small Destroyer Flotilla. In 1917 he took the squadron from the Philippines to the Mediterranean Sea without a single incident or loss of life, a considerable feat of seamanship and navigation, as those five ships were the oldest and smallest destroyers in the Navy, weighing a mere 420 tons each. A few months later, he was assigned to the staff of Rear Admiral William Sims, the commander of the American naval forces attached to the Royal Navy's Grand Fleet, where he remained until the end of the war. It was in this posting, working daily with his British counterparts, that Stark's knack for diplomacy became evident, a talent that would serve him well in the years ahead; ironically, at the pinnacle of his career, that talent would prove to be his most serious weakness as a naval officer.

Like almost all officers in any service, Stark was ambitious—not with a thrusting, overly aggressive, trample-anyone-in-the-way ambition, but with the sort of ambition that naturally comes to a man determined to rise as high as his abilities and connections will take him. It was his good fortune that in 1914 he was befriended by the assistant secretary of the navy, Franklin Roosevelt; neither man had the slightest idea of the Olympian heights of power to which Roosevelt would eventually ascend: at the time, it was simply a case of two men who shared a love of the Navy and got on well together. Two decades would pass before their paths again crossed professionally, but when they did, Roosevelt's familiarity with Stark, knowing that Stark was someone with whom he could work, would be no small factor in his decision to appoint Stark the chief of naval operations.

In a sort of naval *cursus honorum*, much as politicians of the Roman Republic would prove their merit and mettle by holding a succession of increasingly demanding and difficult offices in the hope of one day being elected consul, US Navy officers had to earn the right to fly an admiral's flag, no matter what their political connections might be, and Stark was no exception. After the Great War came to an end, there was shipboard duty as Executive Officer of the battleships *North Dakota* and *West Virginia*, followed by a year of instruction at the Naval War College, then command of the aptly named ammunition ship *Nitro*. Promotion to captain in 1925 came with his posting as the chief of staff to the commander, Destroyer Squadrons Battle Fleet, followed by three years as an aide to the secretary of the navy—this was his introduction to the detailed workings, official and unofficial, of Washington DC.

In the spring of 1933 came the coveted battleship command, the USS *West Virginia*. After a year on her bridge Stark returned to Washington DC, this time as Chief of the Bureau of Ordnance, a post he held for three years; in November 1934 his promotion to rear admiral was approved by the Senate. He went to sea again in July 1938, now a vice admiral posted to the Pacific, this time as the commanding officer of CruDiv 3 as well as the overall commander of Battle Fleet's entire cruiser force. When he was once again called back to Washington, in July 1939, the man who replaced him as Commander, Cruisers, Battle Fleet, was Husband Kimmel.

Stark returned to the nation's capital to take over the office of the chief of naval operations—the CNO—replacing Admiral William Leahy, who was retiring. Today, the posting is almost entirely administrative, but in 1939 the CNO was charged with not only preparing the Navy's war plans and keeping them up to date, but also directing the actual operations—moving the ships to where they could fight the battles—necessary to carry out those plans when the shooting started. He was also expected to ensure that the fleet was up to strength in men, ships, and planes, along with the necessary logistics. This, of course, meant often going to Congress, hat figuratively in hand, for funding, a chore which required someone who would be adept at coping with the often prickly, usually self-important personalities of various influential senators and congressmen. This was an arena where Stark's diplomatic skills would not simply serve him well, but would shine.

By law, only a full admiral—that is, a man with four stars on his shoulder boards—could hold the position of CNO. Promotion in the peacetime Navy wasn't entirely by seniority, but that was always a significant consideration whenever a particularly powerful or prestigious appointment was being made—and no appointment in the US Navy carried more prestige than that of the chief of naval operations: at that time it was the senior uniformed position in the entire service. So it came as a surprise to everyone, including Harold Stark, when President Roosevelt chose him as Leahy's successor, passing over several longer-serving admirals. Not surprisingly, Roosevelt already being known for having a very short way with people who disagreed with him—as Admiral Richardson would soon be able to confirm—there was little opposition expressed about Stark's selection. Once he took over the CNO's duties, Stark adroitly smoothed any feathers that may have been ruffled by his appointment, and proved to be quite capable in his duties.

One of Stark's most important accomplishments was his establishment of a genuine working relationship with Congress, persuading politicians who were habitually tight-fisted in regard to naval and military appropriations, however generous they might be when spending money on social programs, that the Navy's budget requests, especially for building new ships, were both reasonable and necessary. His wartime experience in London served him well in Washington: he astutely approached senators and representatives as fellow professionals, something not all flag officers did, and persuaded rather than demanded or cajoled. He wasn't always successful. In 1939, and again in the spring of 1940, when he asked for an increase in the funding for new shipbuilding even larger than the 11 percent Congress had already passed into law, the answer was "no." The legislators did an abrupt about-face a few weeks later, however, when France surrendered to the Germans and the British Army was driven off the Continent. The result was the Two-Ocean Navy Act, signed into law by the president on July 19, 1940.

From time to time Stark would suddenly but quietly remind the Navy, Congress, and the White House that he was more than just a uniformed bureaucrat, however. The most memorable such occasion was on September 4, 1939, one day after France and Great Britain declared war on Nazi Germany, and a day before President Roosevelt formally declared American neutrality. Acting entirely on his own initiative, Stark ordered the Atlantic fleet to begin active patrols along America's eastern seaboard and in the Caribbean, using ships and planes alike, to prevent violations of the United States' territorial waters. A few days later, Roosevelt publicly announced the establishment of these patrols, implying as he did so that the idea for these operations had been entirely his own—which surprised no one—and declared that they would be collectively known as the Neutrality Patrol. Stark, possibly having taken to heart the lesson of Admiral Richardson's misadventure, said nothing to contradict Roosevelt.

Stark also had a hand in determining the grand strategy which would guide American operations should the United States become involved in the war, willingly or no. He composed a memorandum which was delivered to the White House on November 12, 1941, presenting the four possible strategies available to the United States, lettered "A" through "D." As Stark presented them, "A" was to solely stand on the defensive and protect North and South America; "B" was to take the offensive against the Japanese, committing the majority of America's military resources to the Pacific while defending against German attacks in the Atlantic; "C" called for an equal commitment of resources to both the Atlantic and Pacific; and "D" was the reverse of "B"—take the offensive against Germany and Italy while remaining on the defensive against Japan until the war in Europe was won or America mobilized the strength to take the war to the Japanese.

Stark, sharing Roosevelt's belief that Nazi Germany was the greater threat to Western civilization, strongly endorsed "D", which became known as "Plan Dog"—in the phonetic alphabet used by the US Navy in 1940, A, B, C, and D were "Able," "Baker," "Charlie," and "Dog." Later, the admiral's critics would suggest that his recommendation of Plan Dog, which he knew the president would favor, was an attempt to further ingratiate himself with Roosevelt, but sycophancy was not part of Stark's character. In any case, Roosevelt never formally endorsed Plan Dog, though he concurred with Stark and all of the plan's fundamentals were incorporated in America's grand strategy once the shooting started. Doing so, however, essentially scrapped what had been for the previous 30 years the United States' basic plan for war with Japan, War Plan Orange.

War Plan Orange, often called "Plan Orange" or simply "Orange," was the coordinated blueprint for the Army and Navy to carry out a war with Japan that took its broad outlines from an operational plan drawn up in 1911 by Rear Admiral Raymond P. Rodgers. It was fairly straightforward in concept: it assumed that at the beginning of the war the Imperial Navy would blockade the Philippines and Guam; the American forces there would hold out—theoretically, at least—until relieved by the US Navy. The fleet meanwhile would mobilize on the West Coast, and once a sufficiently powerful force was assembled, sail into the Central Pacific, methodically advancing through various island chains, eliminating any Japanese garrisons it found, on its way to the Philippines. Once the Japanese blockade was broken, the American fleet would turn north to engage the Japanese in a series of battles which would, hopefully, erode and eventually eliminate the Imperial Navy, ending with the Home Islands tightly blockaded, which would make surrender by the Japanese inevitable.

To a remarkable degree, whether intentional or not, Plan Orange in concept mirrored the script established by the Japanese in their planning to lure the US Navy into the requisite "Decisive Battle" which was the dogmatic heart of *Dai Nippon*'s naval strategy. American planning, however, expected to eliminate the Imperial Navy in a series of battles, rather than the sort of naval *Götterdämmerung* the Japanese treasured and so devoutly sought. Attrition was a key element in the planning of both navies, though for some reason the American planners never factored in their possible losses to submarine and air attacks, which had always been integral parts of the Japanese plans. Nor did War Plan Orange make any allowance for any sort of pre-emptive strike by the Japanese against the US Navy as soon as war was declared.

Plan Orange was formally adopted by the Joint Army and Navy Board in 1924, and meticulously revised every year to keep it up-to-date with changes in Japanese and American naval strengths as well as improvements in new technologies, especially aviation. Yet, however much the Army and Navy staffs might tinker with the details, in its fundamentals Plan Orange was as hidebound and archaic as Japan's strategy of the Decisive Battle, a relic of the theories Mahan had formulated when the submarine was no more than a nautical novelty, and there were no airplanes at all. Worse, too many of its premises were built on the assumptions as to what the Japanese *would* do, rather than allowing for what they *could* do.

There is an old military maxim that in one form or another dates back at least to the days of the Greek phalanx, when battles became something more sophisticated than loosely organized gang rumbles: "No plan survives intact for more than five minutes once contact is made with the enemy." In no small part because the men responsible for keeping War Plan Orange "current" forgot this, the stage was being set for the attack on Pearl Harbor: that the Japanese might not prove cooperative in staying true to the script American planners were writing seemed to occur to no one in the War or Navy Departments, and so Plan Orange remained essentially inflexible, and no alternative plans for war with the Japanese were ever developed.

The problem was fundamentally institutional: there was more rumor and speculation than fact in the "intelligence" gathered on Japan's armed forces, while too little attention was given to how Japan's culture and history could and would influence—even dictate—how Japan's leaders, civilian and military alike, perceived threats and challenges, and so prescribe and proscribe their possible reactions and responses. The advice and insight of men who had long studied the Japanese, or even lived in Japan and spoke the language—there were several such officers in both the Army and Navy—went unheeded, or worse, unsought. The stereotypes were too deeply ingrained, and the perception of the Japanese as a people who could only rather ineptly imitate the West wouldn't allow American policy makers or strategists to admit that the Japanese were as capable of producing original ideas and innovations as were Americans: they didn't simply imitate the West, they learned from it. At the same time, no one recognized the insight into Japanese culture and character offered by their martial arts, all of which taught in one form or another how a smaller, weaker man could, with a single swift, sharp strike, disarm or even cripple a supposedly more powerful foe.

Had anyone taken the time to give the situation a long, hard look they would have seen that it moved far beyond bad for the Americans. Having been in place for nearly three decades, War Plan Orange and its inflexibility had forced the Navy's strategic thinking for the Pacific into a well-worn rut, and the idea that the Imperial Navy might suddenly choose not to follow into that rut was inconceivable. But in many ways, even a bad plan is better than no plan, yet when the shooting started and the United States' strategic priorities were reassigned to comply with Plan Dog, the Army and Navy in the Pacific would be left with no viable plans at all.

* * *

When Admiral Yamamoto penned his letter to Vice Admiral Shimada expressing his certainty that Japan could not win a war with the United States, he was sitting in his day cabin aboard his new flagship, the battleship *Nagato*. He had just been named Commander-in-Chief of the Combined Fleet, the most prestigious sea-going command in the Imperial Navy, on August 10, 1939. Ironically, the appointment was both an acknowledgment of his professional skill and stature, and a protective measure meant to save his life—from the Imperial Army.

Absurd as it sounds, it was nonetheless an awkward, even disturbing truth. Yamamoto had continued in his open and rather vocal opposition to the proposed Tripartite Pact with Nazi Germany and Fascist Italy, making it clear whenever the subject came up in conversation that he regarded it as an act of utter folly that could only work to Japan's detriment. He would do so right up until the moment the Pact was signed; once the deed was done he would say nothing more about it, of course, as continuing to protest an accomplished fact was pointless. Until then, however, his attitude had hardly endeared him to the Army hotheads who were pressing as urgently as they dared for Japan to join the Rome–Berlin Axis. They feared that Yamamoto's prestige might be sufficient to sway those Cabinet members who were as of yet undecided into opposing the Pact.

The Army began doing what it could to intimidate him, muzzle him, and restrict his movements, at one point assigning a detachment of *Kempeitai*—a distinctly Japanese blending of military police and Gestapo-like domestic spies—to "guard" his house, and he began receiving anonymous death threats in his mail, personal and official. By sending him to sea, the Minister of the Navy, Admiral Yonai Mitsumasa, was able to keep Yamamoto out of the Army's clutches. Not surprisingly, he faced the prospect of a violent death with a remarkable equanimity, saying, "To die for the Emperor and the Nation is the highest hope of a military man. After a brave, hard fight the blossoms are scattered on the battlefield… One man's life or death is a matter of no importance. All that matters is the Empire. As Confucius said, 'they may crush cinnabar, yet they do not take away its color; one may burn a fragrant herb, yet it will not destroy the scent.' They may destroy my body, yet they will not take away my will." While Yamamoto had grave misgivings as to what end the militarists were driving Japan, his loyalty and patriotism remained unshaken and unimpeachable.[8]

This was why when throughout 1940 certain members of the Cabinet began asking, then demanding, that Yamamoto prepare a plan for a preemptive attack on the United States Navy, he didn't simply dismiss them out of hand. He knew that, if only tacitly, those men had the approval of the emperor who, regardless of whatever circumlocutions were used, actively ruled Japan through them. If the Government believed that a plan should be in place for striking the opening blow in an all-out conflict with the United States, it was because the Emperor believed it to be so. Yamamoto thus felt himself duty- and honor-bound to comply.

The most persistent of these Cabinet officials were Foreign Minister Matsuoka Yōsuke, and General Tojo Hideki, the Minister of War. Matsuoka was something of a mental lightweight, a bit erratic in character, moderately successful as a businessman but in government service always the perennial bureaucrat with only a second-tier talent for diplomacy. The loose cannon in the Cabinet, his preferred method of solving any foreign policy problems was to suggest invading somebody. He owed his position as foreign minister solely to the fact that he possessed tremendous influence in Japan's second-largest political party, the *Rikken Seiyūkai*—his appointment was the bone thrown to its members, who were overwhelmingly conservative, by then-Prime Minister Prince Konoye in exchange for their support in the Diet. Yamamoto could, and did, dismiss him as a minor annoyance.

The Minister of War was a different story. Yamamoto disliked the 56-year-old Tojo, whom he saw as moderately intelligent, reactionary, ruthless, by turns charming and intimidating, and morally ambiguous; in point of fact, Tojo was all of these and more. He was also intellectually lazy and by his own admission possessed of no outstanding innate talents, a shortcoming he countered through sheer hard work. Behind his back, his colleagues and subordinates called him *Kamisori*—"Razor Brain"—not as a mark of his capacity for profound thinking, but rather an acknowledgment of his skill at bureaucratic infighting. The worst of his flaws, which truly handicapped him as Minister of War, was that he never fully grasped how the United States' economy and industry dwarfed those of Japan, with all that implied for the Empire's chances of victory.

Intensely patriotic, ultra-conservative, and, not surprisingly, a fierce partisan of the Army, Tojo, like Yamamoto, saw serving the emperor and the Empire as life's highest calling. He had never held any real political ambitions: he was given the office of Minister of War not because he wanted it, but because he was the Imperial Army General Staff's choice, and could be relied upon to be the General Staff's mouthpiece in the Cabinet. The General Staff had Konoye cornered: if he refused to accept Tojo, his government would collapse before it was even formed, a situation the General Staff could perpetuate until Konoye either gave in and accepted Tojo, or resigned as prime minister. As Konoye still had hope of resolving the increasingly sharp dispute with the United States through diplomacy, and imagining he could keep Tojo on a short leash, he finally relented.

For his part, Yamamoto wasn't disposed to simply refuse Tojo's demand that an attack against the Americans be prepared, or to fob him off by appearing to go through the motions of planning. Like Konoye, the admiral had yet to give up on diplomacy; at the same time he recognized that it would be too late to create a plan only after diplomacy failed. Therefore, he would put together the most effective attack possible with forces available to him, and pray it would never be needed. Yet even as he hoped for a diplomatic miracle, in assessing the overall strategic situation in the summer of 1940, Yamamoto could see it approaching a point where it would begin driving events of its own accord, depriving the Empire of any remaining choices or options but war with America.

In the north, the Imperial Army had hoped to use Manchuria as a springboard for seizing large tracts of resource-rich Mongolia and Siberia; that such an attack was highly unlikely to further provoke the United States did much to recommend it—the mutual non-aggression pact of August 1939 between the USSR and the Third Reich, which enabled the *Wehrmacht* to overrun Poland, had soured the attitude of the American people toward the Soviet Union. But a short, sharp, undeclared border war with the Soviets along the Khalkhyn Gol River in the summer of 1939 quickly put paid to the idea of a northern offensive: the Soviets and their Mongolian allies proved to be much tougher nuts to crack than the General Staff had expected. As valuable as Siberian resources might prove to be in the long run, the effort would be too costly: a prolonged campaign in Siberia would only further deplete Japan's limited strategic reserves of both men and material, with no assurance of ultimate success. The dwindling stocks of oil in particular dictated that any operations to seize the raw materials so desperately needed by the Empire must be swift and decisive.

To the south lay the Philippines, which the Japanese most definitely coveted, and Yamamoto could not imagine any circumstance where an aggressive move against them would not result in Japan and America going to war, no matter how strong isolationist sentiment in the United States ran at that moment. America's international prestige and national honor, about which the Americans could, in their own way, be as prickly as the Japanese, would be at stake. To the southwest, the French in Saigon were proving to be compliant, if not exactly cooperative, in allowing the north half of French Indochina to be turned into a staging area for further advances toward the Kra Peninsula, Borneo, and the Dutch East Indies. They had no real choice, given that three-fifths of France were occupied by the Germans, and the newly created Vichy regime, still in the formative stages, wasn't about to go to war with Germany's most powerful ally.

The Dutch, on the other hand, despite the whole of the Netherlands being under Nazi occupation, showed every intention of putting up a fight if the Japanese made a move on the East Indies, and no one in Tokyo believed for a moment that if the Imperial Army set foot outside of French Indochina toward either of Great Britain's colonies in Burma or Malaysia's Kra Peninsula, sources of the oil Japan desperately needed, the British would simply stand to one side and let those colonies be taken from away from them. Attempting to invade Borneo would bring the Dutch and the British into the fight together—and there was still the question of what the United States would do.

Yamamoto was convinced that even if only Borneo and Malaysia were attacked, bypassing the Philippines, the Americans would not stand idly by while the Japanese overran the British and Dutch possessions, but rather would form an open alliance with Great Britain and the Dutch government-in-exile, and send the whole of Battle Force westward from Pearl Harbor to engage the Imperial Navy. The Japanese would then face a strategic nightmare, as the Empire lacked the strength as well as the logistical capacity to support amphibious operations in the southwest while at the same time defending against an American offensive from the east. Such a scenario could only end very badly for Japan.

The obvious solution, of course, was the preemptive strike against the US Navy that Matsuoka and Tojo were urging. Should the American fleet be hamstrung just as the offensives toward Burma, Malaysia, and the Dutch East Indies were jumping off, Japan would have the time needed to complete those operations, and then bring the full strength of the Imperial Navy to bear on the US Navy once it sorted itself out and began moving westward with a reconstituted battle fleet. Yet, in truth, it was no solution at all, but merely a delay of the inevitable: once the Americans got over the initial shock of being attacked—and they would, Yamamoto was under no illusions about that—the calculus of war would swiftly and permanently shift against the Japanese.

In some ways, that shift began once Roosevelt invoked the Export Control Act. Yamamoto's fear that the momentum of events would soon compel the Japanese to act regardless of the consequences was based on one ironbound deadline: Japan's reserves of oil would be exhausted in 18 months, possibly even sooner. It was absolutely imperative that new sources of oil—whether in Burma, Malaysia, or the Dutch East Indies was immaterial—be seized before that happened, otherwise the Empire would be paralyzed, unable to even defend itself. There was an already-narrowing window where, if the Japanese made an all-out effort, the Allies might be rocked back on their heels long enough for the Empire to settle into its defenses and hope the Allies would accept a *fait accompli*, recognizing that evicting the Japanese from their conquests would be too costly in lives and material to be worth the effort. If the Allies were resolved to fight, however, while the Japanese might win the early victories, they would ultimately lose the war.

Yamamoto was blunt in making this point to Prince Konoye, saying, "If I am told to fight regardless of the consequences, I shall run wild for the first six months or a year, but I have utterly no confidence for the second or third year… I hope you will endeavor to avoid a Japanese–American war."[9]

* * *

In Hawaii, responsibility for the success or failure of any aerial attack on the fleet in Pearl Harbor in early 1941 rested not, as might be expected, on the shoulders of Admiral Kimmel, but with a soldier, Lieutenant General Walter Short. Sixty-one years old, born in the rural Illinois town of Filmore, Short was something of a rarity in the United States Army: a general officer who was not a graduate of one of the six senior military academies. Instead, he took a degree in mathematics from the University of Illinois, which he then taught at the Western Military Academy for one year before accepting a direct commission from the Army as a second lieutenant in March 1902.[10]

Short's career in the years before the Great War, like that of almost every officer in the US Army at the time, can be summed up as "uneventful." Between 1902 to 1916 he was assigned to posts in Oklahoma, the Philippines, Nebraska, California, and Alaska. In the summer of 1916, now assigned to the 16th Infantry Regiment, Short joined in General John Pershing's punitive expedition into Mexico, pursuing the revolutionary Pancho Villa. A year later America was at war with Germany and Short was in France, a captain assigned to the staff of the 1st Infantry Division, developing machine gun tactics and training gunners, earning a Distinguished Service Medal in the process. Such was the rush to get American soldiers into action that thousands of American troops were sent to France with only the most rudimentary training: the instruction they received under Captain Short's auspices was literally a matter of life or death for many of them. His staff work was also good enough to earn him wartime promotion to major, then lieutenant colonel; four days before the armistice he was promoted to colonel.

But there were wartime colonels and peacetime colonels, and when the shooting ended and the US Army returned to its far smaller pre-war size, Short, like thousands of other regular officers who were retained on active duty, reverted to his peacetime rank, that of captain. He didn't remain a captain long, however: he was first assigned to the Army General Services School Fort Leavenworth, Kansas, as an instructor, then within a year went to Washington DC, to work on the War Department's General Staff, where he was promoted to major in recognition of his excellent staff work. Next came an assignment to Military Intelligence, working the Far East desk until 1923, earning a promotion to lieutenant colonel in the process.

Much as command of a battleship was a prerequisite for a naval officer to be considered for flag rank, following the Great War any field-grade officer in the US Army—that is, any major, lieutenant colonel, or colonel—who hoped to one day put up general's stars was expected to complete the course of instruction at the Army War College in Carlisle, Pennsylvania. Short did so, graduating in 1925, and was subsequently posted to Fort Leavenworth as an instructor at the Army Command and General Staff School. The next 10 years were spent in command of successively larger infantry units, interrupted in 1936 by a posting as Assistant Commandant of the Army Infantry School at Fort Benning, Georgia, after which he put up his first star. A second followed in 1940, and it was as Major General Walter Short that he took command of IV Corps that same year.

Short had become friends with George Marshall back when both were first lieutenants serving in the Philippines, and the friendship had endured as the years passed. In September 1939, Marshall, now a major general, was appointed Chief of Staff of the Army by President Roosevelt and raised to the rank of general. One of his responsibilities was selecting corps commanders as well as commanding officers for the Hawaiian, Panama Canal, and Philippine Military Departments, and when Lieutenant General Charles Herron, commandant of the Hawaiian Department, announced that he would be retiring in early 1941, Marshall tapped his friend Short for the post. Now designated a lieutenant general for as long as he held the post, Short formally assumed command on February 7, 1941, a week after Admiral Kimmel took command of the Pacific Fleet.

The Hawaiian Military Department wasn't the most prestigious posting in the United States Army—that status was reserved for Fort Meyer in Washington DC—but in 1941, it was the most important; Roosevelt's decision to make Pearl Harbor Battle Force's main base saw to that. With German submarines running amok in the Atlantic—the U-boats were enjoying what their crews would remember as *Die Glückliche Zeit*, "the Happy Time," that spanned June 1940 to April 1941, during which they sank 1.5 million tons of Allied shipping—there was little chance that the Neutrality Patrols would be scaled back, and quite likely would be increased instead. Which meant, of course, that Battle Force, soon to be styled the Pacific Fleet, would be the Navy's sole line of defense should the Japanese suddenly lunge southward, toward the Philippines and the Dutch East Indies—and the Pacific Fleet would be very much on its own: no help would be forthcoming from the Atlantic.

What made Hawaii so important was that, however grave a threat President Roosevelt might regard Nazi Germany, the *Kriegsmarine* would never possess the sort of large, balanced, and powerful fleet that could bring the war to America's shores. Japan's Imperial Navy was, of course, just such a fleet: should the Japanese attempt any operations against the continental United States, they couldn't ignore the American naval forces at Pearl Harbor. For all of its flaws as a fleet anchorage, the naval base in Oahu offered the US Navy one great strategic advantage: it was perfectly positioned to allow the Pacific Fleet to sever the supply lines of any Japanese naval force moving to strike at the West Coast. Hawaii, then, would be the United States' front line: it was there any Japanese offensive against America would begin, where the earliest and heaviest blows would fall.

This reality had been recognized as early as August 1937, when Army and Navy planners working on the updates to War Plan Orange placed the Hawaiian Military Department in "Defense Category D." This meant that the Hawaiian Islands could be the target of a major attack, and all defenses should be prepared to go into action with little or no warning; this status was reaffirmed in August 1941. According to the Operations section of Plan Orange, the Army's mission in Hawaii was to "Hold Oahu against attacks by land, sea, and air forces, and against hostile sympathizers. Support naval forces in the protection of the sea communications of the Associated Powers and in the destruction of Axis sea communications by offensive action against enemy forces or commerce located within tactical operating radius of occupied air bases."[11]

Fortunately, the islands, specifically Oahu, were well defended from attack by sea, as the Army had been preparing them for decades. The first modest naval facilities in Hawaii were built at Pearl Harbor in 1899, following a recommendation made some years earlier by Major General John Schofield when he was commandant of the US Army's Military Division of the Pacific. Originally designated "Naval Station,

Hawaii," the base began to grow almost immediately, and in 1941 it was still growing. The Army arrived in 1905 and started the construction of Fort Shafter a few miles east of the harbor; three years later Schofield Barracks were built to the north. The island's defenses grew ever more-elaborate as a string of forts and heavy gun emplacements were sited around the island—Forts Armstrong, Barrette, De Russy, Hase, Kamehameha, Ruger, and Weaver being the major installations—along with three naval air stations and four Army airfields, the largest of which were Wheeler and Hickam Fields.

The core of the defense on Oahu was the Hawaiian Division, an infantry unit 13,500 strong that in October 1941 would be reorganized to provide the cadre for two new divisions, the 24th and 25th, which when fully manned would more than double the available troop strength. When Lieutenant General Short took command in February of that year, the Army garrison in Hawaii, including the Army Air Corps, totaled over 35,000 officers and enlisted men, supported by a total of 127 heavy guns—some of them converted 14-inch naval guns—in the forts and coastal batteries, 211 anti-aircraft guns, and 3,000 pieces of field artillery and heavy machine guns. So confident was he of Hawaii's security Army Chief of Staff General George Marshall informed President Roosevelt on April 21, 1941, that, "The Island of Oahu, due to its fortification, its garrison, and its physical characteristics, is believed to be the strongest fortress in the world."[12]

Marshall was, of course, assuring Roosevelt that Hawaii's defenses could repel an actual invasion by the Japanese, but, whether by accident or design is impossible to say, he also implied that the islands were secure from *any* type of enemy attack. In a personal letter written to Short the day he took command in Hawaii, Marshall went even further, saying,

> My impression of the Hawaiian problem has been that if no serious harm is done us during the first six hours of known hostilities, thereafter the existing defenses would discourage an enemy against the hazard of an attack. The risk of sabotage and the risk involved in a surprise raid by Air and by submarine constitute the real perils of the situation. Frankly, I do not see any landing threat in the Hawaiian Islands so long as we have air superiority.

Marshall also emphasized that "the fullest protection for the Fleet is *the* rather than *a* major consideration" for the Army in Hawai.[13]

Short apparently didn't—or couldn't—grasp Marshall's point: it was the Army's responsibility to defend Oahu, and above all Pearl Harbor, from *any* type of attack. To the chief of staff, "the Army" naturally included the Air Corps as well as the ground forces, while to Short "the Army" was the infantry and artillery, with a helping hand lent now and then by other branches. In Marshall's view, "protection for the Fleet" meant that the bombers and fighters of the Hawaiian Air Force were to be the shield interposed between the Navy's ships at anchor in Pearl and any Japanese attack. Short, conversely, took his cue from the first sentence of the Operations Plan directive: "Hold Oahu against attacks by land, sea, and air forces, and against hostile sympathizers." As he saw it, unless they specified otherwise, all subsequent orders were to be carried out in conformity with the requirements of the Operations Plan. He then construed the order in which Marshall noted the dangers of sabotage, air raid, and submarine attack as an official confirmation of how immediate the chief of staff regarded each threat. "Protection for the Fleet," then, for Short meant defending the island of Oahu from a Japanese invasion: his command would be called upon to fight a land battle, not an aerial battle.

Seizing on the phrase "the risk of sabotage," he developed something of a mania for thwarting potential saboteurs: in Europe the havoc supposedly created by "fifth columns" that were said to have infiltrated the civilian populations in countries the Nazis were about to invade was a thought that lurked in the back of most Army officers' minds. Almost 160,000 Japanese nationals and Japanese-Americans lived in Hawaii, a third of the islands' population in 1941; in Short's eyes, any and each of them were simply waiting, bomb in hand, for an opportunity to blow up a radio tower, a truck, a fuel tank—or an airplane.

One of the first, and most readily apparent, measures taken on Short's orders to prevent sabotage was to end the practice of dispersing combat aircraft around the perimeter of the airfields where they were stationed, the standard defensive practice to protect them from an attack from the air. As he saw it, aircraft parked like that would be highly vulnerable to a determined saboteur, and posting an armed guard to watch every one of them—the most logical measure of protection—was a waste of manpower: the men assigned sentry duty could be more usefully put to work elsewhere—training, for example. Instead, the planes would be parked on taxiways and hangar aprons, lined up in neat, compact rows, where they could be more easily protected by fewer guards.

General Short's worries about the vulnerability of his aircraft stemmed from his realization that the state of Oahu's defenses didn't precisely match the rosy picture created by the tinted glasses worn in Washington DC. The garrison was large and well-armed, of course, but he knew that if the Japanese did stage an invasion of the island, or even launched a large-scale hit-and-run raid, they would hardly be so accommodating as to come ashore where the Army's defenses were the thickest, or within range of the largest coastal defense guns and heaviest artillery batteries. They would land wherever they perceived a weakness in the defense, hoping to be able to consolidate a position ashore before the US Army could respond and push them back into the sea.

In any amphibious operation, there is always a span of time when the landing force, having made it ashore, is disorganized and vulnerable to counterattack. Its communications will be spotty and unreliable, units disordered and often scattered, and there are no heavier weapons than what the infantry or marines can carry with them—rifles, grenades, light machine guns and mortars only. The extent of the confusion and how long it lasts will be determined by the strength of the resistance the landing force faces: the task for the defending units on the spot is to prolong the enemy's disarray as much as possible, buying time for reinforcements to arrive and contain the enemy's landing area. Ideally, sufficient fresh units will be able to come forward in time organize and launch a counterattack to drive the enemy back into the sea.

Short, taking counsel of Frederick the Great's maxim that "He who defends everything defends nothing," knew he could not be strong everywhere and that the Japanese would hold the initiative as to where and when they made their landings. It would fall upon the Air Corps, then, flying interdiction missions as a sort of "airborne artillery," to put as much pressure as possible on any Japanese forces that were trying to create a beachhead, bombing and strafing the Japanese troops already on the beaches as well as attacking their transport ships and landing barges. They were no substitute for boots on the ground, especially infantry, in holding a position, but with bomb loads measured in thousands of pounds, the Hawaiian Air Force's B-17s and B-18s could hopefully pin an enemy in place long enough for the infantry to arrive. The Air Corps' part in General Short's plans for defending Oahu would be small, but vital. The real problem, along with Short's anxiety over sabotage, lay in how few aircraft the Air Corps had in Hawaii.

In the four years Lieutenant General Charles Herron, Short's predecessor, commanded the Hawaiian Military Department, he had fought, with varying degrees of success, an ongoing battle to increase the number of bombers and fighters deployed to Hawaii. Better than General Short would do, General Herron had understood that, rather than a supporting arm for the infantry, the Army Air Corps was in truth Hawaii's first and, arguably, most important line of defense: if Oahu was, as the War Plans Division suggested it could be, subjected to a major attack or even an invasion by the Japanese, for the Hawaiian garrison to have any chance of holding the island the Air Corps would have to do more than just interdict enemy beachheads—it would have to inflict significant losses on enemy warships and transports, and do so as far distant as possible from the islands.

Moving Battle Force to Hawaii in the summer of 1940 and making Pearl Harbor its permanent base raised the stakes considerably and at the same time complicated the Air Corps' mission. The Army's bombers would still be expected to act as a striking force against the Japanese as they approached Hawaii, but now its fighters would have to defend the warships against enemy air attack instead of providing protective escorts for the bombers; there were no Navy or Marine fighter squadrons permanently based at Pearl Harbor. Yet when Short assumed command from Herron, the Air Corps had fewer than 250 airplanes of all types in Hawaii, the majority of them obsolete or obsolescent. Two-thirds of the Hawaiian Air Force's bomber strength was made up of B-18s, short-ranged, underpowered, inadequately armed, and while useful for interdiction missions against ground forces, incapable of carrying bombs heavy enough to damage anything larger than a destroyer. The 18th Bombardment Wing's three squadrons of B-17 Flying Fortresses, the most modern and powerful bomber in the world in 1941, were assigned to Hickam Field, but two of the three were soon sent to the Philippines; the War Department then dithered over sending replacements to Oahu.

A similar situation existed for the 14th Pursuit Wing: on paper, it authorized 160 fighters, and on some days sufficient pursuit planes in serviceable condition could be found at Wheeler, Hickam, or Bellows Fields to come close to or actually reach that number. But only a hundred of them were up-to-date P-40s, an aircraft which, in the hands of the right pilot, could hold its own against the Zero; the rest were a mix of obsolete P-26 that would do little more than provide live target practice for Japanese fighter pilots, and near-obsolescent P-36 fighters. Worse, typically a third or more of the P-40s were unserviceable, downchecked by a lack of spare parts or replacement equipment.

The upshot was that, no matter how Short interpreted Marshall's pointed reminder that "the fullest protection for the Fleet is *the* rather than *a* major consideration" for the Army in Hawaii, he had been given a mission which he couldn't fully accomplish out of his own resources. While, as a rule, it's the rare officer at any level of command who ever believes that he has enough men and material available for the job at hand, and that one measure of a good officer has always been how well he carries out his mission with what men and material he does have, no small part of Short's discontent was well-founded. There was nothing the least bit out of the ordinary in tasking an army garrison with defending a fleet anchorage; for that matter, Short's plans for the defense of Oahu could be seen as doing just that. Expecting that garrison to protect the actual fleet while it was inside that anchorage was rather more unusual, almost unique. No matter which was the case, however, the Hawaiian Air Force in strength and readiness wasn't up to the task.

No one was truly at fault for that, everyone was doing what they believed to be the best they could with what they had, but there simply weren't enough planes—or aircrews—to go around. The American aviation industry was still tooling up to produce the ambitious numbers set by the Two-Ocean Navy Act, so that for the time being the production rate for new aircraft, along with the spare parts needed to keep planes flying that were already in service, was little better than it had been in 1939. Likewise, the Army and Navy's aviation training programs were rapidly expanding, but as of yet the available numbers of new pilots, navigators, bombardiers, and gunners was only slowly rising. The priority given in May 1941 by President Roosevelt to the Neutrality Patrol in the North Atlantic only aggravated the problem for the Navy, as it required long-range patrol squadrons from the West Coast, Hawaii, and the Philippines be transferred to the Atlantic Fleet, leaving Honolulu and Manila in particular to scramble for whatever aircraft and crew could be begged, borrowed, or stolen from other commands.

That shortage of patrol planes was critical. Real "protection for the Fleet" began with locating any Japanese naval forces approaching Hawaii as far away from the islands as possible, giving Kimmel time to choose his course of action: sail out to meet the Imperial Navy, stand fast in Pearl, or make for the West Coast. It would be pointless to try to "protect" the Pacific Fleet only after Japanese battleships and carriers appeared off Honolulu where Kimmel's ships could be sunk or disabled piecemeal as they tried to sortie from Pearl Harbor. It was a consequence of that fundamental flaw which Admiral Richardson saw as Pearl's great weakness as a fleet anchorage: the narrow channel that was the harbor's only entrance or exit. The problem was not that simply sinking a single large ship in that channel would block it and either bottle up the fleet inside the harbor or deny access to Pearl once the fleet had sortied. Rather, it was that the channel was too narrow to allow the fleet to sortie *en masse*; warships attempting to leave the harbor would be forced to transit the channel in penny packets, allowing the Japanese to overwhelm them in detail.

This simple bit of geography, then, dictated that any Japanese naval forces approaching the Hawaiian Islands must be located at the earliest possible moment. The best—and most obvious—means of doing so would be through long-range aerial reconnaissance, precisely the sort of mission for which the Navy's Consolidated PBY-4 and PBY-5 patrol bombers were designed. Ideally, given enough PBYs, it would be possible to maintain a 360-degree dawn-to-dusk patrol at the optimum range of 400 miles offshore. To do so would have required upward of 200 of these aircraft, however, and there was a chronic and acute shortage of PBYs, not just in Hawaii but everywhere—there were fewer than 400 of the type in service in the entire navy.

As it was, the Pacific Fleet had just 81 PBYs on strength, with 12 of them stationed at Midway Island, 1,300 miles to the north of the Hawaiian Islands. A squadron of Douglas SBD-2 scout bombers was routinely based at the Marine Air Station at Ewa and could be pressed into service if needed—the "SB" designation stood for "Scout Bomber"—along with a motley collection of other scouting and observation aircraft scattered about the islands. At Admiral Kimmel's direction, the 23 fleet submarines based at Pearl Harbor were added to the mix of scouting forces, but even then only a third of the perimeter around the Hawaiian Islands would have patrol coverage that could reasonably be described as adequate. The B-17s and B-18s of the Hawaiian Air Force, had they been available to the Pacific Fleet, could have significantly increased coverage, although it would have been by no means complete. Still, every little bit would have helped, but it's at this point where utter absurdity enters the narrative: long range reconnaissance patrols over open water were on the list of missions the Army Air Corps was specifically forbidden to fly.

Back in May 1938, in what was as much a publicity stunt to demonstrate the capabilities of Air Corps bombers as it was a training mission, a trio of YB-17s, developmental prototypes of the B-17 Flying Fortress, intercepted the Italian passenger liner *Rex* while she was still 600 miles from the East Coast, inbound for

New York Harbor. Within hours a bevy of admirals invaded the office of Army Chief of Staff General Malin Craig, loudly protesting the Air Corps' action, the then-Chief of Naval Operations, Admiral William Leahy, going so far as to declare that the Air Corps' interception of *Rex* "was in violation of the Navy's prerogative of controlling the sea approaches."[14]

As the admirals saw it, this was the first step in an attempt by the Air Corps to usurp the Navy's traditional role of protecting America's coastline beyond the range of land-based artillery. The admirals proceeded to browbeat Craig into forbidding any Air Corps operations more than 100 miles offshore; long range patrols would be the sole responsibility of the Navy. Six months later, the Air Corps' freedom of action was even further proscribed, when, at the direction of Secretary of War Henry Woodring, the Army was informed that Air Corps bombers could carry out attacks on hostile warships only when specifically asked to do so by the Navy. The situation was absurd—both services were dedicated to defending the United States, yet here were the Army and Navy bickering over where, when, and who would get to shoot at the enemy.

The ugly truth was that, while not as lethal as sometimes was the enmity that existed between Japan's Imperial Army and Navy, there was a sour antagonism between America's Army and Navy that on occasion edged over into outright hostility. Interservice rivalries were a far from new phenomenon, and, if properly channeled, could be healthy, encouraging higher standards of professionalism among soldiers, sailors, and their officers. But in the cash-strapped 1920s and early 1930s, when both services were scraping and scrapping for every elusive dollar, that rivalry turned bitter as each sought primacy of place in the role of national defense and hence the larger share of the appropriations. Eventually the relationship would deteriorate to a point where, in the early years of the Second World War, senior officers were known to openly state their service's enemies as being Washington politicians first; the Army or Navy, as the case may be, second; while the Germans and Japanese would be third on the list.

Fortunately, the worst of the interservice infighting took place in Washington, where political turf wars had always been the order of the day; in local commands around the country somewhat saner heads usually prevailed, though even they weren't entirely free of some of the antagonism. In Hawaii, Short and Kimmel's predecessors, General Herron and Admiral Richardson, had both accepted an informal agreement between Major General Frederick Martin, commanding officer of the Hawaiian Air Force, and Rear Admiral Claude Bloch, commandant of the 14th Naval District, in regard to conducting aerial operations. While flights of any kind past the 100-mile limit were still technically the Navy's bailiwick, in practice both services agreed to ignore at least part of the restriction and carry out attacks on enemy warships wherever they were found; long-range patrols, though, remained entirely in the hands of the Navy.

When he assumed command of the Pacific Fleet, Kimmel had the good sense to allow this arrangement to remain in place; Short, arriving in Hawaii a few days later, chose to leave well enough alone and likewise made no attempt to alter it. On the whole the two men worked well together in the 10 months they held their respective commands, yet, in all that time, Kimmel never requested the use of the Air Corps' bombers to augment his limited number of patrol planes—perhaps, given the Navy's official stance, an understandable if not forgivable omission. Short, less understandably, never offered to make them available.

That may well have been due to the fact that Short seems to never have fully understood or appreciated the airplane and the additional dimensions, figurative and literal, that it brought to warfare; unarguably, he never grasped the concept of "air power." He was an infantry officer, first, last, and always, of the sort who believed that the mission of every other branch of the army—Cavalry, Field Artillery, Air Corps, Corps of Engineers, Quartermaster Corps, Ordnance Corps, Signal Corps, Medical Department, Military Intelligence—was subordinate to and supported that of the infantry. Not long after his arrival in Hawaii, he made six weeks of infantry training mandatory for all Air Corps personnel; a few days later, he issued an order requiring the enlisted men—the armorers, ground crews, and mechanics who kept the Air Corps bombers and fighters armed and flying—to stand guard duty when, where, and as needed at the Army facilities around Oahu, as well as provide manpower for work details. The servicing and maintenance of the aircraft could be done in the men's "off duty" hours. As Short saw it, the "real" work of the Army was done between Reveille and Retreat—that is, between 8:00 AM and 5:00 PM—and no amount of tinkering on gadgets and gizmos would be allowed to disrupt that schedule. Here Short exceeded his brief, as he didn't have direct authority over the Hawaiian Air Force. General Martin, who reported to Short but whose chain of command ran upward to Major General Henry Arnold, Chief of the Air Corps, acquiesced to the first of Short's directives but with Arnold's support ignored the second.

Whatever might have been his reasons, and despite knowing full well of the Pacific Fleet's paucity of patrol planes, Short never recognized just how useful making the Hawaiian Air Force's bombers available would have been to Kimmel. Nor did he ever understand that the Army actually had the means to locate Japanese forces drawing near to Hawaii, specifically an approaching aerial attack. There were six shiny new SCR-270 mobile radar sets on Oahu, each with an effective range, when sited on a well-elevated position, of up to 200 miles; with them came operating crews as well as the requisite communications and plotting equipment needed for a fully functioning air warning system. Five of the radar units were positioned at or near the peaks of carefully chosen mountains, the sixth at Fort Shafter, where together they could have provided complete 360-degree coverage of Oahu around the clock—but didn't. At the specific orders of General Short himself, the radar sets were instead switched on at 4:00 AM every morning, and shut down promptly at 7:00 AM for the remainder of the day. Just as with the enlisted men who kept the Air Corps' planes serviced and flying, by Short's reckoning when the radar operators were carrying out the duties for which they had been trained, they weren't being "real soldiers"—they weren't training on the rifle or grenade ranges, digging entrenchments, or standing guard duty at some warehouse miles from Fort Shafter.

For that same reason the communications center and plotting and intercept station which would coordinate all of the radar sets' reports and direct Air Corps fighters to meet intruding aircraft was never set up; even when the radar equipment became operational beginning in July 1941, it wasn't possible for the operators to make sighting reports directly to anyone who could make immediate use of them. Initially some of the radar emplacements had no radio or telephone equipment at all—the crew of the Opana Point station, for example, was told to use the public telephone at a gasoline station one mile away to report if anything unusual appeared on their set's oscilloscope. Major Kenneth Bergquist, who had been detached from the 14th Pursuit Wing in April to attend the Army's air defense school at Mitchel Field on Long Island, New York, returned to Hawaii in June prepared to set up the plotting and intercept station, only to be told that he was to report back to his original squadron instead—General Short saw no purpose in wasting manpower and material on air defense installations he was convinced would be ineffective.

Nor was that all. General Short never took time to inform Admiral Kimmel that the radar equipment was even on the island, let alone in the process of becoming operational—an error that was compounded by the failure of anyone in Washington to ensure that Kimmel had this information. This despite the fact that the Navy had nearly a year's operational experience with their ship-mounted radar systems, some of which might have been of practical value to the Army's radar technicians. Kimmel himself was, of course, no radar expert, but he was aware of its capabilities, and there were radar experts in the Pacific Fleet who could have made themselves useful to the Army. Certainly it's difficult to conceive of Kimmel being anything less than enthusiastic about having a functional, round-the-clock radar net watching the approaches to the Hawaiian Islands.

Short's failure—there can be no other word for it—to inform Kimmel about the radar wasn't malicious or the by-product of inter-service rivalry. Short said nothing simply because he didn't think it was worth mentioning: he was solidly in the camp of officers who regarded radar as "a freak gadget producing snap observations on targets which may or may not be aircraft," despite all of the evidence to the contrary already accumulated by both the Army and Navy. His was the scorn of an experienced senior officer told to entrust the security of his command and its mission to some rag-tag collection of experimental, unproven hardware.[15]

This is where a large measure—though by no means all, or even the lion's share—of the responsibility for the disaster which would overwhelm Pearl Harbor just a few months hence begins to settle on General Short. He refused to employ all of the tools and weapons which the War Department had assigned to his command for the defense of the Hawaiian Islands. This was because, bluntly put, he didn't know what to do with them. Short was, despite his combat experience in France two decades earlier, an ideal peacetime officer: efficient, conscientious, and hardworking, a master of peacetime bureaucratic procedure—but he was not a thinker. His signal weakness was that he lacked imagination. As the months went by in 1941 and a possible war with Japan became a probable war, then a near-certainty, Short never seemed to fully grasp the strategic and operational reality contained in General Marshal's letter: it would not be Short's infantry units which would be called upon to protect the Pacific Fleet. That mission fell to the Hawaiian Air Force—the bombers of the 18th Bombardment Wing and the fighters of the 14th Pursuit Wing. Instead, Short continued to think in terms of a conventional ground defense of the islands—the threat of aerial attacks on any scale larger than that of nuisance raids just never seemed credible to him.

Meanwhile, the staffs of the Pacific Fleet and the 14th Naval District did the best they could with what they had, maintaining, with only minor changes, the rotation of ships in and out of Pearl Harbor that Admiral Richardson had initiated, in order to keep some of the Pacific Fleet's battleships and most of its carriers at sea as much as possible. Search and patrol efforts focused primarily on the approaches from southwest and west, while patrols to the north and east of the islands were sporadic at best. It was thought that any attack by the Imperial Navy on the Hawaiian Islands would be made by a fleet that staged out of the Japanese-occupied Marshall Islands, directly to the west of Hawaii. If the staff planners guessed right, then Admiral Kimmel would have the time to withdraw the Pacific Fleet from Pearl if he thought it prudent, or he could advance and give the Japanese a most unwelcoming welcome. If they guessed wrong, the fleet—or at least a sizeable portion of it—might well find itself temporarily bottled up inside the harbor until a relief force from the mainland arrived and drove off the Japanese forces. What was certain was that the Imperial Navy's logistics weren't up to the task of keeping a large battle fleet fueled and supplied indefinitely in the waters around Hawaii—if the Japanese sent their battleships to try conclusions with the Pacific Fleet, regardless of the outcome sooner or later they would have to go home. In any event, no one, as of yet, at least, was anticipating the sort of massive, crippling aerial attack Admiral Yamamoto was already contemplating aboard *Nagato* in Yokohama Bay.

* * *

Some months after the attack on Pearl Harbor, Yamamoto Isoroku confided in a letter to a friend that he had begun planning the air strike in mid-December 1940. The date is significant, although it's unclear at this remove whether he meant that it marked the moment he decided that such an attack must be made, or if it was when the basic concept of the attack plan began to take shape in his thoughts. Certainly, the idea of an air strike on Pearl had been on Yamamoto's mind for some time already: there is some evidence that he began giving thought to it in May, and a few tantalizing hints that he had toyed with the idea as early as December 1939. Be that as it may, in early July 1940, only weeks after the US Navy shifted the primary base for its Pacific Ocean fleet from San Diego, California, to Pearl Harbor, and just days after the proclamation of the Greater East Asia Co-Prosperity Sphere, Yamamoto had instructed Rear Admiral Onishi Takijiro to begin exploring the idea of an air strike on Pearl Harbor. Onishi, a fellow naval aviator and a solid if not flamboyant proponent of naval air power, would know the right questions to ask and find the problems as well as the opportunities that only fliers would recognize. Curiously, Yamamoto asked Onishi to go about this task in secret; he offered no explanation as to why, and Onishi didn't ask.

Onishi's report was completed and forwarded to Yamamoto by the end of the month. Onishi was, as Yamamoto knew he would be, blunt and straightforward in his conclusions: an air strike on Pearl Harbor was theoretically possible, given the Imperial Navy's current strength, but losses were certain to be heavy, possibly even severe—when weighed against the estimated damage that would be inflicted on the American fleet, the game wasn't worth the candle. The air war against the Chinese had been far from one-sided, and those navy pilots and aircrew who survived the air battles over Shanghai, Nanjing, and elsewhere had accumulated skills and experience which were literally irreplaceable. Squandering them on a single mission that would not produce decisive results even in a best-case scenario would be, in Onishi's well-considered opinion, the height of folly.

Yamamoto accepted Onishi's report and conclusions, and then to all appearances promptly forgot about both. This was hardly surprising, as there were events and developments which were more immediate and pressing which legitimately required his attention than planning hypothetical air operations. First came the news that America's Congress had passed the Two-Ocean Navy Act, which would in time permanently change the strategic future in the Pacific, followed shortly by President Roosevelt's invocation of the Export Control Act, cutting off Japan from what had been its single largest source of iron, scrap steel, oil, and other strategic materials. Two months later the Imperial Navy was busy supporting the occupation of the north half of French Indochina and the United States government began advising its citizens living in the Far East to return home as expeditiously as possible. The two sides were still talking, of course, though Yamamoto knew that the hardline militants in Tokyo would never accept a diplomatic settlement short of total concession by the Americans to every Japanese demand, something that simply was not going to happen. Anything else meant war, and for that the Combined Fleet had to be ready.

Yamamoto was convinced that the time had come for caution—uncharacteristically for him, but there it was—while the Army, Navy, and politicians alike carefully planned their next moves. A rash act in any sphere just now could have consequences that would lead to national disaster. He very deliberately expressed this in a letter to Vice Admiral Shimada Shigetaro, written on December 10, 1940, saying,

> The probability is great that the launching of our operation against the Netherlands Indies will lead to … war with America, Britain, and Holland before those operations are half over. Consequently we should not launch out on those operations unless we are at least prepared to face such an eventuality, and are, moreover, adequately equipped… The southern operations, unlike the operations in China, will determine the nation's rise or fall, for they will lead to a war in which the nation's very fate will be at stake.[16]

And yet, just a few days after posting his letter to Shimada, Yamamoto had returned to the brash idea of attacking Pearl Harbor, determined to create a viable operational plan. Something happened late in 1940 that galvanized Yamamoto, persuading him that the Pearl Harbor raid, while risky, could be decisive after all.[17]

That "something" was an aerial attack staged by the Royal Navy on the night of November 11–12, 1940, when 21 Swordfish torpedo bombers flew off the aircraft carrier HMS *Illustrious* and successfully attacked the Italian Navy at Taranto Harbor, sinking three battleships anchored there—*Conte di Cavour, Caio Duilio*, and *Littorio*—in exchange for two aircraft shot down, with two of the aircrew killed, two captured. Though *Caio Duilio* and *Littorio* would eventually be raised and returned to service, their loss, albeit temporary, created a window of opportunity for the Royal Navy to shift the balance of naval power in the Mediterranean Sea in Great Britain's favor for at least the next six months; the attack would also have unexpected consequences for both Britain and Japan a year hence.

What immediately caught and held Yamamoto's attention was not that the battleships were sunk, but that the Taranto raid was the first time aircraft attacked and sank capital ships that were manned, alert, and able to defend themselves. In the 1920s various navies had conducted experiments with bombers and torpedo planes attacking old, obsolete battleships or derelict hulks, usually at anchor, some efforts achieving spectacular results, others doing little more than giving the air- and ground-crews the benefit of their exercise. The single constant in all such experiments, though, was that the warplanes were able to make their bomb and torpedo runs free of the distraction and danger of anti-aircraft fire, a detail that battleship advocates claimed, not unreasonably, made such experiments hopelessly unrealistic. Against battleships protected by proper anti-aircraft defenses, so went the refrain, airplanes would be driven off long before they could press home their attacks to inflict serious or crippling damage. Now that claim was proven to be hollow.

The deputy naval attaché at the Japanese embassy in Berlin spent a week in Taranto, surveyed the damage done to *Littorio, Ciao Duilio*, and *Conte di Cavour*, and established exactly how the raid was carried out, then sent to Tokyo a detailed report on the attack. While the report itself did not survive the war, it was written by a professional naval officer to be read by other naval officers, and so some deductions can nonetheless be made as to its contents. One detail which certainly would have been included was that the Italians had confirmed the Royal Navy used their standard Mark XII 18-inch aerial torpedoes in the attack.

That one piece of information may have been what convinced Yamamoto to begin planning in earnest for a massive aerial strike on the American fleet at Pearl Harbor. It laid to rest any lingering doubts that torpedoes carried by aircraft were capable of delivering a punch powerful enough to cripple or even sink a battleship. Aerial torpedoes were readily acknowledged to be capable of sinking merchant ships, which of course carried no armor at all, as well as lightly armored warships, such as cruisers and destroyers. But there were doubts as to how effective they would be against the layered anti-torpedo defenses—heavy bulkheads, internal cofferdams, bunkers, and void spaces—of a battleship's hull. This was because the warheads on torpedoes carried by aircraft were usually only one-half to two-thirds the weight of those on the larger torpedoes carried by submarines, destroyers, and cruisers, which were known ship-killers.

More specifically the British Mark XII was a close equivalent to Japanese Type 91, the Imperial Navy's standard aerial torpedo. This similarity allowed the Japanese to draw some fairly accurate conclusions, based on the damage done to the Italian warships, as to how effective would the Type 91 be against American battleships— conclusions that had the benefit of being based on actual combat performance, not theoretical projections or peacetime tests. The three battleships sitting on the bottom of Taranto Harbor, then, were proof that not only could air strikes be driven home even in the face of determined defenses—Italian anti-aircraft gunners fired upward of 20,000 rounds at the attacking Swordfish, nearly 1,000 rounds for each aircraft, yet could only bring down two of them—but also that the airplane had at last become the battleship's mortal enemy.

With the raid on Taranto fresh in his mind, Yamamoto began working alone on the outline of what would become the "Hawaii Operation," the strike on Pearl Harbor. Hardly had the dust and debris at Pearl Harbor settled a year later than the myth sprang up that the Taranto raid had provided Yamamoto with the idea of attacking Pearl, something that supposedly he had never before considered, a myth that persists to this day. The roots of this fable lay in the obvious but only superficial similarities between the two operations, and in the prejudices toward Asians in general and the Japanese in particular that persisted in most Western nations long after the guns had fallen silent. It simply wasn't possible, so went the conventional wisdom, for the Japanese by themselves to have concocted a plan as original, complex, thorough, and sophisticated as Hawaii Operation; their talent lay in refinement, rather than original ideas. Hence, there had to be a Western origin—the Taranto raid—for the plan of attack.

Such was not the case, however. What the raid on Taranto actually provided Yamamoto is best described as a "proof of concept" rather than the concept itself.

The idea of the Imperial Navy launching an attack on Pearl Harbor dated much farther back than late 1940: it was in 1927 that the first plan for a strike on Pearl Harbor was drawn up—at Japan's Naval War College. There the instructors used highly complex wargames in much the same way that 21st-century military and naval colleges would use computer simulations—to conduct hypothetical exercises, refine general staff contingency plans, and reveal flaws in operational planning. Japan had no intention of going to war with the United States in 1927, of course, but there can be no doubt that the Imperial Navy recognized that such an attack might be called for at least 13 years before Taranto. And, of course, there was Yamamoto's own explorations of an airstrike on Pearl which began no later than July of 1940.

Still, there *was* a kernel of truth in the suggestion that the idea of the attack on Pearl Harbor wasn't original to Yamamoto: there *was* an aerial attack on a naval base which was almost certainly the source for the basic outline of the plan Yamamoto would ultimately produce. The similarities, unlike those between Taranto and the Hawaii Operation, were far from superficial, and included many of the fundamental conditions, requirements, and methods that would be found at the heart of the Hawaii Operation. That plan came from, ironically, the United States Navy, and its target was, of all places, Pearl Harbor. It was the centerpiece of a very large-scale exercise conducted in early 1932 known as the "Grand Joint Army-Navy Maneuvers 4," or "GJE4", which served as a sort of prelude to Fleet Problem XIII, the big Navy show of 1932.

Between 1920 and 1940 the United States Navy conducted a succession of 21 annual fleet-wide exercises known as Fleet Problems, numbered successively. These exercises were drawn up to test the effectiveness of potential adversaries' offensive or defensive strategies and tactics against the US Navy's existing tactical and operational doctrines, as well as critique and refine new tactics, and evaluate new weapons and aircraft. Ships would be assigned to either the "Blue" or "Black" teams, Black always being the enemy forces; the Black team was tasked, naturally, with simulating as best it could the tactics and operations of a specific foreign navy. As the Fleet Problems were often formulated around an attempted invasion of the United States or an attack on one of its foreign possessions, the US Army would sometimes participate in what were rather heroically termed "Grand Joint Exercises."

Held in February 1932, Fleet Problem XIII had as its core premise a war in the Pacific with an unidentified "militaristic, Asian, island nation"—it took little imagination to see that this was a euphemism for Japan—allied with an aggressive European naval power, that had seized control of the Hawaiian Islands. Blue was given the mission of retaking the islands, Black was tasked with repelling any attempt to do so. Since, in a real war, physically recapturing the islands would involve a significant ground campaign, the US Army took on the role of the Black force in this exercise, determined to repel any attempt by Blue to retake the islands. This, then, was what would be known as GJE4.

Blue's commanding officer was Rear Admiral Harry Yarnell, an 1897 graduate of the US Naval Academy, and in 1932 one of the handful of US Navy flag officers who was a qualified naval aviator, having earned his wings 10 years earlier. A staunch though not overly outspoken advocate of the potential of airpower at sea, he saw in the parameters laid down for GJE4 an opportunity to put that potential on full display. Yarnell's orders required him, as a necessary prerequisite to any amphibious attack on the island, to "inflict maximum damage on the PEARL HARBOR NAVAL BASE in order to destroy or reduce its effectiveness;" to accomplish this he was given two fleet carriers, the USS *Lexington* and *Saratoga*, nine battleships, four heavy cruisers, 24 destroyers, and an assortment of support ships and fleet auxiliaries. What Yarnell did with them was a *tour de force* of operational genius which the US Navy subsequently disparaged but the Imperial Navy heeded closely.[18]

Conventional naval wisdom held that Yarnell would be forced to employ his battleships and cruisers to fight their way into Pearl, while the two carriers would be relegated to supporting roles. Yarnell thought differently, and detached the two carriers and a small escorting force from the slow, 21-knot battleship fleet. The carriers raced ahead at 32 knots, undetected by Black scouting units, to reach a point 100 miles north of Oahu where, at dawn on Sunday, February 7, they launched 152 fighters and bombers in an airstrike on Pearl Harbor. The Army airfields scattered around Oahu were the first targets; taken completely by surprise, the Air Corps wasn't able to put up a single fighter in defense. Now it was Battleship Row's turn, and the Navy bombers, dropping sacks of white flour instead of live ordnance, scored hits on four battleships, causing enough damage, in the opinion of the exercise umpires, to sink or incapacitate all of them, in exchange for negligible losses to the attacking aircraft. GJE4 was an unqualified victory for the Blue team.

Or so it seemed, at first. Predictably, the "battleship admirals" categorically refused to accept the umpires' decision. Their reasoning ran the gamut from assorted technical issues to the patently absurd assertion that a Sunday morning was not a "legal" time for an attack. They even resorted to arguing that it was supposedly common knowledge that Asians lacked the degree of eye-hand coordination required to achieve the level of bombing accuracy Admiral Yarnell's pilots had produced. Eventually the umpires, sufficiently cowed by the gaggle of senior officers, reversed their decision, declaring that the Blue strike force had lost nearly a quarter of its number to anti-aircraft fire, and the formerly critical damage done to the battleships was deemed to be "superficial" or "minor" instead. When the umpires original rulings were tossed overboard, with them went any lessons the US Navy might have learned from Admiral Yarnell's audacity and professionalism.[19]

But if the old-school "shellbacks" of US Navy chose to ignore the implications of Yarnell's attack on Pearl Harbor, officers of the Imperial Navy were not so blind. The Americans had made no effort to keep the operations of GJE4—or its outcome—a secret, and Japanese officers who had gathered in Honolulu to officially observe the exercises had been able to watch the attack on Battleship Row from the comfort of the Japanese consulate's lanai. When they returned to Tokyo, those officers reported everything they had witnessed, and the Naval General Staff began drawing conclusions from those reports. The staff findings were then circulated among the officers of the Naval Air Service, including one then-Vice Admiral Yamamoto Isoroku, on whom they made a deep and lasting impression.

Yamamoto spent the last two weeks of 1940 and the first week of 1941 working out how to best adapt Rear Admiral Yarnell's operations in GJE4 to the capabilities and limitations of the Imperial Navy. It was not a matter of merely copying Yarnell's plans detail-for-detail, as there were major technical challenges which the Japanese would need to overcome that had not been factors in the American exercise, especially the thorny problem of refueling light cruisers and destroyers at sea while underway. Yamamoto was confident they would not be insurmountable obstacles, but could be mastered with sufficient time and thought. As for the Royal Navy's attack on the Italian fleet at Taranto, in the end there was very little Yamamoto could glean from it in the way of operational planning, no matter what later myth-making might claim, and yet it did provide him with the last piece to the puzzle of how to ensure that attack would be successful: the performance of the Royal Navy's Mark XII torpedoes, so similar to that of the Imperial Navy's Type 91, confirmed that the attack on Pearl Harbor was now feasible. It was time for Yamamoto's staff to begin work on the detailed planning of the Hawaii Operation, and at the same time make certain the Americans never caught the slightest hint of what was coming.

CHAPTER 4

MAGIC and the Color Purple

Three years before the attack on Pearl Harbor, in the summer of 1938, the United States Navy very quietly moved a special intelligence unit into Fort Ward, an all-but-deserted coastal artillery installation on Bainbridge Island in Washington State's Puget Sound. Built at the beginning of the 20th century, little more than two decades later the fort had been largely abandoned, its 8- and 5-inch guns rendered obsolete by advances in long-range naval gunnery. The Navy became interested in Fort Ward when a series of field tests showed it to be an ideal site for intercepting the Morse code transmissions broadcast from Japan to Tokyo's embassies and consulates around the world. Even better, the listening equipment could be set up in the old Post Exchange, while the existing housing and barracks were refurbished for use by the officers and enlisted men posted there. Apart from erecting a few radio aerials, there was no new construction to draw unwanted attention to Fort Ward's new residents and their purpose: the Navy intended to keep its new installation, designated "Station S," a very closely held secret. The reason for the secrecy was very simple: the Office of Naval Intelligence (ONI) was reading Japan's diplomatic mail.

Military use of codes and ciphers can be reliably traced back as far as the waning days of the Roman Republic—Julius Caesar created his own substitution cipher, which he used in both official communications and private messages; a few centuries later, Arab mathematicians created the first codes. The differences between the two—codes and ciphers—is often subtle, and the two terms are frequently used interchangeably, but in practice use an alphanumeric group to hide the meaning of a whole word, or even entire phrases, while ciphers use the substitution of pre-determined individual numbers or characters to conceal the identity of the individual characters that make up a word. For example, the *code* group for "battleship" could be 61538, while as a *cipher* "battleship" could be "obdp6ax27c"—the actual numbers or characters used in either, of course, would depend on the specific code or cipher employed. One significant difference between the two systems is that in a code, the number of characters in an individual code group bear no relation to the number of characters or even words the group represents—a single four-digit code group could easily be used to convey a set phrase several words in length. One the other hand, in a cipher the number of characters is always identical that of the original message. The two methods can even be combined, so that a message is first encoded, that is, the words of an original message—the "plaintext"—are converted into the appropriate code groups, then the letters and numbers of those groups are enciphered; the text actually transmitted then bears no resemblance whatsoever to the original coding, let alone the plaintext. The process of converting a plaintext into coded or enciphered form is known as encryption; trying to extract the plaintext from an encrypted message while lacking the original code or cipher is called cryptography; drawing useful information from a decrypted message is called cryptanalysis.

Using a code or cipher—or both—requires that both the sender and the recipient possess matching codebooks or cipher keys to "lock" and then "unlock" the message. Both systems have their own peculiar advantages and disadvantages, and for well over two millennia a never-ending game of cat-and-mouse has been played out between cryptographers and cryptanalysts to create and break increasingly more complex and—hopefully—secure codes and ciphers. With the introduction of electrical and then electronic communications, the importance of codes and ciphers increased dramatically, as telegraph wires could be tapped, and it was impossible to prevent wireless transmissions from being intercepted by an enemy, real or potential.

The mission for Station S was to pluck out of the ether encrypted Japanese communications to and from the Washington DC embassy, and pass along by landline the intercepted texts to the Office of Naval Intelligence, where Navy cryptographers would strive to decode and analyze them. The Americans had been surprisingly successful at breaking into Japan's secret traffic, beginning with the diplomatic cipher used by the Japanese delegation to the Washington Naval Conference in 1922. The United States had learned by experience during the Great War the value of good cryptanalysis: it was the coded message from Imperial Germany to Mexico which became known to history as "the Zimmermann Telegram" that provoked America to join the Allies and declare war on Germany in April 1917. The American government's first codebreaking organization, the Cipher Bureau, better known as the Black Chamber, was set up in 1919, a joint effort by the Army and the State Department; it was specifically tasked with breaking the codes and ciphers used by foreign governments for diplomatic communications, something it did with surprising ease during the Washington Naval Conference. Ironically, while this was the Black Chamber's finest hour, it ultimately proved to be its undoing: in 1929, when a new president, Herbert Hoover, took office, his secretary of state, Henry Stimson, declared that "Gentlemen do not read each other's mail," and withdrew his department's funding of the Black Chamber. The War Department, in turn, was unwilling to foot the entire bill for the operation, and closed it down.[1]

But just when the Army appeared to be abandoning cryptanalysis, the Navy's interest in cryptographic intelligence was increasing dramatically. By the time Hoover's successor, Franklin Roosevelt, took office, Japanese and American interests began to grind against one another in the Far East and the western Pacific Ocean, the sort of frictions that create the kinds of crises that start wars. David Kahn, in his biography of Henry Yardley, who organized and directed the Black Chamber, best summed up the sources of the American unease with Japan's ambitions that was growing just at the time when the United States' ability to forestall those ambitions was declining: "[Japan's] belligerence toward China jeopardized America's Open Door policy. Its emigrants exacerbated American racism. Its naval growth menaced American power in the western Pacific. Its commercial expansion threatened American dominance of Far Eastern markets." There were naval officers who, refusing to take the popular Japanese stereotypes at face value, saw a need for accurate intelligence about Japan's capabilities and intentions. As it was all but impossible to introduce intelligence operatives—spies—into a society as racially and culturally homogenous as Japan, other means had to be employed, signals intelligence being the most promising.[2]

It was through a book, *The American Black Chamber*, written by Yardley and published in 1931, that the Japanese first learned that some of their encryption systems had been compromised, and how. Yardley's revelations about his cryptographers' work was an embarrassment to both Washington and Tokyo: the Americans for being caught with their hand in the cookie jar, so to speak; the Japanese for the humiliation of being outsmarted by the *gaijin*. This led to the wholesale scrapping of every code and cipher then in use by the Imperial Army and Navy as well as the civilian government, accompanied by a scramble to find replacements. For the Foreign Ministry, this would be a German-designed machine that the Japanese modified and then issued to its embassies as the "Type A Cipher Machine." American cryptographers soon began calling it simply "RED", because intercepted messages and decrypts were kept in a series of red binders.

RED wasn't a terribly sophisticated enciphering system, even by the standards of the day, and within four years of its introduction it was compromised by three separate cryptographic teams working independently of each other, one British, two American. The Japanese evidently understood RED's limitations, as they began looking to replace it almost as soon as it entered service; the result was a system superficially similar to RED but far more complex, which the Americans christened "PURPLE", again after the color of the binders in which intercepted signals sent in this new system were stored. Based on—but not a copy of—the Enigma machine used by Nazi Germany, PURPLE was introduced in 1938. Given the limitations of the mathematical tools available to cryptanalysts at the time—"entabulating machines," as the first primitive computers would be known were still years in the future—PURPLE was potentially a near-unbreakable cipher system; as it was, it proved difficult enough to crack.

For a time, OP-20-G, the Navy's signals intelligence and cryptanalysis unit, and its newly revived Army counterpart, now known as the Signal Intelligence Service, or SIS, worked in uncharacteristic harmony on the problems presented by the new Japanese codes. Such was the complexity of PURPLE that the Navy's cryptanalysis unit agreed to shoulder the burden of solving the other Japanese encryption systems while the Army's cryptanalysts in SIS worked exclusively on PURPLE. Determined to make PURPLE yield to its efforts, the Army turned William Friedman loose on it.

Friedman, at that time a lieutenant colonel in the Army Reserve, had worked in cryptography and cryptanalysis for more than 20 years, dating back to the Military Intelligence Division of the First World War, and was currently in charge of the SIS. Such was his gift—there really is no other word for it—for cryptanalysis that he was literally "the man who wrote the book" on codes and ciphers, the four-volume *Military Cryptanalysis*, which became and would remain the unofficial "bible" of American cryptography. When the War Department closed down the "Black Chamber," it didn't completely abandon cryptanalysis, although it appeared to the rest of the world to have done so. Instead a small and highly secretive section was very quietly created in the Signal Corps, the Signals Intelligence Service, and in it Friedman and three other very talented analysts went to work. To keep that work as secure as possible, the SIS reported directly to the chief signals officer of the US Army and no one else. For a time not even OP-20-G knew with whom they were working in the initial stages of the attack on PURPLE.

For two years Friedman and his team of cryptographers tried to break into PURPLE, through a combination of herculean mental exertion aided by blinding flashes of insight, and assisted by the poor communication security procedures of the Japanese. Part of the Type A Cipher Machine's design was an electrical plugboard and a series of switches, the settings on which were changed daily according to a prearranged schedule, to ensure that even if one day's communications were compromised, the next day's would be secure. However, there would often be parts of messages—dates, times, station identifiers, names of senders and addressees—that would already be known to the SIS personnel that could provide a baseline for determining a given day's settings. For example, all communications to and from Tokyo and Japan's embassies were time-stamped according to Tokyo time, no matter what the local time might be—the transmission time would be logged by the Navy's radio intercept station on Bainbridge Island, which had transmissions in PURPLE as its priority, and thus be a known value for which the decryption team would look in the messages as they worked out the daily settings. Specific titles, phrases, greetings, and diplomatic courtesies that were frequently used—"I have the honor to inform you" was a common one, "Your Excellency is advised" was another—along with the names of diplomatic personnel, were put to work in the same way.

At one point, the strain was so great that Friedman was hospitalized briefly after experiencing a nervous breakdown, but the effort and sacrifice paid off when, in the summer of 1940, the Army cryptanalysts were able to construct, working entirely from theory and without ever having seen an original example, a fully functional prototype of a PURPLE machine. (In fact, they would *never* see an actual, complete PURPLE machine: at the end of the war the Japanese were able to destroy every example before any of the Allies' intelligence services could lay their hands on one, leaving behind only fragments.)

This breakthrough didn't mean that the Army was suddenly able to effortlessly read Tokyo's diplomatic correspondence—there was the perpetual problem of getting the daily settings right, that was only solved through a trial-and-error process. Then there was the need to correctly translate the text into English: Japanese is a subtle language with both formal and conversational forms, it uses an extraordinary number of contractions and blended words, and it relies heavily on context to convey ideas and information, making the potential for mistranslation problematic under the best circumstances. The solution, of course, was to find military personnel or carefully vetted civilians who were skilled in both formal and conversational Japanese; the challenge was that the number of Americans who were fluent in Japanese was very small.

All in all, extracting useful information from PURPLE was still a formidable problem, but once the actual workings of the Type A Machine were established, the other problems could and would be resolved through dogged hard work. By the summer of 1941, the Army's decryption staff were often reading messages sent from Tokyo to the Washington DC embassy at the same time as the Japanese ambassador read them—sometimes sooner. It was an altogether remarkable achievement, so much so that the entire operation was christened "MAGIC."

The diplomatic cipher been given priority because it was believed that the information in communications between Tokyo and the Japanese embassies wouldn't be as "perishable," that is, become outdated, as quickly as that contained in the Imperial Navy's operational signals. Also, it was hoped that reading the diplomatic correspondence would provide critical insight into Japan's strategic intentions. As it turned out, this was a mistaken assumption—no one in the American government or armed forces realized how deeply the Japanese Army and Navy mistrusted the Foreign Ministry, or just how much information the generals and admirals withheld from the diplomats. It wasn't a wholly false premise, of course, as any insight into the plans and capabilities of an enemy, real or potential, was valuable, and during the war MAGIC would produce unexpected—and critical—information for the Allies. Still, in those last few months of peace between Japan and the United States, because the contents of the MAGIC intercepts offered a distorted and often vague reflection of the political and strategic thinking of Japan's generals and admirals—the men who were actually running the Empire—American officers and diplomats often drew the wrong conclusions and accordingly made flawed plans in response.[3]

Meanwhile, having left the PURPLE cipher in the hands of the Army, the Office of Naval Intelligence (ONI) attacked the codes used by the Imperial Navy. ONI's first success against a Japanese naval code had come in 1923, when, in an operation that could have been the script of a Hollywood motion picture about pre-electronic espionage, a copy of the Imperial Navy's RED code (which was completely unrelated to the diplomatic RED cipher) was "borrowed" from an unsuspecting Japanese naval attaché and photographed. The Japanese had always been sensitive to the physical security of their codes, keeping their codebooks locked away in safes even inside their embassies and secure signal stations on their naval bases, and became near-paranoid in their security measures after learning that RED had been physically compromised. Naturally, then, the US Navy cryptographers couldn't count on a repeat of such a lucky happenstance when the replacement for RED was introduced in 1931, in the wake of the revelations in Yardley's book. As it turned out, the new code, known as BLUE—again from the color of the binders holding intercepted signals—proved to be highly susceptible to a systematic analytical attack, and was broken within two years. Evidently the Japanese had no idea that BLUE was so vulnerable, as the Imperial Navy used it until early 1938, when it was superseded by a code designated BLACK.

BLACK, however, had a short life: late in 1939, a far more complex system, which the Americans, abandoning the use of color identifiers, promptly christened JN-25, as it was the 25th Japanese naval code of any type that OP-20-G had identified; in addition to whatever might be its current operational code, the Imperial Navy had codes that were used exclusively by specific naval departments, while others were reserved for officers who held specific commands or were of flag rank. This time, after having been so lackadaisical about the internal protection of their naval codes, the Japanese became very security conscious indeed and took no chances with JN-25, issuing a revision, which ONI dubbed JN-25a, in December 1940; a second revision, JN-25b, was introduced a year later, just four days before the attack on Pearl Harbor.

The challenge this new system presented the officers and enlisted men in the Navy's cryptography section, along with the handful of civilians who worked with them, was nothing like the one the Army's Signals Intelligence Service was facing. Whereas PURPLE was a *cipher* system, the Japanese Navy—and Army, as well—used a system of *codes*. This meant that there was very little in the detailed work already done by either the Army or Navy that could aid the efforts of the other service. It also meant that Japanese naval communications were far less susceptible to being broken by a mathematical attack, which was the inherent vulnerability shared by all cipher systems. Each version of JN-25 contained roughly 90,000 discrete code groups, each group representing a single word or short phrase, and each one unrelated to the group which came before or after it sequentially—even if the meaning of, say, group 61538 was discovered, it offered up nothing to indicate what 61537 or 61539 might mean. This made breaking into JN-25 an extremely complex and tedious task, especially when the quirks and nuances of the Japanese language were factored in. Compounding that problem, when the revisions went into operational use, even though they were derived from JN-25, the changes made were at once subtle enough yet sufficiently sweeping that most of the work done in cracking the previous version was of little value in decrypting the new one, meaning that the cryptographers had to start more or less from scratch each time.

Breaking into JN-25 and its revisions would rely on accumulating as many messages encrypted in it as possible, until a "critical mass" of messages was reached that could produce results through traffic analysis. As with PURPLE, time-stamps, dates, names, and honorifics were prized, as in this case they formed the basis for that analysis. The context of each signal, as well as the individual code groups within the signals, was examined and cross-referenced with other signals, and slowly, one by one, the code groups began to reveal their meanings.

As far back as 1924, the Navy began building extremely sensitive radio receiving stations at various points in the Pacific, which were then tasked with monitoring Japanese radio traffic. The first was set up in Shanghai, followed by stations in Guam and the Philippines, then on the island of Oahu—the station on Bainbridge Island was the last to be built; OP-20-G itself was located in Washington. They monitored and logged whatever Japanese transmissions they could, slowly accumulating that critical mass of signals. It was a tedious process: because the Imperial Navy conducted few significant fleet operations before December 1941, communications encoded in JN-25 or JN-25a were very limited in number, making meaningful analysis difficult. Orders and messages were usually transmitted by landlines to ships in harbor, and especially sensitive material was invariably hand-carried to its recipient; only when it was necessary to pass messages to ships at sea would JN-25 be used to encode signals. The men and women in OP-20-G simply had to make do with what they had, which meant that in practice only about 10 percent of the traffic was being rendered readable. The immediate intelligence value of what decodes there were was limited; a frustrating, if understandable, limitation, in that it was akin to trying to make sense of a book where only a tenth of the entire text, randomly selected, was readable.[4]

The man who kept this effort going was a career naval officer, Captain Laurence Safford, a Massachusetts-born Naval Academy graduate. He had been the commanding officer of the USS *Finch*, a minesweeper assigned to the US Navy's Asiatic Squadron based in Manila, when just before Christmas in 1923 he received orders assigning him to the Office of Naval Intelligence in the Main Navy Building in Washington DC. Once there, he was to report to the Office of Naval Communications, where he would be given charge of the newly created Research Desk of the Code and Signals Section, usually referred to as OP-20-G, its designator in the Navy's table of organization. At first this assignment seemed unusual to Safford, as he had no special training or experience in codes or signals, and thus had no idea how he would go about "researching" them. However, as is often the case with small naval and military units tagged with vague-but-deadly-dull-sounding titles, there was more to the Research Desk of the Code and Signals Section than met the eye or the ear: the "research" carried out was actually signals intelligence collection through analysis and decryption.

On paper, Safford's mission was to improve the admittedly inadequate security of the Navy's communications systems, overseeing the development of reliable cipher machines and the creation of codes sufficiently robust as to be able to withstand rigorous and sophisticated analytical attacks. In practice, it meant that Safford, who was at first the Research Desk's entire uniformed staff—the word "desk" in this case had been used literally—was not only in the right place for someone of his temperament, he had the opportunity to "write his own ticket," as it were, defining how he and the four civilian technicians working for him, would go about carrying out his mission.

Whether by extraordinary coincidence, or because a senior officer had sensed that Safford was one of those individuals whose personality suited them for cryptographic work, the Navy had neatly slipped a round peg into a round hole. Safford had a restless, probing intellect, and was one of those rare individuals whose mind could be relentlessly analytical even as it was making daring leaps of logic. He quickly realized, of course, that as with all truly effective cover stories, there was a large element of truth in the "official" description of his duties: in much the same way poachers make the best gamekeepers, his cryptanalytic work would, in fact, improve the security of the Navy's communications systems, by designing them to be proof against the types of attacks he carried out on foreign navies' codes and ciphers. As that was best accomplished by skilled technicians acting on suggestions and guidance from a superior officer, it would not require day-to-day supervision in his part. This left Safford free to explore the work of other ONC and ONI sections to see what might be useful, which eventually led him to Room 2646.

Unlike the Royal Navy's Room 40 O.B., which is encrusted with myth and legend, has been the subject of books—fact and fiction alike—as well as motion pictures, and has become something of a romanticized caricature of its real self, outside of the intelligence community Room 2646 in the US Navy's Office of Naval Intelligence remains little known, apart from those individuals with a deep interest in the history of intelligence work. Yet the two facilities were very much akin: Room 40 O.B.—the name comes from its location in the Admiralty's Old Building in Whitehall, London—was where copies of the Imperial German naval codes the Royal Navy acquired by hook and by crook in the early days of the Great War resided and the decryption of German naval signals was performed; Room 2646 was where the purloined copy of the Japanese RED naval code was being painstakingly translated and the mass of intercepted Japanese signals were simultaneously undergoing decryption, a sort of feedback loop that refined the translation at the same time it provided useful intelligence along with further insights into sections of the RED code that had yet to be translated.

"One of the best kept secrets in the US Navy for more than twenty years concerned room number 2646 in the old Navy Building on Constitution Avenue and what went on behind its locked doors," was how Safford would later describe it. For him, assignment to the Codes and Signals Section and discovering Room 2646 together were a sort of epiphany: he had truly found his vocation in the challenge of cryptanalysis. He immediately set about locating other naval personnel, along with carefully vetted civilians, who, like himself, couldn't resist the challenge of trying to resolve what another human being has done their best to render insoluble. Because in addition to being highly intelligent he could also be charming and persuasive, Safford soon convinced his commanding officer, Captain Ridley McLean, to bring all of the ONC cryptanalysis and decryption functions into the Code and Signals Section, under the direction of the Research Desk, and to authorize the construction additional radio interception stations across the Pacific.[5]

In February 1926, new orders arrived for Safford, sending him to sea aboard the battleship USS *California*, then later assigning him to the destroyer USS *Hull* as her executive officer and navigator. By that time, however, he had assembled a small but cohesive unit of cryptanalysts, among whom were some of the most brilliant minds to ever work in the field, who would be at the heart of the most important cryptographic work the Navy would carry out during the Second World War. Staff members in other sections were quick to recognize that the people who worked for the Codes and Signals research desk were remarkable, both for the complexity of the work they performed and for the depth of their dedication to it, often becoming so engrossed in their work that they would forget mealtimes and work through Sundays. Ellis Zacharias, a lieutenant commander who took over ONI's Far East Division shortly after Safford departed, and who would later, as Captain Zacharias, serve as the deputy director of naval intelligence during two of the most critical years of the Second World War and finally retire as a rear admiral, found this first impression of those cryptanalysts unforgettable: "It was an inspiration to watch these people at work, training themselves and improving their art in the secrecy which is part of their craft."[6]

In June 1929 Safford returned to Code and Signals, where he would remain until May 1932. During his absence, the Section had set up a radio intercept school which trained operators to recognize *Wabun*, the Japanese equivalent of Morse code, and quickly and accurately transcribe what they heard; the transcriptions would then be forwarded to OP-20-G. This allowed the Code and Signals Section to expand its ability to monitor and record the Imperial Navy's signal traffic, as the new intercept operators were sent to existing listening stations across the Pacific, as well as new ones as they were constructed; some of the operators were given shipboard duty in the US Navy's Asian Fleet as well as Battle Fleet. In order to keep the exact nature of the training a secret, the radio intercept school's classes were conducted in Quonset huts erected on the roof of the Main Navy building; only instructors and students were allowed access to the huts, and both were forbidden to talk about their duties to anyone outside of the Code and Signals Section. This gave rise to the rest of the Office of Naval Communications to collectively refer to them as "The On-the-Roof Gang." By the end of 1941, 150 Navy signalmen and 26 Marine radiomen had graduated from radio intercept school.

More intercept operators meant more radio frequencies commonly used by the Japanese could be monitored around the clock, a capability which became vitally important when the Japanese introduced JN-25 in 1939. For the first time in more than a decade, save for a few brief interludes, the United States Navy lost the ability to read any part of the Imperial Navy's operational communications—just when the Navy needed as much insight as possible into Japanese plans and intentions. How, if, when OP-20-G could break into JN-25 would be a critical factor in the drama that would play out across the Pacific Ocean in the months ahead. Thus it was important to have more ears than ever before listening for JN-25 encoded signals, as each message could prove to be one more piece of that puzzle.

Safford returned to OP-20-G once more in May 1936, and would remain there for the rest of his naval career. By this time, the Section staff numbered 36, not including the signalmen and radio operators in the rooftop classes, or the radio intercept operators stationed abroad or at sea. The tone of the work being done in the Code and Signals Section had changed in the four years Safford spent at sea: while during the late 1920s and early 1930s no one in the Navy was paying much attention to what foreign navies were saying in their coded communications, by 1936, with Japan's withdrawal from the London Naval Conference and the associated naval limitation treaties, up-to-date and accurate intelligence about the Imperial Navy became a very real concern in Washington DC. OP-20-G would have to expand even further if it were to supply that intelligence.

Safford, who had been promoted to commander upon returning to the Codes and Signals Section, set about combing the Navy for people with the skills and talents necessary to become cryptanalysts—the actual codebreakers—along with intelligence analysts, translators, and clerks, plus the technicians who would take on the task of maintaining and improving the security of the Navy's own signal systems. Fortunately, Safford had a keen eye for talent, so that by the summer of 1940, close to 150 officers, enlisted men, and civilians in three different locations were working under his command and direction, a majority of them assigned to working full-time on the effort to break into JN-25. One of the people Safford brought into—or rather, brought *back* into—OP-20-G was Commander Joseph Rochefort, who had worked in the Codes and Signals Section from 1925 to 1929.

Rochefort was one of the most singular characters to ever serve as an officer in the United States Navy. At the age of 17, after having dropped out of high school while he was living in Los Angeles—he had been born in Dayton, Ohio—he had enlisted in the Navy, hoping to become a naval aviator. That dream never came to be: only months before, the United States had declared war on Imperial Germany, and Rochefort, whose innate intelligence was quickly recognized by his superiors, went to the Stevens Institute of Technology instead, earning a degree in mechanical engineering via an abbreviated curriculum. He was then given an ensign's commission in 1919 and sent to sea as an engineering officer. A few years later, when Rochefort was aboard the USS *Arizona*, his skill at solving crossword puzzles and his mastery of the complex bidding of auction bridge caught the attention of the battleship's executive officer, who, recognizing that Rochefort had a rare talent for both intuitive and analytical thinking, recommended him for training in cryptanalysis.

Rochefort reported to OP-20-G in October 1925, and when Safford departed for sea duty six months later, being the only other commissioned officer on the staff of the Research Desk at the Codes and Signals Section, he found himself in command. He did indeed have a gift for codebreaking, although he wasn't as skilled as Alice Meyer Driscoll, the legendary "Madam X," or Thomas Dyer, but the world of codes and ciphers was not where he truly wanted to be. Rochefort was ambitious, even driven, and kept a keen eye on promotion: he knew that advancement came slowly if at all in obscure, secrecy-ridden naval niches like the Codes and Signals Section—being assigned there was, as he saw it, a major detour on the path to command. He was openly relieved when orders arrived in late 1927 sending him to sea. Ironically, it was during Rochefort's tenure as the commanding officer of OP-20-G that the section scored its greatest success of the 1920s, the black bag operation that secured the copy of the Imperial Navy's RED code.

If Japanese codes were no longer on his mind, Japan was. Plucking him out of the Codes and Signals Section, the Navy sent him on a four-year long assignment to Tokyo, where he was to learn not only the Japanese language, but also as much as he possibly could about the Japanese people and their culture. This was considered a plum appointment—only two officers were selected for it annually—one which usually indicated that the Navy had high expectations for the officer in question. This pleased Rochefort no end, and when he finished his assignment in Japan in 1932, apart from a two-year intelligence assignment in the Eleventh Naval District in San Diego, he spent the next nine years at sea, serving in a succession of staff and department head positions, a typical young officer working his way through the naval *cursus honorum*.

Yet Rochefort was not a typical young naval officer. While by most accounts he was likeable enough, he was also brash and outspoken, sometimes to the point of being abrasive, and while never openly insubordinate, he rarely bothered to conceal his often negative opinions of his peers and immediate superiors. It was hardly the sort of conduct that would win him friends and sponsors who could help him advance his career. But despite knowing that there were senior officers who thought highly of him, Rochefort was a man with a chip on his shoulder: he was a "mustang," the Navy's nickname for an officer who came up through the enlisted ranks. As such, he wasn't part of the fraternity of Annapolis graduates who comprised the vast majority of the US Navy's officer corps, of which some Naval Academy alumni found ways to constantly remind him. While Annapolis did its best to produce graduates who were gentlemen, there were always those boors for whom that translated into snobbery, and who imagined any officer not sufficiently privileged to wear an academy ring to be their inferiors, professionally as well as socially. Rochefort chafed at often finding himself subordinate to such officers, many of whom who lacked both his intellect and competence yet advanced their careers through their academy connections.

Rochefort wasn't without reason for feeling aggrieved at the subtle but real slights he was given. He worked hard to acquire a measure of the social polish the Naval Academy imparted to its graduates and for the most part succeeded. What truly stung, though, was the professional disdain he was frequently offered. There were few cryptographers in the entire Navy who were his equal, he was fluent in Japanese, and he had a rare talent for intelligence work. He had an unnerving ability to take seemingly unrelated and fragmentary bits of information, see that they somehow fit together, and then use them to produce remarkably accurate assessments of the Imperial Navy's plans and intentions. Rochefort was, in the words of Commander Arthur McCollum, at that time chief of ONI's Far Eastern Section, "the only officer in our navy who is a top-flight cryptographer and radioman, and who has a thorough knowledge of the Japanese language."[7]

In February 1941, through a simultaneous appeal to his vanity and his professionalism, Rochefort, now a full commander, allowed himself to be persuaded by Safford to return to OP-20-G in Washington. Safford explained the extent of the troubles his codebreakers were having with the new JN-25a, and that he wanted to set up yet another listening station in the Pacific, this one in Honolulu, that would be for all intents and purposes dedicated to breaking into the Japanese naval code—this would become Station HYPO. The cryptanalysis effort would be split between HYPO and OP-20-G, with help from Station CAST in Cavite, in the Philippines.

That was how Rochefort came to arrive in Honolulu on June 1, 1941, along with a small entourage of intelligence analysts, linguists and codebreakers, many of them hand-picked by Rochefort, the initial staff of HYPO. Working under the bureaucratic cover of the District's Combat Intelligence Unit, with Rochefort officially assigned to be the Combat Intelligence Officer on the staff of Rear Admiral Claude Bloch, HYPO set up shop in the basement of Administrative Building 1 at the headquarters of the 14th Naval District. That basement, which with a mixture of derision, despair, and perverse affection would become known as "The Dungeon," was a single large, windowless, poorly vented room; in it were tables holding dozens of large boxes filled with tabulating machines and stacks of the punch cards that fed them, along with charts and diagrams of varying complexity which charted the progress made on individual JN-25a signals. One door only led into and out of The Dungeon, guarded round the clock by armed Marine NCOs who had orders to shoot without question anyone who attempted to enter the room without authorization. It was here that Rochefort and his staff would not only spearhead the attack on JN-25a, but also produce signals analysis intelligence for Admiral Bloch and Admiral Kimmel.

Six months before Rochefort arrived in Hawaii, and exactly one year before the attack on Pearl Harbor, one of his closest friends reported for duty on Admiral Richardson's staff as Battle Force's Combat Intelligence Officer, Commander Edwin Layton. Rochefort and Layton had first met on board a ship bound for Tokyo, where they were the two officers the Navy selected in 1929 to learn the Japanese language. Three years Rochefort's junior, Layton was a Class of 1924 Naval Academy graduate who, like Rochefort, was expected to have a distinguished career in the Navy. Layton displayed none of the condescension some of his peers had shown to Rochefort, and in the three years the two young officers spent in Japan, they became fast friends. From all indications, it was a meeting of kindred intellects, as Layton would be remembered for being "sharp, quick thinking, fast acting, intuitive, fast to comprehend, and extremely aggressive."[8]

While Rochefort went on to shipboard duty when he finished his studies in Japan, Layton spent a year at the Office of Naval Intelligence before being posted as assistant naval attaché in Peking (now Beijing), China, in 1934. He served as the USS *Pennsylvania*'s gunnery officer before spending another year at ONI; from there he was sent to Tokyo in 1937 as the American embassy's naval attaché. He had the opportunity to meet Yamamoto Isoroku at several official functions, and came away impressed; he considered the Japanese admiral "very capable, a very thoroughly grounded and trained officer" who "possessed more brains than any other officer in the Japanese High Command."[9]

On February 1, 1941, when Admiral Kimmel replaced Admiral Richardson and Battle Force was renamed Pacific Fleet, Richardson recommended that Kimmel keep Layton on his staff; Kimmel did so, and learned very quickly that he had a first-class intelligence officer working for him. In the information presented in his briefings, Layton was always careful to make the distinctions between what was known and what was presumed, assumed, or suspected; he was also not afraid to say so when he didn't know something, rather than hedge or prevaricate, always a rare trait in the world of military and naval intelligence. With HYPO now up and running, and Rochefort providing immediate access to the station's "take" from the signals it intercepted, the daily intelligence briefings for CINCPAC contained what Layton believed to be the best information possible about the comings and goings of the Imperial Navy.

While the attack on JN-25a was HYPO's primary mission, the staff in The Dungeon were able to do more with their intercepts than simply slog away at cracking the Japanese naval code. Traffic analysis could provide considerable insight into Japanese capabilities, and, more important, given that tension between Tokyo and Washington was being ratcheted higher every day, about the movements of the Japanese fleet. It was relatively easy—"relatively" being the key here, as there is nothing truly "easy" in signals intelligence analysis—for the listening stations in Shanghai, Manila, Guam, Bainbridge Island, and Pearl Harbor, using radio direction finding equipment, to make precise cross-cut bearings and pinpoint the positions of Japanese warships. Knowing where the Imperial Navy was keeping its capital ships and aircraft carriers was, unquestionably, a priceless bit of knowledge: given that the best possible speeds of those ships were known, within a knot or two, once an initial position was obtained, it was a matter of simple arithmetic to determine how far they could travel in any given span of time. After a few days of tracking, their probable destinations or objectives could be deduced, by the simple expedient of noting what lay in their path.

Working out which call signs belonged to which ships was often a time-consuming, trial-and-error process, but even then shortcuts sometimes offered themselves up: distinctive "glitches" in equipment—odd harmonics or slightly mistuned transmitters, for example—were as good as fingerprints in identifying certain ships. And then there was the "fist" of individual radio operators: just as every old-fashioned typewriter will leave tiny but unique variances in how it spaces and aligns the letters in the text it produces, every person using a key-type transmitter has minuscule but detectable quirks in how they space the dots and dashes they send; a skilled, experienced analyst will quickly recognize those quirks—and with them the individual working the key. Unlike signals officers, who would move from ship to ship as their careers advanced, enlisted signalmen in the Imperial Navy, like their American counterparts, often spent years aboard the same ship, so that they were more or less permanently associated with specific ships. Some had such distinctive, even idiosyncratic "fists" that they became something of a joke to American naval intelligence. Years after the Second World War had ended, Commander Layton would still remember how the ham-handed senior operator aboard *Akagi* was a constant source of amusement for himself and his colleagues, remarking that "he played that key as if he were sitting on it."[10]

As valuable as it was knowing where the Japanese were keeping their warships, the intercepted signals could be further mined for still more information, of a nature which would be critical to any intelligence staff attempting to predict an enemy's intentions, through a process known as "signal analysis." If "decryption" is the equivalent of surreptitiously opening and reading someone's mail, then when opening the mail isn't possible, signal analysis would be akin to shining a bright light through an envelope to see what parts of its contents can be made readable.

Patterns in the radio traffic—length and types of transmission, the identity of senders and recipients, previously recognized ship identifiers in the texts of messages, as well as the frequency with which those messages were passing back and forth—could reveal when naval forces were being gathered for pending operations or new fleet units were created. Identifying concentrations of supply ships or troop transports was priceless, as those were only brought together when a major operation was imminent. In September 1940, just before the invasion of French Indochina, messages between Tokyo and Japanese warships in the South China Sea as well as naval air bases on the island of Hainan gave the American intelligence services a first-hand look at the pattern the Imperial Navy's signals followed in actual operations. Seven months later, ONI learned through signal analysis that all of the Imperial Navy's fleet carriers had been brought together into the 1st Air Fleet, the single largest concentration of naval air power in the world at the time. In June 1941 the US Navy's listening stations in the Pacific picked out the same pattern of signals that had been noted the previous September, which they took to mean that the Japanese were preparing for another offensive move; sure enough, the remainder of French Indochina was forcibly occupied two weeks later.

Signals analysis meant, then, that even without the ability to decrypt JN-25, the US Navy wasn't entirely bereft of intelligence about the movements and intentions of its Japanese counterpart, at least in approximate terms. There was a dangerous aspect to it however—the US Navy developed practically all of its information as to where the Imperial Navy was going and what it was doing from signals intelligence. That capability, in turn, relied on one condition remaining unchanged: that the Japanese maintain a steady stream of radio communications on which ONI, and specifically OP-20-G, could continue to eavesdrop. If any part of the Japanese fleet suddenly "went dark," that is, imposed radio silence, then as far as the Americans were concerned it would have effectively vanished—and they would have no idea where to look to find it.

* * *

If the staff of both the Office of Naval Intelligence and the Military Intelligence Division felt sharply handicapped by having signals intelligence be their sole source of information on Japanese plans and intentions, their situation in that regard was infinitely better than that of the Japanese, for whom signals intelligence was a dry well. While both the Imperial Army and Imperial Navy had excellent cryptographic sections, the two services' bitter enmity ensured that what little information each had would not be shared with the other, while at the same time guaranteeing that whatever progress might have been made through cooperation between them would never take place.

The Imperial Army's G-2 Operational Bureau was responsible for all army intelligence functions, and its officers focused their efforts on breaking Soviet and Chinese codes and ciphers, a sensible enough decision, given that the war with China as well as the ongoing confrontation along the Khalkhyn Gol River were the Army's responsibility, but they had little time for the sort of signals analysis that was routinely done by their American counterparts in the SIS. Similarly, the Imperial Navy directed its intelligence resources against the United States, as any war with the Americans would, by default, be a naval war. The 10th (later 11th) Section, 4th Department of the Navy's General Staff, had the task of breaking into the US Navy's codes and ciphers, but had very little success in doing so, a problem which would plague the Japanese throughout the Second World War. Minor codes and the American Merchant Fleet cipher would eventually be broken, but the US Navy's operational and strategic signals remained indecipherable.

The Imperial Navy achieved a significant success on another cryptographic front, however: the mid-level Gray and high-level Brown Codes used by the State Department's Foreign Service for communications to and from American embassies proved to be very vulnerable. By the autumn of 1940, both had been thoroughly compromised, of which the State Department remained as blissfully unaware as the Foreign Ministry in Tokyo was that PURPLE had been cracked open. This resulted in, ironically enough, Tokyo and Washington reading each other's diplomatic communications from mid-October 1940 right up through December 7, 1941. How useful that capability would prove to either, however, would be the difference between day and night.

The Americans looked to the MAGIC decrypts for any scrap of information that would point to what the Japanese would do if diplomacy failed—and found very little. Mistrust of the Foreign Ministry ran so deeply in the Imperial Army and Navy that they withheld from the diplomats any sure knowledge of an attack on Pearl Harbor, to the point where they ultimately brought about the failure of Yamamoto's grand design just at the moment the bombs began falling. As for intelligence in the American diplomatic communications which might be of any military value, no one in Tokyo or Yokohama bothered to look for it—they didn't need to. What Yamamoto Isoroku, his planners, and the Naval General Staff would require for the Hawaii Operation was tactical intelligence as to the comings and goings of the Pacific Fleet, what ships were moored where inside Pearl Harbor, where and when long-range reconnaissance patrols were being flown, and the US Army and Navy's general level of readiness. For that, they had a man in Honolulu who, for all practical purposes, lived right next to Pearl Harbor's main gate.

* * *

An announcement appeared in the March 27, 1941, evening edition of Honolulu's Japanese-language newspaper *Nippu Jiji* about the arrival of the "newly appointed secretary of the local Japanese consulate general… His appointment was made to expedite the work on expatriation applications and other matters." Indeed, when the SS *Nitta Maru* tied up at Pier 8 on the Waikiki waterfront that morning, a slightly built, neatly dressed, pleasant-faced young man had been met by no less than Okuda Otojiro, the local Vice Consul. Passing through Customs, the newcomer presented his passport and a letter of introduction identifying him as Morimura Tadashi, 29 years of age and an accredited member of the Japanese diplomatic corps. None of the American customs officials had the least idea that both documents were pure fabrications, as was Tadashi himself: "Morimura Tadashi" had never been in diplomatic service, and he possessed absolutely no secretarial skills—in fact, he didn't even exist. The man's real name was Yoshikawa Takeo, he was an ensign in the Imperial Naval Reserve, and his sole purpose for being in Hawaii was to spy on the United States Pacific Fleet.

For Yoshikawa, this assignment bordered on being a dream come true for a young man who had grown up determined to serve his Emperor in the Imperial Navy, but by a cruel twist of circumstance been denied the opportunity. The son of a Shikoku Island policeman, Yoshikawa had been an honor graduate of the Imperial Japanese Naval College's Class of 1933; his training cruises were made aboard two cruisers, one, *Asama*, a relic from the Russo-Japanese War that had been relegated to training duties. Promoted to ensign, he was sent to Kasumigaura Naval Air Station for pilot training, but while there he developed a stomach ulcer that led to his involuntary resignation, for medical reasons, in 1935. Imagining himself to be disgraced, Yoshikawa Takeo began to contemplate suicide, only to find his career unexpectedly resurrected when he was offered a posting to the Naval General Staff's intelligence. If he couldn't fly for the Emperor he could still serve, and the offer was quickly accepted. He spent four years learning English, studying American society and customs, and becoming a walking encyclopedia on the subject of the United States Navy. In late 1940 he was informed that he would be sent to Honolulu under a diplomatic cover, there to become the eyes and ears of the Imperial Navy, keeping watch on Pearl Harbor.

The Honolulu consulate began making periodic reports to Tokyo about the comings and goings of the American fleet when Pearl Harbor became Battle Force's main base in May 1940. Initially those reports had been the responsibility of the consul-general, Gunji Kiichi, who for the most part relied on local newspapers like the *Honolulu Advertiser* or *Star-Bulletin* for information. As the dailies regularly published the sailing schedules for most of the US Navy's ships based at Pearl, Gunji hadn't been required to exert himself unduly in order to be able to write up those reports. When Gunji was recalled to Japan in September, Vice Consul Okuda Otojiro, a dedicated career diplomat and now the acting consul-general, immediately took up where Gunji had left off. Okuda had never done any military or naval service, which meant that there was always a certain pedestrian quality to his reporting. It also meant that details of the activity in and around Pearl Harbor which would have caught the attention of a professional naval officer often went unnoticed by Okuda; conversely, when he did add extra bits and pieces of information to his reports, they were usually irrelevant or unimportant.

Initially in Okuda's tenure as acting Consul-General, these shortcomings were considered inconsequential, as the very idea of attacking the US Navy at Pearl Harbor wasn't yet being given serious consideration in Tokyo—Okuda's work was good enough for the moment. That changed as Yamamoto began working on the Hawaii Operation. On February 15, Okuda was informed of the applicable paragraphs of a message sent to the embassy in Washington, announcing that Tokyo now required more specific and detailed reports:

> The information we particularly desire with regard to intelligence U.S. and Canada are the following:
> 1. Strengthening or supplementing of military preparations on the Pacific Coast and the Hawaii area; amount and type of stores and supplies; alterations to air ports (also carefully note the clipper traffic).
> 2. Ship and plane movements (particularly of the large bombers and seaplanes)...[11]

Given this new set of priorities, wisdom dictated that a qualified naval officer should be dispatched to Honolulu—the work of an amateur, even a well-meaning one like Okuda, would no longer be sufficient—so that even as Gunji's replacement as permanent Consul-General, Kita Nagao, was informed of his transfer to Hawaii, Ensign Yoshikawa was alerted as to his pending mission to Honolulu. Okuda was relieved when Yoshikawa arrived: his sense of professionalism had been offended by the necessity of sending those intelligence reports to Tokyo, as he rather naively maintained that espionage was beneath the dignity of a career diplomat. It was hardly surprising then when he and Yoshikawa came to mutually dislike one another: the young ensign thought Okuda to be a pompous windbag, while the vice consul, who for some reason imagined Yoshikawa to be his subordinate at the consulate, regarded the naval officer as an intruder in the diplomatic world. Okuda found a thousand different slights to offer Yoshikawa as a consequence, all of them petty, none of them capable of interfering with the ensign's misson. Yoshikawa in turn simply ignored Okuda, and worked directly with Consul-General Kita instead.

With the aid of a few members of the consulate's staff, Yoshikawa quickly learned his way around Oahu and discovered the best ways to observe the details of Pearl Harbor, Hickam and Wheeler Fields, Schofield Barracks, and all of the other naval and military installations scattered around the island. He carefully cultivated the image of a lazy, utterly unambitious young man, more interested in girls and good times than his official responsibilities, on many days not returning to his work at the consulate after lunch, instead gallivanting about Oahu wherever and whenever his whims took him. One of his favorite spots was the *Shuncho ro* restaurant, a Japanese teahouse perched in the Alewa Heights just north of downtown Honolulu, owned by a woman who like himself hailed from Shikoku Island. The upper floor offered an uninterrupted view of the whole expanse of Pearl Harbor, from Hickam Field to the Middle Loch. The proprietress even provided a tripod-mounted telescope to allow her patrons to further enjoy the view, which Yoshikawa found extremely useful.

There were other places where Yoshikawa could make careful observations of the harbor as well as the various Army installations around it, including his own second-floor apartment perched on a mountainside on the northern outskirts of

Honolulu. At least three times he took to the air in civilian aircraft on sight-seeing flights, appearing to be every inch the delighted tourist as he peered down at Ford Island or the submarine base, carefully memorizing the details he saw. An automobile loaned to him by a colleague allowed Yoshikawa to roam farther afield than the limits of the local bus service; day-long excursions aboard tourist boats took him to the other islands when necessary. He was able to make first-hand observations which were invaluable to the staff planners in Tokyo and aboard Yamamoto's flagship, the battleship *Nagato*. He noted, for example, that the battleships along Ford Island's southeast side, were moored side-by-side in pairs, and that those same battleships risked running aground if they tried to enter the shallow waters of Kaneohe Bay, on the east side of Oahu, ruling out the bay as a possible alternate anchorage for the Pacific Fleet. Similarly, a boat ride to Maui allowed him to confirm that no preparations had been made at the Lahaina Roads, a sheltered passage between the islands of Molokai, Lanai, and Maui, for the fleet to anchor there. One observation that immediately caught the attention of Yamamoto and his staff was that almost all of the Pacific Fleet battleships and usually two of its three aircraft carriers, were in port on weekends.

In all of this, Yoshikawa was clever and crafty, having taken to heart advice given to him by the consul-general. Unlike Okuda, Kita was an old hand at the consular espionage game and had been made privy to Yoshikawa's mission before departing for Honolulu, and when the younger man arrived at the consulate, Kita briefed him thoroughly on how to best accomplish his task. Yoshikawa, recognizing the voice of experience when he heard it, paid close attention. Kita emphasized the need to never become conspicuous, never take unnecessary risks, and avoid any temptation to examine restricted areas too closely. Yoshikawa took pains to avoid falling into routines or establishing fixed patterns in his movements that might have given away the game to local or federal authorities. He never took photographs while out and about on his explorations, nor did he take notes, relying on his excellent memory when he wrote his reports. So thoroughly did he conceal his true identity and purpose, that at one point when some of the clerical workers at the consulate wondered how he was able to spend so much time doing so little work, a driver for the consulate remarked that Yoshikawa, whatever he was, certainly was no spy, as he "lacked the sharp eye and the smart gait of a Japanese military or naval officer."[12]

One thing above all Yoshikawa avoided: attempting any sort of overtly illegal act. Given how few real restrictions there were on where he could go and what he could see in and around Pearl Harbor, there was no need to skirt the edge of legality and draw the attention of the American authorities; still, history is replete with tales of spies who, in similar circumstances, for many and varied reasons went that one step too far and were caught out, invariably to their detriment. Not so Yoshikawa, who was content with knowing that everything he needed in order to provide the information requested by Tokyo he was able to obtain legitimately.

This greatly annoyed the Federal Bureau of Investigation, which was responsible for all counter-espionage within the borders of the United States and its territories. Bureau agents had their suspicions about Yoshikawa almost from the day he arrived in Honolulu, primarily because the name "Tadashi Morimura" was nowhere to be found in the State Department's registry of accredited Japanese diplomats. The Americans tailed him for months, yet could never find a pretext by which they could detain and ultimately deport him, however much they may have suspected his actual purpose and activities.

One notable and unexpected detail emerged over the course of Yoshikawa's explorations. As a consular official—Kita had given him the essentially meaningless title of Chancellor as an added layer of cover—Yoshikawa frequently came into contact with Japanese immigrants and first-generation Japanese-Americans. He had hoped to find that they could be useful as guerillas or possibly stage an insurrection should the Imperial Army invade the Hawaiian Islands, much as General Short feared they would, only to be disappointed to find the vast majority of them felt more loyalty to the United States than they did to the emperor and Empire. However low their station might be in America, they felt they had improved their lot over whatever they could have attained had they remained in Japan—a sentiment that would have shocked Short, had he known of it. Yoshikawa, though, as a consequence of what he perceived as their disloyalty, came to regard the *Issei*, as the Japanese immigrants were known, as generally dull and unimaginative, useless for work as saboteurs or spies.

By the beginning of September, Yoshikawa, the handful of consulate staff who assisted him, and a few Japanese subjects hired as drivers and guides, had answered all of Tokyo's queries about the status of the US Army and Navy on Oahu. Now came a subtle change in mission: they would begin providing regular updates on the movement of ships in and out of Pearl Harbor, as well as any changes in the numbers and types of Army Air Corps aircraft at Wheeler and Hickam Fields. Yoshikawa took this to be proof that some sort of raid or attack on Pearl Harbor was in the works; he didn't actually know for certain, having never been apprised of the purpose of his mission in Honolulu.

He had, in fact, become convinced that his mission was a decoy, to draw attention away from another agent or agents who were carrying out a more sophisticated operation. As he later explained it,

> It was Japan's policy to maintain two espionage systems in countries abroad—one run by consulates and the other separate from the consulates and entirely unknown to them. A consulate would indulge only in such espionage activity as could be carried on without compromising diplomatic and consular relations...whereas an extra-consulate organization would carry out "illegal" espionage.[13]

As Yoshikawa saw it, his actions matched those to be expected of a consular intelligence mission, which in fact they did. So then there must be a covert mission on Oahu carrying out the sort of illegal activities he so scrupulously avoided. And yet there wasn't: as impossible it seemed to Ensign Yoshikawa, there was no need for a second set of spies in Hawaii—he was providing the planning staff in Tokyo and Yokohama with everything they required. Whatever the FBI might suspect, the American army and navy apparently had no idea he was there, and certainly didn't know just how good a job he was doing. In one of the many ironies that abounded in the unfolding drama of Pearl Harbor, the US Navy's intelligence officers could have easily discovered both—if only they had been paying attention.

* * *

Much as an archeologist can assert with surety that "X" rarely if ever "marks the spot," experienced intelligence officers will affirm with equal assurance that effective analysis is never a linear process, A leading to B, which leads to C and then D and so forth. Instead it almost always results from making connections between apparently unrelated bits and pieces of information often coming from widely disparate sources—it sometimes seems as though an analyst is adding A to 3, then subtracting a G#, multiplying by 9, then adding C and F to arrive at 42. In other words, it isn't a cleanly logical progression, and it never makes complete sense until the conclusion is reached, at which time it all becomes self-evident and self-explanatory. This was the process by which OP-20-G carried out most of its work, and at which both Commanders Rochefort and Layton excelled.

One of the keys to that process is having access to what analysts call the "raw data" or "raw take," information in precisely the form and language in which it was acquired, rather than having it first interpreted, filtered and reduced to a digest—being given A, 3, G#, 9, C and F, as it were, rather than being presented with A, B, C, D, E, and F in their clean, distilled form. Where and when the data was acquired and how, as well as in what language, and from who and by whom, can sometimes tell an analyst as much as the actual data, and those details themselves become pieces of the puzzle that, while apparently minor, will cause it to hold together and form a coherent whole.

What makes such details important is that they allow the analyst to adjust what is called—and here the intelligence community borrowed a term from the electronics industry—the "signal to noise" ratio, that is, determining how much of the entire spectrum of data collected is actually relevant and useful, and how much of that spectrum is meaningless background chatter. As more extraneous data—the noise—is eliminated, the stronger the signal—the useful information—becomes. The higher that ratio the more confidence an intelligence officer will have in his work, his interpretations, and his conclusions.

In the summer of 1941, Rochefort, Layton, and their staffs at HYPO and CINCPAC respectively, found themselves struggling with a very low signal-to-noise ratio as they were unable to make any significant progress in breaking into

JN-25a. Up until May 1941, Admiral Kimmel's staff had been receiving "sanitized" digests of the intelligence gleaned from MAGIC decrypts, written in such a way that the source of the information couldn't be deduced by reading them. Then abruptly the digests stopped, not for Kimmel alone, but for every other commanding officer outside the continental United States who had previously held some level of clearance for MAGIC. Tensions began to rise between Honolulu and Washington over the evaluation and interpretation of what data there was, as someone in ONI seemed to be playing games with the access to additional sources of intelligence.

In order to properly carry out their mission, Rochefort and Layton needed to be able to see for themselves every bit of intelligence available, preferably in its "raw" form, which might relate to Japan, the Imperial Navy, and any political or diplomatic developments in the state of Japanese–American relations which could have consequences that would affect the Navy. The urgency of that need grew sharply at what was the turning point in America's negotiations with Japan: July 26, 1941, the day that President Roosevelt ordered that all Japanese assets in the United States be frozen, and placed the embargo on the sale and shipment of oil to Japan.

The view from the White House seemed to show that with the stroke of a pen, the president had the Empire boxed in: Roosevelt convinced himself that the Japanese, faced with only three choices—capitulation to the administration's demands, national economic collapse, or war with the United States—would, however reluctantly, accept capitulation. In his ignorance of Japan and the Japanese, he was certain that *Dai Nippon* would allow itself to be intimidated, forgetting that the Empire of Japan possessed a warrior tradition and culture that began centuries before the United States came into existence. Samuel Elliot Morison, in Volume 3 of his *History of United States Naval Operations in World War II*, elegantly sums up the reality of the situation Roosevelt had unwittingly created, saying,

> The oil embargo and assets-freezing order of 26 July 1941 made war with Japan inevitable unless one of two things happened, and neither was humanly possible. The United States might reverse its foreign policy, restore trade relations and acquiesce in further Japanese conquests; or the Japanese government might persuade its army to at least prepare to evacuate China and renounce the southward advance, [an order which would] have been disregarded by an army which, as the facts show, would accept no compromise that did not place America in the ignominious role of collaborating with conquest.[14]

Having lost access to MAGIC just weeks before the president's momentous announcement of July 26, Rochefort and Layton were sharply curtailed in their ability to accurately forecast Japan's military and naval options, and the probability of each, and did so just at a moment when what political intelligence MAGIC provided was even more valuable than purely military or naval information. This arbitrary handicap frustrated and infuriated the usually even-tempered Layton. Inquiring as to why CINCPAC and the 14th Naval District were no longer receiving MAGIC-generated intelligence, he was informed by Commander Arthur McCollum, who had charge of ONI's Far Eastern Section, that

> It does not seem to me to be very practical to build up an organization…which will merely duplicate the efforts of the Intelligence Division in the Department… I believe…that a sharp line should be drawn and a distinction continuously emphasized between information that is of interest and information that is desirable to have on which to base action.
>
> In other words, while you and the Fleet may be highly interested in politics, there is nothing you can do about it. Therefore, information of political significance, except as it affects immediate action by the Fleet, is merely a matter of interest to you and not a matter of utility.[15]

Layton was dumbfounded at McCollum's response, and not merely because of its condescending tone. McCollum was an experienced intelligence officer, not some mere placeholder having his ticket punched at ONI in order to advance his career. He knew the importance of MAGIC to Rochefort and especially Layton, the senior intelligence officer to the man responsible for what was acknowledged to be at that moment the United States' most strategically important command. What Layton could not know—and could not be told, because of the stringent, sometimes bizarre, frequently shifting security measures put in place to protect MAGIC—was that McCollum was not allowed to discuss MAGIC with him, once Admiral Kimmel had been removed from the distribution lists. That was what had prompted McCollum's irritating reply: not only could he not so much as mention MAGIC to Layton, he could not even tell Layton that he wasn't allowed to do so.

If such a situation sounds absurd, it's because it was just that—patently absurd. The United States had never before possessed a secret of such magnitude in all its history, and consequently had little if any idea of how best to protect it while at the same time make the best use of it. This resulted in measures and methods which at times seemed to be lifted straight from a second-rate comic-opera farce.

Like their parent services had done, Army SIS and OP-20-G gradually became rivals. Their decryption work proceeded apace, though at times, the translation backlog became almost overwhelming: there simply were not enough people in the United States, in uniform or out, who could both speak fluent Japanese and pass the background checks necessary to be cleared to work on MAGIC who could be put to work translating the decrypts produced by the PURPLE machines. Rather than focusing their efforts on solving this problem, both offices were increasingly focused on who would accrue the prestige of being the first to deliver the latest or most important decrypts to whom, rather than ensuring that all of the decryptions reached everyone who needed to see them. Eventually toward the end of 1940, SIS and OP-20-G came to an agreement whereby the decryption and translation duties of MAGIC shifted back and forth between the Army and the Navy on a daily basis.

That solved one problem, but there were others. The method for disseminating MAGIC decrypts was ludicrous. The Army and Navy both had distribution lists of senior officers and government officials, along with certain members of their staffs, who were to see anything and everything that MAGIC produced: for the Army that included the secretary of war, chief of staff, assistant chief of staff G-2 (Intelligence), and the chief of war plans. For the Navy, it was the secretary of the navy, chief of naval operations, chief of war plans, and the director of naval intelligence. The secretary of state was on both lists, of course.

Conspicuous by their absence, however, were the president himself, as well as the chief of the army air corps, along with all of the commanding officers of the Army and Navy's overseas commands. Roosevelt had been taken out of the distribution lists in October 1940, when a member of the White House security detail found a MAGIC decrypt crumpled up in a wastebasket in one of the White House offices. There were other officers, none of whom were assigned to an overseas post, who were cleared to see the sanitized digests of MAGIC intelligence, and still others who were permitted to see actual decrypts "as needed," the determination of need being made on a case-by-case basis by the distributing officer of the day.

The decrypts were hand-carried to the recipients by a uniformed courier, who would remain present while the documents were being read; they would be presented one at a time, and when a recipient finished with one the courier would reclaim it before producing the next. Copying was forbidden, as was making notes about the contents; once a decrypt was read, the recipient was not permitted to re-read it, in fact he would never be allowed to see it again. Once all the documents had been presented, read, and retrieved, they would be returned to ONI or MID, where they would be locked away in a safe and never removed for any reason. The entire process was so arbitrary and at the same time so paranoid, that often senior officers and government officials who had not only a legitimate right but an out-and-out need to have access to the information MAGIC produced never saw it. It could not have been any sillier, nor more conducive to reducing MAGIC to the point of near-uselessness if it had been concocted by the Marx Brothers.

Just as bad, there was no procedure for ensuring that those individuals who were cleared to have access to MAGIC were kept up to date as to who else did or did not have such clearance, which sharply restricted the ability of those who were so authorized to discuss the contents with anyone else, lest they compromise MAGIC's security by talking out of turn to someone who wasn't cleared. Hand-in-hand with that went the lack of any process in place for assessing and organizing the intelligence being collected to determine who actually needed to see it, and in what form. There was an incredible volume of information available to ONI and MID, but so rapidly had the American intelligence services expanded—there were more than 700 people, naval personnel and civilians, working for OP-20-G by mid-summer of 1941, for example—the organizational development hadn't been able to keep pace. The result was a degree of confusion that allowed much of MAGIC's potential to go to waste, simply because the right people were not allowed to properly use it.

The single greatest impediment to making full use of the intelligence gleaned from MAGIC, however, was an officer of the United States Navy who, for reasons which are still difficult to parse 75 years later, interfered with and sometimes disrupted the flow of intelligence to ONI as well as to Rochefort and Layton. That officer was Rear Admiral Richmond "Kelly" Turner, the director of the US Navy's War Plans Division. The 56-year-old Turner, who had graduated from Annapolis in 1908, had followed the requisite career path that led to flag rank: shipboard departmental commands and staff appointments, the Naval War College, aviation instruction, various staff duties ashore, assignment as the Executive Officer of a large warship, in his case the aircraft carrier *Lexington*, and finally having command of the heavy cruiser *Astoria*. In October 1940 he was named the Director of War Plans and promoted to rear admiral four months later.

At the War Plans Division, he answered only to the chief of naval operations, Admiral Stark, an arrangement that played directly into some of Turner's worst character traits. While it might be a stretch to call him "enigmatic," there can be no disputing that Turner was a complex individual, possessing an excellent brain, which was unfortunately combined with corrosive ambition and the intolerance of a perfectionist. He fancied himself as someone who knew everything about everything—one wag was heard to remark that the moment Turner boarded a launch to move from ship to shore, he would begin instructing the coxswain on the right way to handle the boat. Arrogant, loud, and foul-mouthed, Turner was accustomed to settling arguments—of which he had many—by the simple expedient of shouting louder and longer than whoever disagreed with him; his notoriously short temper earned him the nickname of "Terrible." And yet there was no denying his intelligence: from 1942 to 1945, he planned and executed a succession of brilliant amphibious operations that drove from the Southwest Pacific into the Central Pacific and then on to the periphery of the Japanese Home Islands; if the invasion of Japan had become necessary, he would have commanded the naval forces in the landing operations. To his further credit, he was an indefatigable worker and apparently had never learned the meaning of the word "fear."

An almost naked lust for power and authority, though, was Richmond Turner's most profound flaw; coupled with his "know-it-all" attitude, it led him to not merely usurp the authority of other officers, but do so in areas where he had no training or expertise, a habit which, in the case of his meddling in ONI's affairs not only contributed to but facilitated the disaster that overtook Pearl Harbor on December 7, 1941.

Within weeks of Turner's arrival at War Plans, the rest of the Division staff had been quietly relegated to minion status, so that "War Plans" came to mean Turner himself. No sooner had he settled into the chair behind his desk than he set about trying to subordinate the Office of Naval Intelligence to his own department, this despite the fact that he had no training in intelligence, nor had he ever in his career held an intelligence posting, at sea or ashore. Of necessity the man responsible for developing the Navy's war plans had to have unrestricted access to any and all intelligence available to the Navy if he were to properly fulfill his duties. Turner, though, began to argue that because his department was responsible for the plans which the rest of the Navy would put into action when a war broke out, the War Plans Division was thus better qualified than any other department or division to best interpret and utilize the intelligence on which those plans were based, modified, and updated—as well as determine who else should or should not have access to the information ONI produced.

It was a specious argument, of course: there were any number of departments, divisions, or senior officers, Army and Navy both, with a need for access ONI's MAGIC intercepts—and the intelligence gleaned from them—whose functions and operations had nothing to do at all with the War Plans Division, but whenever anyone attempted to make the point to Turner, they were literally shouted down. The result was that War Plans' decisions as to who should or should not see the intelligence were completely arbitrary—and often counterproductive. Nonetheless, Turner continued to press his case, although at first he had to be careful not to push too hard: the current director of naval intelligence was Rear Admiral Walter Anderson, and Turner, as mere captain at the time, was not immune to charges of insubordination, however arrogant he might be. Anderson, though, left ONI in January 1941, just as Turner was raised to flag rank himself, which gave him the upper hand over Anderson's replacement, Captain Alan Kirk. Turner bullied and blustered, even threatening to resign his post, if he was not given at least operational control over ONI.

His superior, the chief of naval operations, who should have sat down hard on Turner—or even called his bluff and said he was prepared to accept Turner's resignation—was not the sort of man to do such a thing. Ever the eternal manager rather than a commander, Admiral Stark allowed himself to be intimidated by Turner, so that War Plans took over more and more of the operational functions of the Office of Naval Intelligence, along with those of the Office of Naval Communications, which included OP-20-G. Turner then began making the decisions as to how naval intelligence was handled, including sole determination of who would or would not have access to what intelligence sources, including MAGIC.

Captain Kirk gave up after only eight months on the job as director of naval intelligence, and his successor, Captain Theodore Wilkinson, took up his duties mistakenly believing that ONI's mission was only the collection of intelligence and was in no way responsible for its distribution, an error Turner was not about to correct. Stark, naturally, did nothing to set either man straight on the subject. However this system might have deviated in practice from the organizational ideal, it still could have worked had Turner been willing to accept the recommendation and guidance of the intelligence professionals in ONI. Instead, convinced as usual that he knew better how to do someone else's job, he failed to fulfill the responsibility he had usurped, that of keeping the fleet and naval district commanders properly informed of all the information their intelligence staffs required to anticipate impending Japanese actions—most particularly information culled from the decrypted PURPLE messages passing to and from Tokyo and the Japanese embassy in Washington.

Instead, Turner made his own ineptness evident when on May 5, 1941, Safford's "On the Roof Gang" intercepted a message encrypted in PURPLE sent from Foreign Minister Matsuoka to Ambassador Nomura at the Washington embassy. Once unbuttoned, the message warned "According to a fairly reliable source of information it appears almost certain the United States Government is reading your code messages. Please let me know if you have any suspicion of the above." The language was somewhat enigmatic, as it did not specifically refer to the "'97 Alphabetical Typewriter," which the Americans knew as PURPLE—the Japanese used the same name for both the equipment and the enciphering system. In addition to PURPLE, the Japanese embassy employed a code the Americans had designated J-19; it was used to communicate with the consulates around the country, none of which had PURPLE machines—those were reserved solely for use by embassies. Compared to PURPLE, J-19 was far less complex, and both the Army and Navy cracked it within a year of its introduction.[16]

While it seemed most likely that the message from Tokyo referred to J-19 and not PURPLE, Turner could not count on that being so. Alternatively, it might have been a ruse, an attempt by the Japanese to determine if, in fact, the Americans had broken into PURPLE by suggesting that they knew of it, hoping for some detectable reaction on the Americans' part to confirm their suspicion. Turner wisely assumed the worst, that somehow the Japanese had discovered that the Americans had compromised PURPLE. So far, so good. What he did next, however, was ludicrous.

Rather than initiate an in-house investigation to determine if, in fact, the security around MAGIC had been breached, Turner, with no evidence to support him, immediately became suspicious of security of the two Hawaiian commands, and ordered both Admiral Kimmel and General Short, along with their intelligence staffs, removed from the distribution list of MAGIC decrypts, leaving them to rely on vague or imprecise summations and digests, irregularly supplied. This is where Washington's near-paranoia about the Japanese learning that PURPLE was not invulnerable threatened to make MAGIC counterproductive. The measures being taken to preserve the secret were strangling the secret's usefulness.

In a bitter twist to the plot, it was not a leak or an indiscretion by someone on Kimmel's staff—or Short's, for that matter—that twigged the "fairly reliable source" to the possibility that Japan's highest-level diplomatic communications were not secure. It was Baron Oshima Hiroshi, Japan's ambassador to Berlin, who was reminded in a conversation with a German colleague that the Wehrmacht's often-inept *Chiffrierabteilung* (Cipher Department) had from time to time broken into Japanese cryptographic systems and suggested that the Americans might be able to do the same.

Ambassador Nomura responded to Matsuoka's inquiry by saying "Though I do not know which ones I have discovered the United States is reading some of our codes. As for how I got this intelligence I will inform you by courier or another safe way." When this message was decrypted, ONI and MID held their collective breath, waiting for Tokyo to instruct Nomura to cease using PURPLE and resort to some temporary expedient while an entirely new cipher system was created or, if one was already in the wings, was delivered to the embassy. Either way, the American intelligence community's window into Japan would have been slammed shut for an indeterminate amount of time.[17]

Yet it never happened. So confident were the Japanese that PURPLE was an unbreakable system, a belief that echoed the Germans' confidence in their Enigma machines, with identical outcomes in both instances, that they never contemplated replacing it. Many senior Japanese officials and high-ranking officers would go to their graves decades after the end of the Second World War believing that, no matter what the claims and proofs might be, the Americans had never actually broken any of Japan's codes or ciphers.

Perversely enough, in one way ONI and MID's ability to decrypt PURPLE worked to Japan's advantage. No one in the Roosevelt administration, from the president on down, seemed to fully comprehend the enmity the Imperial Army and Navy held for the Foreign Ministry, or the profound distrust it generated. It simply had no counterpart in American history. The Imperial Army and Navy's saber-rattling was regarded as just that—martial bluster intended to divert the United States' attention and cause the administration to lose its focus in negotiations, so that it wouldn't notice when a clever settlement favorable to Japan of the disputes between Washington and Tokyo was quietly slipped past it. So deeply ingrained in American politicians and senior officers alike was the idea of the military being always subordinate to civilian authority that when America encountered a nation where that idea had never taken root, it was so alien as to be nearly inconceivable.

Nor could Roosevelt and Hull ever quite comprehend that no matter what an honorable man like Ambassador Nomura might say in all sincerity, his words were completely irrelevant if they did not coincide with what the militarists who had the Japanese government by the throat wanted. The president and the secretary of state, while never naive enough to take everything the Japanese diplomats said at flat face value—Roosevelt was far too cunning, Hull far too wise, for that to ever be the case—were convinced that Ambassadors Nomura and

Kurusu were making sincere representations of what the Japanese government genuinely desired. MAGIC told them that, however stubborn, obstinate, and glacial the Japanese might be in their negotiations, from the Emperor down, they wanted a peaceful resolution. Because they trusted MAGIC, in their hopes for peace, Roosevelt and Hull unwittingly gave the Japanese time to finish their preparations for war.

CHAPTER 5

"Climb Mount Niitaka"

America was preparing for war as well, but not with the methodical determination of the Imperial Army and Navy staffs in Tokyo, who were wholly immersed in actively planning for the coming conflict. In Washington DC, the president, Congress, the Army and the Navy were instead all lurching toward war in fits and starts. A major watershed—perhaps the most important of all short of America declaring war on somebody—was reached on March 11, 1941, when Roosevelt signed the Lend-Lease Act into law. Although it would not be until November before the Neutrality Acts were formally repealed, with one swiftly scrawled signature, American neutrality was effectively at an end: the United States government, as well as American businesses and industries, could now legally sell, lend or simply give war materials of any description to any nation the administration declared vital to America's defense.

This was as much a turning point for the United States as had been the Japanese decision to formally join the Axis six months earlier. Sides were being openly chosen, as everyone knew that Roosevelt would never countenance the supply of so much as a single rifle round to Germany, Italy, or Japan. The United States was now in a curious diplomatic state of "non-belligerent non-neutrality": America wasn't actually shooting at anyone—yet—but as Roosevelt, in a nationwide radio address broadcast in late December 1940, had characterized the United States as "the Arsenal of Democracy," there was no mistaking that his administration would stop at nothing short of actual combat operations in its support for the Allies.

Naturally, the fury of the isolationists—especially the tiny but exceedingly vocal handful of "peace at any price" advocates—in denouncing Lend-Lease knew no bounds, but the case for isolationism became increasingly threadbare as the true natures of the Axis regimes manifested themselves to the world. By this time, pure isolationism was for all practical purposes dead: in no way were the American people ready to rush off to war, but the idea the nation could simply ignore anything that happened outside of its borders was at an end. By the spring of 1941, eight in ten Americans believed that the safety of the United States would depend on Great Britain winning the war against Nazi Germany, and just as many were convinced that without Lend-Lease the British would lose. Sixty percent felt that it was more important for the United States to help England win—even at the risk of becoming directly involved in the fighting—than it was to try keep out of the war; seven in ten endorsed the idea of compulsory military training for young American men, as did two-thirds of American high school students. As for the war in Europe, the tide of public opinion had finally, decisively, turned against isolationism.

There was, however, no matching determination in regard to Japan's adventurism in China, Southeast Asia, and the South and Central Pacific. While nearly two-thirds of the American people felt that risking war with Nazi Germany was justified if it kept Great Britain in the fight, the same number saw no reason to risk war with Japan should the Empire forcibly seize French Indochina or the Dutch East Indies. The majority of Americans were closer, geographically and culturally, to the war in Europe than any potential conflict in the Far East. Roosevelt knew this, of course, and shared basically the same sentiment. Which was a large part of why, although as he saw it Imperial Japan was cut from the same bolt of cloth as the Third Reich, he continued to search out a diplomatic solution to the problems in the Pacific. It was an attitude that also fit well with his biases, particularly that Japan could never pose a genuine threat to America in the way he was convinced Germany already did.

February 14, 1941, saw the first face-to-face meeting between President Roosevelt and Ambassador Nomura Kichisaburo, who in November 1940 had replaced Kensuke Horinouchi as Japan's senior diplomatic envoy to the United States. Nomura had retired from the Imperial Navy in 1937, after a 40-year career that saw him rise to the rank of full admiral; he had been Tokyo's military attaché in Washington DC during the First World War and held the foreign minister's portfolio in the short-lived government of General Abe Nobuyuki from August 1939 to January 1940. Nomura was intelligent, approachable, and genuinely liked America and Americans—it seemed likely that his appointment could help ease the increasingly strained relationship between Tokyo and Washington.

The meeting was Nomura's opportunity to formally present his credentials to the president, while for Roosevelt it was an opening to set the tone of Nomura's tenure as Tokyo's representative. Less than three weeks previously, Foreign Minister Matsuoka, in a speech to the Japanese Diet, had openly put the issue on table, saying, "Has America any right to object if Japan does dominate the Western Pacific? ... I wish to declare that if America does not understand Japan's rightful claims and actions, then there is not the slightest hope of improvement of Japanese–American relations." That same day, Joseph Grew, America's ambassador in Tokyo, informed the State Department that he had learned planning was underway for an attack by the Imperial Navy on the US Navy base at Pearl Harbor. Some of this Nomura already knew, and as he genuinely wanted to avoid a war between his homeland

and the United States, he assured Roosevelt that he would do everything he could to resolve the two nations' differences.[1]

A month later there was a second, and this time secret, meeting between Roosevelt and Nomura, intended to be more than a mere formality. The president, while affable throughout their time together, was unusually direct, laying out his belief that Japan's alliance with Germany and Italy was proof that the Empire's expansionism was not driven by economics, despite the repeated claims to that effect coming out of Tokyo, but was outright conquest for its own sake, pure and simple. Tokyo coveted not just the resources of Singapore, the Dutch East Indies, and Indochina but the territories as well. Thus it would be given to Nomura to convince Roosevelt, along with Secretary Hull, that the situation was otherwise—and up to Tokyo to offer up deeds, not words, as proof. Whether or not this was a point at which the war between Japan and the United States might have been averted is, of course, impossible to say: in order to bring about the sort of result Roosevelt and Hull were seeking would have required concessions to be made by both sides, which neither was prepared to offer.

Nomura struggled to find a way to make comprehensible to these two Westerners what was mother's milk to a Japanese: simply giving something away as a "gesture of good faith" was not a negotiating ploy for a Japanese. The loss of face suffered, the insult done to the honor of the Empire in making *any* concession to the United States that did not include a *quid pro quo* of some kind was unthinkable. To do so would give the appearance of Japan being the supplicant to America's benefactor. Nomura was hoping that for their part Roosevelt and Hull might suggest an easing of the embargoes currently in place against Japan, but when no such offer was forthcoming, he spent the next month scrambling to find some basis for negotiation that would be equally acceptable to both Tokyo and Washington DC.

* * *

On April 9 Admiral Nagano Osami took over the duties of the Chief of the Imperial Naval General Staff. The very next day, Yamamoto authorized the creation of the First Air Fleet by combining Carrier Divisions 1 and 2, *Akagi* and *Kaga*, *Hiryu* and *Soryu*, which up to this time had operated independently, into a single formation. This was a major step forward in making the attack on Pearl Harbor a practical proposition: prior to this, the conventional wisdom of naval aviation held that operations should be limited to small, nuisance raids launched by single carriers, providing air cover for the fleet, or carrying out long-range reconnaissance and scouting. By combining the fleet's carriers into a single operational unit, it would be possible to concentrate the navy's airpower and form attack forces strong enough to carry out large scale, decisive actions by themselves, without the need for and far beyond the range of battleships or cruisers.

Command of the First Air Fleet was given to Vice Admiral Nagumo Chuichi. Nagumo seemed something of an odd choice for this new post, as he was a specialist in destroyer and torpedo tactics, but not, curiously enough, a naval aviator; he was, in fact, widely regarded as one of the navy's more conservative admirals. Admiral Yamamoto would have preferred another officer to lead First Air Fleet, and even, at one point, considered taking the command himself; the strict, rarely flouted protocol of seniority in the Imperial Navy, however, dictated that it be given to Nagumo, and Yamamoto chose not to run afoul of tradition—he was courting enough trouble with his own radical ideas naval for strategy and operations.

Graduating eighth in his class at the Imperial Naval Academy in 1908, the 54-year-old Nagumo had followed a career path broadly similar to that of almost all of his Japanese or American contemporaries: a succession of increasingly larger, more powerful seagoing commands interspersed with shore-based postings and staff assignments. He spent two years—1925 and 1926—assigned to a mission to Europe and then the United States, one where rising officers of the Imperial Navy studied the strategies, tactics, equipment, and construction of the world's other great navies. It would be rash to suggest that this posting made Nagumo a more cosmopolitan individual, but one criticism never leveled at him was that he was mentally dull, so that it's not unrealistic to believe that he came to share some if not all of the respect Yamamoto held for the potential military might of the United States, and that such knowledge was responsible for the somewhat lackluster enthusiasm he displayed for Yamamoto's brainchild. If the Hawaii Operation resulted in a disaster for Japan, it would be remembered as Yamamoto's plan, but Nagumo would be forever marked as the man on the spot, in actual command of the doomed fleet. Given his innately glum nature, it would have been difficult for Nagumo to think otherwise.

In any event, Nagumo reached flag rank on November 1, 1935, and was promoted to vice admiral four years later. Although his relationships with his own two sons was awkward and frequently unhappy, within the fleet he acquired the reputation of a father-figure to young officers. He was also known as an admiral who would make himself infinitely familiar with every aspect and detail of any operation assigned to him, though he was not given to petty interference in their execution. While he was hardly an inspired choice for the commanding officer of First Air Fleet, he was a solid, even stolid, officer; that may well have been a factor in his selection for the post, the expectation being that he would serve as a moderating influence on the more zealous airpower advocates among his junior officers, who had a tendency to ascribe capabilities to naval airpower which it clearly did not yet possess.

By the end of the month, the air fleet staff was assembled and began the detailed planning for what was now called "the Hawaii Operation." The Staff Air Officer, responsible for all air operations and plans, was Commander Genda Minoru, a brilliant, colorful, and sometimes controversial pilot who was one of the leading lights of the Imperial Navy's air power advocates. It fell to him and his subordinates to not merely work out the tactics for the attack, but also to calculate the logistical requirements, and find the solutions to any problems that might be encountered in planning and training for the strike. Already three serious obstacles had been identified that if left unresolved would make the attack impossible: how to refuel the carriers and their escorts while at sea; ensuring that the torpedoes used in the attack would run shallow enough so that they wouldn't bury themselves in the mud at the bottom of Pearl Harbor; and developing tactics that would allow accurate high-altitude level bombing attacks.

The second son of five born to a farmer from Kake, Hiroshima Prefecture, Genda Minoru came into the world in 1904 as part of a family of overachievers. His oldest brother was a medical doctor, the third and fourth graduated from Tokyo University, and the youngest became a cadet at the Imperial Army Academy. Minoru graduated from the Imperial Naval Academy in 1924, earned his aviator's wings, and became a fighter pilot; he then promptly formed an aviation demonstration team that was nicknamed "Genda's Flying Circus" which flew all over the Home Islands, extolling to the Japanese public the virtues of and encouraging interest in naval aviation. He then reported to the Yokusaka Air Group as a senior flight instructor, and followed that posting by attending the Naval Staff College, where in 1936 he graduated second in his class. He flew combat missions against the Chinese in 1937, and the next year was sent to London as Japan's naval attaché, finally returning to the fleet in November 1940. This wealth of practical experience, rather than just theoretical knowledge, meant that when Genda talked, subordinates and superiors alike listened, and when he planned, the operations were realistic and practical.

Even more than Yamamoto, Genda was certain that the navy of the future had no place in it for battleships, and that the resources expended on them, especially behemoths like the 64,000-ton *Yamato* and *Musashi*, which he sardonically termed "the Chinese Wall of the Japanese Navy," should be used to build carriers, fast cruisers, and the destroyers which would escort them, along with submarines for long-range attacks on enemy shipping. Going very much against the conventional wisdom of the time, he maintained that should the Imperial Navy be caught up in a war against the navies of the United States and Great Britain, it would need as many carriers, aircraft, and aviators as Japan could produce rather than a big-gun battle fleet.[2]

Yamamoto and Genda first encountered one another in 1933, aboard the carrier *Ryujo*, the young flyer making a positive impression on the admiral. Genda's first encounter with the Pearl Harbor attack came in February 1941, when Rear Admiral Onishi—who knew Genda from his days at Yokusaka—sent instructions to the carrier *Kaga* for Genda to report as soon as possible to the admiral's office in Kanoya. There Onishi showed the younger officer Yamamoto's overall concept for a very large airstrike on Pearl Harbor and asked his opinion of it. Perhaps not surprisingly, Genda had already considered such an operation, and the two aviators traded ideas for the better part of two hours. At the end of the discussion, Onishi told Genda that "I think this is a good plan and should be carried out… Secrecy is the keynote and surprise the all-important factor." Genda agreed, noting that "The plan is difficult but not impossible." Onishi asked him to draw up a detailed operational plan, giving "special attention to the feasibility of the operation, method of execution, and the forces to be used." The admiral expected the results on his desk in 10 days.[3]

When he returned to Onishi's office some days later, Genda presented a document that was astonishing in its thoroughness and insight: going beyond the mere "nuts and bolts" details of an attack plan, it offered up nine essential premises on which the attack must be based if it were to be a tactical, operational, and strategic success. The first was the need for complete surprise, tactically and operationally: if the Americans had any foreknowledge of where and when the strike was to take place, with their defenses on the alert they would have an opportunity to turn the tables on the Japanese and massacre the strike force.

Assuming that surprise was indeed achieved, the first priority of the attack should be the destruction of the US Navy's aircraft carriers. Given Genda's bias in favor of naval airpower, this surprised no one; what gave weight to his argument was his point that regardless of how much damage was done to the American battle fleet, only aircraft could immediately retaliate against the First Air Fleet—the Japanese carriers would be too distant from Oahu for the slow, stodgy battleships to be able to catch them. Likewise, once the carriers were eliminated, the land-based bombers of the US Army Air Corps would have to be put out of action, for the same reason.

For the attack to be decisive, it would have to be overwhelming, which to Genda meant that every one of the Imperial Navy's aircraft carriers must be included in the attack—this was not the place for half-measures. At the time, there were four fleet carriers already in service—*Kaga*, *Akagi*, *Hiryu*, and *Soryu*. Two more, *Shokaku* and *Zuikaku*, were scheduled to join the fleet sometime in late summer or early autumn; Genda wanted them all. Hand-in-hand with Genda's insistence on using every available carrier was his requirement that every available aircraft the ships carried be employed—torpedo bombers, dive bombers, and high-level bombers should all be used. Fighters would also be necessary, both to provide a protective escort for the bombers and torpedo planes should the Americans have an active combat air patrol on station over Oahu, and then, once any fighter opposition was eliminated, add to the destruction using their heavy machine guns and cannon.

The timing of the attack was critical, as it would be a factor in just how alert and ready the Americans would be when the strike went in. The ideal, of course, was a nighttime attack, as the British had done at Taranto, but the Imperial Navy's air arm lacked experience in night operations as well as the precise navigational aids that would be required. There would not be time to develop the necessary equipment and train pilots in its use, so instead Genda recommended that the attack be timed so that the air strike arrived over its targets shortly after sunrise.

One overarching operational deficiency which had to be overcome however much effort was required, was the Imperial Navy's inability to refuel its ship at sea. Theoretically, all the aircraft carriers save *Soryu*, along with any battleships or battlecruisers escorting them, would have the range to steam from the Home Islands to within striking distance of Hawaii and then return, but *Soryu* and any accompanying cruisers and especially destroyers—vital to protecting the fleet from enemy submarines—could not. Yet without that capability the Hawaii Operation would be stillborn, as no admiral of any navy would risk his capital ships on the high seas without proper screening units and escorts. There was no simple "work-around" for this problem, so Navy logistics experts were immediately put to work developing a way to refuel warships on the high seas—without being told why it was necessary.

This was in keeping with the last but most important of Genda's fundamental requirements: absolute secrecy. Even if every other facet of the plan came together perfectly, should the American intelligence services catch wind of it, the entire operation would have to be abandoned. Genda would have been horrified had he known of the warning Ambassador Grew had forwarded to Washington a few weeks earlier that rumors were circulating that just such an attack was being contemplated; fortunately for the Japanese, all Grew heard were rumors, as at that time the plan, such as it was and what there was of it, was little more than a paper exercise, and lacking any sort of confirmation from other intelligence sources, the State Department discarded Grew's report.

The plan Genda drew up specified an attack staged in two waves, with a possible third wave if it was needed. The first wave of the attack would include 40 torpedo planes, 50 level bombers carrying an entirely new design of 1,770-pound armor-piercing bombs specially fabricated from 14-inch battleship shells, and 54 dive-bombers, along with a strong fighter escort. Their mission was two-fold: to sink or cripple as many of the American aircraft carriers and battleships as possible in Pearl Harbor itself, and do as much damage as possible to the military airfields on Oahu, with an emphasis on rendering Hickam and Wheeler Fields completely inoperable. In the second wave would be 81 dive bombers and 54 level bombers, carrying a variety of bombs ranging in size from 125 pounds to 550 pounds. As even the heaviest of these bombs wouldn't be able to penetrate a battleship's deck armor, the orders for those aircraft assigned to Pearl Harbor itself would be to finish off any carriers still afloat and then concentrate on destroying cruisers; it was assumed that all of the battleships present would have already been sunk or crippled by the first wave. The rest of the bomber force would complete the destruction of the American airfields, leaving neither the US Navy or the Army Air Corps with any means of staging a counter-strike against the Japanese carriers.

Three types of aircraft would be used. The first was the most versatile, the Nakajima B5M, best known to history by its Allied reporting name, "Kate." A low-wing, single-engine monoplane, the Kate could serve as a high-level bomber or a torpedo bomber, carrying either a single 800-kilogram (1,770-pound) armor-piercing bomb, a single 250-kilogram (550-pound) bomb along with six 60-kilogram (132-pound) bombs, or a single 450-millimeter (18-inch) torpedo. Fast for its size and reasonably maneuverable, the Kate carried a crew of three: the pilot, the navigator who also served as the bombardier, and the rear gunner who did double-duty as the radio operator. The B5M would soon be outclassed by faster, more powerful aircraft, but in 1941 it was the most advanced torpedo bomber in the world.

The Imperial Navy's front-line dive bomber in 1941 was the "Val," the Aichi D3A Type 99 Carrier Bomber. Like the Kate, the Val was a single-engine monoplane, but it had fixed landing gear, which made it easily identifiable but also gave it a somewhat dated look. Looks were deceiving, however, as for its size the Val was remarkably nimble and could readily "mix it up" with enemy fighters; the aircraft carried a crew of two, and the rear gunner often proved to be an unpleasant surprise for unwary enemy pilots. For its offensive punch the aircraft typically carry a single 250-kilogram bomb slung under its fuselage, as well as a pair of 60-kilogram bombs under each wing. The 250-kilogram weapon could be of either the general purpose type or a semi-armor-piercing projectile; while neither was sufficiently heavy or powerful to inflict significant damage on a battleship, both were a serious threat to cruisers and destroyers, and could be devastating against ground targets.

The third aircraft to be used in the Pearl Harbor attack was the Mitsubishi A6M2 Type 0 Model 21, the legendary "Reisen" or "Zero" fighter. The name came from the "Type 0" designation, "0" being the last digit of the year it entered service, 1940. Powerfully armed with a 20mm cannon mounted in each wing and a pair of 7.7mm machine guns in the engine cowling, they were also fast and agile. Genda had personally seen the Royal Air Force's Hawker Hurricanes and Supermarine Spitfires in action against the *Luftwaffe's* Messerschmitt Bf-109E's during the Battle of Britain, and was convinced that the Zero was superior to any of them—and likewise superior to anything currently in the American arsenal. But the Zero had a deadly flaw, one it shared with the Kate and the Val: in order to achieve the high speed and exceptional maneuverability so prized by Imperial Army and Navy aviators, Japanese aircraft were lightly built and lacked armor protection for the pilot, engine, and fuel tanks. Thus they were somewhat on the fragile side—they could take very little in the way of battle damage and survive. And the Zeroes were far less nimble at altitudes below 10,000 feet, where the US Army's P-40 shone; in short, they could pack a punch, but they couldn't take one. Genda was aware of this weakness, hence the emphasis in his plan on neutralizing American airpower in the first minutes of the attack.[4]

Sometime around March 10 Onishi presented a detailed draft of Genda's plan to Yamamoto; reviewing it together the admirals found the young aviator's work remarkable for being so thorough and comprehensive, as well as, for the most part, realistic in projecting what could be accomplished within the limits of Japan's resources. Decades later, armchair admirals would carp about how Genda's planning didn't follow what would eventually become standard naval air power doctrines and dogmas, but in truth, Genda had no precedents or established doctrines to use as a framework for his plan when turning Yamamoto's concept for the Pearl Harbor attack into a functional, feasible operation. No one had ever before attempted a naval airstrike on such a scale, so that Genda was very much the pioneer and innovator, writing "the Book" as it were, compelled to "make it up" as he went along. That the plan succeeded as well as it did marked it as a work of genius.

There were two parts of the plan, though, where Genda and Yamamoto fundamentally disagreed, and such was the nature of those disagreements that a workable compromise simply did not exist for either man. Genda, ever the air power zealot, took the position that if the American aircraft carriers were not in Pearl Harbor the day the attack was scheduled to go in, then the operations should be cancelled. Sinking battleships and cruisers instead of carriers would be a waste of perfectly good bombs and torpedoes, and needlessly risk the loss of priceless pilots and valuable aircraft. Yamamoto saw it differently—he wanted to smash the entire Pacific Fleet, not just sink carriers. Battleships had been a world-wide symbol of naval power and prestige since the 1880s and the spectacle of half the US Navy's battleships sunk or sinking in the waters of Pearl Harbor, regardless of the fate of any of the aircraft carriers, would, he was certain, prove devastating to America's fighting spirit. The Imperial Navy must "fiercely attack and destroy the U.S. main fleet at the outset of the war, so that the morale of the U.S. Navy and her people would sink to the extent that it could not be recovered." Even if the Americans chose to fight, recovery from such a debacle would only help buy time that the Japanese would use to improve their overall strategic position in the Pacific. Thus Yamamoto's assertion that "We should do our best to decide the fate of the war on the very first day." While Yamamoto was not the sort of officer to insist that his views always be adopted by mere dint of seniority, in this case his opinion prevailed—the attack would be made whether or not the American carriers were in port.[5]

The second point of contention was even more fundamental, involving as it did the overarching purpose of the strike on Pearl Harbor: Genda's perspective on the attack was strategic, while Yamamoto's was operational. Genda saw it as the first phase of an even larger plan, one that would shift the strategic focus of the coming war from Southeast Asia and the Southwest Pacific to the Central Pacific and the Hawaiian Islands—even America's West Coast. There could be nothing "deterrent" about the attack, in his opinion: all-out war with America would be inevitable from the moment the first bomb fell on Oahu. In that case it wouldn't be enough to simply cripple the Pacific Fleet at Pearl Harbor; it would be necessary to seize and hold the Hawaiian Islands. This would not only deprive the US Navy of Pearl Harbor as a forward base for operations westward into the Central Pacific, it would allow the Imperial Navy to use the islands as the springboard for striking at the United States mainland. Faced with the threat—or, worse, the reality—of invasion from the west, the still-woefully unprepared Americans would be quick to make peace and leave Japan a free hand in the Far East.

Yamamoto would have none of it. This was the only part of Genda's plan which was wholly implausible, of that he was certain. Where Genda saw the Pearl Harbor attack as the opening move in a great strategic design, Yamamoto from the first had conceived of it as an operation with limited objectives, put in hand to guarantee the success of a far more vital strategic operation—seizing the Malay Peninsula and the Dutch East Indies, with their priceless oilfields. The Japanese simply didn't have the manpower or the shipping capacity to simultaneously invade Malaysia and the Dutch East Indies—which were still the strategic priority—while staging an invasion of the Hawaiian Islands. Moreover, the task of maintaining a garrison so far from the Home Islands would have strained the Imperial Navy's logistics to the breaking point. However attractive the idea might be in theory, the cold, hard numbers didn't lie: attempting to take Hawaii from the Americans would only cause the Japanese reach to exceed their grasp.

There was another consideration that dictated against such an audacious plan, as well, about which Yamamoto had pondered at length. The Japanese were being taught a lesson in China, one which Japan's leaders, civilian and military alike, seemed unwilling to learn: a sufficiently determined foe who still possessed the means to fight would not be cowed by martial ardor alone. The Chinese, even without a strong industrial base of their own, so that they were entirely dependent on foreign governments to supply any equipment more complicated than basic infantry weapons, refused to acknowledge defeat—they had lost battles, but they had not been crushed, and so they fought on. Similarly, Yamamoto believed that the best outcome Japan could hope for in any war with the United States was a draw, unless the Americans were handed such a devastating defeat—or a series of such defeats—that they would no longer be willing to fight on. The price of such a victory would be so costly—materially, financially, and emotionally—that in his heart of hearts Yamamoto doubted that Japan could afford to pay it. In a letter to Sasakawa Ryoichi, a businessman who led a minor conservative, nationalistic party in the Diet, Yamamoto was characteristically blunt, saying:

> Should hostilities once break out between Japan and the United States, it would not be enough that we take Guam and the Philippines, nor even Hawaii and San Francisco. To make victory certain, we would have to march into Washington and dictate the terms of peace in the White House. I wonder if our politicians, among whom armchair arguments are being glibly bandied about in the name of state politics, have confidence as to the final outcome and are prepared to make the necessary sacrifices.[6]

A few months later, in a letter to his friend Rear Admiral Hori Teikichi where he once again touched on the subject, he would display an uncharacteristic melancholia, writing, "What a strange position I find myself in, having to pursue with full determination a course of action which is diametrically opposed to my best judgement and firmest conviction. That, too, perhaps is fate."[7]

* * *

Throughout the Second World War, the Allies noticed a predilection on the part of the Japanese Army and Navy for overly complicated plans, which often failed because two or more seemingly unrelated elements would interfere with one another, causing the entire scheme to break down. Wherever and whenever this tendency originated, Japan's admirals and generals seem to have come by it honestly, as the same sort of situation was in play in the last months of peace between the Empire and the United States. It was no secret, of course, in the Army and Navy that their senior officers and respective General Staffs reposed little if any confidence in the diplomats of the Foreign Ministry; there was no little justification for this distrust, as historically diplomats of any and every nationality have been notorious blabbermouths. Hence the refusal to inform the Japanese embassy in Washington DC that a highly secret attack on Pearl Harbor was being planned—and the corresponding lack of any mention of it in the MAGIC intercepts.

What Japan's senior officers did not know was that they, in turn, were being systematically deceived as to the efforts being made by Japan's diplomats to secure a diplomatic settlement of the Empire's dispute with the United States. In sharp contrast to the bombast and posturing of men in Tokyo who would never see combat, there were hundreds, even thousands of intelligent, perceptive officers of all ranks in the Imperial Army and Navy who would have to stand into danger in a war with America and had no wish to see it come about. Not that they were cowardly—far from it: the war would prove that, almost to a man, they were incredibly courageous. But like their American counterparts who had no desire to go to war with Japan, these men were professionals, and as such saw no purpose in a war which could be avoided. While there is no equivalent Japanese proverb to the old Roman maxim *Sic transit Gloria*, dying to achieve glory for its own sake had never been a trait the Japanese held to be worthy of emulating. For honor, for the emperor and the Empire, yes, but merely for glory without honor, never.

These men would have been appalled to learn that a consensus was growing in the Government that diplomacy should continue only as a cover for the preparations being made for war. While no one in the Cabinet as yet knew for certain that a plan for attacking the US Navy's Pacific Fleet was being drawn up, the unspoken assumption was such a plan already existed or would shortly be created. The pattern of American demands, restrictions, and embargoes already in place by early April 1941 led to an unspoken consensus in the Cabinet, with which the Emperor fully concurred, that Japan must either become economically self-sufficient or perpetually be at the mercy of foreign powers who could arbitrarily determine to which resources Japan would and would not have access. Here the Japanese were betrayed by their own history, as their experience with the Unequal Treaties and the settlement of the Russo-Japanese War convinced them the Western powers would never deal equitably with the Empire. Consequently, while the Army and Navy were kept busy drafting operational plans to seize those resources for use *if* they were needed, the decisions were already being made as to *when* they would be used.

Thus Yamamoto would be led to believe, even after the *Kido Butai*, the Strike Force, departed the waters of the Home Islands on its way to attack Pearl Harbor, that provision had been made to recall the fleet, up to almost the very last minute if need be, should a diplomatic breakthrough occur and the need for the attack be eliminated. Nor did the deception end with senior officers in the field and fleet: Emperor Hirohito, as aggressive in his own quiet way as any of his admirals or generals, yet understanding as they did not the need to be able to step back from the abyss, even at the last second, insisted on such a recall measure and was assured that one was in place. The truth was, however, once the attack force sailed, the chances of it actually being recalled were already reduced to virtually nil.

As if to further muddle an already complicated situation of who was doing what and why, the Foreign Ministry persisted in undertaking acts of "diplomacy" that seemed calculated to make Ambassador Nomura's efforts in Washington even more difficult. April 13 saw a formal signing ceremony take place in Moscow, as the Soviet foreign minister, Vlacheslav Molotov and Japan's ambassador to the Kremlin, Major General Tatekawa Yoshitsugu, along with Foreign Minister Matsuoka Yosuke, concluded the Japan–Soviet Neutrality Pact, a treaty of mutual non-aggression. This was viewed with particular alarm by the Roosevelt Administration, as less than two years earlier a similar pact between Germany and the Soviet Union had been followed a week later by the Nazi invasion of Poland. The purpose of that pact had been to secure Germany's eastern frontier once Poland was conquered and Hitler turned his attention to the Allies in the West. The question flying up and down the corridors of the White House and the State Department was whether or not a similar scenario was being played out in the Far East: was Japan securing her northern frontier in order to have a free hand in operations to the south, toward Malaysia, the Kra Peninsula, Borneo, Java—and the Philippines?

The answer, of course, was "yes," though the Japanese weren't yet ready to carry out those operations. What they were doing, though, was what boxers call "telegraphing their punches": the preparations for the Empire's next move were so glaringly obvious that some officials in Washington wondered if the Japanese's actions were the product of mere arrogance or an indifference to any reaction by the American government. If it was the former, then perhaps the encroaching embargoes that cut into Japan's ability to sustain her adventurism could take the Empire down a peg; if it were the latter, then it was vital for the administration to buy as much time as possible for America's rearmament plans. Either way, it was essential to keep the Japanese talking.

The problem was finding something to talk about. With Japan's ambitions so nakedly displayed, Ambassador Nomura was hard put to present Secretary Hull with anything that could be a basis for negotiation. Whether by accident or design, Hull came to Nomura's rescue when, on April 16, just three days after the signing of Japan's non-aggression pact with the Soviets, he presented the ambassador with a statement of four principles, informing him that they were to be considered as fundamental to any agreements negotiated between the United States and the Empire. The first three were thinly veiled references to Japan's current situation in China, while the fourth was directed at the looming threat to Southeast Asia and the Dutch East Indies. The principles were, first, a respect for the sovereignty and territorial integrity of all nations; a pledge of non-interference in other sovereign nation's internal affairs; open support of equal commercial opportunity—a call for a return to the "Open Door" policy in China; and finally, no disturbance of the *status quo* in the Pacific except by peaceful means.[8]

A week earlier Nomura had presented Hull with a detailed memorandum offering an immediate settlement of the disputes between America and Japan, one which required that the United States recognize the legitimacy of Manchukuo, accept as accomplished fact further Japanese conquests in China, acknowledge China's status as a Japanese vassal state, and guarantee Japan's access to whatever resources she required from other Far Eastern nations. In return, Japan offered vaguely worded assurances of the Empire's future good behavior. For Hull, this was a clear-cut case of putting the cart before the horse: there was no point to discussing specifics without first establishing the overarching purpose of whatever negotiations might take place.

Nomura seemed disappointed that the secretary of state did not simply accept the Japanese proposal *in toto* and without discussion, but urged Tokyo to endorse Hull's four principles in the hope that the Americans could be finessed into a false position where they were compelled in practice to give Japan a free hand in the Far East, regardless of whatever diplomatic curlicues were in the signed documents. But Foreign Minister Matsuoka dithered, and when his formal reply was sent to Washington on May 3, it neither accepted nor rejected Hull's proposal, instead instructing Nomura to offer up a neutrality pact between the Empire and the United States similar to that which Tokyo had just signed with Moscow. Hull rejected the idea out of hand as patently absurd, which is was: it would have accomplished nothing apart from tacitly endorsing all of Japan's adventures in China as well as tying America's hands when—not if—the Japanese moved southward.

The secretary's patience with Matsuoka, who was rabidly pro-Axis, was wearing thin, as was Roosevelt's, and more than once Hull remarked to Nomura that the foreign minister's aggressive speeches were undermining the credibility of the ambassador's efforts. Unlike Roosevelt, Hull never fancied that he could simply dictate the conduct of foreign governments and their officials, but he did make the point to Nomura, knowing the warning would be duly passed along, that there was little love for Adolf Hitler and the Nazis among the American people. Hence Matsuoka's public expressions of his intensely pro-Axis sentiments were not winning any friends for Japan in the US Senate, which would have to ratify any formal agreements which might be concluded between Washington and Tokyo.

It was with something akin to pleasant surprise, then, when on May 12 Hull received the foreign minister's direct response to the four principles the secretary had proposed almost four weeks earlier. Rather than the outright rejection Hull had expected, Matsuoka offered a counterproposal, which Hull and Nomura informally agreed could serve as the basis for negotiation both men had been seeking. As it stood, Matsuoka's counter-proposal was unacceptable, but it was far from the "take it or leave it" sort of offering that had been typical of Japanese "diplomacy" in the 1930s. Matsuoka candidly stated that his purpose was to prevent the United States from going to war with Germany—this was, he believed, how the Japanese could best aid their German allies—and at the same time compel the Chinese Nationalists to negotiate a peace settlement with Japan, by having the United States threaten to cut off all military aid to Chungking.

For Hull, as with any good diplomat, half a loaf was better than none, though privately he felt less than sanguine about just how realistic Matsuoka's ambitions were, remarking that "Very few rays of hope shone from that document." Still, he and Nomura agreed that the proposal was a starting point for further talks. Matsuoka, though, couldn't keep his mouth shut or his fingers out of the pie: just days before the text of his proposal would land on Cordell Hull's desk, Matsuoka blurted out to His Majesty at an Imperial Conference that "If the United States joins the war Japan must be on the side of Germany and Italy and must attack Singapore. The U.S. entry will prolong the war and there will be a great possibility of a military clash between Germany and the Soviet Union. If that happens, Japan has to abolish its neutrality treaty with the Soviet Union and, joining Germany, advance to Irkutsk." Unfortunately, Matsuoka was prone to speaking the same thoughts in public, without bothering to clarify that he was expressing a personal opinion and not official government policy.[9]

Compounding the problems he was creating, Matsuoka persisted in needlessly meddling in the negotiations between Nomura and Hull, so often revising and amending proposals already under discussion that virtually no progress was being made. An exasperated Nomura warned him that the perception was growing in both the State Department and the White House that, protests to the contrary notwithstanding, the negotiations were a sham, only meant to buy time for the Japanese to finish their preparations for the invasion of the Malay Peninsula, Borneo, and Java. Rumors were beginning to circulate that additional embargoes were being prepared, including one which would be a virtual economic death sentence to the Empire—a complete freeze imposed on all Japanese assets within the United States.

Nomura's words of caution fell on deaf ears, but Matsuoka's increasingly erratic conduct of his ministry's affairs had already made him a liability to the Government. In a personal note sent to the prime minister, Prince Konoye, Ambassador Grew was painfully candid regarding: "The reports which are now reaching the American Government [from Nomura] are so completely contrary to those statements and utterances [by Matsuoka] that the Government of the United States finds it very difficult to believe in the truth of those reports." This was alarming, as Grew's language was barely a step shy of openly accusing Konoye's government of lying about the purpose and sincerity of its negotiations with the United States. The Prince was determined that Japan and America should remain at peace, and Matsuoka's obtuse behavior was finally acknowledged to be one of the major obstacles to achieving that goal.

In the weeks that followed the German invasion of the USSR on June 22, 1941, the foreign minister began publicly calling for a declaration of war on the Russians in order to support the German offensive in the west by diverting Soviet forces to the east, despite Japan's non-aggression pact with the Soviet Union, which Matsuoka had personally helped negotiate. It was clearly time for him to go. In a carefully prepared political maneuver, Konoye resigned on July 16, and as was customary, all his ministers resigned with him; immediately, the Prince was invited to form a new Government, which he did six days later—without Matsuoka, who was not asked to return to the Cabinet in any post; the new foreign minister was Admiral Toyoda Teijiro. Now consigned to the political wilderness, Matsuoka's prestige and influence went into a rapid and dramatic decline—he would never again play a role in Imperial politics—but the damage had been done.

On July 24, 1941, the Imperial Army began moving into the ostensibly still-neutral southern half of French Indochina; upon hearing news of this, without waiting for official confirmation, Roosevelt summoned Nomura to the White House. Present also was the undersecretary of state, Sumner Welles, who was standing in for Cordell Hull while the secretary was recuperating from a flare-up of a chronic lung disease; Roosevelt, however, did all of the talking for the United States, lest there be any mistake about the gravity of what he was imparting to Nomura. The president told the ambassador that if the reports of the Japanese troop movements were true, they could be seen as having only one purpose: to position the land and air forces which would be employed in an invasion of Malaysia, the Dutch East Indies, or even Thailand and Burma. He implied, while carefully avoiding anything that could have been construed as a firm or explicit statement, that should the Japanese make an aggressive move on any of them, the United States, Great Britain, and the Netherlands government-in-exile would declare war on Japan. It was a bluff, of course, although Prime Minister Winston Churchill had earlier that month proposed just such a course of action in response to an appeal from Thailand's prime minister, Phibun Songkhram; Roosevelt had declined, saying he thought it rash and unwise.

Now the president proposed to Nomura that if Japanese forces in Indochina were withdrawn, he in turn would exert himself to obtain a binding declaration from the Chinese, British, and Dutch governments, to which the United States would also adhere, that made Indochina completely neutral and inviolate. The American government would also, Roosevelt assured Nomura, make every effort to persuade the other powers to assure that Japan had ready access to whatever sources of food and raw materials the Empire needed, eliminating the primary incentive for Japanese adventurism. Once again, however, Roosevelt badly misjudged the Japanese character and the extent of his own influence. Wittingly or no, he was doing precisely what Foreign Minister Matsuoka had done in early April: he was expecting the Empire to make material concessions in return for vague promises of American efforts to facilitate diplomatic resolutions which might or might not in fact occur. Worse, he did so in the manner which any Japanese would regard as condescending. Whether Roosevelt did so out of parochialism or simply a misplaced sense of his own importance, no matter how favorably Nomura communicated the proposal to his government, it would be seen in Tokyo as a deliberate slight by the president.

When he sent his digest of this meeting to the Foreign Ministry, Nomura also noted that Roosevelt carefully and deliberately pointed out Japan's dependence on foreign oil, especially oil and fuel imported from the United States. Without actually raising the possibility, the president had implied that the continued flow of oil from America to Japan was far from assured; Roosevelt then went on to say that should Japan attempt to secure by force other sources of oil—explicitly the Dutch East Indies—both the British and Dutch governments would declare war. Should that happen, then in light of America's policy of assisting Great Britain, "an exceedingly serious situation would immediately result."[10]

Two days after his meeting with Ambassador Nomura, on July 26, President Roosevelt signed Executive Order No. 8832, freezing all financial and material assets in the United States belonging to Japanese nationals and businesses in order "to prevent the use of the financial facilities of the United States and trade between Japan and the United States, in ways harmful to national defense and American interests, to prevent the liquidation in the United States of assets obtained by duress or conquest, and to curb subversive activities in the United States." A similar order had been imposed on German assets on June 14, but no one in Tokyo imagined that Roosevelt would move against Japan so quickly.[11]

Despite the timing, imposition of the order had nothing to do with Matsuoka, his antics, or the reorganization of Konoye's government: the legal underpinnings had been in preparation for some months. What triggered such an abrupt reaction by the White House was, of course, the Japanese occupation of the rump of French Indochina on July 24: when the Imperial Navy steamed into Cam Ranh Bay, one of the world's finest deep-water anchorages, Japanese warships were positioned less than 800 miles from the Philippines and were equidistant from Singapore. This placed the Japanese fleet within less than two days steaming time of both; more ominously, the Philippines were now flanked from the west as well as threatened from Formosa to the north.

Executive Order 8832 was tantamount to the Roosevelt Administration finally drawing a line across any potential path to further expansion or conquest. Its effect on Japan was far more profound and immediate than was the order freezing German assets on the Third Reich; when followed on August 1 by the embargo of all oil and petroleum products, it brought the two nations right to the edge of the precipice. The only questions remaining were whether or not a way could be found to step back from that edge, or if one nation would slip and fall into it—or push the other first.

* * *

In late April 1941 Yamamoto sent his senior staff officer, Captain Kuroshima Kameto, to present the plan for the Hawaii Operation to Captain Tomioka Sadatoshi, chief of the Navy General Staff Operations Section, in the hope of convincing him to endorse the plan before its presentation to the General Staff as a whole. Tomioka raised four significant objections: the vital element of surprise would be difficult to achieve; maintaining absolute secrecy while training and preparations were underway would be all but impossible; there was no compelling reason to regard the long-standing plan for a war of attrition against the US Navy as invalid; and, finally, there were no assurances that the practical problems—refueling at sea and developing torpedoes that would successfully run in the shallow waters of Pearl Harbor—could be solved.

For their part, the Naval General Staff, after reviewing the plan, were unconvinced of Yamamoto's premise that the attack would deliver a serious, even crippling, blow to American morale. The staff officers were ill-inclined to give serious consideration to any other operation than the pending offensive to the south, and it was their considered opinion that none of the Imperial Navy's fleet carriers could be spared for what they regarded as peripheral objectives. Yamamoto countered by asserting that by crippling the Pacific Fleet the Pearl Harbor attack would guard the left flank of the southern advance against any unexpected incursions by the US Navy. The conference ended with the issue unresolved for the time being.

In August, Yamamoto tried again. The Naval General Staff was organizing the annual fleet war games, and out of deference to Yamamoto's position as the commander-in-chief of the Combined Fleet agreed that one of the scenarios to be played out would be the Pearl Harbor plan. The plan had been further refined since April, and in July additions and modifications were made: in a subordinate operation, a squadron of fleet submarines would be tasked with taking station outside of the entrance channel to Pearl, poised to torpedo any ships which managed to get underway and out of the harbor during the attack. When the war games began on

September 11, the first exercise was the southern operation, a clear indication of where the naval staff's priorities lay. It was not until September 16 that Yamamoto and a select group of officers had the opportunity, under very secure conditions, to run the simulated attack on Pearl Harbor; the exercise required just over two days to complete, and at its end, the naval staff concluded that the Hawaii Operation was indeed feasible, though extremely risky. The staff officers remained unconvinced, however, that the attack was truly necessary, or that the likely results were worth the risk to the Imperial Navy's carriers.

And yet, a distinct—and different—sense of urgency had suffused these fleet simulations, as on September 6 an Imperial Conference had been held which profoundly altered the direction and priorities of Japan's foreign policy and military planning. The published decision, which bore the emperor's approval and was circulated only to those senior officers and government officials with a "need to know," was utterly unambiguous in its statement of what were termed "Lines of action in Japan's national policy to be pursued according to the changing situation."

> In order to assure self-preservation and self-defense, Japan under the resolve to risk war with America, Great Britain, and the Netherlands, will go forward with war preparation which will be completed sometime toward the latter part of October...
>
> In case there is no prospect by the early part of October of pushing through Japanese claims by diplomatic means...Japan will forthwith decide upon war against America, Britain and the Netherlands.[12]

In short, if the negotiations between Hull and Nomura, which had been plodding along for more than six months, did not miraculously produce some *deus ex machina*-like solution to what was now a crisis, war was inevitable.

It was with this decision looming in the background, then, that the fleet war games were conducted and their results evaluated. On September 24, the Operations Staff of the Naval General Staff held a special conference on the proposed Hawaii attack; in the end the plan was not so much rejected as disregarded—again no formal decision was actually made. Yamamoto was furious: he was determined to have the Hawaii Operation approved. Though he most emphatically did not want to see the Empire go to war with the United States, he was determined that, as the Emperor had chosen war, he would give Japan the best chance it would ever have for winning that war—or at least not losing it. To him, this dithering was dangerous. Every month wasted through hesitation further reduced Japan's reserves of oil, aviation fuel, and other critical materials which, for now at least, were irreplaceable. Aircrew would have to be trained in new torpedo and bombing tactics, the shallow-water torpedoes and high-altitude armor-piercing bombs perfected, the ships that would form the *Kido Butai* readied and refitted as necessary.

By now, in keeping with the Imperial Conference decision, Japan's military preparations for the southern offensive were all but complete. The planning for the southern operation had begun two months before Yamamoto wrote his memo to

Admiral Oikawa in which he first proposed the Pearl Harbor attack; training for the southern operation had begun in March 1941. Units tasked for the amphibious operations were assembled at Imperial Army bases in Japan, south China, and Formosa, while merchant ships were requisitioned and refitted with the specialized equipment they would require to be used as troop transports. A target date for initiating the southern offensive, December 8, had already been established. If the Hawaii Operation was to be simultaneously carried out, it must be approved *now* and preparations begun immediately.

Matters came to a head during a series of staff meetings on October 17 and 18, aboard the fleet flagship, *Nagato*. Yamamoto was convinced that the staff admirals, conservative, traditionalist, and, for all their war-like posturing, fundamentally timid, would never muster the vision or the courage to abandon the dogma of the *Kenta Kassai*, which they had embraced the whole of their professional lives. It would be up to him to drag them, kicking and screaming, into the new era of naval strategy, where the big gun was no longer the arbiter of naval power. Yamamoto forcefully made the case that, regardless of what Mahan had taught a half-century before and whatever had been Japan's experience in 1905, the idea of a drawn-out campaign of attrition with the US Navy had become folly, seeking the Decisive Battle a fool's errand. He reminded them of what they already knew but had, in their feigned martial ardor, come to disregard: even if the emperor's soldiers, sailors, and airmen could consistently inflict higher losses on their American counterparts than they suffered, Japan would still run out of weapons, ships, munitions, and men long before America did so.

Now Yamamoto took the gloves off. Audaciously, almost arrogantly, he pointed directly to the elephant in the room: in the Naval College wargames, to which the staff admirals always looked for confirmation of their strategic and operational ideas, none of the plans the Navy concocted had ever produced a Decisive Battle favorable to Japan. "As I read the results of repeated war games, the Imperial Navy has not once achieved a great victory," he said. The strategy of *Kanto Kassai*, then, was tantamount to conceding defeat before the first battle had even been fought. The only alternative, as Yamamoto saw it, was to abandon the Imperial Navy's traditional defensive strategy in exchange for one that was offensive.[13]

Yamamoto left no doubt that, regardless of whether or not the Hawaii Operation was carried out, there would be war with America once Japan moved into the Southwest Pacific. Let it be so, he argued, but take the war to the Americans—and to the British, Australians, and Dutch simultaneously—rather than wait for it to come to the Japanese, and take it to them on the very first day of that war. Japan needed a strategy that emphasized speed, surprise, and carefully timed attacks on multiple fronts that would disrupt the enemy's efforts to formulate and follow a shared, coordinated strategy of their own, and at the same time inflict serious, even possibly decisive, losses. This was the only way, Yamamoto maintained, whereby the Empire could establish a position, geographically and materially, that would compel the United States and its allies to accept a negotiated peace and concede all of Japan's demands.

Finally, Yamamoto played his ace card. Word began circulating among the Naval General Staff that unless the attack on Pearl Harbor was approved in every detail, Yamamoto and his entire staff would resign. Incredible as it seems, it was this single moment which made the Japanese attack on Pearl Harbor a reality. Had the navy chief of staff, Admiral Nagano, called Yamamoto's bluff, the commander-in-chief of the Combined Fleet would have had no other choice but to carry through with it—the loss of face Yamamoto would have suffered had he tried to renege on his threat of resignation would have left him completely marginalized. Without Yamamoto as the driving force behind the attack, the strike on Pearl Harbor would have never been carried out, and the course—and outcome—of the Second World War in the Pacific would have been dramatically different than it turned out to be. Nagano had no way of knowing this, of course, all he knew for certain was that it was unthinkable for Japan to go to war without Yamamoto at the helm of the Combined Fleet; the plan for the Hawaii Operation was adopted without further debate, and training for the aircrews began almost immediately.

* * *

In the meantime, the Imperial Navy General Staff's Intelligence Section had been busy. In an ironic twist, on September 24, even as the staff informed Admiral Yamamoto that no decision had yet been made regarding the attack on Pearl Harbor, a highly secret "eyes only" message was transmitted to the Japanese consulate in Honolulu, addressed to the resourceful Lieutenant Yoshikawa. It read:

> Strictly secret. Henceforth, we would like to have you make reports concerning vessels along the following lines insofar as possible:
>
> 1. The waters (of Pearl Harbor) are to be divided roughly into five sub-areas. (We have no objections to your abbreviating as much as you like.)
>
> Area A. Waters between Ford Island and the Arsenal.
> Area B. Waters adjacent to the Island south and west of Ford Island. (This area is on the opposite side of the Island from Area A.)
> Area C. East Loch.
> Area D. Middle Loch.
> Area E. West Loch and the communicating water routes.
>
> 2. With regard to warships and aircraft carriers, we would like to have you report on those at anchor, (these are not so important) tied up at wharves, buoys and in docks. (Designate types and classes briefly. If possible we would like to have you make mention of the fact when there are two or more vessels along side the same wharf.)[14]

This message would become known to history as the "bomb plot" —that is, a detailed platting of Pearl Harbor from which targeting priorities could be assigned to the Imperial Navy's torpedo- and dive-bombers. Yoshikawa added a few refinements to the subdivision of the harbor that Tokyo provided, and then proceeded to avail himself of his second-floor perch in his favorite teahouse, and began sending detailed reports.

The US Army's Signals Intelligence Service decrypted the "bomb plot" message on October 9, two weeks after it had been intercepted, and it sent it over to the Far Eastern Section for translation, where it immediately caught the attention of Colonel Rufus Bratton, the section chief. A West Point graduate, Class of 1914, he possessed an insight into the Japanese military which far exceeded that of almost any other officer in the US Army: in the early 1920s, he spent three years in Japan, learning the language, which led to an immediate appointment as assistant military attaché to the embassy in Tokyo. He then spent three years in field commands before reporting to the General Staff School at Fort Leavenworth in 1929; after graduating, he went back to Japan, this time as a student at the Imperial War College. Bratton then remained in Japan as the US Army military attaché, finally returning to the United States in 1937, posted directly to the War Department in the General Staff's Military Intelligence Division as Chief of the Far Eastern Section. His firsthand knowledge of Japan and the Japanese, along with his fluency in their complex and difficult language, virtually assured that Bratton would become part of the select community of individuals granted access to MAGIC.

What stood out for Bratton in the "bomb plot" message was that it was sent only to the Honolulu consulate: Army Intelligence—and ONI, as well—had long been aware that Japanese spies were active in Hawaii, the Panama Canal Zone, the Philippines, and the West Coast, even though their specific identities remained unknown; identical, or at least similar, requests for specific information typically went out at more or less the same time to all of the Japanese agents operating in the United States and America's overseas possessions. Not so this message: no similar instruction was sent to any other Japanese consulate. To Bratton, the Imperial Navy seemed unusually interested in Pearl Harbor, but when he tried to bring this to the attention of his superior, Brigadier General Sherman Miles, the assistant chief of staff for army intelligence, he was met with something akin to indifference: Miles surmised that the Japanese might be contemplating a submarine attack on Pearl, but thought it unlikely. In any case, he reminded Bratton, Pearl Harbor was a Navy base, which made it the Navy's business.

Except that the Navy didn't seem especially interested in the message, either. Bratton's opposite number in ONI, Lieutenant Commander Alwyn Kramer, thought it unusual, but didn't regard it as extraordinary. He did, however, make certain that the decrypt came to the attention of the Director of Naval Intelligence, Captain Theodore Wilkinson, as well as Admiral Turner in War Plans, and the CNO, Admiral Stark; one copy was sent to Secretary of the Navy Frank Knox, another went to the White House. None of the recipients seemed unduly alarmed by the message, and no one thought it necessary to inform Admiral Kimmel—or even Rochefort or Layton—of its contents. Stark was still laboring under the impression that Kimmel's intelligence section was in possession of a MAGIC decryption unit and so was providing intercepts directly to CINCPAC; Turner continued to maintain his stranglehold on who in the Navy did and did not actually have access to MAGIC and refused to forward the message to Kimmel, citing security concerns; Knox and the White House were confident that either Stark or Turner would make certain Kimmel was informed.

While it was reasonable for the president and the secretary to refrain from becoming involved in what was an operational matter, Stark's lapse was less excusable, as it fell upon him as chief of naval operations to be certain—and not merely assume—that all of his fleet commanders had all of the relevant intelligence available to them. But because he was not by nature a "commanding" officer, unlike his eventual successor, the abrasive-but-efficient Admiral Ernest King, currently the Commander-in-Chief, Atlantic Fleet, Stark carefully avoided any word or deed which might appear to encroach on the volcanic-tempered Turner's self-assumed responsibilities. At that moment, however unwittingly, Turner was the best ally the Japanese had in Washington DC, not because he was treacherous, but because his penchant for empire-building and personal ambition prevented critical intelligence from reaching the senior naval officers who most needed it.

Just how critical was the "bomb plot" message became evident when, years later, an incredulous Kimmel learned of its existence for the first time. "With the dispatch of September 24, 1941, and those which followed, there was a significant and ominous change in the character of the information which the Japanese Government sought and obtained," he said. "These Japanese instructions and reports pointed to an attack by Japan on the ships in Pearl Harbor. The information sought and obtained…had no other conceivable usefulness… Knowledge of these intercepted Japanese dispatches would have radically changed the estimate of the situation made by me and my staff… Knowledge of a probable Japanese attack on Pearl Harbor afforded an opportunity to ambush the Japanese striking force as it ventured to Hawaii."[15]

General Short, who, like Kimmel, didn't learn of the existence of the "bomb plot" message until long after the Pearl Harbor attack, was equally emphatic in his agreement with Kimmel's assessment of its significance. He also unerringly pointed out what should have been obvious to everyone in Washington—and should have assured that both he and Kimmel were made aware of the message's existence and content:

> While the War Department G-2 may not have felt bound to let me know about the routine operations of the Japanese in keeping track of our naval ships, they should certainly have let me know that the Japanese were getting reports of the exact location of the ships in Pearl Harbor…

because such details would only be useful for sabotage, or for air or submarine attack on Hawaii… This message, analyzed critically, is really a bombing plan for Pearl Harbor.

Short was kept in the dark because the Army was forbidden to send MAGIC-based intelligence to its department commanders due to the Navy's lack of confidence in the Army's signals security—which in fact was no worse and no better than the Navy's. But the Navy feared that if the Japanese breached the Army's signals and discovered in them information that could only have come from messages encrypted in the PURPLE cipher, MAGIC would become hopelessly compromised and thus useless. It was this sort of rationalizing which highlighted how, for all of its technical expertise, the American intelligence community was, to a considerable degree, still lacking in sophistication. The British, whose Government Code and Cypher School at Bletchley Park had been reading German "Enigma"-enciphered signals for well over a year, had very quickly devised methods of "sanitizing" the information collected from decrypted signals, that is, stripping out anything in a given message, as well as rewording it, so as to eliminate potential clues as to its origin. As a backstop, stories were fabricated—usually involving treachery or ineptitude by Germany's Italian or Hungarian allies—of how the information was gathered that would lead away from the idea that an "unbreakable" cipher system had in fact been broken. It was an ingenious solution which successfully deceived the Germans throughout the war; the American intelligence services had no similar deception plan, and their near-paranoia over MAGIC's security prevented the information it provided from being used to its best effect. This shortsightedness would prove to be very costly.

* * *

Now that the Hawaii Operation was officially approved, training could get underway; over 400 of the Imperial Navy's finest pilots were selected for the mission. Japan's air war over China had not, as is usually implied and sometimes openly stated, been simply a large-scale live-fire training exercise for the Japanese: the naval aviators who would carry out the attack on Pearl Harbor were the experienced veterans, survivors of a bitter and far from one-sided struggle. The highest priority in training was given to the torpedo bomber crews and the bombardiers for the high-altitude level bombers, as these aircraft were expected to be the ship-killers on Battleship Row. Most of the training consisted of "dry runs" where the aircraft wouldn't launch or drop actual ordnance, because both the Type 91 torpedoes and the Type 99 bombs were in short supply. A last-minute modification to the Type 91—installing wooden fins to keep them running stable and true, rather than porpoising or veering off course and not, as is commonly believed, to let the torpedoes run in shallow water, as that problem had actually been solved in 1936—delayed their delivery until early November. Nonetheless, the Japanese aviators spent every available hour in the air, honing their skills however they could.

The officer given charge of the training was Commander Fuchida Mitsuo, who was also designated as the strike leader. Fuchida and Genda had been classmates at Eta Jima, and after graduation in 1924, Fuchida had also become an aviator, but while his friend chose to train as a fighter pilot, Fuchida specialized in bombers. His expertise was such that by 1936, he was an instructor pilot at the Yokosuka training school; he also graduated from the Naval Staff College before being assigned to *Akagi* as her air group commander in 1939. All through October and into November, he pushed his fliers as hard as he dared, demanding what to many seemed impossible levels of near-perfection in their performance. They could hardly complain, however, as Fuchida trained as strenuously as any of his men: he would be flying the mission with them, part of the first wave of the attack. While Fuchida trained the aircrews, Rear Admiral Kusaka Ryunosuke, Nagumo's chief of staff, had performed a logistical miracle in developing a method for refueling *Kido Butai's* warships at sea. Kusaka was one of the unsung heroes of the Japanese attack: he was initially skeptical about the whole idea of an air strike on Pearl Harbor, but once assigned to the operation, never gave Yamamoto or Nagumo anything less than his best efforts; had he not solved the refueling problem, the attack could never have been carried out.

Even as some problems were being solved, though, others cropped up, as the Hawaii Operation acquired a complexity beyond anything Yamamoto had ever contemplated. One subordinate operation in particular which was grafted onto the overall plan of attack at almost the last minute seemed to several officers, most notably Genda and Fuchida, as ill-considered, poorly conceived and a needless threat to the shroud of secrecy which had to be maintained around the attack until the very last minute. This was the plan to use five two-man "midget" submarines to actually penetrate Pearl Harbor and launch torpedoes at high-value targets at the same time that *Kido Butai's* aircraft were striking from overhead.

First built in 1938, these midget subs, designated Type A *Ko-hyoteki* ("scale-covered dragon") had no individual names, but were usually identified by the number of the number of their "mother" submarine. Nicknamed "*tou*" ("tube"), they thus became known as *I-16tou*, *I-20tou*, and so on. Each boat had a length of almost 80 feet and weighed 46 tons, and carried two Type 97 torpedoes, which had 772-pound warheads. Surfaced their top speed was a very respectable 23 knots, submerged they were almost as fast, topping out at 19 knots. But their design had two flaws, neither of which was ever corrected in the more than 400 Type A boats built for the Imperial Navy. The first was that their method of trimming the boat was exceedingly crude: it literally consisted of shifting lead weights by hand back and forth along the keel, a clumsy and imprecise system that could cause the boat to porpoise—unintentionally pop to the surface—or go into an unexpected dive. The second was that they were powered solely by an electric motor, which ran off batteries that occupied much of the hull's interior; the batteries could be exhausted in as little as 55 minutes when running the motor at full speed, and there was no internal recharging system, so the crew had to be extremely careful about conserving their battery power.

Five fleet submarines, *I-16*, *I-18*, *I-20*, *I-22*, and *I-24*, were recalled to the Navy's shipyard at Kure, there to be modified to carry one of these midget submarines apiece on the deck behind their coming towers. Special hatches were rigged to allow the minisub crews to enter their boats while the mother submarine was submerged, so that they could launch undetected. The plan, such as it was and what there was of it, called for the big I-boats to approach Oahu as close as they dared and release the midget subs somewhere along the island's southern coast, where they would then make their way up the entrance channel into Pearl Harbor and, hopefully, wreak havoc on the US Navy's Pacific Fleet from below while swarms of Japanese aircraft did the same from above. After the attack, the crews were to bring their boats back out into open water if they could, and scuttle the little subs; two or more of the mother boats would be standing by at designated rendezvous points to collect them—at least that was the theory. In truth, from the beginning most of the midget sub crews regarded the operation as a one-way mission, with no real prospect of survival or ever returning to Japan; even so, their morale was sky-high.

Genda and Fuchida considered the midget submarine operation ill-conceived and poorly planned, and their shared fury at having it grafted onto the Hawaii Operation was as towering. Both were certain that the US Navy's anti-submarine patrols around the entrance to Pearl Harbor—about which they knew much, thanks to Lieutenant Yoshikawa—would detect the midget subs long before they were able to penetrate the anchorage itself, alerting the Americans to an impending attack and giving them sufficient warning to have their ships at General Quarters, guns manned and ready, by the time the air strike arrived. All it would take would be one alert destroyer skipper or patrol bomber pilot to set the stage for what would be a massacre. By this time, though—late October—preparations for the Hawaii Operation were so advanced and the pace so frantic that their objections were, with exquisite courtesy, brushed aside.

* * *

While *Kido Butai* was being assembled and aircrews trained, the diplomatic charade in Washington and Tokyo continued uninterrupted throughout September and October. It was a surreal situation, as if both sides were speaking the same language, clearly and intelligibly, yet neither were unable to understand what the other was saying. The sticking point was China: the Japanese seemingly could not comprehend that no settlement in the Far East would be acceptable to the Americans as long as any Japanese troops remained in any part of China, including Manchuoko; the Americans could not understand, apparently, that the Japanese would never agree to leave China empty-handed. Prince Konoye had proposed a summit meeting between himself and Roosevelt, Ambassador Nomura formally extending the invitation on August 27, but Roosevelt was adamant that the terms for a Japanese evacuation of China must be agreed upon before the meeting could take place. It never happened, of course, and on September 6, in a tacit acknowledgment that a negotiated settlement between the Empire and the United States had become, for all practical purposes, impossible, the Imperial Conference adopted the resolution that committed Japan to war.

Konoye nonetheless urged that talks between America and Japan continue, holding the war at bay, but he was now a spent force in Japanese politics. While not of the direct imperial bloodline, he was the scion of one of Japan's oldest and most powerful families, the Fujiwara clan, which had played a major, sometimes dominating, role in the Imperial government for more than 1,200 years. At once aloof and Olympian, yet at the same time oddly approachable, Konoye's intellect alone demanded respect; when it was coupled with the power of his house, he expected—and usually received—deference from those around him, especially the ministers in his Cabinet. He had been prime minister since July 22, 1940, an unusually long tenure in Japan's parliamentary landscape, but on October 12, 1941, it came to an end. That afternoon, Foreign Minister Toyoda, War Minister Tojo, Navy Minister Oikawa, and Suzuki Teiichi, who was responsible for the central planning of Japan's economy, met with Konoye at his Tokyo home and respectfully submitted the equivalent of an ultimatum: if Konoye was not prepared to endorse the Imperial Conference resolution, then it was time for him to step aside.

Five days later, Konoye presented his resignation to the Emperor and General Tojo Hideki was appointed as his successor as prime minister. This was a calculated move on the part of Konoye, as he hoped that by placing the burden of resolving the crisis with America firmly on the shoulders of the Army, it would serve as a moderating influence on the men who thus far had avoided taking any responsibility for the crisis their recklessness had created. Instead, the idea backfired, as Tojo, firmly in control—or so he believed, imagining he could ride the approaching whirlwind—now accelerated the pace of events.

On November 4 Togo Shigenori, who had replaced Admiral Toyoda as foreign minister, informed Ambassador Nomura that time was definitely running out, saying "Conditions both within and without our Empire are so tense that no longer is procrastination possible…we have decided, as a result of these deliberations, to gamble once more on the continuance of the parleys, but this is our last effort… If through it we do not reach a quick accord, I am sorry to say the talks will certainly be ruptured, [and] relations between our two nations will be on the brink of chaos." This "last effort" was a proposal by the new Tojo Government which included the evacuation of Japanese forces from southern Indochina; an eventual withdrawal—contingent on an assurance that the United States would cease supplying arms and munitions to the Chinese—of those Japanese troops currently in mainland China except for "North China" and the region along the northern border with Soviet-occupied

Mongolia; an end to all of the American embargoes on Japan; and an assurance by the United States that Japan would have ready access to the oil and rubber in the Malay Peninsula and the Dutch East Indies. "North China" was a euphemism for Manchuoko, of course, which the Empire steadfastly refused to give up.[16]

With Konoye gone and Tojo in his place, Washington grew more apprehensive, and now both SIS and OP-20-G were working around the clock to decrypt and translate the MAGIC intercepts as rapidly as possible. Thus everyone on the distribution lists were able to read Togo's dispatch to Nomura within hours of its transmission, along with one sent the following day, which read in part, "[I]t is absolutely necessary that all arrangements for the signing of an agreement be completed by the 25th of this month." This was the first mention of anything that smacked of a specific deadline in the negotiations between Washington and Tokyo, and as such reinforced the impression made upon Roosevelt and his Cabinet by Konoye's resignation: the last restraining influence on Japan's hard-line militarists had been removed and the pace of events would now be dictated solely by military necessity.[17]

There was no further mention of the November 25 deadline for almost three weeks, but when it did reappear in a MAGIC intercept on November 22, two days after Nomura submitted the formal draft of Japan's latest proposal to Secretary Hull, it suddenly appeared to be even more ominous, if that were possible, than it had on November 4: "There are reasons beyond our ability to guess why we wanted to settle Japanese–American relations by the 25th, but if within the next three or four days you can [conclude a treaty with the Americans], we have decided to wait until that date… After that, things are automatically going to happen." Naturally, no one in Washington, including Ambassador Nomura, knew what was meant by that last phrase, but later that same day, as if to underscore its significance, ONI reported that it had lost track of the Imperial Navy's First Air Fleet.[18]

* * *

First Air Fleet, along with the rest of the ships in *Kido Butai*, had gone into radio silence as the Imperial Navy began a deadly earnest game of cat-and-mouse with the United States Navy and the American intelligence services. This was the first part of an elaborate radio deception operation meant to not only deceive the Americans as to the whereabouts of First Air Fleet, but also disguise the even more crucial fact that the Imperial Navy had shifted its basic strategy from the defensive to the offensive. So vital was the element of surprise that, when the attack on Hawaii went in, the Americans must "never see it coming," as it were—the Japanese Navy had for so long embraced the *Kenta Kassai* strategy that its American counterpart had been lulled into a sense of false security, one that must not be disturbed in the slightest.

While the Japanese didn't know for certain that the Americans were routinely tracking the Imperial Navy's capital ships via their radio transmissions, they assumed it was so—it was hardly a difficult feat, after all. What Imperial Naval Intelligence did was create a false pattern of radio "chatter" that appeared to be emanating from the carriers of First Air Fleet, and began slowly superimposing it over the ships' actual communications to make the American radio intercept stations familiar with it. Stations ashore in Sasebo, Yokosuka, and Kure, along with ships anchored at those bases possessing transmitters of similar types and power outputs to those on the carriers, began a game of "pretend," posing as the carriers, whose radios then went off the air; as far as possible, any equipment "glitches" or operator characteristics peculiar to specific ships were duplicated. When radio direction finding equipment in the Philippines and Guam took bearings on these signals, they showed up quite clearly to be originating in the naval bases. Even the brief loss of signals on November 22 was part of the plan, as there had been at least six instances in the previous eight months where Japanese capital ships had "gone silent," so that when their signals were reacquired a few days later, still in Sosebo, Kure, or Yokosuka, the incident seemed part of a routine pattern. Meanwhile, from naval bases all over Japan, the six aircraft carriers, two battleships, three cruisers, nine destroyers, and eight tankers that would form the *Kido Butai* were already converging on the cold, foggy, windswept fleet anchorage at Hitokappu Bay, far from prying eyes and unwanted curiosity.

* * *

On November 26, 1941, Ambassador Nomura arrived at the secretary of state's office in response to a formal request from Hull. This time he was not alone, as with him was Special Envoy Kurusu Saburo, a career diplomat who had previously been Japan's ambassador to Belgium and then Germany, who had arrived in Washington on November 19. Nomura, who was neither young nor healthy, had finally begun to feel the strain of the interminable negotiations, and requested the Foreign Ministry to send an assistant to shoulder some of the work; Tokyo sent out Kurusu. To the Japanese, as long as he was competent and qualified, a diplomat was a diplomat; to Hull, Stimson, and especially Roosevelt, the choice of Kurusu was regarded as tactless. They saw him as "tainted" by having been Japan's representative in Berlin when the Tripartite Pact was signed; the fact that once Tokyo approved the Pact, Kurusu, as ambassador, was obligated to sign it, seemed lost on them. In any event, Kurusu was clearly Nomura's understudy, and the ambassador continued to be Japan's point man in Washington.

The purpose of this meeting with Hull was to receive the United States' formal reply to the proposal offered by Japan six days earlier. There had been a brief flicker of hope in Washington when the November 20 proposal was presented: for the first time in all of the long months of diplomatic fencing, an offer was on the table where both sides were expected to make a concession to the other, a formula which would satisfy the Japanese sense of honor and present the Americans with a *quid pro quo*. It could almost be called, in some ways, a proposal for a truce between

Japan and the United States. Could it be, Roosevelt, Hull, and Stimson wondered, that the militant General Tojo might accomplish what the moderate Prince Konoye was unable to achieve?

It was not to be so, as the Japanese tried to be too clever by half, hoping to steal a march on the Americans, Dutch, and British when the negotiations inevitably collapsed—an eventuality they had not merely anticipated, but on which they actually based their planning. On November 24, ONI learned from their British colleagues that five troop transports, together with a powerful escort of cruisers and destroyers, had left Formosa and were steaming down the South China Sea, on a course directly for the Kra Peninsula. Suddenly, the meaning behind the phrase in Tokyo's November 22 communique to Nomura that "things are automatically going to happen" after November 25 became far less murky. This was no sudden, impromptu expedition: assembling the troops and shipping, then properly loading the transports for an amphibious assault, had required weeks at a minimum, while the sailing orders would have been issued before the Japanese proposal of November 20 was delivered in Washington.

This infuriated Roosevelt, who took it as the final proof that Japan was no longer negotiating in good faith. The consequences were immediate: he instructed Secretary Hull, who had been drafting a moderately favorable response to the Japanese proposal, to instead take a hard line and make no concessions whatsoever. On the question of China, there was to be no backing away from America's original position: the United States would continue to supply the Chinese Nationalists until every last Japanese soldier, sailor, or airman had been withdrawn from China, including Manchuoko; America also required a complete withdrawal of all Japanese forces from the whole of Indochina. Only when those conditions were satisfied would the process of lifting the American embargoes on Japan begin. In short, Roosevelt told Hull to take the negotiations back to square one. This was the essence of what became known as the "Hull Note" of November 26, 1941.

There was no "or else" to be found in the document Hull presented to Nomura, but when it was communicated to Prime Minister Tojo, his reaction was to declare it an ultimatum. While technically it wasn't, and neither Hull nor Roosevelt had ever intended it to be taken as such, the Japanese Government had painted itself into a corner by allowing the militarists to dictate the course of events by setting hard and fast diplomatic deadlines. In one of his more informal moments with Ambassador Nomura, President Roosevelt assured him that "There are no last words between friends." Tokyo had insisted on having the last word, however, so it's hardly surprising that Tojo and his Government saw in Hull's response, in its explicit rejection of the truce implied in Tokyo's November 22 proposal, an ultimatum-like finality, given the events that had already been put into motion, the "things" that were "automatically going to happen." The Malaya invasion force was on its way southward, and though the Americans had no way of knowing this, the *Kido Butai* had departed Hitokappu Bay the same afternoon that the Hull Note was delivered to Ambassador Nomura; no realistic chance of any last-minute diplomatic resolution now remained. The time had come for the last formality to be concluded before the attack on Pearl Harbor could take place—acquiring the emperor's permission.

The day after Secretary Hull gave his note to Ambassador Nomura, Secretary of the Navy Frank Knox and Admiral Stark were ushered into the office of the secretary of war, Henry Stimson. Already present was Brigadier General Leonard Gerow, Chief of the Army War Plans Division. The Army chief of staff, General Marshall, was in South Carolina, watching the large-scale Army maneuvers being conducted there; Gerow was standing in as his deputy. The purpose of the meeting was straightforward: Hull's rejection—at Roosevelt's orders—of Tokyo's last peace proposal, taken together with the November 25 diplomatic deadline previously set by the Japanese, meant that the Army and Navy had to be prepared for whatever it was that was "automatically going to happen." The president had already made it clear that the American government's policy was to let the Japanese commit the first act of aggression, in whatever form it took, if open warfare broke out: for Roosevelt it was a moral imperative that the nation—and the world—clearly see who was the aggressor in that case.

Letting the Japanese have the first shot did not mean, however, that they were to be given the chance to land a sucker-punch. The Army and Navy had to be warned, on the *qui vive*, as it were, so the issue to be settled was to decide exactly what to tell the generals and admirals of the various commands at home and overseas. Gerow presented to Stimson a draft of an alert message he and Marshall had worked out before the chief of staff left for South Carolina; the secretary read it, made a few minor revisions, and then approved it:

> Negotiations with Japan appear to be terminated to all practical purposes with only the barest possibilities that the Japanese Government might come back and offer to continue. Japanese future action unpredictable but hostile action possible at any moment. If hostilities cannot, repeat cannot be avoided the United States desires that Japan commit the first overt act. This policy should not, repeat not, be construed as restricting you to a course of action that might jeopardize your defense. Prior to hostile Japanese action you are directed to undertake such reconnaissance and other measures as you deem necessary but these measures should be carried out so as not, repeat not, to alarm civil population or disclose intent. Report measures taken. Should hostilities occur you will carry out the tasks assigned in Rainbow Five [the Army's basic war plan] so far as they pertain to Japan.[19]

The dispatch was received in Hawaii at 2:30 PM, and within 30 minutes of it being decrypted, General Short had every military post, facility, and building on Oahu, along with critical civilian installations, under heavy guard. Aircraft not designated for patrol and reconnaissance duties were duly parked where they could be best protected, lined up in neat rows on taxiways and hangar aprons—preventing sabotage continued to be a mania with Short.

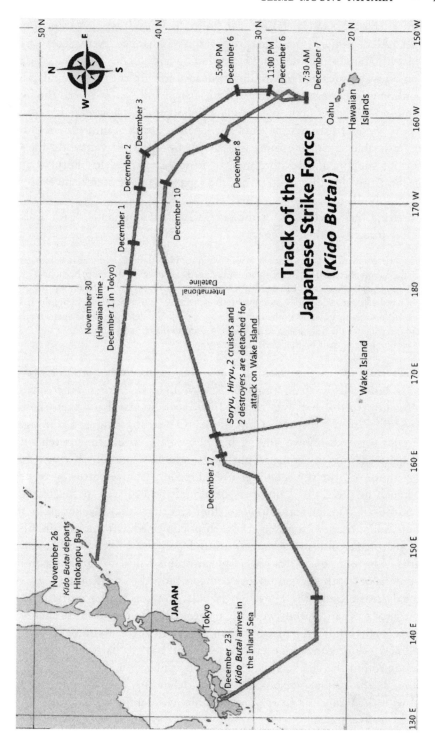

Track of the Japanese Strike Force (Kido Butai)

November 26
Kido Butai departs Hitokappu Bay

JAPAN

Tokyo

December 23
Kido Butai arrives in the Inland Sea

December 17

Soryu, Hiryu, 2 cruisers and 2 destroyers are detached for attack on Wake Island

Wake Island

International Dateline

November 30
(Hawaiian time - December 1 in Tokyo)

December 1

December 2

December 3

December 10

December 8

5:00 PM December 6

11:00 PM December 6

7:30 AM December 7

Oahu

Hawaiian Islands

The General deliberately chose not to go to the full status of what he deemed a Number 3 Alert—where every defensive position was manned, every piece of artillery readied with ammunition standing by, including anti-aircraft guns, and the entire garrison on Oahu prepared for an imminent invasion. To the literal-minded Short, the wording of the message concocted by Marshall and Gerow placed the likeliest flash points 3,000 miles to the west of Hawaii: it logically followed, to him, that the Philippines would be the first target of any Japanese attack against American forces. It was reasonable, then, to assume that the Army would first draw on the Oahu garrison for support and reinforcements—it never occurred to Short, or anyone else in the Army, for that matter, that the Japanese might attack the Philippines and Hawaii both.

In drafting their own alert for the Navy's Pacific Commands, Knox and Stark were more forceful in their language:

> This despatch is to be considered a war warning. Negotiations with Japan looking toward stabilization of conditions in the Pacific have ceased and an aggressive move by Japan is expected within the next few days. The number and equipment of Japanese troops and the organization of naval task forces indicates an amphibious expedition against either the Philippines, Thai or Kra Peninsula or possibly Borneo. Execute an appropriate defensive deployment preparatory to carrying out the tasks assigned in WPL-46. Inform district and Army authorities. A similar warning is being sent by the War Department.[20]

Kimmel's reaction to the warning from Washington was considerably more vigorous and realistic than was Short's, although, in fairness, there was also more for him to do than was required of Short. It may have been the words "war warning" in the dispatch from the CNO—strong language coming from Stark, who was well-known among his fellow flag officers for his tendency to avoid aggressive or antagonistic phrasing—which suggested this was not yet another shout of "The sky is falling!" Aerial reconnaissance patrols were stepped up as much as the limited numbers of aircraft and aircrew permitted; orders went out to all ships at sea to look to their security: strict blackouts, increased lookouts, aerial reconnaissance by those ships equipped with spotter aircraft. The antisubmarine patrols, surface and air, around Oahu were likewise told to be more vigilant. More ominously, they were given orders—not just authorization—to drop bombs or depth charges on any contacts judged to be hostile in any of the restricted areas around the Hawaiian Islands: contacts in the restricted area at the entrance to Pearl Harbor were to be automatically regarded as "enemy" and treated as such. Ships in the harbor were to remain at the "Number 3 condition of readiness"—one gun from each of a ship's anti-aircraft batteries to be manned and ready round the clock. This last was something of a "belt and suspenders" measure, as the primary responsibility for defending Pearl from aerial attack rested with the Army Air Corps, but Kimmel was taking no chances. The fleet in Pearl was irreplaceable.

* * *

As alerts and war warnings flashed outward from Washington DC, the ships of *Kido Butai* labored eastward across the North Pacific. Despite the ocean's name, its northern waters were rarely all that peaceful, and the Japanese fleet struggled against heavy seas, high winds, and near-blinding sleet and rain. Working under strict radio silence since before their arrival at Hitokappu Bay, the ships of the strike force communicated by signal lamp and very low-powered radios with ranges limited to a few miles. Regardless of whatever misgivings he might have had about the Hawaii Operation—now known as "Operation Z" in honor of the Battle of Tsushima, which 36 years earlier had also decided the fate of the Empire—Admiral Nagumo had to feel a deep pride in the professionalism of his ships' officers and crews. None had fallen behind, or wandered off course and become lost, and if the strike force had to be reassembled each morning as the ships had drifted apart in the nighttime to avoid collisions, that was to be expected, and it did no harm to the fleet's progress.

Yamamoto had won his fight to have all six of First Air Fleet's aircraft carriers, *Kaga*, *Akagi*, *Soryu*, *Hiryu*, *Shokaku*, and *Zuikaku*, included in *Kido Butai*. With them went the battleships *Hiei* and *Kirishima*, as fast and powerful as any battleships in the US Navy's Atlantic or Pacific Fleets, but seemingly out of place in company with the carriers. Yet there was a method to this apparent idiosyncrasy: the battleships were there to protect the aircraft carriers should the strike force be intercepted by an American task force, an insurance policy of sorts against an encounter on the high seas with the very American battlewagons the carriers would be attacking—and hopefully sinking—at Pearl Harbor. The Japanese carriers could hold their own against their American counterparts, no one in the Imperial Navy doubted that, but Yamamoto felt it necessary to include a pair of battleships in *Kido Butai* in a tacit admission of a blunt but unspoken truth in First Air Fleet. Despite the success of the Royal Navy's Fleet Air Arm against the Italians in the Mediterranean, and the unexpectedly decisive role some of those same aircraft had played in the destruction of the German battleship *Bismarck* in late May 1941, when *Kido Butai* sortied from Hitokappu Bay a year after Taranto, no battleship underway in open water had yet been sunk by naval aircraft; that it could be done was still an unproven concept.

Taranto had demonstrated that battleships taken by surprise and caught at their moorings were cripplingly vulnerable to aerial attack; the *Bismarck* episode had shown that, with extraordinary luck and the right circumstances, aircraft could cripple a capital ship under way. But however he might welcome whatever good fortune came his way, no admiral worth his shoulder boards ever counted on luck to deliver the enemy into his hands. Gambler though he was, Yamamoto knew well the difference between a calculated risk and sheer foolhardiness. Hence, when

Kido Butai sortied, two battleships went with it—and with the battleships went a battleship admiral, Nagumo. *Hiei* and *Kirishima* were the two finest battleships in the Imperial Navy at the time, yet they were there to be sacrificed if need be, should *Kido Butai* encounter a force of American battleships. They would be expected to act as a screen, drawing the enemy's fire, allowing the carriers to use their superior speed to race out of gunnery range before launching air strikes. This was a duty which Yamamoto knew Nagumo could carry out with skill, and would do so regardless of any personal consequences.

* * *

War with the United States became a certainty for the Japanese Empire on December 1, 1941. That day, at the Imperial Palace in Tokyo, an Imperial Conference was held to make official the decision to carry out the attack on Pearl Harbor. As he had at all but two of these conferences, the Emperor spoke not a word—his silence was a tradition, his will being ascertained long in advance, so that the carefully scripted and rehearsed dialogue between the other participants could flow uninterrupted. Tojo, who presided, went through the motions of explaining the purpose of the conference, then the foreign minister, the minister of war, and the navy minister, along with the chiefs of staff of both services, presented their views on the issue at hand—the question of war with the United States, Great Britain, and the Netherlands. Nothing that was said—or left unsaid—could have changed the preordained outcome: all present voted for war. The Emperor nodded his consent and it was done.

Just after midnight, a special message was picked up by *Kido Butai*'s flagship, *Akagi*: "This dispatch is top secret. This order is effective 1760 on 2 December Combined Fleet Serial 10. Climb Mount Niitaka 1208 repeat 1208."[21]

"Climb Mount Niitaka" was the code phrase instructing Nagumo to carry out the Hawaii Operation. "1208" was December 8 in Tokyo—in Hawaii it would be December 7. The order to attack Pearl Harbor had been given.

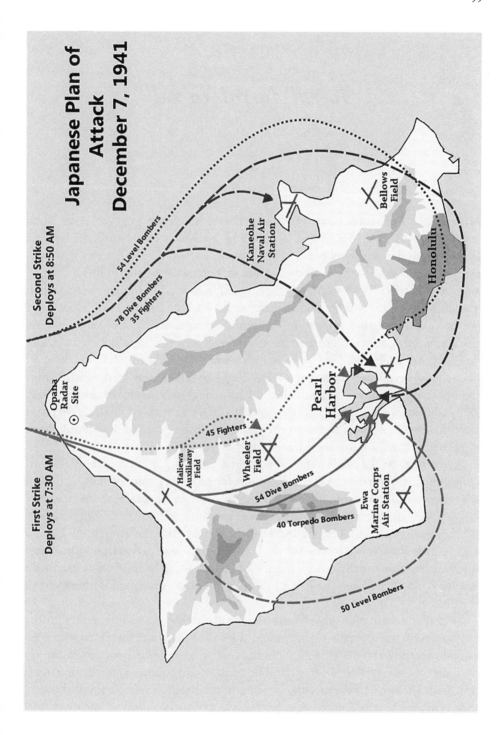

Japanese Plan of Attack December 7, 1941

Second Strike Deploys at 8:50 AM

First Strike Deploys at 7:30 AM

54 Level Bombers

78 Dive Bombers 35 Fighters

Opana Radar Site

45 Fighters

Haliewa Auxiliaray Field

Wheeler Field

54 Dive Bombers

40 Torpedo Bombers

Ewa Marine Corps Air Station

50 Level Bombers

Pearl Harbor

Kaneohe Naval Air Station

Bellows Field

Honolulu

CHAPTER 6

"To-ra! To-ra! To-ra!"

After six days of storm-force winds and heavy, pounding seas, the *Kido Butai* welcomed the strong breezes and long rolling swells that came when the weather eased a bit in the very early hours of December 7. There were still waves that from time to time washed over the bows of the carriers, and the big ships pitched up and down as much as 15 degrees as they passed from crest to trough to crest again. Visibility was 12 miles at best, and the ceiling, that is, the bottom of the cloud layer overhead, was perhaps 5,000 feet. This worried Nagumo's chief of staff, Admiral Kusaka: in his opinion, these were marginal conditions for aircraft operations, and he feared losing pilots and planes to accidents when the strike force began taking off from the carriers. But worrying was all he could do—there was no time to wait for the sea conditions to moderate further, the strike had to be launched this morning. Every additional day, every additional hour, that *Kido Butai* spent this far from Japan and this close to Hawaii increased the chance that the Americans would discover the fleet. So Kusaka fretted and hoped for the best.

Some men, on the other hand, were feeling more and more confident as dawn approached. Commander Ohashi Kyozo, Admiral Hara's chief of staff, had been listening to KGMB throughout the night in *Shokaku*'s operations room; as the hours passed and there were neither changes nor interruptions in the ongoing flow of Hawaiian music, he became increasingly certain that the Americans had no idea of *Kido Butai*'s location nor of the coming attack on Pearl Harbor. On *Akagi*, Admiral Nagumo's intelligence officer, Commander Ono Kanjiro, was keeping a similar vigil: he too was convinced that the Americans suspected nothing out of the ordinary.

Sometime before 5:00 AM, Commander Fuchida awoke, having slept with the assurance of a man literally on a mission; the rest of the strike force's aviators were roused promptly at 5:00, though more than a few had already been awake and up for some time—each man dealt with his pre-mission anxieties and anticipation in his own way. The deck crews, mechanics, and aircraft handlers had been called out of their bunks an hour earlier to begin final checks and preparations on the more than

400 planes that would be launched this morning. As if in some well-choreographed dance, engines were spun up and final adjustments made, bomb- and torpedo-release mechanisms were cycled and checked to make sure they functioned smoothly, fuel was topped off and ammunition loaded; the flight decks were walked from bow to stern to make certain they were clear of obstructions and debris, the aircraft brought up from the hangar decks and "spotted" at the stern of each carrier according to the assigned sequence for takeoff.

Munitions handlers brought bombs and torpedoes up from the magazines, dollied them to the waiting bombers, dive bombers, and torpedo planes and hoisted them into place, while armorers then methodically worked their way through the ranks of aircraft, carefully installing fuzes on the torpedoes and bombs. Each armorer and his assistant were like small islands of calm in the controlled frenzy of activity on the carriers' hangar decks. First the armorer would use a special wrench to remove the plug where the fuze would be inserted into the bomb or torpedo. He would then hand the wrench to his assistant, who in turn would hand him a fuze. The armorer would slide the fuze into place, then hold out his hand for the special wrench, with which he would tighten down the fuze. No one *ever* dared disturb an armorer or his assistant while they were performing this task—the consequences of a slip of the wrench or a joggled elbow or a hand twitching from surprise could be catastrophic. Once the armorers were finished, the aircraft handlers began moving the planes onto the elevators which brought them up to the flight decks.

The aircrews, showered and dressed in fresh underwear and clean uniforms, made their way to the Shinto shrines that were carried by all ships of the Imperial Navy. There, after tossing back a ceremonial cup of *sake*, a pilot, navigator, or radio operator-gunner would stand before the shrine, clap his hands once to be certain that the *kami* (spirit) who inhabited the shrine was paying attention, and offer up a prayer for the mission's success. The airmen then went to breakfast, where the carriers' cooks had prepared a surprise for them: *sekihan*, a dish of *mochi* rice and red *azuki* beans, traditionally reserved for particularly auspicious occasions—the red color of the beans was considered an omen of good luck.

In *Akagi*'s officers' mess, Fuchida joined Lieutenant Murata Shigeharu, finding the young pilot in a particularly good humor, and was greeted with the words, "Good morning, Commander! Honolulu sleeps!"

"How do you know?"

"The Honolulu radio plays soft music. Everything is fine." Murata, like Commander Ohashi, was convinced this continued display of peacetime normality could only mean that the Americans suspected nothing.[1]

After finishing off his breakfast, Fuchida had to tend to one last formality— receiving official permission from the *Kido Butai*'s commanding officer to carry out the attack. He found Admiral Nagumo seated at a table in *Akagi*'s operations room; saluting, Fuchida said without preamble, "I am ready for the mission."

"I have every confidence in you," Nagumo replied, rising to give Fuchida a firm handshake.[2]

Final mission briefings for the airmen came next: course, airspeed, altitude, and formation details were confirmed, along with the meteorologists' predictions as to the weather conditions over the targets. Also included was the latest intelligence from Honolulu, forwarded by Combined Fleet, courtesy of Ensign Yoshikawa.

> Vessels now at anchor in Pearl Harbor consist of eight battleships and two heavy cruisers. No balloons, no torpedo-defense nets deployed around battleships. No indications observed from enemy radio activity that ocean patrol flights are being made in Hawaiian area. *Lexington* left harbor yesterday [December 5] and recovered planes. *Enterprise* is also thought to be operating at sea with her planes on board.[3]

Yoshikawa had been quite positive in reporting that the ships in Pearl Harbor would be at the "Number 3 condition of readiness," which required only one gun from each of a ship's anti-aircraft batteries be manned and ready—for many ships, this meant only a single gun. It was not an unrealistic precaution, however: once the fleet was in harbor, the primary responsibility for its air defense fell on the Army Air Corps. That was why the Army had nearly 400 aircraft, half of them fighters, stationed in Hawaii.

The absence of any of the American carriers was disappointing, of course, but that did nothing to alter the mission: the strike on Pearl Harbor would go forward, part of Japan's great strategic plan for simultaneous attacks, advances, and offensives in the Pacific, Southeast Asia, and China—part of a larger war that Japan was already fighting. Finally, an imperial rescript was read out to the crews of all the ships of *Kido Butai*. The Emperor declared that, "The responsibility assigned to the Combined Fleet is so grave that the rise and fall of the Empire rests on what it is going to accomplish." Hirohito assured the sailors and airmen that he was confident of the fleet's success, "thus destroying the enemy and demonstrating its brilliant deed throughout the world."[4]

Dawn was still an hour away when the aircrew were dismissed to man their planes. Admiral Nagumo, having offered one last word of encouragement to his pilots, was on his way to *Akagi's* flag bridge when he encountered Commander Genda. For a moment the older man said nothing, perhaps contemplating how events were about to pass beyond both his control and his experience. Finally, he murmured, "I have brought the First Air Fleet successfully to the point of attack. From now on, the burden is on your shoulders and the rest of the flying group."

"Admiral, I am sure the airmen will succeed," Genda responded.[5]

On the flight decks the engines of the waiting aircraft were restarted and the airmen clambered aboard. Commander Fuchida had just stepped up onto the wing of the Kate bomber in which he would be flying when his crew chief ran up and held out a *hashimaki*, the traditional Japanese warrior's headband, saying, "This is a present from the maintenance crews. May I ask that you take it to Pearl Harbor?" Deeply honored by the gesture, Fuchida bowed to the man, then proudly donned the headband before climbing into the cockpit.[6]

At 5:50 the fleet altered course 90 degrees to port, bringing the ships' bows into the wind, and increased speed to 24 knots. A string of signal flags appeared at *Akagi*'s masthead, instructing the carriers to prepare to launch aircraft; above them all flew the four-color "Z" flag that flew from Admiral Togo's flagship *Mikasa* at the Battle of Tsushima. By tradition, the Z flag meant, "The fate of the Empire rests on the outcome of this battle. Let each man do his utmost." It was the most powerful exhortation to victory in the whole of the Imperial Navy's lexicon. As the flag was hoisted, the plane handlers, mechanics, and armorers, along with whatever crewmen could break away from their duties to watch the air strike take off, broke into repeated cheers of "*Banzai!*". At 6:00 AM the flags were lowered, meaning "Execute the command," and on the foredeck of each carrier an air operations officer swung a green lantern back and forth.

Now all eyes were on *Akagi*'s flight deck. The first group of aircraft to take off would be her fighters, led by Lieutenant Commander Itaya Shigeru. Seeing the green light waving, Itaya carefully timed the rise and fall of the pitching deck, pushed his throttle forward, the plane handlers pulled the chocks away from the wheels of his pale gray-painted Zero, and the fighter surged forward. The flight deck was crowded, giving Itaya only a short run to get airborne. His plane dipped low as it rolled off the bow and anxious crewmen on *Akagi* held their collective breath, anticipating the worst, but seconds later Itaya was soaring upward, and the next fighter began its takeoff run.

Zeroes were taking off now from all the carriers, and once the last of them was airborne, on *Akagi*, *Kaga*, *Soryu*, and *Hiryu* the Kates fitted out as high-level bombers were the next to take off. This included the aircraft in which Fuchida was flying, piloted by Lieutenant Mutsuzaki Mitsuo; once airborne, Fuchida's Kate took the lead position in the growing formation. They were followed by the torpedo-armed Kates, which because of the weight of the torpedoes, required the longest takeoff runs. *Shokaku* and *Zuikaku* would send up Val dive bombers instead of Kates. Two aircraft, a Val from *Zuikaku* and a Zero from *Soryu*, had to abort with engine problems, but less than 20 minutes from the moment that the "execute" signal had been given, a total of 183 of the 185 bombers, torpedo bombers, and fighters of the first wave of the attack specified by Genda's plan circled above *Kido Butai* then turned southward and vanished in the pre-dawn twilight.

The rapid, flawless launch of so many aircraft had been an incredible sight, such that no one had ever before witnessed, and it was a soul-stirring experience. Otherwise staid and dignified officers cheered and capered like schoolboys, the crewmen shouted themselves hoarse; Commander Tsukamoto Hoichiro, *Shokaku*'s navigation officer, would remember this morning as the greatest day of his life. Even

Admiral Nagumo appeared satisfied, although he was so stoic, even by Japanese customs, that it was hard to tell for certain. Admiral Kusaka, on the other hand, felt such a relief that there hadn't been a single plane lost during takeoff, despite the sea conditions, that he trembled like a leaf as the built-up tension left his body. Embarrassed at what he regarded as a lack of self-control, he slumped down in a chair on *Akagi*'s bridge (some would later say the deck), Buddha-like and began to meditate.

Even before the last plane of the strike force was out of sight, *Kido Butai* was turning back to the south: there was a second wave of aircraft to be armed in the carriers' hangers and then positioned on the carriers' flight decks and there was no time to waste in doing so. Resuming a southerly course put the seas on the ships' port beam, changing the pitching motion into a roll—still somewhat uncomfortable but it made moving the aircraft about considerably easier. The plane handlers and armorers set to with a will, and by 7:00 AM the second wave was ready. At 7:05 the carriers and their escorts once again turned eastward, into the wind, and began launching aircraft.

As the strike force formed up behind him, Commander Fuchida told his pilot, Lieutenant Mutsuzaki, to begin climbing to an altitude of 3,000 meters—slightly less than 10,000 feet. As his Kate ascended, Fuchida concentrated on his navigation. For the time being it was enough for Mutsuzaki to maintain a heading of 180E—due south; he would need to be more precise only as they drew nearer to Oahu. Now came the hard part—the waiting: Pearl Harbor was the better part of two hours' flying time distant, and there was nothing for Fuchida to do until the island of Oahu came into sight. For the moment he was little more than Lieutenant Mutsuzaki's passenger.

It was probably best for Fuchida's peace of mind that he knew nothing of an incident that had occurred while he was still asleep in his bunk aboard *Akagi*. In Washington DC a string of intercepted diplomatic messages were being decoded that, despite the remarkably successful efforts by the Imperial Navy to keep the Foreign Ministry in the dark about the attack on Pearl Harbor, could compromise the secrecy of Operation Z. If the Americans put the pieces together properly, those messages would give the defenders in Hawaii a window of opportunity to be ready and waiting for the Japanese attack.

* * *

At 20 minutes to midnight—2:40 AM in Washington—Station S on Bainbridge Island intercepted the final part of Signal Number 902, a 14-part message sent to the Japanese Embassy in Washington. Like the other 13 parts, the text was in English, and the contents of the message were quickly forwarded by teletype to Naval Intelligence. The language in the concluding part was uncharacteristically blunt for the Japanese, fond as they usually were of circumlocution and indirection.

Obviously it is the intention of the American Government to conspire with Great Britain and other countries to obstruct Japan's efforts toward the establishment of peace through the creation of a New Order in East Asia, and especially to preserve Anglo-American rights and interests by keeping Japan and China at war. This intention has been revealed clearly during the course of the present negotiations.

Thus, the earnest hope of the Japanese Government to adjust Japanese–American relations and to preserve and promote the peace of the Pacific through cooperation with the American Government has finally been lost.

The Japanese Government regrets to have to notify hereby the American Government that in view of the attitude of the American Government it cannot but consider that it is impossible to reach an agreement through further negotiations.[7]

Over the course of the next hour, Part Fourteen was followed by four more messages to the embassy, all of which were forwarded to Washington. Unlike the text of the 14-part message, which had been transmitted in English, these new messages reverted to Japanese, which required translation after being deciphered. Two of them were simple expressions of gratitude to Nomura and his staff for their work, along with regrets that the negotiations had been unsuccessful, but Number 907 had specific instructions for Ambassador Nomura: "Will the Ambassador please submit to the United States Government (if possible to the Secretary of State) our reply to the United States at 1:00 p. m. on the 7th, your time." Number 910 was even more intriguing: "After deciphering part 14 of my #902 and also #907, #908 and #909, please destroy at once the remaining cipher machine and all machine codes. Dispose in like manner also secret documents."

All 14 parts of Number 902 were decoded and waiting on his desk when Lieutenant Commander Kramer arrived at his office at 7:30 AM in Washington. Numbers 907 and 910 were still being translated—it would be 9:00 AM before they were complete—so he was unaware of their contents when he set out to distribute copies of the 14-part message to Admiral Stark, the White House, and the State Department, where he also met Secretary Knox and handed him a copy of the message.

Stark, after reading the message Kramer delivered, called Commander McCollum and Captain Wilkinson into his office, where the three men tried to gain an insight on what might be the meaning, implications, and possible consequences of the message. It was suggested at the time—and later, as well—that the note was simply a termination of negotiations between Japan and the United States, but McCollum, with his deeper knowledge of Japanese culture, immediately saw that it went further than that. Now that he had the last part of the message in his hands, the rest of the document at last made sense to him, and he drew Stark's attention to "the virulence and tenor of the language." He understood the sense of insult the Japanese felt at the repeated rejection of what they saw as reasonable compromises: having decided that diplomacy was now useless, they would seek other means of resolving the differences between the Empire and the United States. Faced with a choice between a shameful capitulation and war, they felt they had only one choice. Either Wilkinson or McCollum, later no one could remember which, put into words what all three men were thinking: the final paragraph of the note "was enough to indicate that we could expect war." Yet, whomever it was who uttered those words failed to press his case vigorously enough to Stark. Wilkinson suggested that a warning be sent to Pearl Harbor, but Stark, for reasons he never explained, hesitated. In the end, nothing was done, at least for the moment.[8]

Colonel Bratton, who arrived at his office at about the same time Kramer was leaving his, was handed the translations of Part Fourteen, as well as Numbers 907 and 910 at about 9:00 AM. Number 907, the instruction to Ambassador Nomura to deliver the complete message at 1:00 PM Washington time, "stunned me into frenzied activity because of its implications," Bratton later recalled. It was immediately clear to him that this was not mere capriciousness: the delivery of the note at a specific time on a specific day could only mean that it was tied to other events—the November 22 message from Foreign Minister Togo to Nomura declaring that if negotiations were not successful, "things are automatically going to happen" suddenly took on a far graver and more immediate significance.

Adding to Bratton's almost instant certainty that the Japanese were going to attack an American military or naval base at or shortly after 1:00 PM was Signal Number 910. The destruction of code books, cipher machines, and classified documents was standard operating procedure for the embassy and consulates of any nation about to go to war. Such actions would serve no purpose if the Japanese were to continue to look to diplomacy for a resolution of their disputes with the Americans, but clearly they had decided that the time for diplomacy was past, which left only one alternative.

Bratton wasted no time in trying to contact the Army chief of staff, General George C. Marshall, along with the assistant chief of staff for war plans, Brigadier General Leonard Gerow, and Brigadier General Sherman Miles, the assistant chief of staff for intelligence. An orderly at Marshall's quarters at Fort Myer informed Bratton that Marshall was out horseback riding, as was his habit on Sunday mornings. The colonel told the orderly that it was vital that General Marshall call him as soon as he returned, trying to impart to the man a sense of the urgency he felt. Apparently the orderly was either unimaginative or unimpressed, as it was 10:30 before Marshall returned Bratton's call.

Gerow couldn't be located at all, but when Bratton called Miles and explained in a general way that a very urgent situation had developed—he couldn't be specific, as, for security reasons, he refused to discuss MAGIC intelligence over an open telephone line—Miles agreed to come into his office immediately. Once there, he read the 14-part message, along with Numbers 907 and 910, and agreed with Bratton, first that "war is likely because of the language used by the Japanese," and second, that "something is going to happen coincident with 1 o'clock Washington time." At 10:30 General Marshall finally called Bratton, and after hearing much the same general expression of urgency that Bratton had offered Miles, he informed them that he was coming to the War Department to discuss the situation in person. Now all Bratton and Miles could do was wait.[9]

By now Commander Kramer had his own copies of Numbers 907 and 910, and like Bratton, realized that something was very much out of the ordinary, although he did not immediately leap to the same conclusions as his Army counterpart. Still, that 1:00 PM delivery time for the message struck a jarring note. Whenever a signal was intercepted that contained a specific time in the text, Naval Intelligence routinely converted it to local time for Washington, the West Coast, Honolulu, Manila, and Tokyo—Tokyo because no matter where they were, ships of the Imperial Navy conducted operations in accordance with Tokyo time. Now Kramer performed that conversion for 1:00 PM Washington time: it would be 10:00 AM on the West Coast; 7:30 AM in Honolulu (in 1910, Hawaii's time zone had been set at five and one-half hours behind the Eastern Zone, and remained that way until 1947); 2:00 AM December 8 in Manila; and 3:00 AM December 8 in Tokyo. The reason for this little exercise was to determine if there was a military significance to any time cited in a message—sunrise, for example, which was an optimum time for launching attacks.

Then Kramer remembered the report of Japanese troop transports moving down the coast of French Indochina, Malaysia almost certainly being their destination. The 1:00 PM deadline in Washington would be 2:00 AM in Malaysia on December 8; the moon would be three-quarters full, sunrise would be around 6:30—nearly ideal conditions for a surprise amphibious operation. The same would apply to Manila if the Japanese were contemplating moving into the Philippines. That loomed larger in Kramer's thinking than 7:30 in Honolulu, even though early Sunday morning would be the time the officers and crews of the ships in Pearl Harbor were likely to be at their least vigilant.

Whatever was going to happen, wherever it happened, Kramer couldn't prevent it, the best he could do was provide warnings. When he delivered copies of the new decryptions to Admiral Stark's office, he was met by Commander McCollum, and made a point of drawing McCollum's attention to the delivery time of the diplomatic note specified in Number 907. McCollum in turn made the same point to Stark—Kramer was now on his way to the State Department, and from there to the White House again—pointing out that "if an attack was coming, it looked like…it was timed for operations in the Far East and possibly Hawaii." The last was clearly an afterthought, and neither McCollum nor Stark pursued the idea that Pearl Harbor might be the target. Strangely, Stark never seemed to grasp the full significance of the instruction to the Japanese Embassy staff to burn their secret papers and codes.

This was the moment that the harsh, unforgiving light of reality revealed the great flaw of Harold Stark's character: he was a man unaccustomed to command unexpectedly thrust into a command role. The *compleat* peacetime admiral—part consummate uniformed bureaucrat, part charming diplomat—in his experience as chief of naval operations when working with Congress as well as his subordinates he had learned to command by consensus rather than imperative, to use the prestige but not the power of his position. An excellent manager yet not truly a leader, he was too wont to hesitate and hedge when faced with the need to make a consequential decision—which is where he found himself now.

Stark hesitated, faced with having to choose whether to act or not act on what was little more than the shared hunch of Wilkinson and McCollum: whether or not to issue alert orders for both the Pacific Fleet and the Asiatic Fleet and accept the risks—except that for Betty Stark the risks of being right never seemed as great as the risks of being wrong. He'd put every ship and naval base from the West Coast to the Philippines on alert on November 24, then followed it up with the "war warning" sent out on November 27, yet in the end the anticipated crisis had been a damp squib. There were only so many times, he was sure, he could cry "Wolf!" before his fleet commanders began to mistrust his judgement, and Harold Stark would not be known as an admiral who jumped at shadows and twitched at loud noises.

No one would or could ever suggest that General George Marshall was indecisive, but the aura of Olympian detachment that he habitually radiated was often both intimidating and maddening, to which Brigadier General Miles and Colonel Bratton could testify as fact this morning. Marshall arrived at the War Department at 11:25 AM, a full 75 minutes after his telephone conversation with Bratton. When the two officers entered Marshall's office, the chief of staff was reading the entire text of the 14-part message and declined to be interrupted; despite Bratton and Miles' efforts to bring messages 907 and 910 to his attention, he wouldn't look at them until he had finished all 14 parts of the diplomatic note. However, once he did read 907 and 910, there was no need to prod him into action. He agreed with Miles and Bratton that a specified delivery time for the diplomatic note was definitely significant, and asked the two officers for their thoughts as to what that significance might be. Bratton and Miles made it clear that they were in agreement: they were convinced that "it meant Japanese hostile action against some American installation in the Pacific at or shortly after 1 o'clock that afternoon." General Gerow, accompanied by Colonel Charles Bundy, Chief of the War Plans Group, walked in as Miles and Bratton were making their case, and when they finished Gerow told Marshall that he was in complete agreement with them.[10]

So far the Americans had put together the pieces correctly, but now came the real challenge—deducing the target. There was nothing in any of the PURPLE traffic that ever gave a hint of where the Japanese might strike first, so who to alert? The Philippines seemed to be the most vulnerable: they were less than 300 miles from Formosa, already within range of Japanese bombers, and there was no reason why the troop transports last seen off the coast of Indochina that everyone had assumed were headed southwest toward Malaysia could not have suddenly turned east instead—at their last reported position those transports were actually closer to Manila than they were to Kota Bharu, which ONI had presumed was their objective. Given the operational challenges created by the distances involved, some sort of attack on the Panama Canal Zone, the West Coast, or Pearl Harbor was much less likely—but not impossible. It was General Miles who proposed the simplest, most obvious, and most effective solution: warn them all simultaneously.

Marshall considered that for a moment, then reached for the telephone and called Admiral Stark: using the same sort of roundabout manner that Bratton had employed when with him earlier that morning, Marshall was able to impart to Stark what were his intentions. Stark demurred, telling Marshall that "we've sent them [the Pacific commands] so much already"—meaning warnings of possible hostile action by the Japanese—that he was reluctant to send another. Marshall, showing no outward reaction to Stark's hesitance, ended the call. A few moments later, the General's telephone rang—it was Stark. He'd suddenly concluded "that there might be something peculiar in the Japanese Ambassador calling on Mr. Hull at 1 P.M." and that he concurred with Marshall's decision, asking if the chief of staff would tell his overseas commanders to pass the warning to their Navy counterparts. Marshall agreed, hung up, pulled a blank sheet of paper in front of him and began writing out the warning message in longhand.[11]

> The Japanese are presenting at 1 P.M. Eastern Standard Time, today, what amounts to an ultimatum. Also they are under orders to destroy their code machine immediately. Just what significance the hour set may have we do not know, but be on alert accordingly. Inform naval authorities of this communication. Marshall.[12]

Marshall handed the paper to Bratton, telling him to take it to the War Department's Signal Center next door and have it sent "at once by the fastest safe means." As Bratton was on his way out the door General Gerow called out, "If there is any question of priority, give the Philippines first priority." The time was 11:55 AM—6:25 in Pearl Harbor.

In the Signal Center Bratton encountered Lieutenant Colonel Edward French, the officer in charge. Handing French the handwritten message, he blurted out "The Chief of Staff wants this sent at once by the fastest safe means!" French took one look at Marshall's scrawling handwriting and asked, "Will you help me get this into readable script? Neither I nor my clerk here can read General Marshall's handwriting." Bratton read it out to the clerk, who typed up a fair copy, which Bratton then approved, leaving the enciphering and transmission to French.

Returning to Marshall's office, Bratton was asked by the chief of staff how long it would take for the message to be delivered to four Pacific commands. Bratton doubled back to the Signals Center, then came back to Marshall with the answer: it would take about three minutes to encode the message, eight to transmit it, and the recipients would have it in their hands in twenty. That seemed to satisfy Marshall, but what Bratton did not tell him was that the signal would still require decoding after being received. It would be very close to the 1:00 PM deadline by the time the message was actually read by the commanding officers in the Philippines, the Canal Zone, the West Coast, or Pearl Harbor.

Now the fortunes of war—or soon-to-be war—turned on the United States Army and Navy. The transmission to the Caribbean Defense Command, which was responsible for the Panama Canal Zone, was made flawlessly, as was the one to Manila. But poor atmospheric conditions made reception at the Presidio in San Francisco sketchy at best, and it was impossible to get through to Hawaii for the same reason. It might have been possible for the Navy's more powerful transmitters to break through the scatter and static, but whether because of professional rivalry—why should the Navy succeed where the Army couldn't?—or simply because it never occurred to him, French didn't ask his naval counterpart for assistance. Instead he chose to send Marshall's alert by Western Union to San Francisco, where RCA, who had transmitters four times as powerful as the War Department had in Washington, would complete the transmission as a radiogram. They would blast through the interference by sheer brute force. The message would reach the RCA office in Honolulu at 7:33 AM Hawaiian time.

* * *

In the Japanese Embassy, a little more than a mile from where General Marshall and his officers were sending out warnings in reaction to the 14-part note and its follow-on messages, a harried Okumura Katsuzo was laboriously pecking away at his typewriter to produce a serviceable copy of that note for presentation to Secretary of State Hull at 1:00 PM. The language was not the problem—the text of the note had been transmitted in English to be certain that it said precisely what the Foreign Ministry wished it to say, rather than rely on possible mistranslations in Washington—and Okumura himself was quite fluent in English. (He would later become Emperor Hirohito's personal translator.) The obstacle was Okamura's lack of typing skills: he was barely passed what the Americans called "the hunt and peck" level of competence.

Ambassador Nomura, ever the optimist, telephoned the State Department to request a meeting at 1:00 PM with Secretary Hull. On the Sundays when he went into his office, Hull usually left for the day at noon, but today he agreed to linger a bit longer. He knew why Nomura wished to see him, of course, and had already read the Japanese response to the November 26 proposals, but to protect MAGIC, he had to play out the charade and pretend he had no foreknowledge of the note's contents. Nomura, having no idea that his own government was using him as a patsy, was pleased to find Hull willing to be so accommodating. Now, if only Okumura could finish the typing in time.

The willy-nilly way the 14 parts of the message had been transmitted only compounded Okumura's difficulties: sent out of sequence and at irregular intervals—sometimes with hours between transmissions—the process of deciphering the various parts, assembling them into their proper order, and confirming that the message was indeed complete and correct had consumed valuable time. Had the parts of the message been sent in order, Okumura could have begun typing up the copy for Secretary Hull as soon as Part One had been processed. As it was, he hadn't been able to begin until he had the complete text in his hands. It was becoming increasingly unlikely that he would be finished in time for the note to be delivered at 1:00 PM.

These were merely technicalities, however: the root of Okumura's problems lay in Tokyo, where the Foreign Ministry had been as clumsy in playing its part in Operation Z as the Imperial Navy had been elegant—and for this clumsiness the navy had to bear the lion's share of the blame. Determined to keep the veil of secrecy wrapped around the Pearl Harbor mission, the navy had refused to inform the Foreign Ministry that such an attack was being planned, let alone about to be carried out. Foreign Minister Togo might use phrases such as "things are automatically going to happen" when communicating with Ambassador Nomura, but even Togo didn't know what any of those "things" were. Consequently, he couldn't communicate to Nomura how necessary, how urgent, it was that the 1:00 PM delivery time for the message over which Okumura was laboring be met, that it was, for the Imperial Government, an absolutely inflexible deadline. The relationship between the civilian and military components of the government had deteriorated so badly that professional naval officers refused to trust their equally professional diplomatic colleagues: convinced as they were of the depth, strength, and superiority of their own patriotism, they could not recognize, let alone acknowledge, that it could be matched by anyone not wearing a uniform. It was an attitude that created the present crisis, would cause this day to be remembered as one that would "live in infamy," and ultimately cost Japan dearly in blood and treasure.

* * *

The USS *Ward* wasn't quite ready to be called "elderly," but she was far from a young ship. Built and commissioned in 1918, she was one of hundreds of "flush deck and four pipe" destroyers built by the US Navy during the Great War, and her initial service life had been brief, spending just three years in commission before being laid up in reserve in 1921. Twenty years later, she was back in harness, reactivated and recommissioned, as part of the navy's emergency expansion to meet the growing threat to American maritime interests in the wake of Nazi Germany's victories in western Europe. Armed with a quartet of 4-inch guns, 12 torpedo tubes, and a pair of depth charge racks at her stern, she could make a top speed of 35 knots; while a shade slower and less heavily armed as the Navy's newest destroyers, *Ward* was, despite her age, still a potent combat unit.

Her captain was as new as his ship was aging. The executive officer on the destroyer *Cummings* only a week ago, Lieutenant Commander William Outerbridge had taken command of *Ward* just two days earlier, on December 5, and this morning was his first operational patrol as the destroyer's skipper. *Ward* was assigned to the Channel Entrance Patrol, keeping an eye on the "defensive sea area" at the entrance to Pearl Harbor, an area where friendly submarines were required to travel on the surface: any submerged subs detected in the defensive area were to be regarded as hostile and treated as such.

Whether it was because of a naturally conscientious nature, or because of his position as *Ward*'s newly minted commander, Outerbridge took his responsibilities very seriously. At 3:57 a signal lamp on the coastal minesweeper *Condor* began flashing a message to *Ward* that she had spotted what might be a periscope in the defensive sea area. Outerbridge immediately had his destroyer begin searching the area, only to come up empty-handed after an hour's effort.

At 6:30, though, *Ward*'s helmsman noticed something strange in the water near the tug *Antares*, which was towing a 500-ton target. He asked the quartermaster on watch, who had a pair of powerful binoculars, to take a look. Dawn was just breaking, and in the growing light the quartermaster saw something he didn't recognize about 1,500 yards off *Antares*'s starboard quarter and pointed it out to the Officer of the Deck (OOD), Lieutenant Oscar Goepner. The OOD took one look and then called out, "Captain to the bridge!" Outerbridge appeared almost instantly—he'd been resting in the chartroom—raised his own glasses and studied the strange object for a few seconds. It looked like, he decided, the conning tower of a small submarine, but neither he nor Goepner had ever seen a submarine like it—whatever it was, it definitely wasn't an American boat.

By now the sub had taken up a position between *Antares* and the target she was towing, showing every intent of following the tug into Pearl Harbor, and the tug's crew finally noticed it. *Antares* signal lamp began flickering, asking *Ward* to investigate Overhead, a PBY Catalina from Patrol Squadron 14 appeared and dropped a pattern of smoke floats to mark the submarine's position. The pilot in command of the patrol bomber, Ensign William Tanner, likewise thought the unknown object was a submarine, but for some reason his immediate reaction was that the boat was in trouble and needed assistance.

Outerbridge knew better and didn't hesitate: at 6:37 he ordered *Ward* to go to General Quarters, then rang down to the engine room for "All Ahead Full." In minutes the destroyer was making 25 knots, and as she closed on the sub, Outerbridge gave the order to open fire. Gun No. 1, the forward 4-inch mount, was the first to get into action, firing off one round at 6:45. That first shot missed, but the crew of Gun No. 3, the portside 4-incher, did better. *Ward* closed so quickly on her target that by now the submarine was barely 50 yards away, and Gun No. 3's shot hit it squarely at the base of the conning tower. The shell didn't explode—hardly surprising, as some of the ammunition in *Ward*'s magazines was as old as the ship—but the concussion from the impact likely killed the two crewmen, Ensign Hiroo Akira and Petty Officer Second Class Katayama Yoshio, and the shell itself ricocheted off a frame member and punched a hole in the submarine's keel. The boat immediately lost speed, took on a heavy list to starboard, and began to submerge. Charging forward, *Ward* almost ran it down, and dropped a full pattern of depth charges over the spot where the submarine had last been seen. Overhead, Ensign Tanner suddenly realized what Lieutenant Commander Outerbridge already knew—that the submarine was in the defensive sea area and it most definitely did not belong there. He swooped down low and added a pair of depth charges to the attack.[13]

At 6:53 Lieutenant Commander Outerbridge sent a message in the clear to the 14th Naval District Headquarters at Pearl Harbor, announcing, "We have dropped depth charges upon sub operating in defensive sea area." Determined to make certain that his superiors understood that *Ward* hadn't been chasing shadows, Outerbridge sent another message hard on the heels of the first: "We have attacked, fired upon, and dropped depth charges upon submarine operating in defensive sea area." Likewise, Tanner dutifully reported the action to the operations center at Kaneohe Naval Air Station. About 20 minutes later, *Ward*'s sonar operators reported a contact, although whether this was the same submarine or not was impossible to tell. Not taking any chances, Outerbridge ordered another pattern of depth charges rolled off the destroyer's stern, and was rewarded with a large oil slick burbling to the surface.[14]

That seemed to put an end to the immediate submarine menace, but *Ward*'s already busy day was far from over. The restricted area around the entrance to Pearl Harbor was attracting a lot of unwanted attention this morning, and no sooner had *Ward* finished its depth charge run than one of her lookouts sighted a white sampan in the area. Outerbridge swung his ship around to investigate. It was probably only a local fisherman trying to sneak in to net a larger catch—the waters around the harbor entrance had some of the richest fishing grounds around Oahu—but after the incident with the unidentified submarine, Outerbridge was taking no chances. When *Ward* overhauled the fishing boat, a white flag suddenly appeared at its stern, and *Ward*'s executive officer ordered the sampan into the harbor, where the local authorities, naval and civilian, would sort out the situation.

It was 7:00 AM and the Japanese strike force was one hour away from Pearl Harbor.

* * *

At that moment, four B-17Cs and eight B-17Es, each spaced about 10 minutes apart, were roughly 175 miles north-northeast of Hawaii, on their way to Hickam Field; they had taken off from Hamilton Field, California, around 6:00 PM the previous evening. The twelve bombers were part of the American buildup in the

Pacific, reinforcements for the Army Air Corps in the Philippines. As originally scheduled, a total of 16 B-17s were to make the flight, eight aircraft coming from the 38th Reconnaissance Squadron from Albuquerque, New Mexico, the other eight from the 88th Reconnaissance Squadron from Fort Douglas, Utah. In order to save weight, which in turn meant saving fuel, the B-17s each carried only five crewmen instead of their normal complement of ten: the pilot, copilot, navigator, engineer and radioman; the bombardier and four gunners that were normally part of B-17 flight crews would fly out later on ordinary transports. The aircraft carried their bombsights and machine guns aboard, but none were mounted and there was no ammunition. Modifications made to the bombers to give them the range for the 2,400 mile flight to Honolulu included installing long-range fuel tanks in the bomb bays; even with the extra fuel, takeoff from Hamilton Field had been delayed by strong head winds until just after sunset.

Major General Hap Arnold, Chief of the Air Corps, made a point of visiting the bomber crews before they flew out to impress upon them both the urgency of their mission and the potential danger they faced. The flight leader, Maj Truman H. Landon, asked General Arnold why, if the flight was so dangerous, none of the guns were mounted and there was no ammunition. Arnold explained that the real danger would be during the later parts of the trip, on the way to the Philippines; the first leg, to Hawaii, was the longest, which meant that the B-17s needed to carry as much fuel as possible. After the aircraft arrived at Hickam the guns would be properly mounted and provided with a full supply of ammunition. Making the point for Arnold, three of the bombers had to abort their takeoffs from Hamilton Field with minor engine problems, while a fourth turned back not long after departure, also with engine problems. The B-17 was a remarkably reliable aircraft, but those four aircrews had taken no chances: there was no such thing as a "minor problem" when flying across almost 3,000 miles of open water.

* * *

At 12:30 PM—7:00 AM in Hawaii—Okumura was still typing. Ambassador Nomura looked in on Okumura from time to time, as if to hurry him along in his work, but finally resigned himself to the fact that, though the young man was doing his best, the fair copy of the note to be delivered to Secretary Hull would not be ready by 1:00. Nomura was compelled to call Secretary Hull once more and request that their meeting be delayed by 45 minutes.

* * *

As the bombers and fighters of the strike force moved steadily southward, Commander Fuchida experienced a moment that he took as a particularly good omen. The sun suddenly broke through the cloud cover, throwing out spray of sunrays that to Fuchida resembled nothing so much as Japan's national flag. Filled with an unexpected pride in his homeland, and feeling the power of the air armada surrounding him, he was moved almost to tears, thinking, *Oh, glorious dawn for Japan!* After a few minutes the clouds closed up again, and Fuchida dutifully turned his attention to his navigation. He had a sudden inspiration and tuned his plane's radio to the frequency for KGMB—if the Honolulu station was still broadcasting, the strike force might be able to "ride the beam," as it were, all the way into Pearl. Sure enough, the strains of Hawaiian music came through his headphones, and he told Mutsuzaki to get a bearing on the signal and follow it.

* * *

Private Wilfred Burke, an aircraft armorer assigned to the 72d Pursuit Squadron at Wheeler Field and billeted in one of the tents along Wheeler's flightline, was somewhat less than enthusiastically rolling out of his cot at 7:00 AM. Sunday was the only day of the week Burke was permitted to sleep late, and he resented being deprived of the opportunity. But he'd made a promise to Sergeant Forest Wills that he would go to church with him, and Burke was a man of his word. He valued Wills' friendship and was surprisingly touched that Wills was, in Burke's words, "sincerely concerned with my spiritual welfare, having observed that I was a worthless fellow given to drinking beer." Church call would be at 8:00, so there was time for Burke to first have breakfast; once he was shaved and dressed he strolled over to the mess hall. Sergeant George Van Gieri, who had the desk sergeant duty at Wheeler Field's guardhouse, was posting the last of 80 guards assigned duty on the base. Most of them were out on the flightline, where they were to keep a protective eye on the fighters parked there, lest some nefarious foreign-born civilian try to sabotage them.[15]

* * *

At 7:00 AM, aboard the USS *Nevada*, the Assistant Quartermaster of the Watch awakened Ensign Joseph Taussig, Jr., who rolled out of his bunk and began to ready himself to take over the duties of the Officer of the Deck (OOD) for the forenoon watch at 8:00. Weekends in port were excellent opportunities for freshly minted "nuggets," as young officers like Taussig were known, to gain some experience—and confidence—standing watches: there was very little danger of them making dangerous mistakes, especially in peacetime. Taussig, who had graduated from Annapolis that spring, was acutely aware that he was as green as grass—in fact, he had only qualified as OOD in Port the previous day. As far as the Navy was concerned, he was barely competent to tie his own shoes without being under the respectfully watchful eye of some senior chief old enough to be his father. Yet he wasn't a complete nautical neophyte. Taussig came from a naval family; Joseph Taussig Sr. was a vice admiral who had only retired in September, and had commanded the first American destroyer squadron to be stationed in Great Britain in the First World War. Perhaps most important of any of the lessons learned from his father, Young Taussig knew how to act like an officer—and he took his responsibilities very seriously.

The Navy's standard practice for a change of watch was for the relieving officer to report for duty 15 minutes before the official handover. This way the officer being relieved could brief his replacement on the current standing orders, the status of the ship, sea and weather conditions, course and speed if the ship was under way, and any special orders, instructions, or departures from standard operating procedures. Taussig planned to report to the current OOD a bit earlier than usual, the better to make certain he got everything right as he began is very first watch as OOD. He knew that, on his orders, the engineering crew was preparing to fire a second boiler as soon as the watch changed, shifting the steam load so that the current working boiler could be shut down for maintenance. While he would do none of the actual work, as the OOD he would be responsible for making certain that changeover went off without a hitch.

There was an additional motive for Taussig, who had hidden a mischievous streak, to have that second boiler lit off, apart from giving the appearance of a conscientious, efficient young officer. The engineer who would supervise lighting the boiler had been a drafting instructor at Annapolis when Taussig was a midshipman, and had been prone to loudly and caustically predicting that Taussig would never graduate from the Academy. Giving him the chore of lighting a boiler on what would have otherwise been a quiet, uneventful forenoon watch was a reminder of how wrong the engineer had been.

Taussig's first duty would be to command the "Morning Colors" ceremony at 8:00 AM, when the United States flag would be hoisted at the jackstaff on *Nevada*'s fantail, the extreme stern of the ship. *Nevada* had one of the best ship's bands in the fleet, and whenever the battleship was in port, "Morning Colors" were carried out to the accompaniment of the band playing "The Star Spangled Banner"—this morning would be no different. In fact, Taussig's only worry at the moment was that he wasn't certain exactly what size ensign to hoist for a Sunday morning. He made a mental note to have someone go forward and check with *Arizona*'s color party to make certain.

While Ensign Taussig was being roused out of his bunk, Lieutenant Lawrence Ruff, *Nevada*'s communications officer, was climbing a ladder (which is what the Navy called a flight of stairs) up the side of the hospital ship *Solace*. Ruff wasn't ill — he and his friend, Father Drinnan, *Nevada*'s chaplain, were attending church services on *Solace* this morning. As he climbed, Ruff noted that, apart from some clouds over the Koolau Mountain Range to the east, the sky was clear and there was a gentle easterly breeze blowing across the harbor: it promised to be another day in paradise.

Aboard *Arizona*, her captain, Franklin van Valkenburgh, was preparing for a busy day—despite it being a Sunday. The previous evening, the repair ship *Vestal* had eased alongside *Arizona* and tied up. Curiously, while all the other ships along Battleship Row were moored facing west, *Vestal* was facing east, so that she was sitting portside-to-portside with *Arizona*. Captain van Valkenburgh's ship had just returned from extended exercises at sea and was scheduled for some long overdue maintenance. By the end of the week, she would be moving into the 1010 Drydock, where her sister ship, *Pennsylvania*, was now sitting, but before that happened, *Vestal*'s crew would dismount and unwind the enormous armatures on *Arizona*'s electric generators. The task was scheduled to begin Monday, and van Valkenburgh planned to oversee the preliminary work that would be done today.

He was proud of his ship and his profession, and he had a sense that war with Japan was much closer than many of his fellow officers imagined. A month earlier, in a letter to an aunt in Milwaukee, Wisconsin, he'd written, "We are busy training, preparing, maneuvering, doing everything we can to be ready to move on to Singapore, if need be. Most of our work we are not allowed to talk about off of the ship. I have spent 16 to 20 hours a day on the bridge for a week at a time, then a week of rest, then at it again. Our eyes are constantly trained Westward, and we keep the guns ready for instant use against aircraft or submarines whenever we are at sea. We have no intention of being caught napping…"[16]

* * *

Ward's signals about the submarine incident went directly to the 14th Naval District, where at 7:12 AM they arrived on the desk of the watch officer, Lieutenant Commander Harold Kaminsky, a reservist who had enlisted in the navy as a seaman during the First World War, and been offered a commission to return to active duty in late 1940. There was something in the way that Outerbridge had worded his signals—specific yet concise—that convinced Kaminsky this incident was not a case of a nervous new skipper being trigger-happy. He decided that the District commander should know about the incident, but wasn't able to reach Rear Admiral Bloch's aide. So he informed Admiral Kimmel's assistant duty officer, Lieutenant Commander R. B. Black, then telephoned Admiral Bloch's chief of staff, Captain John Earle. Earle, who was still in bed when Kaminsky called, was unimpressed by *Ward*'s reports. He was sure that this was, as he put it, "just another of those false reports" that had plagued the Pacific Fleet for the past month, and told Kaminsky that he needed confirmation of the incident before he would take any further action. A few moments later, however, at 7:12, Earle called Admiral Bloch directly, and the two men briefly assessed the reliability of *Ward*'s report. Having been told by Kaminsky that the fleet commander's office had already been notified, they decided to "wait for further developments."[17]

At about the same time that Captain Earle and Admiral Bloch were conferring, the duty officer at CINCPAC, Commander Vincent Murphy, was being informed by Lieutenant Commander Black about the *Ward* incident. Murphy was getting dressed when Black's call came through; his first reaction was to tell his assistant to contact Kaminsky and learn whether or not Admiral Bloch had been informed. Black couldn't reach Kaminsky, neither could Murphy when he tried—the telephone line was busy—so Murphy instructed Black to begin plotting the positions of *Ward*, *Antares*, *Condor*, and the unidentified—and still hypothetical—submarine; he would come directly to Fleet Headquarters once he was dressed.

No sooner had Commander Murphy walked into his office at 7:30 than his telephone rang. The call came from Lieutenant Commander Logan Ramsey, the operations officer for Patrol Wing 2, based on Ford Island. Murphy barely had time to answer before Ramsey blurted out that one of his PBYs from Patrol Squadron 14 had sunk a submarine "one mile off the entrance to Pearl Harbor."

"That's funny," Murphy replied, "because we got the same sort of message from one of the DD's on the inshore patrol."

Ramsey considered this for a second, then said, "You'd better get going. I'll be down at my Operations Center soon." Hurriedly throwing on some civilian clothes, Ramsey drove to the main administration building on Ford Island and immediately began working on a search plan for his PBYs: they would first patrol the northeast approaches to Hawaii, rather than from the west or southwest, as navy planners had come to believe that to be the most likely direction from which an enemy attack would appear.[18]

As soon as Ramsey hung up, Murphy called Admiral Kimmel's quarters and spoke directly to CINCPAC himself. Kimmel's reaction to the submarine report was curiously ambivalent: he had been getting ready for a game of golf with General Short when Murphy called, but the plans for the golf outing were quickly abandoned as Kimmel announced he would be coming to Fleet Headquarters instead. Yet, despite the reports from Outerbridge and Tanner that seemed to confirm each other, Kimmel wasn't completely certain that there had actually been an enemy submarine in the defensive sea area at the entrance to Pearl Harbor. His skepticism was understandable, if not entirely excusable: as he put it, "We had so many... false reports of submarines in the outlying area, I thought, well, I would wait for verification of the report."[19]

Kaminsky's telephone had been busy because he had contacted Commander Charles Momsen, 14th District's operations officer, to pass on details of the submarine incident. Next came a call to the local Coast Guard station to alert them to the sampan being brought in by *Ward*. Momsen called Kaminsky at 7:25 with orders for the destroyer *Monaghan*, which had the ready-duty watch inside the harbor, to contact *Ward* about the submarine and be ready to put to sea, and finally, Kaminsky was to contact the station that controlled the anti-submarine net at the entrance to Pearl Harbor to confirm that it was closed—and if it wasn't, to close it immediately.

* * *

In the berthing spaces on the battleship *Oklahoma*, the crewmen not on watch had enjoyed the extra hour of sleep that they were allowed on Sunday mornings. Now they were rousing themselves, many preparing to go ashore; there were more than a few who had particularly enjoyed themselves on liberty last night in Honolulu's bars and dives and were less than enthusiastic about the new day; their less hungover shipmates were inclined to leave them to their misery. Among the early risers were those paying particular attention to their uniforms, buffing up the shine on their shoes, making certain their whites were immaculate, as they prepared for church call; some were going to services ashore, a large number of the Catholics would be attending Mass aboard their ship. Lieutenant Aloysius Schmitt, *Oklahoma*'s 24-year-old Catholic chaplain, was popular with the crew: along with the insight and compassion essential to his calling, he had a ready wit and lacked the stuffy, stodgy demeanor these men found typical of far too many clergy—Schmitt understood that the men in his flock weren't plaster saints.

Conspicuous among the men preparing for church call was Edward Slapikas, a balding Seaman First Class who gloried in the nickname "Curly." He turned to William Schauf, known to his messmates as "Popeye," and told him that he was glad Schauf was going to church. Schauf replied that he went to church every Sunday, so why should today be any different?

"We hope you go to confession, too, Popeye!" a gunner's mate called out.

"I don't have nothing to confess, except I'd like to pop you one!" Schauf grinned back.

Seaman Second Class Everett Gunning had a date this morning with a girl named Eleanor. Marion Athas was waiting on the weather deck near *Oklahoma*'s Turret Number Three for liberty call to sound. Gazing up at the Curtiss observation plane, an OS2U Kingfisher, perched on the catapult atop the turret, he wondered what it would be like to pilot an airplane like that. Standing not far from Athas, Daniel Weissman, Seaman Second Class, was getting impatient: ever since *Oklahoma* had been returned to Pearl Harbor in October after having a propeller shaft replaced in San Francisco, he'd spent every minute ashore possible. Hawaii and especially Honolulu fascinated him: it was like living in Paradise. When Slapikas came on deck, Weissman called out, "Hey, Curly, how long do you think we'll stay in Pearl Harbor?"

"Forever," Slapikas muttered.[20]

* * *

Ten thousand feet above the deep blue waters of the Pacific Ocean, the first wave of the Japanese strike force was 100 miles north of Pearl Harbor, 75 miles or so from the north shore of Oahu. KGMB continued to obligingly play its steady stream of Hawaiian music for Major Landon's inbound B-17s, never imagining that the signal was also guiding in 183 Japanese bombers and fighters to their target. While

Admiral Kimmel and Commander Vincent were conferring about the reports of the submarine incident, scout planes luanched earlier from the cruisers *Tone* and *Chikuma* were making reports of their own. *Chikuma*'s aircraft informed Commander Fuchida that "nine battleships, one heavy cruiser, and six light cruisers are anchored in the harbor," followed by a summary of the weather conditions over the target. The scout from *Tone* was able to confirm that there were no American ships at Lahaina Roads, which, while disappointing, simplified Fuchida's mission, allowing him to abandon the alternative plan of attack he had created with Genda for such an eventuality. Neither aircraft made any mention of enemy air activity, which an increasingly optimistic Fuchida took as an indication that they hadn't been spotted—so far, it seemed, the Americans had no idea the strike force was approaching Oahu.[21]

Or at least Fuchida so believed; had he known the truth his optimism would have evaporated instantly. A US Army radar station had spotted the approaching Japanese formation more than 30 minutes before the two scout planes made their reports, when the Japanese bombers and fighters were still 150 miles out from Pearl Harbor. Fortune or Fate had handed the Americans one last opportunity to avert a disaster. Privates Joseph Lockhard and George Elliot had the duty at the Opana Point radar station this Sunday morning, Lockard as the radar operator, while Elliot was the plotter and motorman—which meant that he had the task of charting on the map any contacts the station picked up while also keeping the gasoline engine-powered generator up and running. In practice the two men shared their responsibilities, an arrangement that allowed Elliot to acquire some practical experience operating the set—he had barely two weeks experience in radar operations, but was eager to learn.

Their equipment was what the Army knew as a SCR-270-B Radar Unit; by the standards of 1941, it was a state-of-the-art device, with an effective range of between 150 and 200 miles, depending on atmospheric conditions. Signal returns were displayed on a 5-inch oscilloscope, showing up as vertical lines or "blips" on the screen—the height of a blip above a white baseline on the oscilloscope screen indicated the strength of the return, which in turn indicated the size of the object detected. Standard operating procedure called for the station to power up at 4:00 AM and shut down at 7:00 AM, but this morning the truck which was coming to collect the two privates was late, so Elliot decided to keep the set running until their transportation arrived, allowing Lockard to explain the finer points of interpreting the blips and sorting out genuine returns from the false ones that appeared on the scope from time to time.

At 7:02 a huge return unlike anything Elliot had ever seen suddenly appeared on the scope, just on the edge of the SCR-270s detection range. Elliot looked up at Lockard and asked "What's this?" Lockard, thinking that the equipment was either malfunctioning and giving a false return, began fiddling with the unit's controls, then ran a quick test of the set, but when the test indicated that the radar was functioning perfectly, he came to the conclusion that what he and Elliot were seeing was a huge formation of aircraft. Elliot, as the plotter, worked out that the blip was on a course just three degrees east of due north, roughly 137 miles away; he suggested that they call the Information Center at Fort Shafter and report what they were seeing.

"Don't be crazy!" was Lockard's reply. "Our problem ended at seven o'clock." Elliot was insistent though and after a few minutes Lockard gave in. No one answered the telephone at the tactical plot, so Elliot then called the center's main switchboard: the operator, Private Joseph McDonald, explained that the six men who normally worked the plot were at breakfast. Elliot asked McDonald to have whoever was in charge at the Information Center call Opana Point as soon as possible—he was looking at the biggest radar signal he'd ever seen and he didn't know what to do about it. He gave McDonald the blip's course and estimated distance, which McDonald duly wrote down, intending to hand it off to the Information Center staff when they returned from breakfast. It was then that he noticed that the center wasn't completely deserted—Lieutenant Kermit Tyler was sitting at the plotting table.

Tyler, who had been in the Army for four years, was waiting to be relieved at 8:00 AM. He was an Air Corps fighter pilot temporarily assigned to the Information Center in order to learn how to use the information supplied by radar signals to vector intercepting fighters to their targets. He was the only officer on duty at the moment, but the morning had been quiet to the point of being dull, which was to be expected of a Sunday. McDonald passed Elliot's message on to Tyler, suggesting that the plotters be called back, just in case there was something special about this incoming flight of aircraft. Tyler didn't think the situation was worth the effort but McDonald suggested that the lieutenant speak to Elliot personally.

At 7:20 Tyler called Opana Point. Lockard answered, and quickly gave Tyler the bearing and distance of the contact, remarking that it was "the biggest sighting he'd ever seen." But he forgot to tell Tyler that the strength of the return indicated that there were more than 50 aircraft in the formation approaching Oahu. Had he done so, Tyler's response would likely have been very different. As it was, Tyler suddenly recalled that flight of 12 B-17s inbound from San Francisco: if they were on schedule they would be approaching Oahu right about now, and on roughly the same course as the formation of aircraft on Opana Point's scope. That had to be what Elliot and Lockard were tracking.

"Well, don't worry about it," Tyler said and hung up. Fascinated, Lockard and Elliot continued to watch their 'scope as the formation of aircraft grew steadily closer until the signal was lost in the ground clutter 39 miles out.[22]

Had Tyler shown a little more initiative—and to be fair, this was only his second day at the Information Center and no one as yet had really explained to him what were his duties—he could have informed the 14th Pursuit Wing of the Opana Point contact, where—hopefully—an information copy would have been forwarded to CINCPAC. Together with the submarine incident it might have proven persuasive enough to Kimmel for him to order the fleet to go on full alert and send the ships in Pearl Harbor to General Quarters before the Japanese arrived—then again, it may not. But whatever the case may have been, once again Kimmel was dogged by his old nemesis: the information he needed wasn't getting to him, or else it was arriving too late.

Not that there was much of anything the 14th Pursuit Wing itself could have done about the Opana Point report. At Wheeler and Hickam Fields, where all but a comparative handful of the Army Air Corps' P-36 and P-40 fighters were based, the aircraft which were supposed to defend the Pacific Fleet when it was in port were sitting in neat rows, scores of them lined up wingtip-to-wingtip, on taxiways and aprons in dutiful compliance with General Short's Alert No. 1, the better to protect them from sabotage. There was no Combat Air Patrol (CAP) flying, there were no fighters on ready alert, prepared to take off with only a few minutes' warning, and no pilots on duty to man them if they were. Most of the planes had no fuel in their tanks, none had ammunition loaded in their guns. In short, the 14th Pursuit Wing was impotent and helpless.

* * *

The clouds that earlier had presented Commander Fuchida with such a beautiful representation of Japan's national flag were now becoming a problem, as the farther south the Japanese strike force flew, the denser the cloud cover became. Fuchida began to be concerned that he might not know when the formation made landfall on Oahu's north coast: that was where Genda's plan called for the strike force to break up into its specific attack groups; missing it would seriously disrupt the timing and coordination between the groups of fighters, bombers, and torpedo planes. Worse, if there were heavy clouds over Pearl Harbor, the dive bombers and level bombers would be unable to see their targets. Ironically, it was KGMB that solved this part of Fuchida's problem for him: at 7:35 an announcer at the Honolulu radio station broke into the music broadcast with weather information meant for the approaching B-17s. The pleasant measured voice announced "partly cloudy skies mostly over the mountains, ceiling 3500 feet, visibility good."

The rest of Fuchida's dilemma was resolved moments later when a break in the clouds revealed in the distance successive lines of breakers running up onto a narrow beach, with the northern end of the Ko'olau Mountain ridge rising steeply behind it. A decision point was rapidly approaching for Fuchida—he would have to decide if the strike force had truly achieved surprise or if the Americans had somehow anticipated what was coming and were ready for the Japanese. If the Americans were taken unaware, Fuchida would fire off a single black smoke flare, known as a "Black Dragon." The torpedo bombers would attack first, followed by the high-level bombers, then the dive bombers would go to work; the fighters would continue to fly top cover. If surprise was lost, Fuchida would fire two Black Dragons, and the fighters and dive bombers would swarm the American airfields, bombing anti-aircraft guns and destroying as many enemy fighters as possible before they could get airborne—only then would the torpedo planes and high-level bombers begin their attack runs. It was a decision that had to be made carefully. But not yet, not yet. Fuchida wanted to be absolutely certain before committing to one or the other.

* * *

Seaman Leslie Short had duty in the foretop on *Maryland*: not wanting to waste an opportunity, he was busily addressing Christmas cards. On *Arizona*, the ship's band, still smarting from being eliminated from the "Battle of the Bands" by the band from *Pennsylvania* the night before, when everyone *knew* they should have won, was assembling on the fantail for Morning Colors while the Marine color guard formed up. Bosun's Mate First Class John Anderson was supervising a work detail that had just finished sweeping the fantail and now was setting up chairs for the morning's church service; his twin brother Delbert was still in his bunk below deck. Carl Christiansen was waiting for his brother, Edward, to reappear from below (there were 38 sets of brothers aboard *Arizona*); they were going ashore together, but suddenly Edward had announced that he'd left something important behind in his bunk and went to fetch it.

At Wheeler Field, Private Henry Woodrum arrived at the mess hall and for once wasn't faced with waiting in a seemingly endless line of hungry soldiers to get breakfast—there were only four men ahead of him. Woodrum was pleased but not surprised: the barracks where he slept had a lot of empty bunks this morning, evidence that most of the enlisted men who had gone into Honolulu the previous afternoon hadn't yet bothered to return. Making his way quickly through the chow line, Woodrum settled down to enjoy a leisurely breakfast.

* * *

Fuchida studied Pearl Harbor through his high-power binoculars. There was no anti-aircraft fire, no fighters in the air, no sudden surge of activity from the ships below. *Have these Americans never heard of Port Arthur?* he wondered in amazement. Now he made his decision. Despite the odds against them, the Japanese had accomplished the near-impossible: the Americans were about to be taken by surprise. Turning to his wireless operator, Fuchida nodded for him to send the signal to attack: "*To! To! To!*"—the first syllable of *totsugeki*, attack!

Opening a panel in the Kate's canopy, Fuchida thrust the muzzle of his flare pistol through it and pulled the trigger, shooting off a single Black Dragon. As the formation began to break into its component parts for each stage of the attack, he noticed that one of the group of fighters wasn't moving into its assigned position—the flight leader, Lieutenant Suganami Masaharu, had missed the signal. Fuchida fired a second Black Dragon, which Suganami saw, but so did Lieutenant Commander

Takahashi Kakuichi, who led the dive bombers. Takahashi misjudged the interval between the two flares and thought Fuchida had fired the signal for "Surprise lost." He immediately put his wing over and headed for Wheeler Field, followed by half the dive bombers—the other half headed straight for Hickam.

Frustration flared momentarily in Fuchida as the carefully choreographed plan of attack fell apart. In the whole of the planning, preparation, and execution of the entire Japanese attack, it was only that instant of miscommunication that went irrecoverably wrong. Yet, after a moment, Fuchida realized that, in the carnage and chaos about to erupt, it really didn't matter. Turning once more to his wireless operator, he told him to send the signal that would inform *Kido Butai* that complete surprise had been achieved. The man immediately began to tap out a single word, repeated three times.

"*To-ra! To-ra! To-ra!*"[23]

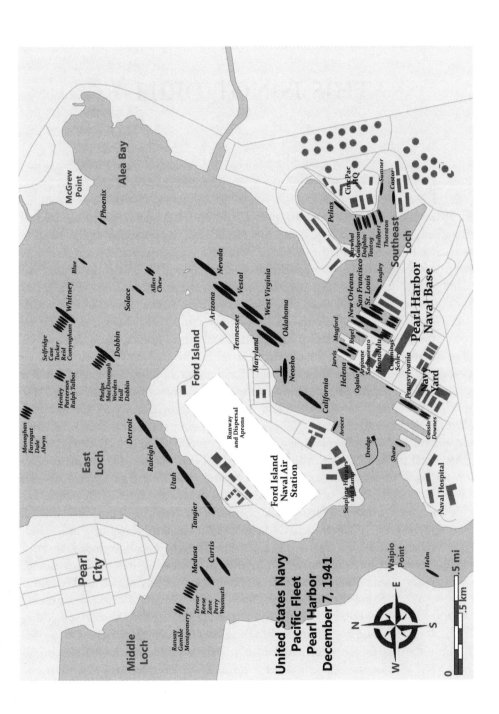

United States Navy
Pacific Fleet
Pearl Harbor
December 7, 1941

CHAPTER 7

"THIS IS NOT DRILL!"

Surprise was indeed total and complete. All around Pearl Harbor the sound of aircraft engines at full throttle began to be heard, but they were too distant to seem menacing. High overhead, the Japanese formations began to break up as the carefully organized flights turned toward their assigned targets on Battleship Row, Ford Island, Kaneohe and Ewa Air Stations, or one of the army air fields—Wheeler or Hickam. They swooped down, hawk-like, toward their targets. Thirty-nine torpedo-armed Kates wheeled northwest to begin their attack runs down the Southeast Loch, straight toward Battleship Row. Torpedo bombers from *Soryu* and *Hiryu*, 16 all told, lined up to attack the American aircraft carriers that were supposed to be moored on the north side of Ford Island. The high-level bombers, Fuchida's aircraft among them, swung wide to the west of the harbor, then turned northeast to line up with Battleship Row—they would fly down its length, hammering the American warships' decks with massive 1,760-pound bombs even as the torpedoes from *Kaga* and *Akagi*'s Kates were exploding against the battleships' hulls. Some of the Zero fighters maintained their altitude, flying "top cover" to protect that attacking dive- and torpedo-bombers from any American fighters that might get into the air; the rest peeled off to begin strafing the American airfields.

It was the dive bombers that struck first, however. Vals from three carriers—26 from *Kaga*, 25 from *Zuikaku*, and 27 from *Shokaku*—roared down on Ford Island, Wheeler Field, and Hickam Field respectively. The first bomb exploded on Ford Island, cratering the seaplane ramp. In the Command Center on Ford Island, Commander Logan Ramsey, hearing a plane flying low overhead, looked out a window in time to see what he thought was a cocky Army Air Corps pilot showing off for the Navy's benefit. His consternation turned to alarm when he saw "something black fall out of that plane," plummet to the ground, and explode. It was 7:55 AM. Instantly Ramsey understood that Pearl Harbor was under attack—he recognized the aircraft as a Japanese dive bomber; running to the communications room, he ordered the radiomen there to send a plaintext FLASH message to every US Navy ship and base: AIR RAID ON PEARL HARBOR X THIS IS NOT DRILL.[1]

Frank Erickson, a coast guard lieutenant, the duty officer at Ford Island's Naval Air Station, had been watching through the window of his office as the three-man Marine color guard took its post for Morning Colors. There were two heavy explosions and Erickson rushed to the door just in time to see a Kate—the Rising Sun on its wings clearly visible—fly past 1010 Dock and release its torpedo, which ran straight and true into the side of the battleship *California* and exploded. Unfazed, the trio of Marines hoisted the colors as smartly as ever, even as the alarm for "General Quarters" was sounding. They then dashed off to their battle stations.

While Commander Ramsey and Lieutenant Erickson were quick to grasp what was happening, for most Americans in and around Pearl Harbor that morning comprehension was slow in coming. It took time, minutes for some, seconds for others, to realize that what they were witnessing was unlike anything they had ever before experienced. Human nature being what it is, when confronted with the unthinkable, people took refuge in explanations for what they were seeing and hearing—some mundanely familiar, some downright bizarre—that allowed them to, momentarily at least, avoid acknowledging harsh reality. Aboard *California*, Pharmacist's Mate William Lynch heard someone remark, "The Russians must have a carrier visiting us. Here come some planes with the red balls showing clearly." Fireman Frank Stock, on the repair ship *Vestal*, thought that the planes diving and buzzing over Ford Island and Battleship Row were participating in an unannounced drill; he noticed big red disks painted on them and thought that the Army had gone all out in making this exercise as realistic as possible.[2]

On the north side of Ford Island, anti-aircraft gun crews on the light cruiser *Raleigh* watched as eight torpedo bombers, followed closely by eight more, flew out of the valley that opened onto the East Loch and began what looked like attack runs. Ensign Donald Korn, who was about to go off watch, thought the aircraft belonged to the Marine Corps, and that he was watching a training exercise. Thinking that this was an opportunity for *Raleigh*'s gunners to get some extra training of their own, he called out for them to track the oncoming aircraft. On Ford Island itself, when one of the big PBY hangers was blown apart by a bomb, Seaman Robert Osborne, who was convinced that this was an unannounced drill staged by the Army to test the Navy's readiness, thought that the Air Corps armorers had made a dreadful mistake, muttering to himself that "Somebody is going to catch hell for putting live bombs on those planes."[3]

Aboard *West Virginia*, the OOD, Ensign Roman Brooks, knew something was wrong, even if he wasn't sure exactly what. He hadn't seen any bombs or torpedoes—or even aircraft—but when smoke and flames erupted from 1010 Dock directly across the channel from where he stood on *Wee Vee*'s deck, he reacted immediately. Switching on the ship's 1MC—the internal loudspeaker system—he called out, "Away the Fire and Rescue Party!"

At Hickam Field, ground crews were waiting for the 12 B-17s flying in from California, while Colonel William Farthing, the base commander, took station in the control tower so as to have a grandstand seat as the heavy bombers made their landings; he was joined by Colonel Cheney Bertholf, Adjutant General of the Hawaiian Air Force—for seasoned aviators like Farthing and Bertholf, who had learned to fly in the days of wood-and-canvas biplanes, the arrival of a dozen B-17s was an impressive display of American airpower. Farthing spotted a long line of aircraft bearing down on Hickam from the northwest—*not* the direction from which the B-17s would be approaching—and instinctively took them to be planes from the Marine aviation detachment at Ewa, as they often flew over Hickam when they staged mock attacks on the ships in the harbor. This led him to casually remark to Bertholf, "Very realistic maneuvers. I wonder what the Marines are doing to the Navy so early on Sunday?"

Everything would change the instant that first bomb exploded on Ford Island at 7:55. As far as the Army and Navy were concerned, though, it was still peacetime, which meant that it was expected that all of the usual peacetime routines, the drill and ceremony, the spit and polish, would be carried out. Even as the first Val dive bombers were releasing their lethal payloads on Ford Island, a blue preparatory flag indicating five minutes to "Morning Colors" was run up the signal tower at the Navy Yard, and was promptly acknowledged by every ship in the harbor raising an identical signal. Aboard *Nevada*, moored at the far end of Battleship Row, directly astern of *Arizona*, the ship's 23-member band was already assembled on the quarterdeck, along with a Marine honor guard. Band Leader Oden McMillan was keeping a close eye on his watch, just in case Ensign Taussig was off his mark, but when he heard a muffled explosion come from Ford Island he looked up in time to see dirt and debris being thrown up at the far end of the island, followed by a succession of explosions, each one seeming to be getting closer to *Nevada*.

The 16 Kate torpedo bombers first seen by Ensign Korn aboard *Raleigh*—eight each from *Soryu* and *Hiryu*—had been given the mission of attacking any American aircraft carriers in the harbor, which were routinely moored on the north side of Ford Island, known as "Carrier Row." With the carriers absent, 12 of the Kates broke off their attack runs and sought out their secondary targets; the other four dropped their torpedoes on the ships occupying the carrier moorings—the cruisers *Raleigh* and *Detroit*, and the target ship *Utah*.

Three of the four torpedoes found targets: two struck *Utah* and one hit *Raleigh*'s port side, exploding in her after boiler room; *Detroit* went unscathed. *Raleigh* immediately took on a sharp list, severe enough that her officers and crew feared she might capsize. Within minutes of being hit, the ship lost all power as water entered ruptured fuel lines and doused the fires in the forward boiler room. The General Quarters alarm sounded and damage control parties, cooly directed by *Raleigh*'s skipper, Captain Bentham Simons, began working feverishly but methodically to keep the ship stable and afloat, starting with counterflooding to reduce the list. The next priority was to somehow restore power and get her pumps working: if they could get ahead of the inrushing water, there was a chance they could save the ship. Incredibly, despite the damage done, none of her crewmen were killed and only three were wounded.

Utah would not be so lucky, however. Despite specific orders from Commander Genda not to waste torpedoes on her—Ensign Yoshikawa had made it clear *Utah* was no longer an active battleship—the flight leader of the four attacking Kates apparently decided those reports were in error. The two torpedo hits blew open her port side, and, like *Raleigh*, she immediately took on a hard list. At the same time she started settling by the stern, and her chief engineer, Lieutenant Commander Solomon Isquith, the senior officer aboard, gave the order to abandon ship. As the list increased, heavy baulks of 6-inch by 12-inch wood that protected *Utah*'s decks when she was a target during gunnery practice broke free and began sliding toward the water, creating a potentially lethal hazard for the crewmen trying to scramble to safety. Fortunately none of them were struck by the heavy timbers, although Lieutenant Commander Isquith was almost trapped in a passageway when one of them blocked a hatchway he was trying to use to reach the upper deck. Almost all of *Utah*'s crew were able to scramble to safety before she capsized, but 64 were lost nonetheless. Sixty-three were either killed by the exploding torpedoes or subsequently died of wounds. The 64th was Chief Watertender Peter Tomich: he remained aboard the sinking ship in order to shut down the ship's boilers and prevent further explosions when the cold harbor water rose to meet them. Tomich would be posthumously awarded the Medal of Honor for his sacrifice.

The other 12 Kates went swooping over Ford Island and made for the berths outside the 1010 Dock, where the fleet flagship—the USS *Pennsylvania*—was usually tied up. This particular morning *Pennsylvania* was *in* the 1010 Dock; the light cruiser *Helena* was moored in her berth, with the minelayer *Oglala* tied up alongside. On *Helena*'s signals bridge, Signalman's Mate C. A. Flood was startled to see explosions on Ford Island, then noticed strange planes beginning to swarm across Pearl Harbor. He shouted down to the Officer of the Deck, Ensign William Jones, who immediately sounded the General Quarters alarm, then announced over the ship's 1MC, "Japanese planes bombing Ford Island. Man all battle stations and break out the service ammunition!"[4]

Only one of the Kates dropped its torpedo; deprived of yet another target, the other 11 made a wide, sweeping turn around the Southeast Loch looking for targets of opportunity. That one torpedo found its mark, however: it passed directly under *Oglala* and exploded against *Helena*'s starboard side, flooding the cruiser's aft boiler room and forward engine room, and the ship ominously began listing. As it passed overhead, the Kate's rear gunner sprayed both ships' decks with machine-gun fire; the strafing and the explosion took the lives of 20 of *Helena*'s crew.

That same torpedo stove in *Oglala's* hull, even though it didn't directly hit the minelayer: the blast was powerful enough to spring sections of her shell plating, and she started rapidly taking on water. The shock also knocked out the ship's electrical power and disabled her pumps. *Oglala* had originally been built as a New England coastal steamer and bought by the Navy in 1917 to be converted into a minelayer. This meant that she lacked the sort of comprehensive watertight integrity a purpose-built navy ship would have possessed. With the pumps inoperative there would be no way to stop the flooding, and the ship would sink.

Crewmen below decks who weren't yet aware that Pearl Harbor was under attack thought that one of her boilers had exploded. As luck would have it, *Oglala* was the flagship of the US Navy's Pacific Fleet Mine Force, and the force commander, Rear Admiral William Furlong, was aboard; he immediately recognized the torpedo bombers that zoomed overhead as Japanese. He also happened to be Senior Officer Present Afloat (SOPA), which meant that he was at that moment in command of all Navy ships and their crews inside Pearl. He immediately ordered a general signal hoisted: "All ships in harbor sortie."[5]

All the way back on *Nevada's* fantail, where Band Leader McMillan was waiting, the drama that was unfolding at the 1010 Dock was invisible, although the explosions were getting closer and more frequent. The minute hand of Ensign Taussig's watch finally touched "12" and he gave the command "Execute!" The colors were run up the jackstaff at the fantail and McMillan gave the downbeat that cued *Nevada's* band to begin playing "The Star Spangled Banner." The musicians were perhaps a dozen measures into the anthem when a Kate swept out of the Southeast Loch, dropped its torpedo in *Arizona's* direction, and zoomed over *Nevada's* fantail. As it swept by, the rear gunner opened fire, but managed to miss not only the entire band, but also the whole of the Marine honor guard. Given that the American flag was shredded by bullets, however, this was probably intentional.

McMillan kept directing and the band kept playing, never missing a beat even when McMillan hesitated for an instant, until they had finished the national anthem. Then musicians, Marines, and musical instruments scattered in all directions as the men ran for their battle stations. Up on the bridge, *Nevada's* bugler was preparing to play the call to General Quarters when Ensign Taussig ran up, snatched the bugle out of his hands and threw it over the side: the time for such formalities and curlicues was over. He sounded the alarm for General Quarters instead, and the raucous "Clang! Clang! Clang!" rang throughout the ship.

Vestal's alarm actually sounded first, perhaps two minutes before *Nevada's*. As the torpedo planes that had made the abortive run on Carrier Row roared across Ford Island, her OOD, Chief Warrant Officer Fred Hall, recognized the red *hinomaru* identification markings. "Sound General Quarters," he bellowed to the quartermaster. "Those are Japanese planes up there!" The quartermaster froze in disbelief and Hall set off the alarm himself. *Vestal* may not have been a warship *per se*, but her crew

Emperor Hirohito: Despite post-war efforts to present him as little more than a figurehead, he was fully briefed on and personally approved the Pearl Harbor attack.

President Franklin Roosevelt: Walking a political tightrope between America's isolationists and interventionists, he focused so intently on stopping Nazi Germany that he was all but blind to the Japanese threat in the Pacific.

Admiral Yamamoto Isoroku: Though he was adamantly opposed to the idea of going to war with the United States, he planned and directed the attack on Pearl Harbor, seeing it as Japan's only chance to buy time for a negotiated peace.

Admiral Husband Kimmel: Commander-in-Chief of the Pacific Fleet on 7 December 1941, his superiors withheld critical intelligence he needed to protect the fleet at Pearl Harbor.

Vice Admiral Nagumo Chuichi: A cautious and conservative admiral, he also possessed the moral strength to make hard decisions.

Lieutenant General Walter Short: The quintessential peacetime general, Short was utterly inadequate to the task of preparing his command for its mission to defend Pearl Harbor from aerial attack.

Lieutenant Commander Fuchida Mitsuo: At one time an instructor in horizontal bombing at the Imperial Naval Academy at Eta Jima, Fuchida was assigned the task of coordinating the aerial tactics of the attack on Pearl Harbor.

(L–R) Japan's Ambassador Nomura Kichisaburo, US Secretary of State Cordell Hull, and Special Envoy Kurusu Saburo: The three men worked feverishly to find a diplomatic solution to the growing crisis between Japan and America, none of them knowing that the Japanese military had already made the decision to go to war.

IJNS *Akagi*: Vice Admiral Nagumo's flagship for the Hawaiian Operation, she was converted from a battlecruiser to a carrier while still under construction, and was the Imperial Navy's first fleet carrier.

IJNS *Kaga*: Regarded as a half-sister to *Akagi*, she was Japan's second fleet carrier.

IJNS *Soryu*: The first of the Imperial Navy's "second generation" of aircraft carriers.

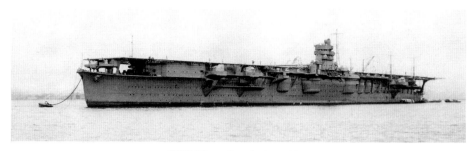

IJNS *Hiryu*: *Soryu*'s sister ship.

IJNS *Shokaku*: One of the Imperial Navy's newest carriers, she joined the First Air Fleet in August 1941, followed a month later by *Zuikaku*.

IJNS *Zuikaku*: As with her sister, *Shokaku*, *Zuikaku*'s inexperienced aircrews were assigned to the less demanding mission of attacking the American airfields on Oahu.

USS *California*: The flagship of Battle Fleet, the battleship component of the Pacific Fleet, she was sunk by two torpedoes.

USS *Arizona*: Few ships have died as violently as *Arizona*, whose forward powder magazine blew up when hit by a specially made Japanese bomb.

USS *Maryland*: Tied up inboard of *Oklahoma* on Battleship Row, she suffered only minor damage in the attack.

USS *Oklahoma*: Hit by as many as seven torpedoes, she capsized in less than 12 minutes.

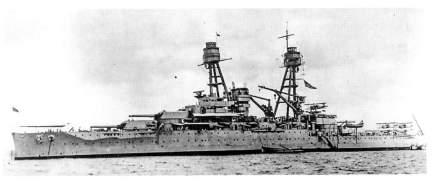

USS *Nevada*: Sister ship of *Oklahoma*, she was the only battleship to get underway during the attack.

USS *Pennsylvania*: Sister ship to *Arizona*, at the time of the attack she was in drydock, which protected her from Japanese torpedoes.

USS *Tennessee*: Moored inboard of *West Virginia*, she was struck by two bombs of the same type that destroyed *Arizona*; fortunately, both proved to be duds.

USS *West Virginia*: Struck by at least five torpedoes, quick counterflooding prevented her from capsizing like *Oklahoma*.

Curtis P-36 Hawk: Though obsolescent at the time of the Pearl Harbor attack, the few P-36 fighters that got airborne tangled fiercely with Japanese bombers and fighters.

Curtis P-40B Warhawk: An in-line engine development of the P-36, with the right pilot at the controls, the Warhawk proved it was able to go toe-to-toe with the Zero.

Aichi D3A "Val": Despite its somewhat dated appearance, the nimble Val was arguably the best dive bomber in the world in 1941, and would remain in front-line service until 1944.

Mitsubishi A6M "Zero": Fast, highly maneuverable, and heavily armed, the Zero was the most dangerous fighter in the world in 1941.

Nakajima B5N "Kate": Capable of carrying either bombs or a single torpedo, the Kate was the Imperial Navy's premier attack aircraft.

Japanese pilots being given a final briefing just moments before taking off from *Akagi*'s flight deck.

Zeroes on *Akagi* ready for take-off. They will be part of the second attack wave to strike Hickam Field.

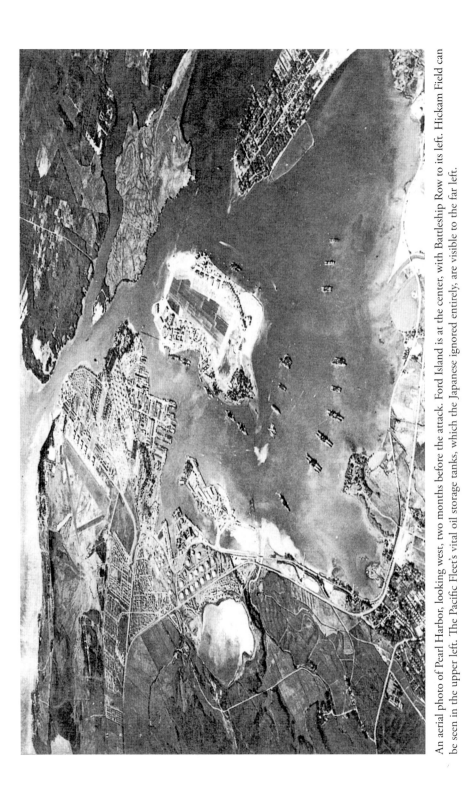

An aerial photo of Pearl Harbor, looking west, two months before the attack. Ford Island is at the center, with Battleship Row to its left. Hickam Field can be seen in the upper left. The Pacific Fleet's vital oil storage tanks, which the Japanese ignored entirely, are visible to the far left.

The attack begins: Clearly visible are plumes of water sent up by torpedoes striking *West Virginia* and *Oklahoma*.

The attack on Battleship Row: Oil slicks can be seen spreading from *West Virginia* and *Oklahoma*, both of which are beginning to list to port. In the background, smoke is rising from burning aircraft and buildings at Hickam Field.

Wheeler field under attack: The fighter planes parked in neat rows as an anti-sabotage measure provided easy targets for Japanese dive bombers and fighters.

California, sunk at her moorings by a pair of torpedoes that tore huge holes in her port side. The resulting flooding caused the loss of all power to her guns and pumps.

Nevada sorties: Hit by one torpedo and five bombs, she is visibly down by the head as she steams past Battleship Row.

The forward magazine of the destroyer USS *Shaw* explodes. Incredibly, only the ship's bow was destroyed in the blast. It was replaced and she went on to earn 11 battle stars in the Pacific War.

Battleship Row after the attack: *Maryland* sits behind the keel of the overturned *Oklahoma*, while astern can be seen the sunken *West Virginia* and the cage masts of *Tennessee*. The smoke is from burning fuel oil flowing out of the wreck of *Arizona*.

Arizona explodes: 500 tons of propellant powder have been detonated by a single 1,600-pound Type 99 bomb.

The wreck of *Arizona*: The forward superstructure collapsed when the battleship's bow was blown apart by the exploding powder magazine. The fires aboard her burned for two days after the attack.

(L–R) *West Virginia*, *Tennessee*, and *Arizona* the day after the attack. *Arizona* is still burning fiercely; her flag still flies at her stern.

responded with an urgency any of the battleships in harbor that morning would have envied: by 8:05, *Vestal*'s single 3-inch AA gun and the handful of machine guns she mounted were all furiously banging away at the attackers.

By then all across Pearl Harbor all hell had broken loose. A dozen torpedo-armed Kates turned into the far end of the Southeast Loch, settled scant feet above the water, and bore down on Battleship Row. These were *Akagi*'s aircraft, led by Lieutenant Commander Murata Shigeharu. They separated into two flights of six, with Murata's section of three Kates and Lieutenant Goto Jinichi's trio of aircraft in the lead. The target for Murata's section was the battleship *West Virginia*; Goto's headed straight for *Oklahoma*. All three torpedoes from Goto's section hit home.

Lieutenant Goto would leave a terse, tense account of what that targeting run was like and what was expected of the torpedo bomber crews in making their attacks:

> Three things were the key elements to the attack: speed must be 160 knots, the nose angle zero [that is, perfectly level], an altitude of 20 meters [65 feet]… I didn't have time to say "ready" so I just said "fire!" The navigator in the back pulled the release lever. The plane lightened with… the torpedo being released. I kept on flying low and flew right through, just above the ship…[6]

Two torpedoes from Murata's section hit *West Virginia*—the third may have buried itself in the harbor bottom or it may have struck the ship and not exploded, as a dud torpedo was later found in *Wee Vee*'s hull. In any event, there were a few anxious seconds for Murata as he waited for his observer to tell him whether or not he'd scored a hit. When a waterspout erupted against the battleship's hull, the observer yelled "*Atarimashita!* [It hit!]" then on Murata's instructions tapped out a message to the waiting aircraft carriers of the *Kido Butai*: "Torpedoed enemy battleships. Serious damage inflicted." The modified fins worked. The effect on the American warships would be devastating.[7]

Oklahoma and *West Virginia* both began listing to port. On *Oklahoma* the General Quarters alarm began clanging and a voice that no one could later identify (it may have been Ensign Herbert Rommel) but everyone remembered announced on the 1MC, "Man your battle stations! Real planes! Real bombs! This is no shit!" Her commanding officer, Howard D. Bode, was on *Maryland*, which was moored inboard of *Oklahoma*; command responsibility at that moment fell on the shoulders of her executive officer, Commander Jesse Kenworthy. When the air raid warning went off, he was on his way aft to "officer country" on the Second Deck; he turned around and began running forward, heading for the conning tower, shouting for the crew to go to battle stations and set Condition Zed. Lieutenant Goto's three torpedoes hit *Oklahoma* before Kenworthy could reach the bridge, and he felt the deck beneath his feet shifting as the battleship began to list.

Ray Richmond was a Yeoman First Class, an administrative clerk who handled the paperwork of *Oklahoma*'s daily operations. He was showering, planning on going on liberty in Honolulu, when the Japanese attack began. "Suddenly it felt as if someone had picked up the ship, shook it, and dropped it. I hit the overhead"—"overhead" being the Navy term for ceiling. His first thought was that this was another "surprise attack" by the Army, but the sandbags Army bombers dropped to simulate hits never shook *Oklahoma* like this. Then came another shudder, followed by the sound of the ship's bugler, Marine Corporal Richard Fisk, blowing the call to General Quarters. Instinct and training took over for Richmond as he bolted for the door out of the shower room. "I was naked as a jaybird, but I went to my battle station on Number 5 Port 5-inch, 51-caliber gun." Richmond felt the battleship shake yet again then start heeling to port—then the power failed and the lights went out.[8]

West Virginia's commanding officer, Captain Mervyn Bennion, was in his quarters, and had just finished putting on his uniform when the alarms started going off; like everyone else aboard, he was startled to hear "Away the Fire and Rescue Party!" come over the 1MC. He was on his way to the bridge when "General Quarters" was called: instantly he knew that, whatever it was that was going on out there, it wasn't some harbor incident or shipboard accident: *West Virginia* would be fighting. He changed direction slightly and made for the conning tower instead.[9]

Commander Roscoe Hillenkoetter, *WeeVee's* Executive Officer, was also dressing in his cabin when the call "Away the Fire and Rescue Party" went out at 7:55. Just as the "General Quarters" alarm went off, his marine orderly rushed in and announced, "The Japanese are attacking us!" Hardly had the words left the Marine's mouth than Hillenkoetter felt two heavy shocks come from somewhere deep in *West Virginia's* hull; to him, it seemed as if they were somewhere forward on the port side. By the time he reached the quarterdeck, the ship was already leaning heavily to port.[10]

When the fire and rescue party was called away Lieutenant Claude Ricketts left his breakfast at the wardroom table; he was scrambling up a ladder leading to the quarterdeck when "General Quarters" went off, and he felt *West Virginia* shaking. Not knowing that the ship had been torpedoed, he thought the vibration might be caused by near-misses from falling bombs. Rickett's usual battle station was up on the boat deck, in the starboard anti-aircraft battery, but at the moment he was the senior gunnery officer aboard: after telling Ensign George Hunter to get the guns firing as soon as possible he went to the conning tower where the fire control position was located. By now *WeeVee* had taken on a noticeable list, and the power had failed, taking down all communications within the ship save for a handful of sound-powered telephone circuits. As soon as Captain Bennion arrived, Ricketts, who had been the ship's damage control officer before he was promoted, asked, "Captain, shall I go below and counterflood?" Bennion replied, "Yes, do that," and Ricketts took off aft.[11]

A few decks below the bridge, Seaman Second Class Stuart Hedley was buttoning up his dress blues when the call for the fire and rescue party came over the 1MC. A moment or two later, the ship's bugler blew the call to General Quarters and Hedley's training took over. Running for his battle station in Turret Number 3, he dashed out onto the open quarterdeck and saw Japanese planes coming from seemingly every direction. "I saw a torpedo plane going over us," he remembered later, "and the pilot was laughing like anything." He quickly climbed the ladder that ran up the back of the turret to a hatch on the bottom of the gunhouse—the huge, heavily armored moving structure of the turret that enclosed the breeches and elevating gear of the big 16-inch guns. Twenty-seven men were stationed in each gunhouse, and once the last man was inside Turret Number 3, the hatches were dogged down tight and the men waited for orders.[12]

On *Tennessee*, the senior officer aboard this morning was Lieutenant Commander John Adams, Jr., the gunnery officer, as her captain and executive officer had gone ashore the previous evening and not yet returned. When "General Quarters" was sounded, he made a beeline from his cabin to the bridge; on the way he ran into—literally—Marine Captain Chevey White. Shouting to make himself heard over the alarms and explosions, Adams told White to "get the ship in condition Zed [i.e. set water-tight integrity] as quickly as possible." White rushed off to begin passing the word.[13]

Up at the lead end of Battleship Row sat Vice Admiral William Pye's flagship, *California*. Pye was the commanding officer of Task Force 1, which included all of the Pacific Fleet's battleships, and was also Admiral Kimmel's second-in-command; as such he had been given the same intelligence briefings that Kimmel received. Less than 24 hours earlier, when Commander Layton delivered a report of Japanese troop transports moving toward Malaysia, Pye had wondered aloud if the Japanese might turn east and attack the Philippines instead, then dismissed the idea, declaring flatly that, "The Japanese will not go to war with the United States. We are too big, too powerful, and too strong." Now, as if to prove the admiral wrong, almost at the same moment *Oklahoma* and *West Virginia* were hit by Murata and Goto's two flights of Kates, two Type-91 torpedoes slammed into *California*'s port side just seconds apart.

While none of the battleships in Pearl Harbor that morning were truly prepared for an aerial attack, *California* was more vulnerable than the others. She was one of several ships scheduled for a complete keel-to-mast top inspection scheduled for Monday, and the preparations made for it had critically compromised her watertight integrity: six manhole covers giving access to her bilges and double bottom had been removed entirely, while another 12 had been loosened to make access to those areas easier as the inspection progressed. The two torpedoes that struck her ran slightly deep, and by pure ill-luck they detonated not against *California*'s armor plate and anti-torpedo bulges—the kind of protection which had so far saved *Oklahoma* and *West Virginia*—but instead exploded below the armor, against the relatively thin shell plating at the turn of the bilge, where the ship's side curved into the bottom of the hull.[14]

Two gigantic holes were ripped open in the battleship's bottom, the first under *California*'s bridge, a gaping wound 10 feet high and 24 feet wide. The second, located aft beneath Turret Number 3, was almost identical in size. The flooding was swift and extensive: water rushed into the ship's three lowest decks, aided by the missing manhole covers, and *California* soon took on a five-degree list to port. The center engine room (technically the Central Motor Room, as *California* had turbo-electric propulsion) was soon awash—it would later flood completely—several of the fuel bunkers had ruptured and were contaminated by seawater, and the ship began losing power.

A repair party was working on *California*'s third deck, under the supervision of Gunner Jackson Pharris, when the first Japanese torpedo hit almost directly below. The men were bounced off the bulkheads and overhead by the blast, but somehow most of them survived, including Pharris. Feeling the ship begin heeling to port, he detailed some of the shipfitters in the work party to begin counter-flooding, directing them to which forward compartment on the starboard side were to be opened to the sea. (Up on *California*'s bridge Ensign Edgar Fair was sending damage control parties to the stern for the same purpose.) Water was rising onto the third deck, but more dangerous was the fuel oil leaking from the ruptured bunkers, as crewmen began passing out, half-strangled by toxic fumes. Pharris half-led, half-carried several men out of contaminated compartments as he brought the rest of his work party up to cleaner air. Once there, he began looking for another job to do.

One of the compartments threatened by the rising water was an air compressor station that was vital to the ship's defense: like all American battleships, *California*'s anti-aircraft gun mounts were powered by compressed air. As the water rose, the crew manning the station were forced out—all, that is, save for Machinist Mate First Class Robert Scott. He refused to abandon the compartment, for as long as there was an air supply to them, the guns could keep firing. He shouted out to his crewmates "This is my station and I will stay and give them air as long as the guns are going." Much as Chief Tomich aboard *Raleigh* was doing at almost the exact same moment, Scott was making the choice between duty and safety. Duty won out. Like Chief Tomich, Scott would be awarded a posthumous Medal of Honor.[15]

Overhead, Scott's self-sacrifice wasn't wasted as *California*'s 5-inch anti-aircraft guns began banging away at the swarming Japanese aircraft. Getting those guns into action had required remarkable exertion from *California*'s crew. With the power gone, the ammunition hoists that brought up the shells and propellant charges from the magazines stopped working. A call went out for volunteers to form a human chain from the forward magazine and up four decks to the anti-aircraft guns. Gunner Pharris joined in, despite the injuries to his back and the oil fumes he'd earlier sucked into his lungs. Standing on a narrow vertical ladder, he helped pass the 52-pound shells for nearly an hour before he finally collapsed from oxygen starvation.

Guns on other ships were firing now as well: the 3-inch batteries on the cruisers *Raleigh* and *Detroit*, *Vestal*'s solitary 3-incher, the heavier 5-inch mounts on *Helena*, *West Virginia*'s heavy four-barreled 1.1-inch heavy machine guns. Nicknamed

"Chicago Pianos" the 1.1-inch guns were carried by most of the battleships, and generally known to be unreliable—but this morning most of them worked superbly. On the bridge of the destroyer *Bagley*, Seaman Frank Johnson manned a .50-caliber machine gun and hosed a Kate from nose to tail, sending the bomber tumbling into the harbor. On both *Maryland* and *Nevada*, crewmen in the "birdbaths" perched on the heavy fighting tops of the ships' masts blazed away at the Japanese with .30- and .50-caliber machine guns. Atop *Maryland*'s mainmast, Leslie Short, Christmas cards now forgotten, brought down a Kate that had just dropped one of the torpedoes that struck *Oklahoma*.

Not that it was easy getting guns into action. This was the peacetime Navy, after all—or had been until just a few minutes earlier—and the peacetime procedures on which the Japanese had so heavily factored into their planning worked against the American sailors, just as the Japanese had hoped. Only a handful of guns were manned and ready in the entire harbor, and their ammunition was limited. The problems gun crews encountered attempting to get more shells would have been farcical under almost any other circumstances. On battleships, cruisers, destroyers, oilers, tenders, repair ships, ready ammunition boxes and magazines were securely locked, with the keys nowhere to be found. Hammers, fire axes, cold chisels, prybars, hacksaws, all were brought to bear; a gunner's mate on *Pennsylvania*, who had been aboard the USS *Panay* when that gunboat was bombed by the Japanese in 1937, loudly declared that he wasn't going to be caught again unable to shoot back—and began knocking locks off magazine doors with a sledgehammer.

A supply officer on Ford Island refused to issue ammunition without being presented with a properly filled-out requisition form. Boatswain's Mate Thomas Donohue, a gun captain on *Monaghan*, was literally flinging wrenches at low-flying Japanese airplanes, shouting down in frustration to the men in the magazine for them to start sending up shells and powder charges, exclaiming, "I can't keep throwing things at them!" The ammunition problem on *Oklahoma* approached the surreal: fighting against the battleship's increasing list, Boatswain Adolph Bothne reached the superstructure deck and produced a hammer and chisel, which took care of the locks on the ready ammunition boxes. But then Bothne discovered that "after they had the ready boxes open there and the ammunition out they had no air to load the guns, and one of the men said there was no firelocks on the guns." *Oklahoma* had ammunition, but nothing with which to shoot it—and no power for the guns: the second torpedo had caused the power to fail throughout the ship.[16]

Down by the Navy Yard, in the Southeast Loch, gunners aboard the cruisers *St. Louis* and *San Francisco* seethed with frustration as *Kaga* and *Akagi*'s torpedo planes flew past: they had perfect, almost point-blank shots—and nothing to shoot. *St. Louis* was on "limited availability" while a new radar set was being installed; only one of her anti-aircraft guns was working. *San Francisco*'s situation was even worse: she was undergoing an overhaul, which meant her anti-aircraft battery had been removed and the ammunition stored ashore until the work was complete. A third cruiser, *New Orleans*, was tied up between *St. Louis* and *San Francisco*, her sister ship, but her turbines and boilers were being repaired, so there was no power for the ammunition hoists: the ready boxes held 25 shells each, and once her gunners fired off those, there were no more coming up from the magazines.

Still, some guns *were* firing, and the speed and fury with which the American gunners responded made an indelible impression on their Japanese antagonists, none more so than Commander Fuchida.

> Dark gray bursts blossomed here and there until the sky was clouded with shattering near-misses which made our plane tremble. Shipboard guns seemed to open fire before the shore batteries. I was startled by the rapidity of the counterattack, which came less than five minutes after the first bomb hand fallen. Were it the Japanese fleet, the reaction would not have been so quick...[17]

But there were too few guns firing from too few ships to drive off the swarming Japanese bombers and torpedo planes. Hardly ten minutes had passed since the first bomb fell on Ford Island, yet already two cruisers had been crippled and three battleships were in danger of sinking. There would be far worse yet to come.

* * *

For the attack on the Pacific Fleet to succeed, total mastery of the air by the Japanese was vital. Achieving complete surprise gave a tremendous advantage, of course, but for the Japanese to keep it, the Americans could not be allowed to get their own fighters into the air in any significant numbers. To make certain of this, the strike force hit hard at the army and navy air bases, determined to destroy on the ground as much American air power as possible.

The Japanese struck Wheeler Field first. Approaching from the north, the dive bombers split into two groups: 26 Vals, led by Lieutenant Takahashi, continued south to attack Hickam Field; while Lieutenant Sakamoto Akira took the remaining 25 into Wheeler. Surprise was complete: no one on the ground saw them until they were lining up to make their bomb runs. The dive bombers' priorities were the gasoline storage dump, the aircraft hangars, and the sheet metal, electrical, and machine shops. Releasing their bombs from 500 to 1,000 feet, the first wave scored direct hits on Hangars 1 and 3—the explosion that tore apart Hangar 1 was so violent that it seemed as if the entire building was lifted off its foundation. One bomb obliterated the upper floor of the 6th Pursuit Squadron's barracks. After completing their bomb runs, the pilots began making strafing passes on the parked aircraft. Once Lieutenant Commander Itaya Shigeru, in command of the fighter escort, realized that the Americans had no CAP airborne, he let his pilots loose on targets on the ground. The Zeroes came in low and hot, racing toward the dispersal areas where 39 P-36s and 99 P-40s were obligingly lined up, sitting ducks for the strafing Japanese aircraft.

The pilots barely had need to aim as they walked short, sharp bursts of 7.7mm machine gun and 20mm cannon fire into the ranks of the hapless airplanes. General Short, so determined to protect those planes from sabotage, had delivered them up to the bombers and fighters of the Imperial Navy; the Zeroes 20mm cannon shells punched fist-sized holes in aircraft and tore apart spars and stringers in their targets' airframes. The machine guns were even more dangerous to the grounded American fighters: the Japanese had set up the ammunition loads in the Vals and Zeroes so that the guns fired in a repeating sequence of two armor-piercing rounds, one tracer round, followed by two more armor-piercing rounds and one tracer, then two armor-piercing, and one incendiary round. The armor-piercing bullets would puncture the nearly-empty fuel tanks and the tracer and incendiary rounds that followed would ignite the fumes in the tanks into fireballs, or set the leaking aviation gasoline ablaze. Flames would quickly spread to aircraft parked alongside or behind a burning plane, which once they were well and truly alight, would ignite still others. Soon Wheeler's flightline was filled with scores of burning fighters.

Colonel Willian Flood, the base commander, was chatting with some friends in front of his quarters when the attack began. Seeing a bomb hit near the depot area, his first thought was much like that of Seaman Osborne on Ford Island—somebody on maneuvers had goofed and dropped live ordnance. But when a flight of Zeroes sporting red *hinomaru* sped by barely 50 feet above the ground, he knew better: Wheeler was under attack. He rushed down to the flightline where he was greeted by the sight of wrecked hangars and burning aircraft. Somewhere an air raid warning siren began wailing.

Private Henry Woodrum was making his way down the serving line and hadn't heard the siren when an aircraft roared low overhead and an explosion shook the entire mess hall. Thinking that a plane had crashed, someone behind Woodrum said, "Boy, that lieutenant sure hit hard!" Just then, Woodrum turned to a window and saw a khaki-colored airplane climbing away from Wheeler, the large red disc clearly visible on its wings. "That's no crash," he shouted. "It's the Japs!" At that a stampede for the door started; Woodrum ran through the kitchen and out onto the loading dock, just in time to see a Val diving in his direction. The bomb exploded close by, blowing him back through the kitchen and into a walk-in cooler. Woodrum took a moment to clear his senses, then dashed back out onto the loading dock and ran to the 14th Pursuit Wing headquarters.[18]

After breakfast, Private Burke saw that it still wasn't time for church call, so he joined a handful of other soldiers in the open quadrangle in the middle of the tent area "shooting the bull," as he put it. As they talked, they noticed a formation of planes pass overhead in the direction of Pearl Harbor. Someone remarked, "It's the Navy," but they were all surprised when black puffs of anti-aircraft fire appeared in the sky above Pearl. Then they realized that there were planes overhead that were diving on Wheeler Field. This time someone said, "It's the Japs!" and the men scattered when one of the aircraft began diving down toward them. Burke, thinking the Japanese wouldn't waste bombs or ammunition on housing tracts, made for the married NCOs' quarters. A bomb exploded somewhere behind him but he was untouched, and as soon as he reached the nearest house he put his back to the wall and stared out at the wreck of Wheeler Field. The Japanese were still strafing any aircraft that appeared operational, as thick, oily smoke began to rise from the ruins of the hangars and workshops, while most of the P-36s and P-40s were burning fiercely.[19]

One P-40 that wasn't burning was the aircraft assigned to First Lieutenant Teuvo ("Gus") Ahola of the 19th Pursuit Squadron. Hearing explosions and machine-gun fire, he looked out the window of his quarters, saw smoke rising from Wheeler and then caught sight of a Zero overhead—he headed straight for the flightline. Reaching his P-40, he climbed aboard, started the engine, and began to taxi toward one of the revetments along Wheeler's perimeter. Getting into the air to tangle with the Japanese was out of the question, as all of his fighter's ammunition had been unloaded before it was parked on the flightline—yet another of General Short's "anti-sabotage" precautions. An enemy plane turned toward him—Ahola would never be certain if it was a Zero or a Val—and his first thought was "I'll ram the SOB!" Fortunately for Ahola the fabric on the elevators of his P-40 had been burned away, so he wasn't able to get it off the ground. Instead he had to content himself with pulling into a revetment as he'd originally intended, where, after a few hours' work, his aircraft would be one of the few serviceable Army Air Corps fighters in the whole of the Hawaiian Islands.[20]

It was the sound of "people running, yelling, aircraft everywhere…" that awakened Harry Kilpatrick, a private in the 696th Ordnance Company. No one had to explain to him what was going on, however: "It took only seconds to realize this wasn't the Navy giving us one of their Sunday morning buzz jobs." He and several of his buddies ran to the weapons shop, only to find it locked—that problem was solved much the same way as the ammunition problem aboard the battleships down in Pearl Harbor. Once the locks were removed, Kilpatrick began handing out weapons to anyone who wanted one, no questions asked—later he would recall that "This was the first time in my nearly 11 months in the service that paperwork and signatures were ignored." The ordnance men reserved a water-cooled .50-caliber for themselves and set it up just outside the shop, shooting at every Japanese plane that passed by. Their ammunition supply was limited, but at least they were doing *something*.

Henry Woodrum never made it to the 14th Pursuit Wing Headquarters. As he ran past a construction site, he saw dirt being kicked up around him and realized that he was being strafed. A quick dive behind a stack of two-by-fours took him out of the line of fire, and when he looked over the top of the lumber pile he saw what looked to be every building along the flightline burning. Others had the same idea as Woodrum and were taking shelter among the stacks of lumber, but it wasn't long before the Japanese spotted them and raked the construction site with machine-gun fire as they flew past. Woodrum never forgot one soldier, a lad about 20 years old, who treated the whole incident as if it were a lark—then died without making a sound when a machine gun bullet caught him in the chest. Another was shot when the men huddled among the stacks of lumber decided to make a run for the ground floor of the barracks, 30 yards away.

Inside the barracks, someone had opened up the armory, and a steady stream of soldiers were passing through, grabbing any weapon that was handy. Medics were collecting the dead and wounded from the upper floor, while outside a line of wounded men was forming in front of the dispensary; blanket covered bodies lay on the lawn. There was a grim urgency about most of the men moving through the barracks, but there were some inside who said and did little or nothing, some stunned, others confused, some reduced to helplessness by the sight of friends and fellow soldiers killed before their eyes.

Woodrum picked up a Springfield rifle and then, when a technical sergeant learned that he'd just spent two years in the infantry, detailed Woodrum to show a handful of aircraft mechanics how the '03 Springfield worked. While Woodrum talked, the sergeant, named Henderson, went in search of ammunition; he returned with a case of ammo and the mechanics pried it open, loaded their weapons, then filled their pockets with loose rounds. Henderson posted the mechanics along the perimeter of Wheeler, then told Woodrum to stay close, saying, "You may have showed those guys how to fire an '03 but I don't want any antsy mechanic around me when it [the attack] starts again." Minutes later a trio of Japanese planes flew over Wheeler and began strafing again. Henderson began shooting at the Japanese, while Woodrum herded a group of small children that were standing along the street, watching the action, into a nearby house.

He ran back to Henderson's position just in time to watch a dogfight between a Zero and one of the handful of P-40s that had been able to get airborne that morning. The Zero lost the fight and when it crashed a great gout of black smoke rose into the air. A few minutes later another Japanese plane went down, this time crashing near the front gate of the base. Then a huge four-engine airplane appeared overhead and it seemed as though everyone at Wheeler who had a machine gun or a rifle opened fire on it. Fortunately, most of them were poor shots, which made Woodrum and others like him who recognized the aircraft start shouting to cease fire. It was an American B-17.

* * *

The flight from California for Major Truman Landon's 12 B-17s had been remarkable only for the fact that it was utterly unremarkable: the Army Air Corps was quickly learning that the big Boeing bomber was an amazingly tough and reliable machine. At 7:45 Oahu came into view and Captain Carmichael tried to contact the air controllers at Hickam Field, but his transmission was too garbled for anyone at

Hickam to understand. (Radio transmission and reception conditions—what the Army and Navy called "atmospherics"—would vary wildly all day.)

Just as the bombers were crossing the coast, a handful of fighters suddenly appeared—Landon and his aircrews thought they were an escort out from Hickam. (The P-36 had a radial engine just as did the Zero, from a distance a mistake in identity was easily made—especially when no one aboard the B-17s expected to encounter Japanese warplanes.) It wasn't until the fighters turned to attack the bombers that American flyers realized their error, and the 12 B-17s scattered, taking whatever evasive action they could. Ordinarily this would have been the worst possible maneuver—the B-17, especially the latest E model, was designed to fly in formation where the bombers' guns could have interlocking fields of fire to provide mutual defense, hence the nickname "Flying Fortress"—but as none of the aircraft in Landon's flight had their guns mounted, it was a clear case of "every plane for itself." Most of them firewalled their throttles and continued straight on for Hickam, hoping for the best.

Some of the crew aboard the bombers could see Hickam now—the thick, roiling clouds of smoke were hard to miss—and some wondered if a drill or exercise was underway. Sergeant Albert Brawley was certain that the rows of burning aircraft were the result of a pilot crashing on the flightline; Lieutenant Bruce Allen didn't even realize the fires were actually at Hickam—he was sure that the smoke came from sugar cane fields nearby being burned off. It wasn't until the pilots began asking the flight traffic control at Hickam for landing instructions that the truth was confirmed for them. Up in the tower, Captain Gordon Blake, the base operations officer, displayed a remarkable *sangfroid* as he provided the usual wind speed and direction information, then added that the air base was under attack by "unidentified aircraft."

Lieutenant Allen was the first to land, and he did so without incident. Captain Raymond Swenson's B-17C followed Allen's, but it caught fire when a stray round from a Zero ignited the emergency flares—the magnesium in the flares eventually burned the plane apart amidships. All but one of Swenson's crew survived—the lone loss was the flight surgeon, First Lieutenant William R. Schick, killed during one of the Zeroes' firing passes. Major Landon was next, making a textbook landing—with three Zeroes on his tail.

First Lieutenant Robert Richards, piloting a B-17C, tried to land at Hickam, but there were too many Japanese fighters in the way, so he turned toward Bellows Field and tried to make a downwind landing. He came in too fast and overshot the runway, his B-17 ending nose-down in a ditch at the edge of the airfield. Zeroes repeatedly strafed the plane, leaving it so badly damaged that it never flew again, yet by some miracle no one aboard was wounded or killed.

The remaining two B-17s in the first flight landed more-or-less safely at Hickam, though all were damaged to some extent; the other six B-17s were only minutes behind them. Army photographer Lee Embree was sitting in the waist gun position of one of the bombers in the second group, and managed to take photos of a pair of D3A dive bombers making a half-hearted firing pass at his plane—not knowing if the big bomber was armed, the Japanese pilots chose not press their attack. Embree would later recount how the Vals "passed us so close on the left, I could see the pilots' faces. They were grinning from ear to ear." The pilots of two of the B-17s gave up trying to land at Hickam Field, flew to Wheeler, which was still under attack, and eventually put their aircraft down at the small auxiliary field at Haleiwa. First Lieutenant Frank Bostrom's bomber was repeatedly jumped by Japanese fighters each time he attempted to land at Hickam, so he flew off to the north, eventually making a forced landing on a fairway at the Kahuku Golf Course with only minor damage. (A week later, repairs to the bomber complete, Bostrom flew it out.) Captain Carmichael also decided to give Hickam a pass, peeled off and made for Haleiwa. One of the remaining two B-17s eventually landed at Hickam Field in a lull between attacks, while the last one landed at Wheeler then flew on to Hickam later in the day.

* * *

When the B-17s flew into Hickam, they found that airfield being hammered every bit as heavily as Wheeler.

Captain Russell Waldron, CO of the 31st Bomb Squadron, was still in bed when his six-year-old daughter ran into the room announcing that "They're firing at Fort Kam!"—Fort Kamehameha, south of Hickam Field. Hearing the explosions for himself, he got up and looked out the window just in time to see a pair of airplanes flash by. Dressing quickly, he ran outside, saw still more planes, all headed staight for the naval base, and thought "They're having an exercise here, and they never told us about it!" As he watched, some of the aircraft dropped torpedoes, and though he couldn't see where they hit, heard still more explosions and saw heavy black smoke rising above Pearl Harbor. Suddenly everything clicked into place as he recognized the national marking on the planes circling overhead: "This is for real! The Japanese are attacking us!" He drove over Hickam's flightline, where he found almost all the aircraft parked there already on fire or shredded by strafing runs—fewer than a half-dozen were in any condition to be salvaged, let alone sent airborne. As he watched, several Vals made another pass down the flightline, their rear gunners firing at anyone on the ground they spotted.

Captain Laverne Saunders was dressed for mass and was collecting the Sunday newspaper when he heard an explosion come from the direction of Pearl Harbor. At first thought it was Navy engineers carrying out a demolition for some construction project or other, but a pair of Japanese torpedo bombers flying 50 feet overhead told him otherwise: he saw the Rising Sun insignia on the planes overhead and "knew we were at war." Making sure that his wife and two sons were safe indoors, he jumped into his automobile and raced over to Hickam's flightline—he was the commanding officer of the 23rd Bomb Squadron—only to find that a bomb had exploded in the hangar housing his B-17 and set the bomber afire. He drove down to the consolidated barracks, parked, and ran to the far end where his men were quartered to tell them to get out to the hangar line to save the airplanes.

One of Captain Saunders' pilots, Second Lieutenant Lee Metcalfe, was standing on the second floor balcony of the Bachelor Officers Quarters, contemplating breakfast at the Junior Officer's Mess, when he looked up and saw aircraft he didn't immediately recognize push over into powered dives above Hickam Field. His first thought was that he was watching a mock attack where the Navy flyers were putting extra effort into making it realistic; when one of the planes pulled out of its dive seemingly just above his head and he saw the Rising Sun insignia on its wings he knew that this was a real attack on the airfield. When he saw Hangar 17 burning, he ran down to the flightline, hoping to make himself useful, though he had no idea how—he'd graduated from flight school only a month ago.

On the flightline, Technical Sergeant Arthur Townsend commandeered a truck and asked Second Lieutenant John Roesch for help in collecting ammunition and machine guns. Roesch climbed in and off they went, dragged as many weapons and as much ammunition as they could from Hickam's armory, and passed them out to soldiers who were sheltering in bunkers on the airfield perimeter. Keeping one of the machine guns for themselves, they set it up on the far side of the field and began hammering away at the Japanese. Their weapon was a water-cooled .50 caliber machine gun, and the water kept boiling out of the cooling jacket as they fired. Townsend pulled off his First World War-vintage tin hat, put a round from his own .45 pistol through it, and used it to scoop water from puddles that were nearby—the hole in the helmet served as a funnel to pour fresh water into the cooling jacket of the machine gun, which they kept firing until they ran out of ammunition. Both Sergeant Townsend and Lieutenant Roesch later received the Silver Star for actions.

General Jacob Rudolph, CO of the 18th Bomb Wing, had scheduled a training flight for this morning for new, inexperienced pilots to familiarize, and 24 of those young men were in Hangar 11, pre-flighting a dozen B-18s prior to rolling them out onto the apron and starting the engines. Hangar 11 was one of the first buildings hit by the Japanese dive bombers—the explosion killed 22 of the 24 pilots. Out in front of the hangar, Master Sergeant David Jacobson was changing a tire on one of the B-18s when a Val scored a direct hit on the airplane; his body was never found.

As at Wheeler, the big hangars were priority targets for the Japanese—but the pilots' marksmanship was somewhat erratic. Hangars 7 and 11 were completely destroyed and 15 suffered heavy damage, while 9 and 17 were slightly damaged and Hangars 3 and 5 were untouched. But while some of the hangars survived, most of the bombers they served and sheltered were either burning or had been smashed beyond repair. By the end of the attack only a handful of B-17s and none of the B-18s would be serviceable.

When he arrived at the hangar line, Captain Saunders found his men waiting for him but the hatches on the bombers were locked—yet more of General Short's measures to prevent sabotage—and the keys were in the armament section, which had been obliterated by a bomb. Saunders didn't hesitate: he told his men to shoot the locks away, then taxi the aircraft to the dispersal area, where they then proceeded to hoist bombs into the bomb bays using ordinary block and tackle. It was a dangerous and back-breaking task, but the loading carts had been damaged beyond use. It took the better part of the morning, but they were able to get three B-17s armed.

As Lieutenant Metcalfe neared the flightline, he saw body parts lying where a bomb had exploded, his first exposure to the reality of war. He heard a B-17 approaching and turned toward it in time to see the big aircraft abort its landing attempt and pull up to go around again, a Zero on its tail. On the second attempt the B-17 was able to land, but the Zero was still there, still shooting. As the bomber came to a stop, a burst of machine-gun fire from the Zero set it on fire. The crew ran from the plane as it burned and eventually broke apart—it was Captain Swenson's B-17.

The Japanese targeted Hickam's huge consolidated barracks as well—it would gain the reputation of the single most-heavily bombed building in the entire Pearl Harbor attack. Its reinforced-concrete construction actually withstood most of the bombs dropped on it, but it did have weaknesses. The big mess hall located at the center of the barracks was one: the first bomb to strike the barracks crashed through the roof and instantly killed 35, wounding scores of others; the concussion killed all the Chinese cooks who had huddled for protection in a walk-in freezer.

The sound of heavy artillery awoke Private Ira Southern—at least that's what he thought it was. Mumbling about how target practice shouldn't be held on Sunday mornings, he got up to look out the window. The first thing he saw was an airplane diving down toward the barracks; as he watched, a bomb fell from beneath the aircraft, and seconds later the engine repair depot across the street vanished in a flash of flame and smoke. Aircraft mechanic Robert Chase, assigned to the 23rd Bomb Squadron, was jolted out of a deep sleep when Japanese bombs exploded on and around the barracks, and enemy planes began strafing runs up and down the flightline.

William Melnyk and two friends had an early breakfast and now were sitting on their bunks in the big barracks when they heard a low-flying plane pass by; someone remarked, "It looks like the Navy is practicing dive bombing us again." Hardly had the words left the man's mouth than there was a loud explosion. They rushed out to a stairway landing just as a bomb hit Hangar 7 and exploded, blowing them all off the landing onto the ground. The squadron first sergeant yelled for everybody to get out of the barracks, and soon there were scores of men milling about on the parade ground, Melnyk and his friends among them. It was too tempting a target, and one of the D3As strafed them, the rear gunner raking the men as they scattered.

When he heard someone shout to evacuate the barracks, Russell Tener of the 18th Bomb Wing pulled on a pair of trousers, scrambled down the stairs, and ran out onto the parade ground—to be greeted by bombs falling and machine gun bullets whizzing by in every direction. As he watched men around him fall to the ground and never move again, he began to think he would be next—his idea of joining the Army so that he could live in Hawaii at the government's expense suddenly seemed like a bad idea. He ran toward the base chapel, only to find that it had taken a direct hit. His best friend, Joe Nelles, was the Catholic chaplain's assistant; Nelles had been inside the chapel, preparing the altar for mass.

First Sergeant Carlos McCuiston was standing in the street in front of the barracks when he was blown off his feet by the blast from a bomb. Rising, he began to run for cover when he noticed two dead airmen were lying face down. "One had both legs severed at the buttocks. His blood had soaked the ground. The other had a massive head wound from an object which had passed through him from the left temple to just above the right ear, and his brains were lying on the ground." The sight shook the veteran soldier so badly that he failed to notice that the left sleeve and front of his shirt were bloodstained from wounds of his own, which, fortunately, turned out to be minor.[21]

Some men panicked, other didn't, many felt a sudden surge of fury—and some shamed themselves. When the Post Exchange (PX) was hit by a bomb, an airman dashed into the wrecked building, only to emerge moments later with a case of beer under one arm and several cartons of cigarettes under the other. Running across the parade ground with his loot, he became the target of one of the strafing Zeroes, which cut him down in mid-stride, scattering cans of beer and packs of cigarettes in every direction. Nor was this an isolated incident: when Private Southern returned to the barracks after the attack, he found his squad bay virtually untouched—but his locker had been rifled and several small valuables were missing.

For some, the sights, sounds, and imminent danger of the attack were too much for them endure. A young, somewhat foppish second lieutenant, green as grass, was found hiding in a bomb storage area, weeping with fear; one PFC, at once crying and helplessly raging, had to be evacuated to the mainland after the attack, where years of psychiatric care awaited him. A senior officer, who afterward no one would identify by name so as to save him from further humiliation, "went all to pieces after the attack and had to be sent back to the states on a stretcher."[22]

But for most, there was a sudden, desperate, almost primal need to strike back at their tormentors. In the chaos of explosions, yammering machine guns, and shouted orders, men instinctively headed for Hickam's armory, where they broke the lock on the door, then the locks on the weapons racks. Their anger almost palpable, they loaded Springfield rifles and M1911 pistols, then filled bandoliers with extra ammunition, while shrapnel, bomb fragments, and broken glass flew past, and ran out of the barracks onto the parade ground, where they began shooting furiously if ineffectually at the Japanese planes.

Some were taking the attack personally, as well: when the Vals demolished the new enlisted men's beer garden, the Snake Ranch, a truck company first sergeant reached his breaking point. Shaking his fists in the direction of the offending aircraft, he shouted, "You dirty SOBs! You've bombed the most important building on the post!" (The only thing that could be salvaged from the wreckage was a 78 rpm record, "San Antonio Rose." Later, when the Snake Ranch was rebuilt, it was the only music men who had been at Hickam on the day the field was attacked allowed to be played.)[23]

Technical Sergeant Wilbur Hunt set up 12 .50-caliber machine guns in bomb craters near the barracks, but had no gunners for them. The Japanese provided the men he needed: a stray bomb blew off a corner of the stockade, and the prisoners rushed over to Hunt. To a man they declared they were ready to be put to work, thereby confirming what Hunt had always suspected: the ones who get into trouble are the ones you want with you when things get tough.

The toughest man at Hickam Field that morning might well have been a "mild-mannered private first class who was an orderly room clerk." Minutes after the attack began, he climbed into a B-18 parked in front of one of the hangers, loaded the .30 caliber machine gun in the nose, and opened fire on any Japanese plane that flew past. His aim was unsteady—he wasn't a trained gunner—but he kept it up as long as his ammunition lasted, long after a Zero's incendiary bullets set the B-18 on fire, long after the fire cut off any possibility of escape: witnesses said he never seemed to make an effort to get out of the burning plane. Finally the flames engulfed the nose, and after a few moments the machine gun stopped. Not long after that, so did his screams.

Sergeant Stanley McLeod and Corporal William Anderson stood on the parade ground blazing away at the attackers with a Thompson submachine gun until they were both cut down by a strafing Zero. No one knew how he'd managed it, but one man had carried a machine gun to the roof of an undamaged hangar and opened fire on passing Japanese planes. One machine gun stood in the center of the parade ground without any protection around it—a suicidal position. That didn't stop a corporal from the 19th from running out onto the parade ground to help man the gun. Halfway there he was caught by a strafing Japanese plane, fell, got up, and fell again, mortally wounded.

Two men set up a machine gun on an anti-aircraft mount on the baseball field, between home plate and some trees along the edge of the field. A flight of high-level bombers appeared overhead and walked their bombs across the field, wiping out the gun and the would-be gunners manning it. Seemingly inexplicable, the reason the baseball field was bombed only became clear when a targeting map was found in the wreckage of one of the Japanese dive bombers. Hickam Field's fuel storage tanks were to have originally been built on the site of the baseball field, but another location was eventually chosen. The Japanese pilots believed that the baseball diamond was an attempt to camouflage the location of the storage tanks. Ensign Yoshikawa had missed the change in plans.

CHAPTER 8

"A Devastating Sight..."

The attacks on Battleship Row, Ford Island, and the Navy Yard seemed to increase in fury even as the first moments of surprise passed. More torpedo-armed Kates—at least two dozen of them—were already coming down the Southeast Loch, straight toward *Oklahoma* and *West Virginia*, while above Waipio Point the high-level bombers—15 from *Akagi*, 14 from *Kaga*, 10 each from *Soryu* and *Hiryu*—were wheeling past the harbor entrance and forming up to begin their bomb runs down Battleship Row.

As Commander Hillenkoetter worked his way along *West Virginia*'s starboard side he felt another heavy shock from a torpedo hit—her third—and the battleship's list continued to grow. The pair of OS2U Kingfisher observation planes on top of Turret Number 3 burst into flames, and Hillenkoetter organized a firefighting detail to contain the blaze. A fourth torpedo hit the ship, this one striking almost directly below the mainmast, just forward of where he was standing. The explosion sent him sprawling, and by the time he regained his feet, the deck was tilting almost 20 degrees to port. Using a sound powered telephone, he tried to contact Central Station, the nerve center of the ship's damage control system, to pass the word to begin counterflooding, but he wasn't certain if anyone heard him.

Lieutenant Commander John Harper was in Central Station, and he didn't hear Commander Hillenkoetter—then again, he didn't need to. He'd felt the shocks from the exploding torpedoes as he made his way down to "Central," and by the time he arrived the list had reached 15 degrees and was still growing. Ensign Archie Kelley, the Assistant Navigator, was giving the order to set Condition Zed just as Harper arrived—Kelly was still very new to Central Station and Harper admired the young officer's foresight and initiative.

Harper tried to use the 1MC to make a general announcement that all the starboard void spaces were to be flooded, but before he could do so, the power failed and the loud-speaker system went dead. Two damage control parties, using sound-powered phones, reported that they were counterflooding some of the void spaces under the direction of Lieutenant Ricketts, much to Harper's relief: by this time the list had grown to something between 25 and 28 degrees. The counterflooding slowly brought the *WeeVee* back to a 21-degree list to port—not good, but an improvement. At least she seemed stable.

Everyone seemed to have counterflooding on their mind because the list created multiple problems—serious problems—for *West Virginia* and her crew. Aside from the difficulty men had keeping their footing on the slanting decks, the angle created problems for the air-powered training and elevating systems on the anti-aircraft guns. The turntables on which the guns sat were thrown off-balance, and the sharper the list the harder the training gear had to work to turn the gun mount—eventually there would be a point where they would simply lack the power to do so. The elevation problem was one of straightforward geometry—with a 25-degree list, the barrels of the guns couldn't be raised high enough to shoot at the Japanese: as it was, only the starboard AA guns could be brought to bear now. Then there were the ammunition hoists, which could malfunction or jam if the angle was too great. And in the back of everyone's mind was the very real possibility that, if left unchecked, the list would grow until *West Virginia* simply fell over on her side and capsized—"turned turtle" was the way seamen put it.

Oklahoma was dying. She had already taken three torpedoes—the first two amidships, the third forward, below Turret Number 2—and started listing alarmingly. Then the roll to port slowed, almost stopped, as the battleship's righting moment, the inherent stability given a ship by its buoyancy and hull design, caused the ship to try to right herself. Now a fourth torpedo slammed into her. But this one was different, louder, more powerful—to some of her crew, it seemed that the ship shook harder with this impact than it had when the first three torpedoes hit her. It certainly seemed that way to Seaman First Class James Bounds in the aft steering room: "I noticed other torpedo hits, but I noticed the first three more than anything else, and then there was an extra loud one…it shook the ship, then we got one or two more after that…but they wasn't as powerful as that one." Commander Kenworthy, *Oklahoma*'s XO, made specific mention of it in his action report nine days later: after methodically noting the first three torpedo hits, he singled out the fourth as being different from the others: "As I attempted to get to the Conning tower over the decks slippery with oil and water, I felt the shock of another very heavy explosion on the port side." Stephen Young's description was more dramatic: "The fourth torpedo hit the ship hard, above the armored belt this time because of the *Oklahoma*'s heavy list to port. The ship rocked from side to side… An almost inaudible moan sounded through the lower decks as the…insides absorbed the impact… The ship was going fast."[1]

Commander Kenworthy found Lieutenant William Hobby, *Oklahoma*'s first lieutenant and damage control officer, on the starboard side of the weather deck, and the two officers quickly briefed each other on the condition of the ship. It wasn't good: even though the roll to port seemed to have slowed or even stopped, without power it was impossible for *Oklahoma* to defend herself. Counterflooding might restore her trim somewhat, but if she took any more damage, she would sink—it would only be a question of whether she capsized or simply settled to the bottom of the harbor. Either way, it was time to get the men off. And then came that fourth torpedo. In his official report, Hobby noted that, "There was an explosion around the port side of the forecastle, which I thought was a bomb hit. [Hobby was mistaken; it was a torpedo. No bombs struck *Oklahoma* during the entire attack.] There was another shock and concussion and vibration, and fuel oil splashed in streams over everything topside."[2]

Exactly what created that fourth explosion remains a mystery, but it was incredibly powerful, rocking and shaking the entire ship, so much so that it stood out distinctly in the memories of survivors. Stephen Young had erred in one detail: whatever hit *Oklahoma* did not strike the ship above her armor belt—salvors would discover that it hit the belt directly: the explosion actually *cracked* the 13-inch-thick armor plate. It may be that by some freak chance two torpedoes dropped by the swarm of Kates flying struck *Oklahoma* at the same instant only a few feet apart, or it could have one of the massive Type 95 torpedoes fired by the midget submarine *I-16tou*—or it could have been some as yet unexplained phenomenon. Whatever its cause, that blast sealed *Oklahoma*'s fate: the battleship instantly lost whatever righting moment she had and what had been a slow roll to port now became increasingly rapid—and unstoppable. At least two more torpedoes hit *Oklahoma*, possibly as many as five—by now the water of the Southeast Loch was practically alive with torpedoes rushing toward Battleship Row.

Two of them hit *West Virginia* within seconds of each other, the first slamming into her side below the mainmast, the second striking her stern, blowing off her rudder. Up in the conning tower, Captain Bennion and Lieutenant Commander Thomas Beattie, *Wee Vee*'s navigator, couldn't talk to Central Station or the anti-aircraft batteries: they had no knowledge, beyond what they could see for themselves, of the damage done to the ship, or of whatever success the damage control parties might be having. Bennion had sent Lieutenant Ricketts on his way to start counterflooding, but he didn't know that Lieutenant Commander Harper had already ordered all the starboard voids flooded. Likewise, he could do nothing to coordinate the fire of the ship's AA guns. Beattie suggested that they move out of the conning tower to the starboard side of the bridge and set up messenger communications—runners—and try to save the ship. It was about that time that, high overhead, unseen by Bennion or Beattie, a formation of high-level bombers was beginning to fly down the length of Battleship Row.

The 49 Kates sorted themselves out into nine five-plane V's, the final four aircraft following in trail in a truncated V of their own. Commander Fuchida gave up the lead of the formation to Chief Petty Officer Watanabe and his crack bombardier, Petty Officer Aso, sliding back into the number two position in the lead V. Each five-plane section would release its bomb when the bombardier for that section's lead plane released his. Flying at 10,000 feet, the altitude needed for the big 1,700-pound Type 99 bombs to reach maximum velocity—and penetration—the bombers would make as many passes as the bombardiers needed to get properly lined up on the targets. Fuchida's section was making its first run over the American battleships when a small cloud drifted in just before Aso pulled his release lever, obscuring the ships below and spoiling his aim, so his section of Kates had to go around again. Someone in one of the following sections, though, got very, very lucky on their first pass.

This Sunday aboard *Arizona* started out like countless Sundays before it. Men not on watch or about to go on watch were relaxing their bunks (for officers) or hammocks (for enlisted men), were writing letters, eating breakfast, preparing to go ashore, or tending any one of a hundred personal details. Just before 8:00 AM, though, things began to change—and then quickly went straight to hell. On the forecastle, Seaman First Class Clay Musick heard a loud explosion on Ford Island and looked up as a plane with Japanese markings flew low overhead. Even before the air raid siren sounded he was running for his battle station, an ammunition hoist in one of the anti-aircraft magazines. He had just started feeding shells upward when he felt the ship shudder as the first bomb exploded in the water just off *Arizona*'s port bow.

Seaman First Class Donald Stratton was bringing some oranges to his friend, Harl Nelson, who was in *Arizona*'s sickbay, which was on the Second Deck, just forward of the Turret Number 1 barbette, when General Quarters sounded. Errand and oranges forgotten, he ran for his battle station, the port AA director, a large, box-like apparatus perched on the left side of the sky control platform, the topmost level of the superstructure, right by the foremast.

James Lawson, Gunner's Mate Third Class, was strolling back to his deck division's quarters when he heard a loud *thump!* outside the ship. Thinking it must be Army Engineers working on some construction project or other, he didn't pay it much attention, but the odd noises continued. Curiosity piqued, he looked out the porthole just in time to see a torpedo hit *West Virginia*. General Quarters sounded and a voice came blaring from the 1MC: "General Quarters! This is not a drill! All hands to General Quarters!" Coffee and paper went flying as Lawson took off for Turret Number 4, only to find when he got there that the hatch was dogged down tight from the inside. The Japanese planes—Lawson recognized the red circles in their wings—were strafing the open decks and for a moment he felt terribly vulnerable. Then he was up on his feet, grabbing a fire axe mounted on the base of Turret Number 3, and running toward the nearest bollard where one of the lines tying the repair ship *Vestal* to *Arizona*'s side was secured. If Captain van Valkenburgh wanted to get his ship under way, she wouldn't be able to move until all of those lines were cleared away. Lawson didn't know that the ship didn't have steam up and *couldn't* move, but *Vestal*'s crew would soon be grateful for Lawson's impetuosity.

Vestal had been spared from the torpedo-bearing Kates, but the high-level Kates were a different matter. Two of the huge Type 99 bombs, clearly meant for *Arizona*, hit the repair ship squarely. The first hit her forward, penetrating three decks before it exploded in a stores hold and started a large fire—a repair ship, as could be expected, carried a significant volume of flammable materials. The second hit just aft of the superstructure, passed through the carpenter shop and the shipfitter shop, and plunged straight through the bottom of the ship without exploding, leaving a five-foot hole behind it. The only other damage it caused were smaller holes in *Vestal*'s decks and hull. That fire started by the first bomb, however, quickly grew in intensity, and *Vestal*'s captain, Commander Cassin Young, ordered the forward magazine flooded to prevent *Vestal*'s anti-aircraft shells from cooking off. A few moments later, as a precaution, he had the after magazine flooded as well.

The air raid siren interrupted breakfast for Lieutenant Commander Samuel Fuqua, *Arizona*'s First Lieutenant and Damage Control Officer. Grabbing the telephone on the wardroom wall, he ordered the OOD to sound general quarters, then ran out onto the quarterdeck to make certain Ensign Davison got the word. A low-flying Val zoomed past, spraying *Arizona*'s deck with machine-gun fire—Fuqua thought it was no more than a hundred feet above the water. He ran for cover and had almost reached the starboard gangway when he was blown off his feet and knocked unconscious: *Arizona* had taken her first bomb hit.[3]

That bomb glanced off the face of Turret Number 4, punched through the Main Deck and the Second Deck and was stopped by the five-inch-thick armor of the Third Deck before it exploded, starting fires there and on the deck above. The blast vented through the hatches around Turret Number 4 and shattered the O2U Kingfisher floatplane on the catapult atop Turret Number 3, igniting the aviation gasoline as it spilled out; the ship was hurt, but not critically damaged.

Arizona fought back. Up on the sky control platform, spotters were feeding range and speed estimates on the planes overhead into the anti-aircraft directors, which in turn supplied the AA guns with elevations and bearings. At each of the eight 5-inch AA guns was a ready box of ammunition that held 25 shells; the guns began firing as soon as the high-level bombers were spotted. The rounds in the ready boxes were quickly used up and fresh shells were slow in coming up from below. Ensign Frank Lomax, the portside AA Director Officer, went down to the magazine to see if the men there could speed up the resupply. He was never seen again.

Two more bombs barely missed the ship. One fell into the water between *Arizona* and *Vestal*, just abreast of the battleship's mainmast. The other, falling just off the port bow, threw up a very large waterspout when it exploded, causing some of *Vestal*'s crewmen to believe—mistakenly—the battleship had been torpedoed. Despite the damage she'd taken, so far the big ship was holding her own against the attacking Japanese.

Then, at 8:08, *Arizona*'s luck ran out.

The 1,770-pound Type 99 bombs were stopgap weapons, their design a flawed concept produced out of equal parts embarrassing necessity and wishful thinking. After the attack on Pearl Harbor they would never be used in combat again: the modified 14-inch shells proved too unreliable. But when they worked properly, they were devastating in their effect.

Few ships have died as swiftly, as brutally, or as spectacularly as the USS *Arizona*. Only HMS *Hood*, blown up in a gunnery duel with the German battleship *Bismarck*, or the three British battle cruisers immolated at Jutland, ever matched the ferocity of her destruction. The second Type 99 bomb to hit *Arizona*, falling from 10,000 feet, took 23 seconds to reach its target. It struck her foredeck on the starboard side, abeam of Turret Number 2, penetrating the thin steel of the Upper Deck, then punching through the Main Deck and Second Deck, finally exploding when it struck the armor of the Third Deck. The blast ignited black powder launching charges used in *Arizona*'s two aircraft catapults—a fire flared up and spread, reached an open hatch or a vent in one of the magazines filled with the propellant charges for the ship's 14-inch main guns, and flashed through it. Seven seconds after the bomb hit, 1 million pounds—500 tons—of propellant powder exploded.

Seaman Artis Teer on *Nevada* saw *Arizona* "jump at least 15 or 20 feet upward in the water and sort of break in two." As she did, a huge gout of flame—orange, yellow, white—burst out from beneath Turret Numbers 1 and 2, growing until it enveloped the forward half of the ship, rising 600 feet into the air, throwing out glowing white fireballs—still-burning bags of propellant—while a thick, oily jet of black smoke shot up from her funnel. (This would later give rise to the myth that *Arizona* had taken a bomb "straight down her stack.")[4]

The shock wave from the explosion was felt all across Pearl Harbor—sailors on *Tennessee* later claimed that it actually bent bulkheads on their ship. Ten thousand feet overhead, Commander Fuchida's aircraft rocked so violently that he thought it had been hit by anti-aircraft fire. Destroyers in the East and Middle Lochs strained against their lines briefly as the shock wave passed over them. A 10-foot high wave surged outward across Battleship Row. *Vestal* heeled sharply to starboard (she was still moored portside-to-portside with *Arizona*) even as the blast snuffed out her fires as if they were giant candles—her captain and almost every other crewman on her open decks were blown off the ship and into the water. Wreckage, debris, bits of machinery, and body parts were thrown high into the air, thudding down on the surrounding ships and on Ford Island.

The forward 200 feet of the ship was instantly torn apart, the sides of the hull blown outward, the one-inch steel shell plating being ripped from the hull frames and peeling back like flayed skin, the frames themselves shattered. Internal bulkheads were ruptured or torn away. Turret Numbers 1 and 2, along with the conning tower, collapsed downward 30 feet—the supporting structure had disintegrated in the blast; the superstructure and tripod foremast sagged forward at a 45-degree angle, stopped from falling any further by the wreckage below; the hull itself was all but torn in two, just aft of the Turret Number 2 barbette.

In that instant, almost 1,200 men were dead or dying. Almost no one whose battle station was forward of the mainmast survived. A sheet of flame swept over the navigating bridge, where Captain van Valkenburgh was trying to pass orders via the telephone: he and his quartermaster were incinerated. All that was ever found of the captain were two buttons from his uniform jacket and his Naval Academy class ring—it had been welded to a bulkhead by the heat of the blast. On the signal bridge, one deck lower, Admiral Kidd, who had just ordered the fleet to sortie, suffered the same fate—like van Valkenburgh, no trace of him was left save for his class ring, found fused to the central support of the foremast. The officers and enlisted men in the forward turrets, the shell and powder magazines, the handling rooms, the sickbay, the communications center, the forward boiler rooms, all were dead before they could realize they were dying.

But there was a handful of men still alive in *Arizona*'s superstructure. Ensign Douglas Hein was standing at the back of the navigation bridge when he heard the quartermaster tell Captain van Valkenburgh a bomb had struck Turret Number 2. Then "the whole bridge shook like it was in an earthquake, flame came through the bridge windows which had been broken by gunfire." The superstructure lurched forward and down and Hein fell to the deck, badly burned; seeing the portside door to the bridge had been blown open, he staggered through it, worked his way down the wildly tilted ladders that led to the Upper Deck, made his way aft and down to the quarterdeck.

Seaman Russell Lott's battle station was in the port anti-aircraft director on the sky control platform, one deck above the navigating bridge. During General Quarters, as many as 30 crewmen were stationed at sky control: each of the two fire-control directors were manned by six operators, while a dozen or more spotters stood on the open platform. When *Arizona*'s magazine exploded, the spotters were either killed in the blast, blown overboard, or plunged into the inferno below when the superstructure collapsed. The housing of the Mark 28 director provided a measure of protection for the men inside, but it was far from perfect: flames flashed through ventilation hatches and the apertures used by the director's optics, leaving all the men inside burned, some severely. They were alive, but trapped atop the precariously leaning superstructure, surrounded by flames on the levels below—the metal ladders leading off the platform were of no use, they were literally too hot to touch. They could see crewmen below them trying to escape the fires, some of them burning like human torches, staggering across the decks until they collapsed.

With Lott was Donald Stratton, Petty Officer Earl Riner, who was in charge of the director and its crew, Bosuns Mate Second Class Alvin Dvorak, Lauren Bruner, Fire Controlman Second Class, and Harold Kuhn, like Stratton a Seaman First Class. Kuhn's burns weren't as serious as the others', while Bruner had been hit in the leg by a metal fragment when he was climbing up to the sky platform. Stratton was in terrible shape: his uniform had caught fire and his arms, legs, and back were a mass of second- and third-degree burns.

A gust of wind pushed away the smoke around them and they saw a sailor on *Vestal*'s bridge, directly opposite where the six *Arizona* crewmen were stranded. It was Joseph George, a Bosun's Mate Second Class, and fortunately for the men on the sky platform, one of the strongest men in the whole of the Pacific Fleet. Shouting and waving, they got his attention and called for him to throw a line across. It took George three tries, but he succeeded in getting a messenger line over to the *Arizona*, which was quickly secured and then followed by a much heavier line, one strong enough to carry a man's weight.

One of *Vestal*'s officers came up to George while this was going on and told him to cut the remaining lines that tied his ship to *Arizona*. The repair ship already had problems of its own, and now the thick, heavy fuel oil leaking from *Arizona*'s ruptured bunkers was alight, threatening to engulf *Vestal*. Wordlessly, George looked at the officer, then at the men on the sky platform, then back at the officer, who walked away at that point. Meanwhile, Harold Kuhn swung himself out on the heavy line George had passed across and started to pull himself hand-over-hand across the 50 feet that separated the two ships. Stratton followed Kuhn, then came the others, one at a time, with George shouting encouragement the whole time: "Come on, now! You can make it! Keep going!" Lauren Bruner was the last man to leave the sky platform—one of the last men to leave *Arizona* alive.[5]

With its internal bulkheads shattered, torn apart, or knocked down, the forward half of the ship began rapidly flooding, dragging *Arizona* down to the bottom of Pearl Harbor. Back on the quarterdeck, Louis Conter, Quartermaster Third Class, could feel the ship settling beneath his feet, listing, sinking into the harbor. On the Upper Deck, which the crew had taken to calling the Boat Deck, there was a solid wall of flames just ahead of the mainmast; the handful of survivors from the forward part of the ship began to trickle onto the quarterdeck, many of them heading straight for the deck edge and the deceptively cool embrace of the harbor waters. Private James Cory, one of the few Marines on board still alive—only 15 of *Arizona*'s 88-man Marine detachment would survive—remembered them vividly: "These people were zombies, in essence. They were burned completely white. Their skin was just as white as if you'd taken a bucket of whitewash and painted it white. Their hair was burned off; their eyebrows were burned off… Their arms were held away from their bodies, and they were stumping along the decks."[6]

There was one small group survivors that arrived on the quarterdeck smudged and smoke-stained, nursing a few minor burns but otherwise unhurt—the Marines from the secondary fire control position located in the mainmast's boxy fighting top. Major Alan Shapley had been enjoying his last morning aboard *Arizona* when the ship went to General Quarters. He'd been transferred to the 2nd Marine Division and relieved the previous day by Captain John H. Earle, Jr. His only reason for remaining aboard was that he played first base for the Marine detachment's baseball team, which was to play the Marines from the carrier *Enterprise* later that day—the fleet championship was on the line. All that was forgotten, though, as Shapley rushed to his battle station, the secondary fire control, reached by climbing an eighty-five foot ladder attached to one leg of the tripod.

Above him on the ladder was Second Lieutenant Carlton Simensen, *Arizona*'s junior Marine officer. Simensen had almost reached the searchlight platform halfway up the mast when the first bomb to hit the ship struck aft and exploded. Steel splinters ripped into the young officer's chest; Simensen continued climbing until he reached the platform, but there he collapsed and died—one of the splinters had pierced his heart. All Major Shapley could do was push Simensen's body aside and keep climbing.

Reaching the fighting top, Shapley realized that he had an incredible view of the entire attack. Then, just as he was catching his breath, the second bomb hit *Arizona* and the powder magazine exploded; Shapley was one of those who thought she had taken a bomb straight down her funnel. A moment passed, then, as the heat from the flames that enveloped the superstructure became increasingly uncomfortable, he looked at the eight Marines around him and said simply, "We might as well go below, we're no good here."

As the Major and his men now descended the ladder, they could feel its metal getting hotter with every foot. When they reached the searchlight platform, one of the sailors manning the position shouted, "You can't use the ladder!" meaning it was too hot to touch. At that, Private First Class Kenneth Goodman vaulted over the platform railing and landed on the roof of Turret Number 3, spraining an ankle but somehow avoiding more serious injury. Shapley and the rest of his men found that the sailor was wrong and used the ladder to finish their decent. Once on the quarterdeck, Shapley sought out the senior officer present, which turned out to be Commander Fuqua, to report what he had seen of the destruction of the forward half of the ship.

When Commander Fuqua regained consciousness he had set about doing what he could to save his ship—or what was left of her—long enough to get her surviving crew off. (It literally *was* "his" ship now: with Captain van Valkenburgh dead and Commander Ellis Geiselman, the Executive Officer, ashore, Fuqua, as First Lieutenant, was in overall command of *Arizona*.) At the Naval Academy, he had earned a reputation for being unflappable; he set about proving the truth of it now. For Fuqua, Major Shapley's quick, frank briefing on the condition of the ship forward of the quarterdeck was confirmation that the time had come to abandon *Arizona*. To prevent the stunned and horribly injured survivors from jumping into the water and drowning, Fuqua called out to QM Conter, "Lay the injured on the deck until we can get them off!" Then he organized a fire-fighting party to contain the aviation gasoline fire on the quarterdeck and hold back the encroaching flames from the Upper Deck long enough for an orderly evacuation.

There was no pressure in the water mains for the fire hoses, so Fuqua told a half-dozen crewmen to find as many CO_2 extinguishers as possible. They found a total of 14 and together fought a rear-guard action against the fires. Fuqua finally ordered "Abandon ship!" and Conter went in search of any surviving crew that might still be below. Many had already vacated the lower decks when the power went out and water began flooding in, but there were some who were trapped, the rising water having cut off their only routes to the decks above. Then there were those who, with months and years of discipline overriding their instincts, were simply waiting for orders. Most of the men in Turret Numbers 3 and 4, the magazines and handling rooms, machinery spaces, and storerooms on the Third Deck had no idea what had happened or was happening. Electric power abruptly cut out, so they were without communications with the rest of the ship and were dependent on the fitful light of a handful of "battle lanterns," the Navy's standard battery-powered emergency lights. Something was clearly wrong, but what—and what to do about it?

Gunner's Mate Lawson's experience was typical. After hacking away the last of the stern lines that tied *Vestal* to *Arizona*, he ducked through a hatchway that led to another way into Turret Number 4's shell handling room. He was puzzled when the ship didn't get underway as he'd expected—Captain van Valkenburgh certainly knew that a motionless ship was a sitting duck for *any* kind of attack. He realized that *Arizona* was in trouble when the men in the powder handling room one deck below began shouting, "We're getting water and it's coming pretty fast!" The officer in command of the turret told them to move up to Lawson's level, but the water kept rising and in minutes both handling room crews were climbing up into the gunhouse.

They seemed safe enough for the time being. It made sense to stay put, as they could hear machine gun bullets bouncing off the turret armor as the Japanese planes intermittently strafed *Arizona*'s decks. Lawson took a quick look through a viewport in time to see a Filipino mess steward get hit in the back and fall to the deck, dead. The ship shuddered and groaned as it settled—everyone realized by now that she had sunk to the harbor bottom—and the water stopped rising before it reached the gunhouse deck.

Now their lives were threatened from another quarter, however: when the water reached the racks where the emergency batteries were stowed, it mixed with the acid in the batteries, producing chlorine gas. Their eyes and noses stinging, the men labored to breathe. As Lawson remembered it, "The fumes were so bad I was sitting there in the pointer's chair with a t-shirt over my nose, saying, what do we do next? The division officer was absolutely worthless—he didn't know what to do either. We had no communication with the bridge, we couldn't ask anyone what was going on. We were just sitting there in limbo. We knew we'd been hit bad."[7]

After just a few minutes, though it seemed much longer than that, the men decided they'd had enough and told the division commander that they were evacuating the turret, orders or no orders. The officer, whether bowing to the inevitable or relieved that the decision had been made for him, agreed. Scrambling out the hatch at the rear overhang of the gunhouse, they were greeted by the sight of a broken, burning ship. Some of the men rushed to the base of Turret Number 3, where a pair of life rafts were stowed, undid the lashings, carried the rafts to the deck edge, and dropped them in the water; normally, *Arizona*'s aft freeboard was between 15 and 20 feet, depending on how deeply she was loaded—now it was only four.

As he was herding crewmen together on the quarterdeck for evacuation, QM Conter opened one last dogged-down hatch on the starboard side near Turret Number 4. It led to an escape shaft from the starboard engine room and was almost completely flooded. In it were four men clinging precariously to the ladder welded to the shaft wall, standing with their heads thrown back so that their faces were above water—barely. They couldn't get the hatch open from inside the compartment and had been minutes away from drowning while within inches of safety.

Conter and the able-bodied men not fighting the fires helped the most grievously burned and injured into the few boats that had pulled alongside *Arizona*'s stern. There hadn't been time to launch the ship's boats: at first all that were available were the launches which only moments before had been collecting crewmen who had liberty or were going ashore for church services, and a few captains' and admirals' barges. The crew of the hospital ship *Solace*, moored off the east end of Ford Island, sent over as many of their own boats as could be manned, but it took some minutes for them to arrive. Bosun's Mate DeWayne Barth stood at *Arizona*'s fantail, pushing into the water whatever life rafts and floats he could find. When the quarterdeck was awash, most of the battleship's remaining crewmen who hadn't found a place in a boat decided to try to swim to Ford Island, a few made for *Nevada*. Some had no choice: Glenn Lane, for example, had been toppled off the deck and into the water by the blast from the magazine—now he found himself swimming in water covered with a thick scum of black bunker oil. Boats from the hospital ship *Solace* retrieved as many of these swimmers as possible. Commander Fuqua and QM Conter were able to get all of the burned and bleeding survivors from the forward part of the ship away from *Arizona*—Fuqua estimated that there were 70 all told—and when the last boat, a captain's barge, pulled away, the last man to leave the ship was Fuqua.

While *Arizona* was dying, the high-level Kates, including Fuchida's, that hadn't released their bombs on the first pass over Battleship Row circled wide to the north and now were lining up for a second run. The anti-aircraft fire was becoming more intense and more accurate—Admiral Kimmel's insistence on months of unrelenting drills and practice was paying off—as gouts of dark gray smoke began bursting around and among the bombers. Fuchida's Kate suddenly bounced and shuddered as if whacked by a giant club; looking around, he heard the radioman saying that there were holes in the fuselage and the rudder cables had been damaged. Matsuzaki still had control, however, so the plane kept its position in the formation. (Fuchida and his crew wouldn't know until they were back aboard *Akagi* just how close they had come to personal disaster: the rudder cable had been all but severed—only a few strands of wire were holding it together. Had those wires failed, the plane would have become unflyable and crashed.)

Fuchida concentrated on the bomb run, anxiously watching the lead plane. Chief Petty Officer Watanabe held his aircraft steady and this time Petty Officer Aso was satisfied with what he saw through his bombsight. "This time the lead bomber was successful, and the other planes of the group followed suit promptly upon seeing the leader's bombs fall," Fuchida wrote later.

> I immediately lay flat on the cockpit floor and slid open a peephole cover in order to observe the fall of the bombs. I watched four bombs plummet toward the earth. The target—two battleships moored side by side—lay ahead. The bombs became smaller and smaller and finally disappeared. I held my breath until two tiny puffs of smoke flashed suddenly on the ship to the left, and I shouted, "Two hits!"
>
> When an armor-piercing bomb with a time fuse hits the target, the result is almost unnoticeable from a great altitude. On the other hand, those which miss are quite obvious because they leave concentric waves to ripple out from the point of contact, and I saw two of these below. I presumed that it was battleship *Maryland* we had hit.[8]

Though there would be no way to know for certain whose bombs hit and whose missed, what wasn't in doubt was the result: a pair of bombs hit *Tennessee*, two struck *West Virginia*, and one hit *Maryland*.

Yet, once more luck seemed to change horses in mid-stream, as the Type 99 bombs, one of which had delivered such awesome and awful devastation to *Arizona* only minutes earlier, now failed miserably. *Tennessee* was hit squarely atop both Turret Number 2 and Turret Number 3, yet instead of exploding deep with the turret barbettes and producing a volcanic eruption when both the forward and after magazines exploded with even greater force than what *Arizona* had suffered, the bombs broke up on impact, barely penetrating the turrets' armored roofs. The bomb that struck *Maryland* and hit her forecastle did explode, but it caused only minor damage; a near miss at the bow did further damage to the shell plating. One of the two that hit *West Virginia* was a dud, later found buried in wreckage on the Second Deck, having somehow plunged through the searchlight platform, signal bridge and main deck without exploding. The other bomb landed squarely on the roof of Turret Number 3, but broke up on impact. After the fate suffered by *Arizona*, it was almost an anti-climax. Fuchida, of course, was certain that the hits he saw on "*Maryland*" had in fact exploded deep within the ship and done crippling damage.

Such over-optimism was understandable. Why would he not think it to be so? Even from 10,000 feet he could see that the forward half of *Arizona* was a mass of flame and smoke, *Tennessee* appeared to be burning as well (it was actually the pall of smoke and the burning bunker oil flowing out of *Arizona* that he mistook for fires on *Tennessee*), *West Virginia*'s deck was awash, and *Oklahoma* was rapidly turning turtle.

Almost as though the sight of *Arizona*'s destruction was too much to bear, in the seconds that followed *Oklahoma* seemed to give up the fight and her roll to port picked up speed. On *Maryland* crewmen hastily grabbed firefighting axes and hacked away at the heavy mooring hawsers that tied the two ships together to prevent *Oklahoma* from being pulled into *Maryland*'s port side as the sinking battleship continued to roll. When the list reached somewhere between 35 and 40 degrees, her righting moment vanished, her last vestiges of stability were gone, and she reached the point of no return. On Ford Island, Esther Molter cried out to her husband, Chief Petty Officer Albert Molter, "Al, there's a battleship tipping over!" Molter rushed to the window where his wife was standing and together they watched *Oklahoma* capsize, "slow and stately," as Molter later recalled, "as if she were tired and wanted to rest."[9]

In what seemed to add insult to injury, two final torpedoes hit her, this time above the armor belt, driving deep into her hull before exploding, compounding the damage already done. Within minutes *Okie* lay on her beam ends, oil gushing from ruptured bunkers and fractured fuel lines, the portside faces of the big, box-like mast tops slipping into, then vanishing beneath, the surface of Pearl Harbor. Her roll would finally stop when first those mast tops and then her superstructure dug into the harbor bottom.[10]

Scattered across the keel were hundreds of her crewmen; hundreds more bobbed in the water around the ship, or found a place in one of the handful of boats floating by. Inside her hull another 500 men—a quarter of *Okie*'s complement—were trapped in a bizarre world where down seemed up and up seemed down. With the power gone, the only lighting inside the ship came from whatever battle lanterns were handy, casting strange, murky shadows that only deepened the crewmen's disorientation. Seamen and officers alike found themselves fighting for life as they were trapped in unfamiliar spaces with the water rising about them; more often than not they struggled to survive in total darkness. Seaman First Class George Murphy was lucky enough to find a battle lantern as he was bobbing about in the darkness, caught in an air pocket in the sickbay, trying to figure out where he was. Not realizing the ship had actually turned over, he couldn't recall any compartment that had a tile ceiling—he didn't know he was looking up at the operating room floor.

When seawater began rising in Turret Number 4's powder handling room, Seaman Stephan Young thought it was overflow from counterflooding in some of the portside void spaces. It was only when the water continued to rise, the list never stopped growing, and the thousand-pound shells started toppling from their racks in the magazine directly above, making a hell of a din, that he and the 30 or so other sailors in his division realized that *Oklahoma*—and themselves—were in mortal danger. They were trapped in an air pocket deep inside the ship with no way out within the upturned hull. Faint yells told them that other crewmen survived in an adjoining compartment. In the flickering light of a battle lantern and with water up to their chests, the men could do little but bang on the deckplates above them with hammers and hands.

Oklahoma was still turning when Shipfitter Second Class Wayne Vickery, making a beeline for the upper deck, almost ran over a group of sailors who inexplicably had huddled to pray in a Third Deck gangway. His voice mixing consternation, disbelief, and anger, he bellowed, "Pray later! Get your asses off the ship!" That startled the men into movement, and Vickery followed them as they fled upward. Just as he was climbing one final ladder, the last of the torpedoes to hit the ship exploded, knocking him back down to the deck. By now the ladder was almost upside down, impossible to climb, but someone overhead threw a line down to Vickery, who pulled himself up to the hatchway and onto the open deck.

Yeoman Richmond, like scores of his crewmates, was groping his way through the darkness, trying to stay ahead of the rising water. He was one of the lucky ones who somehow found his way to a compartment with a hatch to the open deck. Willing hands were reaching down into the hatch from above and pulling up the sailors who had already gathered there—the men doing the pulling were Commander Kenworthy and Lieutenant Commander Hobby. When it was Richmond's turn, they couldn't reach him—Richmond stood only five feet, two inches tall. Kenworthy told him to go to the starboard side, crawl through one of the 5-inch gun casemates, and get out that way.

Richmond did so, but once there, he found himself 20 feet above the water, with the broad expanse of the ship's anti-torpedo bulge in the way. He jumped as far as he could but came up short, landing hard on his lower back. Years later he described that moment, saying, "I felt a shock of intense pain, I couldn't feel my legs, and I had to use my arms to scoot down the hull… Then I slid into the oily water and ducked under."

Richmond had learned his lesson the hard way, but survived it—barely. (He would later find out he had broken his back when he landed on *Oklahoma*'s hull.) Others weren't as lucky: Wayne Vickery, catching his breath after his hand-over-hand climb from the deck below, watched sailors jumping into the water on the port side of the ship, because it was easier to reach, never realizing that *Oklahoma* was about to roll over on top of them. He shouted at them to stop but they couldn't hear him over the cacophony of aircraft engines, explosions, anti-aircraft fire, and the din of the sinking ship itself. Turning away, Vickery climbed up the slanting deck to the starboard deck edge. There he found dozens of seamen doing exactly what Ray Richmond had done—trying to jump out far enough to clear the hull before hitting the water. Too many of them were diving blindly, unable to see what was below the surface because a thick coat of oil from *Oklahoma*'s bunkers was spreading across the water. The men were hitting their heads, knocking themselves unconscious, or possibly even killing themselves, when they fell short and struck the side of the ship. Vickery bellowed (he apparently had a powerful voice) for the men to sit down and slide along the plating until they reached the water. Taking his own advice, he scooted down *Oklahoma*'s side and into the water, where he calmly waited to be picked up by one of *Maryland*'s boats.

The first inkling George DeLong, a Seaman First Class, had that Pearl Harbor was under attack was when the torpedoes began blowing holes in *Oklahoma*'s side and the ship suddenly lurched to port. He was in the crew's bunking space in Steering Aft, down on the Third Deck, along with seven other crewmen. With so many of the void spaces opened up for next day's inspection, the flooding spread rapidly, and some of the men came close to panicking when they realized they were trapped. The power failed, leaving them in a darkness that was relieved only by the glow of a single flashlight; the noise was deafening as everything loose inside the ship began shifting while *Oklahoma*'s roll increased—then got louder still as equipment and machinery broke loose from their mountings and crashed into bulkheads and overheads. Water began pouring into the compartment through a two-foot square air vent; DeLong and the others struggled to block it by stuffing a rolled-up mattress into the vent, finally securing the mattress with a wooden Acey-Deucy board they lashed into place on top of it. Now came the hardest task of all—waiting. They had no way out, no way of knowing how long their air would last, or even if anyone knew they were there. From time to time one or another of the eight men would bang out an "S O S" on one of the bulkheads, hoping someone would hear and come looking for them.

When the attack began, Ensign John England, who was just four days shy of his 21st birthday, was in *Oklahoma*'s communications center—her radio room—on the Third Deck, just aft of the Turret Number 2 barbette. He'd volunteered to take the watch for a friend who'd gone ashore this morning to meet family visiting from the mainland. The torpedoes hit, the power failed, and the ship began her roll to port; England was able to find his way through the darkness to reach the Upper Deck, then realized that none of the other men in the radio room had followed him. He went back down and led three of them out, one by one—no one will ever know why he did it that way, because when he went back to the radio room a fourth time, he never returned. His body was never identified.

With the power gone, it took time for the order to abandon ship to spread. By the time word reached the gun turret where Seaman First Class James Ward was stationed, the list was already sharp and water was rising in the turret. Ward found a flashlight, and it gave off just enough illumination to allow the men in the turret to find a way out of their crazily canted surroundings. Man after man passed Ward, who calmly held the light, making no move to get out himself. Whether he just waited too long or was overwhelmed by a sudden inrush of water will never be known, but Seaman Ward was not one of the men who made it out. He had been in the Navy exactly one year and two weeks.

Ensign Francis Flaherty died the same way, using a battle lantern to show the men in his gun turret the way out. Chief Carpenter John Austin, trapped along with several of his crewmates in a pitch-black compartment half-filled with water, found a porthole in *Oklahoma*'s outer bulkhead. He was able to guide 15 of the men to it, all of whom were able to swim to the surface. Austin himself was never seen again.

There were so many men in the water around *Oklahoma* that it looked like a public swimming pool on a summer holiday. Marine Private Ray Turpin was not a strong swimmer, and he hesitated at the idea of joining that thrashing throng. Instead he walked up the quarterdeck as the ship rolled, and found himself standing on *Okie*'s starboard side when she finally fell over onto her beam ends. He heard someone close by shouting for help and when he turned around was startled to see a sailor with his head and shoulders sticking out of a porthole. Carefully walking over to him, Turpin pulled the man out, only to find another seaman behind him rising up through the port. Three more followed, although getting the fifth man out was a challenge. "The last guy, his name was Bob Burns…he was a little larger and had a little more weight on him than the skinny little recruits that just came in. So I had a little trouble getting him through the porthole." Turpin shouted for help and a sailor rushed over. "The two of us, we each had an arm and were trying to move him out," Turpin he said. "The poor guy. We were about to pull his arms out of their joints. He'd scream and we'd let up. And he'd say, 'don't stop. Keep pulling.' We finally got him out."[11]

The Marine and the sailor succeeded in pulling Burns through the porthole in part because someone underneath Burns was pushing him up as they pulled. That someone was Lieutenant Aloysius Schmitt, *Oklahoma*'s Chaplain. He had just celebrated his last Mass aboard her, as he was being transferred to duty ashore in the week ahead. When the torpedoes hit and the lights went out, Schmitt, shepherd that he was, gathered as many men as he could find and led them to a starboard-side compartment, where they used a porthole to escape the ship. That became more and more difficult as *Oklahoma*'s list grew, until it became nearly impossible when the porthole was overhead.

Just then Turpin came along and lent a hand. Father Schmitt tried to follow Seaman Burns, but the breviary he'd stuffed in a back pocket caught on the porthole frame, and he had to drop back into the compartment, gesturing for the other men to go ahead of him. Lending a hand whenever he could, Schmitt was able to help at least a dozen more of *Okie*'s crew escape the rising water—at the cost of his own life. A month later, at a Protestant memorial service in San Francisco, a Jewish sailor would stand to tell the story of how he owed his life to the sacrifice of a Catholic priest.

Meanwhile, it was time for Ray Turpin to get off the ship. Seeing a 3-inch line still tying *Oklahoma* to *Maryland*, he swung onto it and began to pull himself across, only to have one of *Maryland*'s seamen cut the line—on orders from the bridge—when Turpin was just a few feet shy of her hull. He dropped into the oil-covered water and began floundering about. "I went into the water with all this 3-inch line on top of me. I had a hard time figuring out which way was up," he said later. "I finally popped up and there was a sailor in the water who was a good swimmer. I told him I wasn't a very good swimmer. So he helped me over to the *Maryland*, where there was a 1-inch line hanging from the deck." Using that line to pull himself up to the deck, he found one of *Maryland*'s anti-aircraft guns crewed by fellow Marines and immediately joined them, passing ammunition. Ray Turpin finally had a chance to fight back.[12]

When she finally stopped rolling, *Oklahoma* was lying upside down at a 135-degree angle, only the dull red of the starboard half of her hull bottom now visible. Astern of her, *West Virginia* was clearly sinking, but the kind of counterflooding that *Okie*'s crew had never had the chance to begin was keeping *WeeVee* more or less upright. There was one beneficial consequence to her situation: the rising water flooded the ship's magazines, no small concern given what had happened to *Arizona*. When the attack began and *West Virginia* went to General Quarters, Stu Hedley, his friend Walter Crosslin, and the other 25 men in Turret Number 3 had nothing to do but wait for orders which were unlikely to come—there would be no targets for the 16-inch guns in an air raid. They felt the ship shake repeatedly as Japanese torpedoes slammed into her port side and felt the battleship begin listing to port. Crosslin suggested they find out what was happening outside, and uncovered one of the sighting periscopes—just in time to watch *Arizona* explode. They saw equipment, machinery, bodies, and parts of bodies being thrown in every direction, some of it raining down on *West Virginia*'s quarterdeck. Shaken by the sight, Crosslin told the rest of the crewmen that they were better off staying put inside the gun turret for the time being.

Over on *Tennessee*, the Type 99 bomb that hit her Turret Number 3 split open and the explosive filling, rather than detonating, caught fire, rendering the left-hand gun useless and killing four men in the process—a fifth would die later that day; they were the only fatal casualties aboard *Tennessee* in the entire attack. The bomb that landed atop Turret Number 2 punched a hole in the gunhouse roof but broke apart as it did so—there wasn't even so much as a fire with this one. But it did send fragments of the turret's armor screaming in every direction, some of them striking *West Virginia*'s bridge. One, about four inches square with razor-sharp edges, tore across Captain Bennion's mid-section, cutting a deep gash. With a groan Bennion collapsed to the deck, bleeding heavily.

A runner got word of Bennion's injury to Lieutenant Ricketts, who sent a Pharmacist Mate to the bridge to do what he could for the captain. Lieutenant Commander Johnson, the ship's communications officer, brought Doris Miller to the bridge to help carry Captain Bennion to the upper deck, three levels down. A

Mess Attendant Second Class—at the time one of the very few ratings in the Navy open to black sailors—and *West Virginia*'s heavyweight boxing champion, Doris Miller stood six feet, three inches tall and weighed over 200 pounds: if anyone could bring Captain Bennion off the bridge, it was him. But an oil fire at the base of the superstructure blocked the only route down from bridge that Miller could have used while carrying Bennion, so he and another sailor moved the captain to a sheltered spot behind the conning tower.

The Pharmacist Mate did what he could for Bennion, who was still conscious and lucid despite the excruciating pain of his wound. The captain insisted that he be kept informed of the condition of his ship and continued to give orders. He instructed one of the ensigns with him on the bridge to make certain that all watertight doors and hatches were secured; later he ordered *West Virginia*'s anti-aircraft gun crews to move over to *Tennessee*. That ship still had power for her guns—*WeeVee*'s people would be more useful over there.

With nothing more to be done for the captain for the time being, Lieutenant White and Ensign Victor Delano, with help from Miller, loaded the two .50 caliber anti-aircraft machine guns mounted on the bridge, just aft of the conning tower. Delano stepped away for a moment to check on Bennion, and was surprised to hear "his" gun begin firing: Miller had seized the grips of the big machine gun and pressed the firing stud—even though he'd never been trained on .50 caliber, he already knew how to shoot: he'd helped feed his siblings back home in Waco, Texas, by hunting small game with a .22 rifle. "It wasn't hard," said Miller shortly after the battle. "I just pulled the trigger and she worked fine. I had watched the others with these guns. I guess I fired her for about 15 minutes. I think I got one of those Jap planes. They were diving pretty close to us." Miller kept shooting until he ran out of ammunition; whether he actually shot down one of the Japanese attackers has never been confirmed, although no one aboard *West Virginia* ever put in a formal claim.[13]

Lieutenant Ricketts came back to the bridge, and together with Miller and two officers, made another attempt to get Bennion off the bridge by lowering him down to the upper deck on a makeshift stretcher. When that effort failed, Lieutenant White, Miller, and a signalman were able to carry the captain one level higher, to the navigation bridge, to get him out of the thick oily smoke that had begun roiling through the lower superstructure. By this time, Captain Bennion was losing consciousness; he died a few minutes later.

One level above Captain Bennion, on *West Virginia*'s range finder platform, Ensign George Hunter was stunned by what he saw as he looked out across Pearl Harbor: "It was a devastating sight. Forward of the *West Virginia* the *Oklahoma* lay bottom up. Inboard of her the *Maryland* was putting up a tremendous volume of fire. I wondered what the 'rump-rump' noise was and suddenly realized it to be the *Maryland*'s 1.1" guns which proved extremely effective. Astern of us the *Arizona* was a mass of flame."[14]

Far below where Ensign Hunter stood, well forward on the Hold Deck, the very lowest level of the ship, Seamen Ronald Endicott, Clifford Olds, and Louis Costin were caught in the inrush of water that followed the first torpedo hits. All the ladders and hatches to the decks above were aft of them, and by the time they realized what was happening, the flooding had cut them off. They took refuge in a storeroom, which by pure good luck was stocked with emergency rations, fresh water, and a handful of battle lanterns. As *WeeVee* settled to the bottom of Pearl Harbor, leaving her quarterdeck submerged and her foredeck awash, her gun turrets and superstructure above water, the three sailors could only wait, hoping someone would hear them banging on the bulkheads and come to their rescue.

The men in Turret Number 3 finally decided to get out while the getting was good: despite Commander Hillenkoetter's best efforts, the fire started by the fuel from the two shattered float planes perched on the turret catapult was getting out of hand. The Type 99 bomb that landed on the turret roof allowed some of the burning gasoline into the turret, where it ignited the glycerin in the recuperator (the cylinder which controlled recoil) on the left-hand gun, causing a flash fire that killed 11 men. That was enough for Stu Hedley and his buddy Crosslin: Crosslin said, "Stu, let's get the hell out of here!" and the surviving crewmen pushed and shoved their way through the escape hatches in the underside of the gun house.

Hedley and Crosslin ran over to the starboard side of the quarterdeck, prepared to dive into the water between *WeeVee* and *Tennessee*. One look convinced them that this was not a good idea—the burning oil from *Arizona*, mingling with the bunker fuel leaking from *West Virginia* herself, was already starting to flow around the stern, and the water itself was littered with debris, some of it large enough to do a man injury if he struck it while diving in. Hedley's first thought was to do as a lot of other crewmen were doing: swing onto of the heavy hawsers that tied *West Virginia* and *Tennessee* together and pull himself across, but no sooner had the idea occurred to him than one of the Kates came zooming along between the row of battleships, machine gun rattling, strafing the men who were clinging to the lines. Hedley watched as dead and wounded shipmates fell into the water and changed his mind. Instead, he and Crosslin ran out on the barrel of one of the 5-inch guns, dove into a patch of open water, and swam over to *Tennessee*. When they hauled themselves aboard, they were told to get over to Ford Island. "'How?' I asked a chief petty officer. 'Swim, you idiot!' We stripped down and jumped into the water and swam to the beach of Ford Island. Every time I came up to breathe I inhaled hot, burning air." By the time Hedley reached the shore, *West Virginia* was resting upright on the bottom of Pearl Harbor.[15]

At his battle station atop *Tennessee*'s foremast, Seaman Jack Evans' view was in some ways even better—and more distressing—than that had by George Hunter aboard *WeeVee*. A Seaman Second Class, he was one of a half dozen aircraft spotters who worked with the telephone talker connected to the anti-aircraft fire control. This morning there were more enemy planes roaring about than he could report, some actually flying so low Evans could look down at them. "We were about 122 feet off the water and could see everything. My job was to report aircraft to the fire control center phone talker. I saw plenty. I looked north toward the center of the island and watched the smoke rising from Wheeler Field and Schofield Barracks. To the east past the *West Virginia* and *Oklahoma* a really big column of smoke was rising over Hickam. I saw this one plane with fixed landing gear fly right over our bow."[16]

Evans didn't bother to look astern—there was really nothing he could see there: heavy smoke from the mass of flames that engulfed *Arizona*'s superstructure along with even thicker, blacker smoke billowing up from the burning bunker oil that coated the water around the wreck completely obliterated the view astern of *Tennessee*'s mainmast. Moving with the outgoing tide, the burning oil was creeping closer to her stern, threatening the lives of the men swimming in the open water between her and *West Virginia*, sheets of flame flowing around and past *Tennessee*'s stern.

Those fires were an even more immediate threat to *Vestal*. The old repair ship—launched back in 1908, she was the oldest ship in the harbor, save for the minelayer *Oglala*—had taken a pounding when *Arizona* blew up. Hull plates were buckled, frames distorted, seams sprung open. There was no immediate panic among the crew—there was surprisingly little panic anywhere in Pearl Harbor this morning— but they were definitely nervous. No one aboard knew if Captain Young was still alive, or, if he was, where he might be found, and the executive officer was convinced that the flooding would soon sink the ship. He had a point: *Vestal* was taking on more water than her working pumps could handle. If he couldn't save the ship, he would at least save the crew—the word went out to abandon ship.

Down in the engine room, the chief engineer began stoking the fires in *Vestal*'s one working boiler, trying to raise enough steam to get the ship under way. When a runner brought down the order to abandon ship, it appeared that the effort had been wasted, and the engine and boiler rooms were evacuated. Hardly had they reached the main deck when they were greeted by an apparition from the underworld standing in the starboard gangway. "Where the hell do you think you're going?" the figure shouted in a voice loud enough to be heard above the guns and explosions going off around *Vestal*.

"We're abandoning ship!"

"Get back where you belong! You don't abandon ship on me!" It was the captain, Commander Young, soaking wet and covered in black fuel oil.[17]

After being blown off *Vestal*'s deck and into the harbor, he'd swum back to the repair ship's starboard side, where he found a rope ladder hanging down that led to the starboard gangway. He clambered up it and took back command of his ship. A fair man, he never said a word in reproach to his executive officer: the decision to abandon *Vestal* wasn't a wrong decision, it just wasn't the one Cassin Young would have made. Ordering the engineering crew to go below again, he set about getting

Vestal away from the burning wreck of the *Arizona*. Any remaining lines to the battleship were cut, and a harbor tug was signaled over to help pull the ship clear of her mooring. In the engine room, the chief engineer had barely a quarter of the steam pressure normally needed to turn the engines, but he somehow managed to get them started and *Vestal* began to move, however slowly.

She was still taking on water faster than her pumps could manage and began to take on an ominous list to starboard. Her crew did their best to plug leaks and shore up weak bulkheads, but there was no denying that *Vestal* was sinking. Young, not wanting to try anything fancy as the ship's rudder wasn't working—the bomb hit aft had damaged the steering gear—had the tug guide his ship straight past the battleship *Nevada* and across the east end of Pearl Harbor, where he dropped anchor off McGrew Point. There *Vestal* slowly settled to the bottom, sitting securely upright on a sandbar.

At the west end of Battleship Row, *California* was slowly sinking to the harbor bottom: water was flowing into her hull faster than her pumps could eject it. Her Executive Officer, Commander Earl Stone, finally arrived on board—he and Captain Joel Bunkley, as well as Admiral Pye, had all been ashore when the attack began—and took charge of the damage control efforts. There was precious little he could do, though: when ship lost power, the pumps stopped, and *California* began to list ominously. Meanwhile the Vals continued their relentless dive-bombing attacks, one of which scored a direct hit that crashed through the ship's Upper Deck close to the starboard side of the forward superstructure. This bomb penetrated all the way to the Second Deck before detonating, killing 50 of *California*'s crew while starting a serious fire in the ship's interior. At this point, the best Stone could hope to do was prevent the battleship from turning over, instead settling on the harbor bottom on something like an even keel. To do that, the crew had to be told to set Condition Zed, but Stone was handicapped by the same problem that had plagued the officers on *West Virginia* and *Oklahoma*: the loss of power took down most of *California*'s internal communications; using voice-powered telephones and runners, Stone did what he could to pass the word. With all the ship's electric lights out and oil fumes spreading throughout the lower decks, *California*'s crew struggled in the darkness and foul air to close enough watertight doors and hatches to keep their ship from capsizing.

At the opposite end of Battleship Row, *Nevada* so far had been spared the same degree of attention the Japanese were giving the ships moored ahead of her. Ensign Taussig had hardly finished calling the ship to General Quarters when the Marines in the "birdbath" on the mainmast fighting top opened fire with two .50 caliber machine guns, and the ready gun in each of the port and starboard anti-aircraft batteries began banging away at the Japanese torpedo bombers. Taussig raced up *Nevada*'s superstructure to the starboard anti-aircraft director and plugged into the sound-powered telephone network that connected the anti-aircraft guns and gave them the ability to concentrate their fire on specific targets. The problem this morning was that there were too many targets, too close and moving too fast—there were more Japanese planes swarming over Battleship Row than the system could accurately track.

That didn't stop *Nevada*'s gunners from taking down at least two of the Kates. One appeared to be making a torpedo run on *Arizona*—*Nevada*'s gunners claimed that one exploded in mid-air. The second Kate was aiming for *Nevada* herself when machine-gun fire shredded it. The gunners were an instant too late in getting that one, though: the pilot dropped his torpedo a second before his plane spun into the harbor. The torpedo ran straight and true, and hit *Nevada*'s hull abreast of the forward gun turrets. The ship rocked as the warhead exploded, and sagged slightly to port, but the anti-torpedo blister on the battleship's lower hull did its job and despite a hole 40 feet long and 30 feet wide being torn open in the outer plating, none of the ship's vitals were breached. As they flew past *Nevada*, the Kates that had already dropped their torpedoes strafed her decks with their machine guns.

It may have been one of those bullets that drilled through Joe Taussig's left thigh, or it could have been a splinter from a bursting AA shell; it might have been a fragment from the decks or hull of *Arizona*, which had just exploded. Whatever it was, it knocked the young ensign to the deck and smashed the fire control computer in the director. Suddenly deep in shock, his leg shattered and nearly severed, the ensign felt no pain, and only after a few seconds did he notice that his left foot was lodged up under his armpit. Taussig commented absently, "That's a hell of a place for a foot to be."[18]

Collapsing to the deck, Taussig refused to be evacuated from the director platform, and instead tried to continue to direct the anti-aircraft guns, although most of the telephone lines had been cut. He also sent a runner down to Central Control with orders to start counter-flooding on the starboard side aft and bring *Nevada* back onto an even keel. Either the runner got it wrong or Central Control misunderstood the order, as damage control parties were sent forward instead, and flooded the trim tanks in the starboard bow, giving the ship a distinct bow-down trim.

Over on *Solace*, Lieutenant Ruff, like so many others that morning, saw explosions erupting on Ford Island and immediately thought, "Uh oh, some fool pilot has gone wild," imagining a terrible training accident had happened involving live ordnance. It wasn't until he saw *Arizona* all but vanish in a searing yellow flash that he realized Pearl Harbor itself was under attack. (Not far from where Ruff was standing, a visiting army physician, Dr. Eric Haakenson, was filming the attack with a hand-held 8mm movie camera—and by chance had the lens pointed at *Arizona* just as she blew up.) Ruff ran down the accommodation ladder on *Solace*'s side, jumped into a waiting launch and ordered the coxswain to take him back to *Nevada*. The trip across the harbor seemed to take forever, but at last the boat pulled up to the battleship's stern and Ruff jumped onto the landing platform of the boarding ladder.

Running up to the quarterdeck, Ruff ignored the chaos around him as he made for the ship's radio room. Halfway there, he nodded absently in passing to Ensign Charles Jenkins (known for some reason as "Pops"), then abruptly stopped and turned around, heading for the navigation bridge. He'd realized that the radio room could function perfectly well without him, but with *Nevada*'s captain and executive officer both ashore, most of the officers remaining on board were mere ensigns: Lieutenant Commander Francis Thomas, *Nevada*'s first lieutenant and damage control officer, was going to need all the help he could get.

Already standing on the navigating bridge as if he owned it was Quartermaster Chief Robert Sedberry, a careerist who had spent a dozen years in the Navy. Sedbury had already notified the engine room to be prepared to get under way—he'd seen the signal for all ships to sortie hoisted by Admiral Furlong on *Oglala*. Here Ensign Taussig's mischievous initiative paid an unexpected dividend, as that second boiler was already coming on line: just one of *Nevada*'s six boilers couldn't raise enough steam to move the ship, but two boilers could—barely. When Lieutenant Ruff appeared, Sedbury gave him a quick, concise briefing on what he knew of *Nevada*'s condition as well as Admiral Furlong's order to sortie. As Ruff saw the situation, if *Nevada* was ever going to make a run for the open sea, the sooner she got moving the better, before the Japanese could do any further damage.

Ruff called down to Commander Thomas in Central Station, the main damage control center, and explained the situation. Thomas agreed that *Nevada* should get under way as soon as possible; he also knew that when she did, his place had to be on the bridge, not buried on one of the lower decks. He confirmed that the firefighting parties had all been properly dispatched and that the counter-flooding measures were underway—he hadn't yet caught the error in where the flooding was being done—then set out on the 80-foot vertical climb up the access trunk out of Central Station, through the conning tower and onto the navigating bridge.

Once there, he confirmed everything Ruff had told him, then called down to engineering to be prepared to "answer bells"—that is, respond to engine orders. Chief Sedbury took his place at *Nevada*'s wheel, Thomas nodded to the quartermaster manning the engine telegraph, who twice worked the brass handles back and forth, the "Stand By" signal for the engine room. Then Thomas gave the order: "Helm amidships. Slow astern." At 8:25 AM, *Nevada* began moving.

It was then something very strange seemed to happen. Almost as if on cue, just as suddenly as they appeared the Japanese were gone, their bombs and torpedoes exhausted. By 8:40 AM, the last aircraft of the first wave of the Japanese attack was winging away from Pearl Harbor. Behind them, Fuchida's bombers, dive bombers, torpedo planes and fighters left two cruisers and a minelayer heavily damaged, a target ship sunk, and, most critically to the objectives of the attack, three battleships damaged—*Tennessee*, *Maryland*, and *Nevada*; three sunk—*Oklahoma*, *West Virginia*, and *California*; and the blasted, blazing wreck that had been *Arizona*. Wheeler and

Hickam Fields were devastated, the hangers and machine shops blasted, blazing ruins, and more than half their fighters and bombers had been reduced to wreckage or blazing hulks. The stunned, tired, and frequently burned and bloody defenders had been given what would be a short-lived reprieve, as high overhead Commander Fuchida's Kate remained behind, circling at better than 10,000 feet. He was waiting to watch what would happen next.

The second wave was on its way.

CHAPTER 9

Inferno

The tens of thousands of men and women in and around Pearl Harbor watching the Japanese warplanes disappear over the mountains had no idea that their respite would be short lived; they were fervently hoping they had seen the last of their tormentors. All around them were scenes for which "chaos" was hopelessly inadequate to describe. Great, roiling clouds of thick, bitter, black smoke, columns of red and yellow flames at their hearts, spread the length of Battleship Row, hundreds of tons of bunker fuel burning uncontrollably as it oozed around the hulls and superstructures of sunken or immobilized battleships. Within those broken ships lay hundreds of dead sailors and marines; hundreds more were wounded or injured, many likely to die if help didn't reach them soon.

At Hickam and Wheeler Fields, the shattered aircraft hangars, demolished buildings and barracks, and long flight lines marked by burning and smoldering wrecks of bombers and fighters were testimony to both the intensity and precision of the Japanese attack. Officers and enlisted men, pilots and groundcrew alike began working through the wreckage and debris, looking for wounded and injured men, laying out bodies in neat rows on the concrete aprons and taxiways. In the distance, to the east, north, and west, smaller yet still ominous columns of smoke were rising: while spared the concentrated fury of the attacks on Wheeler and Hickam, most of the secondary Army airfields and Navy air stations scattered across Oahu had received their own measure of attention from the Japanese.

Oil-soaked survivors from the sunken ships on Battleship Row wandered aimlessly about Ford Island, which was a shambles. Eleven bombs had exploded on the island, most of them in and around the seaplane base at the west end; it had been one of the prime targets for Lieutenant Commander Takahashi's dive bombers. Hanger 6 was burning fiercely, as were most of the 36 PBY's stationed there. When *Arizona* blew up, she settled across the main that supplied Ford Island's fresh water, leaving the firefighting crews with no way to extinguish the fires; the best they could do was to try to contain them and push what aircraft that could be saved away from the flames.

More worrisome was the situation in which the tanker *Neosho* found herself: most of the 143,000 barrels of aviation gasoline her crew had begun pumping into Ford Island's huge storage tanks at midnight were already off loaded when the first wave of Japanese planes began their attack: had she still been half or even one-quarter full she would have been a huge fire hazard, which would have been bad enough. But now, with some of her tanks empty save for gasoline vapors, she was not only still an enormous fire hazard, but she was, under the right—or wrong—circumstances, potentially a gigantic floating bomb. The crew, keeping anxious eyes on both the flaming bunker fuel being pushed by the wind and tide along Battleship Row toward *Neosho* and the fires on Ford Island, were working feverishly to disconnect the pipes that attached the ship to Ford Island's pumping station so the ship could pull clear of both hazards.

On Battleship Row, launches, cutters, and barges darted back and forth, plucking men out of the oil-slicked water. Many of them were put ashore on Ford Island, those who were injured were carried over to the hospital ship *Solace*, or rushed to the Naval Hospital that sat beside the entrance channel to the harbor, whichever was closer. Some men insisted on going back aboard their ships, or one of the others if theirs was sunk or abandoned, to help with damage control and to fight fires.

What was absent was any widespread sense of panic: there was fear, shock, confusion, anger—but little panic. Most moved and acted with a sense of purpose that would have given the likes of Tojo Hideki, Sugiyama Hajime, and Matsuoka Yosuke in Tokyo pause to reflect on their presumptions of Americans as lax, timorous, irresolute. There would be no lack of trepidity shared among the higher echelons of the War and Navy Departments in the weeks to come, but the first flicker of a cold, dangerous determination to repay with interest the self-styled, latter-day *samurai* of *Dai Nippon* for lives lost and damage done could be seen in those moments between the departure of the first wave of enemy aircraft and the arrival of the second. How the men in Washington DC would react remained to be seen; for the men at Pearl Harbor, the decision had been made before the attack was over.

* * *

Admiral Kimmel's quarters, sitting on the gentle slope of the Halawa Heights, just above CINCPAC Headquarters at the base of the Southeast Loch, always offered a sweeping, breathtaking view of the whole of Pearl Harbor. The view this morning was indeed breathtaking as usual, but in the worst possible way. Kate torpedo bombers lining up their approaches to Battleship Row, Val dive bombers on their way to Hickam Field had roared over Kimmel's house as the attack began, and the admiral, still doing up the buttons of his tropical white uniform jacket, had run out onto the front lawn and watched as his fleet was decimated—*California* and *West Virginia* settling to the harbor bottom, *Oklahoma* slowly rolling over to port, and of course, *Arizona* was immolating herself with a magazine explosion. Legend has it that when he recognized the red *hinomaru* on the attacking aircraft, Kimmel exclaimed in puzzlement, "How could they possibly be Japanese planes?"

As with Yamamoto's epigram about a sleeping giant, the remark is almost certainly apocryphal, as Kimmel didn't need to have it explained to him how the Japanese bombers and fighters reached Pearl Harbor. Still, he must have wondered how they got there without anyone in Washington or Hawaii even suspecting they were on their way. Yet, for the moment, at least, the answer was irrelevant.

Kimmel's car pulled up in his driveway, and as soon as the admiral's door closed, it began rolling again, on its way to CINCPAC Headquarters. Kimmel knew that there would be little he could accomplish there except collect the bad news; no matter what he did today, this battle was lost. That meant that he had to begin preparing to win the next one.

* * *

Even as the second wave of aircraft was approaching Oahu, one part of the Hawaii Operation had already well and truly run its course: the attempt to attack the Pacific Fleet from within Pearl Harbor by the quintet of midget submarines. In contrast to the success of the airstrike, this phase of the operation had been a near-total failure. It had been an audacious undertaking, in some ways more daring than attacking the Pacific Fleet from the air, but it had also been far too ambitious, a clear-cut case of reach exceeding grasp.

All of the five Type A submarines were lost, just as those in Tokyo who had planned the mission had expected. What they never anticipated was that three of them would be sunk or abandoned without ever having an opportunity to fire their torpedoes, while a fourth would be rammed and sunk by one of its targets; only one Type A was able to successfully attack the enemy's warships.

The first to die were the *I-20tou* and its crew; shelled and depth charged by the USS *Ward*, it sank three miles south of the entrance to Pearl Harbor. The *I-22tou* was run down and sunk by the destroyer *Monaghan* inside Pearl Harbor—the submarine's commander, Lieutenant Iwasa Naoji, was crushed in the collision, while his helmsman, Petty Officer Sasaki Naokichi, was permanently pinned in the wreckage. *I-18tou* sank in relatively shallow water just outside of Keehi Lagoon, three miles east of the entrance to Pearl Harbor. The boat had been damaged, though not catastrophically, in a depth charge attack, most likely one dropped by the destroyer *Helm*, and here began one of the many minor mysteries of the attack on Pearl Harbor.

When the wreck of the *I-18tou* was discovered in June 1960, the conning tower hatch was found undogged, that is, the heavy clips, called "dogs," that pulled the hatch tight against its coaming to make a watertight seal, were undone, something that could only have been accomplished from inside the boat. But there was no trace of the two crewmen, apart from a few articles of clothing and some personal effects; both torpedoes were still in their tubes. Equally curious, the fuses on the scuttling charges had not been lit. The most plausible scenario for the situation as it was found was that the damaged *I-18tou* began taking on water, which the crew couldn't stop; they were able to surface their boat before its reserve buoyancy was overcome by the flooding, with just enough time for the commander to undog and open the hatch—and in their haste to escape they forgot to light the fuses on the little submarine's scuttling charge. At that moment, though, the two crewmen, Lieutenant Funuro Shigemi and Petty Officer Yokoyama Shigenori, vanished without a trace. Their bodies were never found, they weren't captured by the Americans, they never returned to Japan. They were probably trying to make their way to shore—after all, the plan to be picked up by either *I-68* or *I-69* hadn't changed—when they were swept away in the surf, eventually drowning or dying of exposure far out to sea.

I-24tou's mission was a failure almost from the moment the little submarine was released from the deck of *I-24*. Its gyrocompass stopped working, leaving the crew unable to navigate; Ensign Sakamaki Kazuo, the commander, and Chief Warrant Officer Inagaki Kioshi, the helmsman, tried to find the entrance to Pearl Harbor by dead reckoning, but only succeeded in twice bouncing off reefs along the Oahu shore before running aground on a third reef, this one to the east of the harbor channel, just as the USS *Helm* came charging out of Pearl and opened fire with her 5-inch guns. A pair of near misses jarred the little sub free of the reef, but the two crewmen were knocked unconscious in the process, and the boat drifted out into the surf, where the current gradually carried it around to the east side of the island.

When they finally regained consciousness, sometime after midnight on December 8, Sakamaki and Inagaki realized that their batteries were almost exhausted, and without a working compass they had no chance of making a rendezvous with *I-68* or *I-69*. A PBY was circling overhead, obviously lining up to drop depth charges, so they ran *I-24tou* aground and abandoned it, Sakamaki lighting the fuse on the scuttling charge before climbing out of the sub. *I-24tou*'s luck held true to form, however: the demolition charge inside the boat never detonated. Sakamaki managed to stagger through the surf and collapsed in exhaustion on the beach, so he didn't realize the charge had failed to explode until it was far too late to do anything about it. When he awoke in the morning, he found Inagaki's body lying nearby in the sand; how and when the helmsman died remains uncertain, as some accounts claim he drowned trying to swim ashore, others stating that he had been shot in the head. If the latter is true, Inagaki most likely took his own life rather than subject himself to the disgrace of being captured by the Americans. For himself, Sakamaki had no choice in the matter, as within moments of coming to in the sand, he was taken prisoner by Sergeant David Akui of the Hawaiian National Guard, whose infantry squad had been asigned to patrol along this particular stretch of beach. Sakamaki became the United States' first Prisoner of War in the newborn conflict between America and Japan.

Enough evidence has accumulated in the years since the attack to make the case that *I-16tou*, alone out of all of the midget submarines, succeeded in penetrating the defenses of Pearl Harbor and carried out an attack on the battleships of the Pacific Fleet. At 10:40 PM the night of December 7, the Type A sub's crew chief on *I-16* was sitting in the big submarine's radio room, listening on the dedicated set used by the smaller boats. Without warning, he heard the word "Success" tapped out twice in *Wabun* code; because the message came on the frequency assigned to *I-16tou*, the transmission could have come from no other source. A few hours later another message was picked up, this was saying "Unable to navigate." After that, silence.

Sixty-eight years later, the wreck of a Type A submarine lying three miles off the entrance to Pearl Harbor was identified as *I-16tou*. It had been lying there, along with hundreds of tons of scrap steel, since 1944, part of the aftermath of the West Loch Disaster on May 21 of that year. *LST-353*, loaded with drums of gasoline and crates of mortar ammunition, blew up when the cargo was mishandled, destroying herself and causing six other LST's to sink. Unknown to anyone, one of them sank on top of the remains of *I-16tou*, which had been scuttled in the West Loch three years earlier. Operations to remove the wrecks and clear the West Loch basin began almost as soon as the last fire was extinguished, and as the broken hulls and fractured keels were dredged up, the wreck of *I-16tou* was brought up with them, carried outside the harbor, and dumped into the ocean. The hulk of *I-16tou* was immediately recognized for what it was—a Japanese midget sub—but because Operation FORGER, the invasion of the Marianas Islands, was set to begin just three weeks after the disaster, no one had much time for documenting its fate. Damage to the hull clearly showed that it had been scuttled and not sunk by an American warship, but what became of Lieutenant Commander Yokoyama Masaji and Chief Warrant Officer Soyeda Udamu remains unknown—no mention was made one way or the other if the remains of the crew were still inside the Type A when it was dredged up in 1944.

How *I-16tou* came to be in the West Loch was ultimately easy to deduce. Yokoyama, in what must be regarded as a brilliant piece of seamanship, brought his unwieldy boat into Pearl Harbor, and just as dawn was breaking, carefully positioned *I-16tou* in the Southwest Loch, where he had perfect shots at *Oklahoma* and *West Virginia*. When the first wave of Japanese aircraft struck, he fired both torpedoes, scoring a hit on *Oklahoma*, that devastating fourth detonation which sealed the battleship's fate. The other torpedo missed its target; it was found when *WeeVee* was being refloated, lying in the mud on the harbor bottom. In a report sent to the Navy Department by Admiral Chester Nimitz, the warhead was stated to weigh almost 800 pounds, confirming that this was a Type 97 torpedo, which only the Type A submarines used in the attack on Pearl Harbor.

His two torpedoes spent, Yokoyama took advantage of the massive confusion created by the airstrike and maneuvered *I-16tou* into the West Loch, where he and

Soyeda waited for an opportunity to escape. That night he sent his two signals to *I-16*, the second apparently being Yokoyama's way of admitting that the little boat's batteries were close to exhaustion and no longer had enough power to leave Pearl Harbor and reach the rendezvous. Sometime thereafter, *I-16tou*'s scuttling charge was detonated, although whether or not the two crewmen abandoned their boat first or chose death before the disgrace of capture will forever remain unknown—like the men who were aboard *I-18tou*, no trace of *I-16tou*'s crew would ever be found.[1]

But all of that was still in the future when sharp eyed observers on Ford Island and aboard the ships in Pearl Harbor spotted a horde of black specks coming over the mountains to the north and east, steadily growing larger. The Japanese were back.

* * *

Kido Butai's six carriers began launching the second wave of Japanese aircraft, 171 in all, at 7:15 AM, to cheers from the plane handlers, mechanics, armorers—and the carriers' crewmen— as loud and enthusiastic as they had been for the first. To the immense disappointment of their pilots and bombardiers, four of the planes, three Vals and one Zero, had mechanical problems and were forced to abort their takeoffs. That left 54 Kates, 78 Vals, and 35 Zeroes that swiftly coalesced into a single large formation before heading south, with the Kate of Lieutenant Commander Shimazaki Shigekazu, Fuchida's second-in-command, taking the lead. By 8:45 it made landfall on Oahu, and just as the first wave of Japanese planes had done, the formation began to break up as smaller groups of one or two squadrons each peeled off toward their assigned targets.

The closest was the seaplane base at Kaneohe Bay, on Oahu's east coast. Kaneohe had already been hit hard in the first wave of the Japanese attack: Genda's plan designated the base as a priority target despite its relatively small size, as Kaneohe was home to three full squadrons of PBY's. The long-range patrol bombers were sure to be the first aircraft the Americans would send out to search for *Kido Butai*. It's likely that the first attack of the day was actually made at Kaneohe by the first wave—in the chaos that swept over Oahu that morning, people had more important things to do than keeping track of precisely what took place when.

In any case, just before 8:00, nine Zeros swooped down on the base and in the space of 10 minutes had destroyed or damaged most of Kaneohe's 36 PBY's. Like everyone else on the ground that morning, the pilots, observers, gunners, and ground crew of Patrol Squadrons VP-11, VP-12, and VP-14, were taken completely by surprise. The sound of aircraft engines overhead elicited a few barbed comments about Army Air Corps flyers, but it wasn't until the first of the Japanese fighters nosed over and began shooting up the flightline that they realized they were under attack.

That was when Chief Petty Officer John Finn first realized it as well. Still in bed with his wife alongside him, he had been looking forward to a rare drowsy, undisturbed Sunday morning when the gunfire and explosions began. He jumped up, dressed hurriedly, and rushed over to the flightline, where some of the PBY's were already burning. Groundcrew and aviators scrambled to get their hands on whatever weapons they could, and Finn, who was an aircraft ordnance specialist, commandeered a Browning .30 caliber machine gun from one of the base's painters. He dragged out a tripod normally used for gunnery training and set it up in front of the hangars, then loaded and charged the Browning, and began hammering away at every Japanese plane on which he could draw a bead.

As one Zero pulled out of its dive, multiple machine guns opened up on it, and the aircraft staggered under the weight of fire it was taking. As his plane clawed for altitude, the pilot must have realized that it had been fatally damaged, because he abruptly pitched the nose over and dived straight for Kaneohe's three hangars. If they were his target, he was unlucky—or else he lost control of his plane—as it overshot the hangers and plunged into a hillside just beyond them, blowing up on impact.

Chief Finn watched the Zero dive to its destruction, then turned his attention back to the remaining Japanese planes. It seemed as if all the Zero pilots were determined to stay until they had exhausted their ammunition, and they made repeated strafing runs across the Kaneohe air station. As runners brought out fresh belts of ammunition, Finn stayed behind that machine gun for almost 45 minutes, keeping up a steady, accurate fire. "I was out there shooting the Jap planes and just every so often I was a target for some. In some cases, I could see their [the Japanese pilots'] faces. I don't know if I hit any of them, but I sure fired at every Japanese plane I saw," was how he would remember that morning.[2]

As abruptly as they had appeared, the Japanese vanished around 8:30, and everyone at Kaneohe began fighting the fires and trying to save those few PBY's that hadn't been blown apart and could be repaired. Now, 20 minutes later, more Japanese planes appeared and another attack began, and CPO Finn, having been given some rough-and-ready first aid, returned to his Browning .30 machine gun, where he once again fired at every plane he could see. By the time the second attack was over he had been wounded 21 times. Most were caused by bomb fragments and flying debris, but at least two were from bullets—one that passed straight through his right foot, another hitting his left arm, leaving it hanging limp at his side.

This time the Japanese had brought bombers—nine Kates, each carrying a single 550-pound bomb and a pair of 132-pound bombs, accompanied by an equal number of Zeroes. The second attack finished what the first had begun: Kaneohe's Number 3 hangar took a direct hit from one of the large bombs; the rest tore up the ramp leading into the bay, along with the machine shop and the dispersal areas. Twenty-seven of the air station's PBY's had been destroyed, while six others were damaged—at the end of the day, the only planes based at Kaneohe that were untouched were the three out on patrol during the attack.

Sitting just a few miles down the coast from Kaneohe, Bellows Field got off lightly when the first wave of Japanese aircraft struck Oahu—a single Zero fighter, piloted by Lieutenant Tadashi Kaneko, made a few strafing passes, but caused neither casualties nor damage. This was fortunate for Lieutenant Richards and his crew, as their B-17C came barreling into Bellows just after the single Zero left. One of the 12 Flying Fortresses that just arrived from the West Coast, Richards had been forced to divert from Hickam when the formation flew right into the middle of a war. Determined to get his aircraft down on the deck as quickly as possible, Richards brought the big bomber in fast and hot—too hot, as it turned out: the B-17 went skidding off the end of the runway and stopped, nose down, tail up, when it ran into an earthen embankment. The damage was fairly minor, though, and the plane could have been salvaged, except that just minutes after Richards and his crew scrambled to safety, the Japanese returned, this time in strength.

Bellows wasn't as lucky as it had been in the first attack. Eight Zeroes zoomed in low and shot the B-17 to pieces, then banked sharply and dove on the 12 P-40s that were parked in a neat formation beside the runway. The 44th Pursuit Squadron had moved to Bellows earlier that week for air-to-air gunnery training, but at the moment all of its aircraft were sitting with their fuel tanks empty and ammunition unloaded; some even had their guns removed for cleaning. Working frantically under fire, at the cost of five wounded, ground crews were able to get three P-40s fueled and armed, but all three were shot down as they were taking off; two of the pilots were killed, the third was seriously injured. By the time the Zeroes flew away, all of the Army Air Corps' planes at Bellows were either destroyed outright or damaged badly enough to render them unusable. Meanwhile, the rest of the second wave of Japanese aircraft—45 Kates and 78 Vals, along with 27 Zeroes—was bearing down on Pearl Harbor.

* * *

Edwin Hill was 47 years old, and he had spent the last 30 of them in the United States Navy. He was *Nevada*'s Chief Bosun, her senior enlisted man, an old salt of the sort who younger sailors regard with awe—Chief Bosuns were rumored to discuss naval policy with God, on a first-name basis. He knew his ship intimately, and it was his business as Chief Bosun to know everything that went on aboard her. It wouldn't have escaped his notice, then, that, unlike all the other warships tied up on Battleship Row, *Nevada* had *two* hot boilers, not just one, and he understood that any battleship sitting motionless while under attack was just a big, fat, juicy target.

No one would ever know just how he learned that Lieutenant Commander Thomas and Lieutenant Ruff were going to try to get *Nevada* under way—but, being a Chief Bosun, he did. He began gathering men to cast off *Nevada*'s mooring lines while the two officers, along with Quartermaster Sedberry, were working out exactly how they would get the ship away from her berth. Under normal conditions, getting *Nevada* out of her berth and under way required having steam up in at least four of her six boilers, the assistance of four tugs, a half-dozen spotters on the navigating bridge along with a harbor pilot and the navigator, with the Captain on board to supervise the entire evolution. What Thomas, Ruff, and Sedberry were about to attempt violated just about every peacetime regulation on the books for normal ship operations, but then, conditions were hardly "normal" and peacetime had ended about 30 minutes earlier.

Chief Bosun Hill sent one work party aft, where they jumped into the water, clambered up onto the mooring quays, and cast off the heavy mooring lines; he led the forward line party on the quay himself. Burning oil from *Arizona*'s ruptured bunkers spread toward them and bullets from strafing Japanese airplanes flew everywhere, mixed with the fragments of the anti-aircraft shells that burst high overhead, but Hill and his men got the lines undone. Hill waved to the bridge to signal that *Nevada* was clear of her moorings.

Thomas, Ruff, and Sedberry were ready. The first step in getting *Nevada* out of her berth would be to move the ship back far enough to be certain she would swing clear of *Arizona*'s stern, so Sedberry called out to the quartermaster at the brass engine room telegraph, who rang down for "Slow Astern" on both engines. For a few moments nothing happened, but the men on the bridge knew that it took time to get 30,000 tons of battleship moving, and *Nevada* started slowly easing astern. When Sedberry estimated that the battleship's stern was nearly touching the floating dredge pipeline that trailed out from Ford Island, he called for "All Stop!" Ruff, acting as navigator, used the starboard pelorus just outside the pilothouse to take bearings on structures on Ford Island he felt confident wouldn't be obscured from view by the smoke rising up from the burning bunker fuel. They would be his navigation markers, helping him fix *Nevada*'s position down to the yard as she moved along Battleship Row. At that point Sedberry, his eyes on the helm indicator and compass card only, would be steering the ship solely by helm orders from Lieutenant Commander Thomas; Thomas' orders would be based on crossbearings taken by Ruff from his sightings on those markers. Given Pearl Harbor's shallow bottom, and that maneuvering a battleship even under ideal circumstances was extraordinarily tricky—the momentum of 30,000 tons of moving steel was immense, and had to be factored into even the slightest change of direction—Ruff wanted to be absolutely certain *Nevada* stayed in the deepest part of the channel.

Once he was sure of his fixes, Ruff nodded to Sedberry, who called for "Slow Ahead" on the starboard engine and "Slow Astern" on the port. The bow began to swing clear of *Arizona*'s stern and Sedberry stopped the engines briefly, then ordered "Slow Ahead" on both and applied a touch of starboard rudder to make certain *Nevada*'s stern stayed well clear of *Arizona*'s burning wreck. It was a close thing even then: it seemed to Commander Thomas that he could have reached out and lit his cigarette with *Arizona*'s flames. But *Nevada* cleared the blazing wreck, and at 8:45 she was officially under way.

Chief Bosun Hill was thrilled to see his ship begin pulling away from her moorings, but then realized that *Nevada* was getting under way without him. Not thinking twice, he leaped back into the harbor and began swimming as hard as he could, determined to catch the ship before she could get away. Here luck was with him, as he reached *Nevada* just as she began moving ahead; someone on deck tossed down a Jacob's ladder and in short order Hill was back aboard.

It wasn't until *Nevada* began easing her way down the South Channel that the full extent of the awful spectacle along Battleship Row was finally revealed to the men aboard her. *Arizona* was an inferno, forcing *Nevada*'s sailors manning the starboard anti-aircraft batteries to shield the shells from the heat with their bodies, fearing that the rounds might cook off. The deck crew managed to throw lines to three of *Arizona*'s sailors who had been blown overboard and now were treading water, bringing them aboard before the men were overtaken by burning fuel oil. Wet, filthy, and mad as hell, the trio was promptly assigned by Bosun Hill to one of the 5-inch AA guns. Several of Ruff's US Naval Academy classmates had been aboard *Arizona*, and he could only wonder if any of them had survived her destruction.

Next came *West Virginia*. It was clear that multiple torpedo hits had torn open her port side: she was visibly settling onto the bottom of Pearl Harbor, but thanks to rapid counter-flooding was still on a more-or-less even keel. All that could be seen of *Oklahoma* was perhaps a third of her red-painted hull—the men on *Nevada* had no idea that nearly 500 of *Okie*'s crew were trapped inside that overturned hull. Moored inboard of *West Virginia* and *Oklahoma*, *Tennessee* and *Maryland* had escaped the barrage of torpedoes, but both had taken bomb damage and now were threatened by the burning oil flowing out of *Arizona*'s ruptured fuel bunkers. As *Nevada* approached the end of Battleship Row, *California* came into view, the flagship of the battle fleet. Flames surrounded her and she, too, was settling to the bottom.

By now people on Ford Island, in the 1010 Dock, on the damaged and sunken battleships, in every corner of Pearl Harbor, were watching *Nevada*'s progress down the channel. Each of them knew that what they were seeing was impossible, there was no way any of the ships on Battleship Row could have gotten underway so quickly. Yet they could not deny the evidence of their eyes: there she was, majestic as only a battleship could be, gliding along the South Channel. On Ford Island, Seaman Thomas Malmin caught a glimpse of her gray hull and superstructure standing in stark contrast against the thick black smoke, then saw, streaming brightly in the morning sun, the ensign on her fantail that young Joseph Taussig had hoisted only an hour before and yet already a lifetime ago. In that moment, Malmin understood as he never had done before what inspired Francis Scott Key to write "The Star Spangled Banner." However it might ultimately end, for those watching *Nevada*'s sortie, in those few moments it became an act of sheer bravado, a moment of unalloyed courage, that one great act of defiance thrown up in the faces of their

Japanese tormentors that would, as much as the immolation of *Arizona*, becoming a defining moment of the attack on Pearl Harbor.

Nevada cleared the end of Battleship Row just before 9:00 AM. Now all that lay between her and the entrance channel to the harbor was the dredge *Turbine* and its pipeline, which was anchored on to Ford Island. That was a problem, though, as the pipeline stretched more than halfway across the South Channel and there was no time to move the dredge or disconnect the pipe. Somehow, Quartermaster Sedberry would have to steer the battleship through the narrow space between the dredge and the concrete face of the drydock complex in the Navy Yard. That would have been a remarkable bit of ship handling on a normal day—and this wasn't a "normal" day. To make matters worse, as *Nevada* was approaching the dredge, time ran out for the ship and her crew: the second wave of the Japanese attack had just arrived.

* * *

This time the Japanese didn't have surprise on their side.

Every gun that had ammunition and power on every ship still afloat and able to fight began firing at them. With the anti-aircraft guns out of action on five of the eight battleships in port that morning the barrage was nowhere as intense as it could have been—and as it would have been when the first wave attacked, had the fleet been alerted in time. Nonetheless, the gun commanders, gunlayers, fuze setters, and ammunition passers who were still in action were now working in a smooth, disciplined rhythm, as the habits acquired in months of training and drills asserted themselves, and what guns there were quickly made themselves problematic for the Japanese flyers.

The seaplane tender *Curtiss* had been one of the few ships able to get underway during the first attack, and despite her small anti-aircraft battery—she carried just four 5-inch guns and four quadruple 40mm mounts—her crew began throwing up as much AA fire as they could almost as soon as the first Japanese aircraft was identified. She'd barely missed being torpedoed by one of the Japanese midget submarines and now, as the second wave of Japanese aircraft appeared, she was back in the thick of the action. Her gunners quickly brought down one of the Vals, would claim a hit on a Zero, and they definitely got a piece of a second dive bomber, but not before it was able to release its bomb. The projectile hit *Curtiss* just aft of midships and started fires in her hangar and on the main deck; the offending dive bomber crashed into the harbor just off her port side. The Japanese fliers quickly decided they'd had enough of the unexpectedly fierce seaplane tender and turned their attentions elsewhere; *Curtiss'* crew turned to fighting the fires and soon had them under control—but the ship had paid for its temerity, at a cost of 19 dead crewmen and many more injured.

A few hundred yards to the east, the crew of the light cruiser *Raleigh* were still fighting to keep their ship afloat. The torpedo she took in the first minutes of the attack created problems that were all out of proportion to the actual damage done. It had hit the cruiser's port side almost squarely amidships, and knocked out the fires in the forward boilers—which just happened to be the ones online at the time—causing her electric generators to abruptly stop turning. Without power the ship's pumps could do nothing to stop the flooding, and the inrush of water was so powerful that several critical watertight doors couldn't be closed because of the pressure. *Raleigh*'s list to port grew ominously, and the crew began throwing overboard whatever seemed like excessive topweight—the two Kingfisher observation planes, the portside triple torpedo tube mount, both bow anchors, reels of cable, just about anything moveable that wasn't shooting back at the Japanese went over the side.

When the second wave of Japanese aircraft appeared overhead, one of the Val dive bombers swooped down on *Raleigh* and dropped its 550-pound bomb. The pilot's aim was good, his luck less so: either the bomb's fuze was faulty or it simply hit in the wrong spot on the ship, but whichever was the case, it penetrated three decks and passed through *Raleigh*'s starboard side without exploding; it finally detonated when it hit the water. The cruiser had been saved by pure good luck, as the bomb actually struck only a few feet from the stowage tanks for the floatplanes' aviation gasoline—had it exploded then, the consequences for the cruiser would have been catastrophic. Eventually the "black gang" was able to get steam up in the after boiler room and start the after generators, while topside the crew lashed the ship to a pontoon barge which kept *Raleigh* afloat long enough for her pumps to get ahead of the flooding and the damage control teams could restore some of her buoyancy. The cruiser would live to fight another day.

What might have happened to *Raleigh* had that bomb gone off near the aviation fuel was amply demonstrated on the other side of Ford Island, in the massive 1010 Dock of the Navy Yard. The cluster of ships moored in and near the yard acted like a sort of magnet for the bombers of the second attack wave: the battleship *Pennsylvania*, the Pacific Fleet's flagship, was up on blocks in the 1010 Dock, along with the destroyers *Downes* and *Cassin*; tied up nearby were the cruisers *Helena*, *New Orleans*, *Honolulu*, *St. Louis* and *San Francisco*. Scattered among the cruisers were a half-dozen destroyers; a seventh destroyer, *Shaw*, was perched in the floating drydock at the north end of the Navy Yard.

Pennsylvania, of course, was the prize. The only battleship in Pearl Harbor that morning not moored along Battleship Row, she had gone through the first attack almost unscathed. Now, though, the Japanese dive bombers of the second wave turned their full attention on her. A handful of torpedo-carrying Kates in the first wave had tried to blow open the massive caisson that closed off the huge drydock, but failed. Had they succeeded, the enormous, near-instantaneous inrush of water would have severely damaged the battleship—refloating a ship in drydock was a precision operation that usually took the better part of an entire day to accomplish without accident—driving her down onto the two destroyers laid up ahead of her and possibly even tipping onto her beam ends as she struck them. That opportunity was missed, though, so now it was up to the Vals and Kates and their 550-pound bombs to do as much damage as they could to the flagship.

It was the two destroyers, *Downes* and *Cassin*, that bore the brunt of the attacks on the 1010 Dock, however. Several bombs exploded around *Pennsylvania*, but only one struck her directly. At least three bombs hit the destroyers, though, including one that detonated squarely between the two and ruptured one of *Downes'* fuel bunkers, setting the oil aflame. What hadn't happened to *Raleigh* now happened to the two destroyers: the fire spread rapidly, burning hot enough to cause *Downes'* second bunker to burst, spraying burning fuel oil across the inside of the drydock and forcing both destroyers' crews to abandon their ships. The warheads on at least two torpedoes cooked off, one exploding so violently that it blew a thousand-pound section of a torpedo tube deep into *Pennsylvania*'s forecastle. By the time the fires burned out, both destroyers were structural wrecks.

As for *Pennsylvania* herself, she was in an especially awkward position. Not only was she immobile, but with the water drained from the 1010 Dock and the ship resting on enormous iron blocks set up on the floor of the dock, her anti-aircraft guns were actually *below* the upper coaming of the drydock walls, meaning the gun crews weren't able to see approaching planes until they were almost on top of the ship. The spotters and the men manning the anti-aircraft director gear up in the superstructure did their best to provide ranges and bearings, but there were so many Japanese aircraft swarming over the harbor that it soon became a hopeless task. The gunners got off a shot whenever they could, but they rarely had more than a second or two to track an enemy plane before it vanished again.

One man *could* see the Japanese bombers as they began their bomb runs and dives on *Pennsylvania*, a civilian by the name of George Walters. He was the operator of the enormous electric crane that sat on rails embedded in the concrete structure of the 1010 Dock which ran its entire length. Watching the AA gunners vainly trying to shoot back at their attackers, he had the sudden, slightly crazy idea that he could help them defend their ship. Jumping into the cab of his crane, he began to run it back and forth along the wall of the dock, swinging the crane head around in whatever direction he saw an approaching Japanese aircraft. He fancied that by interposing his crane between them and their target, he would distract the pilots and throw off their aim.

Whether or not his ploy actually succeeded no one would ever know—none of the Japanese pilots made mention of it when they returned to their carriers—but the gun crews on *Pennsylvania* eventually caught on to the fact that the crane's movements were giving them a few vital seconds' warning of where the next Japanese plane would appear. Witnesses later claimed that one Val, flying a bit too low, snagged its landing gear on the crane's cables—its wheels torn off and heavily damaged, the plane crashed on Hospital Point. Walters' luck ran out when a bomb exploded at the base of his crane taking it out of action and nearly flinging him out of the cab. He later came to in the Navy Hospital, astonished at his own survival: "Why God protected me, I don't know," he told the medical staff. "But He must have had a reason."[3]

As determined as they were to cripple *Pennsylvania*, the Japanese aviators only managed a single direct hit on the battleship. At 9:06 a bomb glanced off the concrete wall of the dock and plunged through the deck plating on the battleship's boat deck, exploding in the casemate of the Number 9 5-inch gun, wiping out the entire gun crew. By the time the attack ended, *Pennsylvania*'s casualties would total 15 dead, 38 wounded, with another 14 crewmen missing.

Even though it seemed to the men aboard *Pennsylvania* that every Val and Kate overhead was targeting their ship, not all of the Japanese pilots ignored their orders to concentrate on the cruisers in the harbor. A bomb exploded in the narrow stretch of water between *Honolulu*'s port side and the concrete pier where she was tied up, shaking the entire ship. The blast stove in several of her hull plates and punctured two of her fuel bunkers; her forward magazines were flooded and both forward gun turrets lost power. For all that, not a single man in her crew was killed or wounded in the course of the entire attack.

St. Louis was tied up outboard of *Honolulu*, her boilers at stand-by, her powerplant shut down, electrical power being supplied to her by the shipyard. Her lookouts spotted the first wave of Japanese planes almost as soon as they came over the mountains to the north and west of Pearl Harbor, but no one aboard recognized them as Japanese until one of the Kates swept down the Southeast Loch, roaring past the cruiser's stern, and launched its torpedo at *Oklahoma*. Finally realizing that Pearl Harbor was under attack, *St. Louis*' crew went to General Quarters. Seeing Admiral Furlong's signal "All ships in harbor sortie" go up, Captain George Rood wanted to get underway immediately. That was easier said than done, but the crew set to with a will; while the engineers began spinning up the generators, those men not manning the anti-aircraft guns began clearing away anything that tied the ship to the dock or *Honolulu*. One shipfitter took a cutting torch to the gangway and in a few minutes it fell into the water with a rattling crash; another cut away the fresh water supply pipe, and as the generators came online, other crewmen broke the electrical connections to the dock and cut away the mooring lines.

While all this was going on, *St. Louis*' gunners were banging away at Japanese planes that flew past. They claimed one probable kill in the first wave, but once the torpedo bombers made their runs down the Southeast Loch, not many aircraft flew within range of the cruiser's guns. Not so when the second wave arrived: with the cruisers now the main target of the Japanese aviators, *St. Louis*' guns found plenty of airplanes at which to shoot. They claimed two more "probables" before the ship was ready to pull away from the dock—no small feat, as the circuit breakers for the elevation and training gear in the AA guns were all ashore, being refurbished—the gunners had to rotate and elevate the guns by hand. They were still doggedly firing away when, at 9:31, *St. Louis* backed away from the pier into the Southeast Loch, swung her bow around and, as Captain Rood ordered "FULL AHEAD," charged out into the South Channel, headed for the harbor entrance and the open sea.

No one would have criticized the crew of the heavy cruiser *New Orleans* had the men simply walked off her decks and over to other ships, hoping to make themselves useful there. Like most of the other cruisers in the Navy yard that morning, *New Orleans* was drawing her electrical power from the Navy yard, as all her boilers were shut down and her engines were undergoing repair—one entire turbine was being readied for replacement. The situation went from bad to worse when a near-miss severed the electrical feed to the ship just minutes after the attack began, leaving the engineers down in the engine room to work by flashlights and battle lanterns as they tried to restore power. Up topside crewmen who could find rifles and pistols began taking pot shots at low-flying Japanese planes—for the moment they had nothing else with which to fight back. With no electrical power at all, *New Orleans'* situation was even worse than *St. Louis'*—not only did the guncrews have to manually elevate and train the 5-inch/25 AA guns, the ammunition hoists couldn't be used to bring up fresh rounds from the magazines. This meant the 54-pound shells had to be physically carried topside one by one. *New Orleans'* crew met the challenge head-on: every man who wasn't working in the engine room, firing an anti-aircraft gun, or busy with some other essential job immediately fell into one of the lines snaking from the AA magazines to the upper deck, passing fresh ammunition as rapidly as they could. It was here that one of the most memorable moments of the entire Pearl Harbor attack took place.

Lieutenant (j.g.) Harold Forgy was what sailors irreverently called a "sky pilot," a chaplain. Classified as "non-combatants" by the Hague Conventions and the Geneva Accords, chaplains were forbidden to carry, fire, handle, or in any way serve or service any weapon of any description. Strictly speaking, this also meant that Chaplain Forgy wasn't allowed to join in any of the lines of crewmen passing ammunition to the anti-aircraft guns. But Forgy was a good officer: he wasn't about to stand idly by, hobbled by a technicality while his shipmates were grunting, sweating, straining to keep up a steady flow of shells for the anti-aircraft guns. So he passed out oranges and apples, carried fresh water, offered a word of encouragement where he thought it was needed, made small jokes where he could. At one point, with a wry grin, he remarked to a handful of crewmen that, "We can't have church this morning, men, so praise the Lord and pass the ammunition."[4]

New Orleans might have been in a poor condition to fight back, but *San Francisco's* situation was even worse. She would go on to earn 17 battle stars in the war that had just begun, but at the moment she was as good as helpless. Almost all of her anti-aircraft guns had been removed to be either overhauled or replaced—two twin .30-caliber machne-gun mounts were the only serviceable weapons aboard the cruiser—and her engineering machinery had been taken apart for repairs and rebuilding. She had no power, no lights, no guns. Most of her crew went over to other ships that did have working guns and made themselves useful.

What no one realized until after it was all over was that, for all of its apparent fury, this attack on the cruisers wasn't doing all that much damage, at least not compared to the first wave. In part this was due to the relative inexperience of this group of Japanese aviators—most of these aircraft came from the brand new carriers *Shokaku* and *Zuikaku*, and the pilots lacked the *sang froid* of their fellows from *Kaga* or *Akagi*. They were also put off by the unexpected intensity of the American's anti-aircraft fire: the Navy gunners weren't shooting down all that many planes, but they were disrupting bomb runs, disturbing the bombardiers' aim, and causing more than a few young dive bomber pilots to break out of their dives prematurely. Until, that is, those pilots saw *Nevada*.

* * *

Nevada's sortie would be remembered by the Americans as the single most stirring incident of the entire morning of December 7, 1941, and with good reason. But while she was the only battleship to get underway during the Japanese attack, she was not the only warship to pull out of her berth and head for the open sea—for that matter, she wasn't even the first: *Helm* and *Monaghan* were already underway when the first bombers arrived. With orders to concentrate primarily on battleships and cruisers, the Japanese aviators had paid very little attention to most of the destroyers in Pearl Harbor that morning, which suited the crews of the little ships just fine. A typical US Navy destroyer weighed between 1,000 and 1,500 tons—a mere fraction of a behemoth like *Pennsylvania* or *Nevada*—and bombs which only dented battleship armor could blow a destroyer apart. Still, the small size brought with it certain advantages, one of them being that a destroyer could get underway with a single working boiler, something no battleship could do. Scattered around the East Loch, a handful of "tin cans" prepared to do just that about the same time that Commanders Ruff, Thomas, and Quartermaster Sedberry were working out the details of getting *Nevada* away from her berth.

The destroyer *Blue*, moored just off McGrew Point was the first to get moving; at 8:40 she cast off her lines and began steaming westward through the South Channel. As she passed down the shambles of Battleship Row, here and there a cheer went up from the battered warships' crews, who took the destroyer's passing as a small but meaningful act of defiance, a lower-case edition of the grand statement soon to be made by *Nevada*. *Blue* was the first of an irregular, rag-tag procession of six destroyers that had been at anchor when the attack began and managed to put to sea while the bombs were still falling.

As on the bigger ships, weekends in port were normally the days when a destroyer's complement of ensigns, usually only three or four, could gain some experience standing watches, and December 7, 1941 was no different. What was exceptional was that those young, unseasoned officers reacted, quickly, decisively, and with a self-assurance that should have been beyond their years: *Blue* was under the command of Ensign Nathan Anders, the senior officer aboard *Dale* was Ensign Frederick Radel, Ensign James Benham, a 24-year old assistant engineer, took command of *Farragut*, and Ensign Stanley Caplan was acting as the captain of *Aylwin*. *Ralph Talbot* and *Patterson* both put to sea with junior officers in command, though they were a bit more senior and experienced lieutenants; together with *Helm* and *Monaghan*, they formed an anti-submarine screen outside the entrance to Pearl. It wasn't much of a combat force if a squadron or two of Japanese battleships and heavy cruisers were lurking in the waters around Oahu, but it would have to do.

* * *

The destroyers making their way down the entrance channel blazed away furiously with every gun that could be brought to bear on the Japanese planes overhead, but the enemy fliers ignored them, as every Japanese pilot with a bomb still slung beneath his plane focused on a much bigger, more important target—the battleship *Nevada*. The next 20 minutes would be the old warship's Golgotha: Vals lining up on *Pennsylvania* pulled away and dove on *Nevada* instead; 29 Kates from *Kaga* diverted their bomb runs from the cruisers in the Navy Yard to line up on the battleship as she threaded the needle between the dredge *Turbine* and the floating drydock. High overhead, watching *Nevada*'s slow progress down the South Channel, Commander Fuchida willed his pilots on, thinking "Ahh, good!... Now just sink that ship right there!" in the hope that in doing so they could block the harbor entrance. In quick succession *Nevada* was hit by five 550-pound bombs. Standing on *West Virginia*'s bridge Ensign Victor Delano saw a huge explosion erupt in *Nevada*'s bow, and the whole ship seemed to lurch upward and shake violently with the blast. One of the bombs had punched through the forecastle deck and exploded near the fuel tank holding the aviation gasoline for *Nevada*'s spotter planes; white-hot flames shot skyward as the fuel and fumes ignited—these fires would burn for two days before they were fully extinguished. But *Nevada* would be spared the sort of immolation that had consumed *Arizona*: all of the ammunition and propellant charges for her main guns had been offloaded days earlier. Another bomb hit the ship near Turret Number 1 and tore huge holes in the main and upper decks; splinters and fragments tore into the anti-aircraft gun crews, leaving so few uninjured that sometimes three men were doing the work of seven. Vals and Kates that had already dropped their bombs swooped low over *Nevada*'s decks, raking them with machine-gun fire, cutting down anyone not taking cover.[5]

Nevada wasn't the only ship to suffer during this onslaught, as a few bombs that missed the battleship still found targets. Sitting perched high and dry inside the floating drydock as *Nevada* passed by was the destroyer *Shaw*, undergoing repairs to her hull. A trio of bombs struck her forward superstructure, two of them wrecking the machine-gun platform, the third crashed through the port bridge wing and exploded against her deck. Her forward fuel bunkers were ruptured and the leaking oil immediately caught fire, which spread quickly and within minutes was burning out of control. An attempt was made to localize the fires by flooding the drydock, but failed; by 9:25 *Shaw*'s entire bow was engulfed in flames and the order was given to abandon ship.

On board *Nevada*, Ruff and Thomas, with the enthusiastic vocal support of young Ensign Taussig, who was lying on a stretcher nearby, still believed that they could reach open water. Almost as if he could read their minds, Vice Admiral William Pye, the commander of Battle Force itself, quickly put paid to that idea: standing on the admiral's bridge of the battleship *California*, herself on fire and sinking, he had a perfect view of the fury raging about *Nevada*, and saw that she was in far worse condition than those on board could realize. He had also just been informed that the destroyer *Monaghan* had encountered a midget submarine on the other side of Ford Island, and suspected that there were other Japanese subs lying in ambush outside the harbor entrance. Signal flags quickly ran up *California*'s yard arms with instructions for *Nevada* to remain in Pearl.

Orders were orders, and Ruff, disappointed, was left with no choice, so he turned to Sedberry and Thomas for advice on what to do and how to do it, deferring to the men's experience and seamanship. They quickly agreed that the best course of action was to move the ship as near as possible to Hospital Point, beach her on the east side of the channel, and drop anchor. *Nevada*'s list was problematic, as no one knew just how severe the flooding might be—the Navy didn't need another capsized battleship in the harbor. Once she was safely aground, there would be no chance of *Nevada* heeling over onto her side. Bosun Hill took a work detail forward to drop the bow anchor when Ruff gave the signal to do so, and another work party headed aft to ready an anchor at the stern as well. Sedberry, of course, manned the helm, and Thomas handled the engine orders. At 9:10 *Nevada*'s bow drove into the sand-and-mud shallows off Hospital Point—so-called because the naval base's medical center sat just above it—and once he was confident the ship was firmly aground, Thomas rang down "Finished with engines."

The Japanese weren't finished with *Nevada*, however. They swarmed in once more, some ferociously strafing *Nevada*'s decks while others dropped their bombs, determined to mete out as much punishment as possible to the ship that had denied them such a golden opportunity. One hit at the base of the funnel, starting a small fire and blasting hot gases through much of the ship's ventilation ducting. Three bombs fell toward the bow, landing almost simultaneously; two missed close aboard, tossing columns of water high into the air, while the third landed squarely on the forecastle, wrecking the anchor windlass, wiping out most of Bosun Hill's work detail, and blowing Hill overboard. When his body was found, though, it was discovered that he hadn't died in the explosion: he'd been hit multiple times by one of the strafing Vals just before the bomb struck.

The powerful current moving down the channel now took hold of *Nevada* and swung her almost 180 degrees, pushing her starboard side into the muddy east bank of the channel. Ruff turned aft, waving his hat over his head to the seamen at the stern, who knocked free the shackles holding the anchor in place. The chain rattled loudly enough as it ran out to be heard above the din of aero engines, exploding bombs, and chattering machine guns, and then, as recorded in *Nevada*'s log, at 9:40 the battleship "was grounded between the floating dock and channel buoy #24, starboard side to the beach on an even keel." The ship wasn't entirely out of harm's way, but at least now there was no danger of her sinking.

That *Nevada* had stayed in the fight so long was due in large part to one man, Warrant Machinist Donald Kirby Ross. As the ship made her spectacular run down the South Channel, he was at his duty station, the forward dynamo room, deep within her hull, where two of *Nevada*'s four vital electrical generators were located. The generators supplied more than just electricity for the lights, they were the power supply for the ship's pumps, her firefighting systems, the shell-hoists, and the compressors that supplied air for the training and elevating equipment on the anti-aircraft guns. By throwing switches and opening or closing circuit breakers—some carrying loads of over 450 volts each—Ross could route power away from *Nevada*'s damaged sections, shunt additional power anywhere throughout the ship as it was needed, and shift loads between the generators to prevent them from overheating and failure. This morning those generators meant life or death for *Nevada*.

Just one day shy of his 31st birthday, Ross was a thoughtful man who had escaped an unhappy childhood and teen life to find a home and a purpose when he joined the navy at the age of 18. He was young for someone holding a warrant rating—that denoted exceptional levels of technical competence and leadership—but today he would prove the Navy's confidence in him had been well-founded. When the bomb that struck *Nevada*'s funnel exploded, Ross was standing beneath one of the main air trunks that supplied fresh air to the dynamo room, directly in the path of the searing wave of toxic gases that filled the compartment. Half-blinded, choking, Ross ordered everyone out of the dynamo room, then began transferring control of the forward generators to the aft dynamo room. He used a telephone to stay in contact with his crew outside the compartment, but after 15 minutes the line seemed to go dead without Ross reporting that the forward control room was secure. Fearing the worst, the crew reopened the heavy watertight door leading into the compartment, and found Ross alive but passed out across a switch panel. He was carried outside and corpsmen immediately began working to revive him; they succeeded, but to their astonishment, Ross insisted on returning—alone—to the 140-degree heat of the control room to finish the job he'd started: the aft control room couldn't fully take over until the forward room was properly and completely shut down.

Once again Ross collapsed in the heat, but not before he finished the final steps in securing the forward dynamo room. This time he was carried to a sheltered area of the upper deck, where he could breathe fresh air. The worst of the Japanese attacks on *Nevada* were over by this time, but Ross insisted on receiving regular reports about the ship's generators and electrical system. When he was told that smoke was filling up the after control room, he forced himself to his feet, brushed off the hands that tried to restrain him, and headed below—mostly by feeling his way down, as he hadn't bothered to mention to anyone that the gases in the forward dynamo room had left him almost totally blind. When he reached the aft control room he ordered everyone out until the smoke had cleared. The last man to leave the compartment was, naturally, Ross himself, who carried an unconscious sailor across his shoulders in a fireman's lift. Exhausted, Ross collapsed for the third and final time.

* * *

Shortly before *Nevada* grounded on Hospital Point, the fires in the floating drydock reached *Shaw*'s magazine, and the forward part of the ship erupted in a spectacular explosion. Shortly thereafter, the old minelayer *Oglala*, whose crew had been fighting a steady but losing battle against an ever-increasing list, finally gave up and with a groan of straining steel rolled onto her port side. Officially, the cause of her loss was reported as flooding due to stove-in shell plating caused by the torpedo exploding against the hull of the cruiser *Helena*, but more than one old sailor would insist that the old ship "had a nervous breakdown and died of fright."[6]

The blast from *Shaw*'s exploding magazine was almost like a gigantic exclamation mark for the attack on the fleet anchorage: with their ordnance expended, most of them out of ammunition, and many perilously close to the point of no return on fuel, by twos and threes the Japanese aircraft broke off their strafing runs and headed northward. The last to leave Pearl Harbor itself was Commander Fuchida, who took the time to make one last survey of the damage his fliers had done. Even absent the American carriers, it was clear the US Navy's Pacific Fleet had been crippled. Where and how Japan would exploit that advantage was not his decision to make; for the time being he could take pride and satisfaction in a job well done.

It's possible that on some abstract level, Admiral Kimmel was able to appreciate the competence and professionalism the Japanese displayed in carrying out their attack, but if it were so, he gave no indication of it. Standing in his office in CINCPAC Headquarters, watching the methodical destruction of his fleet, he knew that, no matter how strongly General Marshall may have made the point to General Short that the Army was responsible for the defense of the Pacific Fleet while it was in harbor, he was also watching the destruction of his own career. Earlier, between the first and second waves of the Japanese attack, he briefly disappeared into his private office, where he took off his tunic and carefully removed the four-starred shoulder boards of a full admiral. When he returned to the staff office wearing the twin stars of a Rear Admiral—his permanent rank—Chief Yeoman Kenneth Murray cried out, "Oh, hell, no, Admiral!" to which Kimmel replied "Oh, hell, yes, son!" He already knew his days as CINCPAC were numbered. Not long afterward, as he once again stood by the window, this time listening to his aides read off damage reports, a spent .50 caliber bullet crashed through the glass and struck Kimmel, leaving a black smudge on his spotless white tunic, tearing a hole in the fabric, and leaving a painful welt on the admiral's chest. Picking it up, Kimmel looked at the small lump of lead for a moment, then murmured, "It would have been more merciful if it killed me."[7]

* * *

The second wave of the Japanese attack also struck Wheeler and Hickam Fields. The first strike, of course, had caught the Hawaiian Air Force completely by surprise: no combat air patrol had been up, and no fighters on any sort of ready alert status, prepared to take off on just a few minutes notice; with only a handful of exceptions, all of its fighter strength was effectively immobilized and disarmed. What air defense the Army Air Corps was able to mount was uncoordinated and very, very limited: a total of 14 American pilots would make it into the air and engage the Japanese on this morning.

Which did not mean that the Japanese had it all their own way: those 14 pilots gave a good accounting for themselves, and offered up a few surprises for the Imperial Navy's veteran fliers. The exact details of just what happened when are confused, in no small part because aircraft were taking off from three separate airfields more-or-less simultaneously, and because those pilots and ground crewmen involved had more pressing matters to hand than making precise time entries in logbooks. It's generally agreed, though, that the first American pilots to get airborne were a pair of second lieutenants, George Welch and Kenneth Taylor; when they realized Wheeler Field was under attack, they drove Taylor's automobile hell-for-leather to the small auxiliary airfield at Haleiwa, where their P-40s were waiting. A few days previously, their squadron had rotated to Haleiwa for gunnery practice, a detail that had escaped Lieutenant Yoshikawa's attention, so no Japanese aircraft had been diverted to attack the site.

A telephone call from Welch before he left Wheeler alerted the ground crew at Haleiwa to have a pair of fighters ready—fueled, armed, and with their motors running—by the time the two pilots arrived. They were wheels up at or about 8:30, and headed straight for the newly completed Marine air station at Ewa, where they could see the Zeroes of the first attack wave still busily strafing the two squadrons of Navy torpedo- and dive-bombers stationed there. Welch and Taylor immediately began to mix it up with the Japanese over Ewa.

While the Zeros were decidedly more nimble than the P-40s, the Japanese pilots, accustomed to dogfighting with outdated or obsolescent Russian-,

Italian-, or American-built aircraft in China, found the big Curtiss fighter an unexpected handful. With the pilot armor, self-sealing fuel tanks, and robust construction the Zero lacked, the P-40 could take far more damage than the Japanese expected it could and keep flying and fighting. In turn, it carried enough firepower—especially the pair of heavy .50-caliber machine guns in the nose—to critically damage the lightly built Zero with just a few hits. Another advantage the P-40 enjoyed was that, at altitudes below roughly 10,000 feet, its thick wing generated more lift than the Zero's thinner wing: while the Curtis fighter couldn't out-turn a Zero, it could roll far more quickly, an advantage a skilled pilot could use to evade enemy fire. Finally, the heavier P-40 could outdive the Zero, giving the American pilots an opportunity to break off an engagement if they got into too much trouble.

Taylor and Welch saw what they estimated to be a dozen Japanese aircraft lining up for, from the look of the burning planes on the ground, their second or third strafing run on the airfield at Ewa. Like a pair of aerial gate-crashers, they cut into the line and began shooting at anything sporting red *hinomaru* on its wings, each pilot scoring a pair of kills almost before the Japanese realized someone was shooting back at them. Taylor put a burst of fire into a third Zero and watched it nose over into a dive, trailing smoke, but didn't see it crash; he later claimed a "probable" for this one. The action was so intense that both pilots quickly found themselves low on ammunition, so they broke away from the fight and made a beeline for Wheeler, where, during the relative calm between the storms of the first and second Japanese attacks, their P-40s were rearmed and refueled.

Wheeler, of course, had seen more than its share of excitement in the first wave. Despite the suddenness and ferocity of the Japanese airstrike, a handful of pilots tried to get airborne and engage the attackers; only a few succeeded. Most of the P-40s at Wheeler were destroyed outright or too badly damaged to fly, leaving perhaps a dozen Curtiss P-36s airworthy. Ground crew and pilots worked hard and fast to get them fueled and their ammunition loaded, while First Lieutenant Lewis Sanders pointed to three of his more experienced pilots—Othneil Norris, John Thacker, and Philip Rasmussen, all second lieutenants—and told them to get airborne as quickly as the aircraft were readied. Lieutenant Norris' parachute had a faulty harness, and he went looking for a replacement; it was an impulsive decision that probably saved his life.

In the two or three minutes Norris needed to find a fresh 'chute, Gordon Sterling, Jr., another second lieutenant, saw Sanders, Thacker, and Rasmussen begin taxiing to the runway, spotted Norris' P-36 sitting unoccupied with the motor running, and clambered aboard. When the plane's crew chief rushed up, Sterling handed his wristwatch to the astonished sergeant, shouting over the sound of the motor, "Give this to my mother. I'm not coming back," and then rolled out onto the taxiway behind Sanders and the other two pilots. Sanders led the flight east toward Kaneohe, just as the second wave of Japanese planes began their attack. Sanders didn't hesitate: he nosed over and latched onto the tail of Kate, taking it down with a well-aimed burst of fire, pulled up and began looking for another target.

Rasmussen saw another Japanese plane on its way down—he wasn't able to identify the type—with Sterling right behind it. A Zero tucked in on Sterling's tail and began shooting, and Sanders rolled in behind the second Zero and opened fire. Rasmussen watched as all four aircraft plunged toward the ocean. The first Japanese plane and Sterling's P-36 hit the water only a few seconds and a few hundred yards apart—Sterling had been shot down by the Zero on his tail; his body was never found. Rasmussen watched as Sanders' P-36 hammered the fighter that downed Sterling; the Zero begin smoking, but Rasmussen didn't see if it crashed or somehow evaded Lieutenant Sanders and limped away to safety, as he suddenly found himself very busy.

Rasmussen's morning had literally begun with a bang, when the sound of the first bombs falling on Wheeler Field jarred him out of a sound sleep. Not bothering to change into a flight suit or even regulation khakis, he strapped his .45 caliber pistol to the outside of his pajamas and ran to the flightline, where he encountered Lieutenant Sanders and minutes later found himself airborne, winging toward Kaneohe Bay. He charged his guns, which promptly began firing of their own accord: before he could pull the charging handles again to clear the guns, a Kate flew directly in front of him, straight through the stream of bullets, and exploded. Climbing to gain time to clear his guns, he caught a glimpse of Lieutenant Sterling crashing in the ocean, then was jumped by a pair of Zeroes. Briefly, he was the center of a lot of unwanted attention, as at least five Japanese fighters made firing passes at him, one coming so close that Rasmussen was convinced the Japanese pilot was trying to deliberately ram him. Hit repeatedly, the P-36 miraculously took no critical damage, but being so heavily outnumbered, Rasmussen knew this was a fight he couldn't win. Though not as fast in a dive as the P-40, the P-36 could still easily outdive the Zero, and Rasmussen took full advantage of this to shake off his pursuers, plunging into a low-hanging cloud bank. When he pulled out of the dive, Rasmussen found could barely control the aircraft, so he returned to Wheeler, where he landed with no brakes, an ineffective rudder, and a deflated tailwheel. After the attack, several people tried to count the number of holes in the wings and fuselage of Rasmussen's plane—no two tallies agreed, but all the totals were right around 500.

Lieutenant Thacker was seething with frustration. Unlike Rasmussen, whose guns began firing on their own, Thacker couldn't get his guns to fire at all. Most likely the armorers at Wheeler, desperate to get any fighters into the air, had created a misfeed when loading the ammunition for the P-36's pair of nose-mounted machine guns, which then jammed when Thacker tried to fire them. He did what he could, making repeated passes at Kates and Zeroes, trying to break up their attack runs, but he knew it was only a matter of time before some sharp-eyed Japanese pilot realized that the American pilot wasn't actually shooting at anyone and got the better of him. Thacker broke away from Kaneohe and returned to Wheeler.

That left Lieutenant Sanders all by his lonesome—not a pleasant place to be when surrounded by the best pilots in the Imperial Navy. After splashing the Zero that shot down Lieutenant Sterling, he found himself tangling with another Japanese fighter who was all but flying rings around Sanders' P-36. Knowing this engagement could end only one way if he tried to dogfight with the Zero, Sanders dove away and flew back to Wheeler. He and his three pilots had done their best—and paid the price for it—but as Sanders flew off, the Japanese continued to methodically demolish Kaneohe Air Station.

Welch and Taylor, meanwhile, had landed at Wheeler, each taking on fuel and a fresh supply of ammunition. Now they raced down the runway, trying to get airborne before the bombers in the second wave of the attack, which had just arrived overhead, began dropping their bombs. Taylor barely got his landing gear up before he settled in behind what appeared to be the last plane in a string of Vals lining up on Wheeler's east–west runway. He didn't see the Zero that in turn latched onto *his* tail and began shooting. Holes began appearing all over the P-40 and Taylor was nicked in the left arm, but the armor plate behind his seat saved his life long enough for Welch, who saw Taylor get bounced by the Zero, to swing around and shoot the Japanese fighter out of the sky. Taylor could still fly and fight, his aircraft hadn't taken serious damage, so he and Welch continued their lopsided battle against the Japanese aircraft over Wheeler and Ewa. Taylor damaged another Kate, but was too busy to note if it crashed or was able to stagger away, while Welch scored a confirmed kill on another Zero, bringing his total for the day to four.

Back at Haleiwa, fighters were taking off as fast as pilots showed up. Lieutenants John Dains and John Webster went roaring away in P-40s, while Lieutenants Harry Brown and Robert Rogers got into the air in a pair of P-36s. At Wheeler Field, Lieutenant Norris had found another parachute and another P-36 and took off with Lieutenant Malcolm Moore as his wingman. After an inconclusive skirmish with Japanese bombers over Kahuku Point, Brown and Rogers formed up with Moore and Webster and headed west. At Kaena Point, they damaged one enemy aircraft and shot down another; Moore and Brown gave chase to a Kate that they damaged but couldn't finish off. Low on fuel, the four pilots split up, Moore and Brown making for Wheeler Field, Rogers and Dains landing at Haleiwa. Dains, who had shot down one Japanese plane over Ewa, wasn't willing to wait for his P-40 to be refueled, so he took off in a waiting P-36.

Sadly, that proved to be the young aviator's undoing. He joined up with George Welch, who was still flying a P-40, and together they swept from Ewa to Kaneohe, but by now the Japanese were well to the north, on their way back to their carriers. Welch and Dains returned to Wheeler Field, and there Army gunners opened fire on Dains, whose aircraft exploded and crashed, killing him instantly. The men at Wheeler were understandably trigger-happy by this time, and seeing the radial-engined P-36 flying alongside the inline-engined P-40, they mistook Dains aircraft for a Japanese fighter—all the Japanese planes in the air over Hawaii that day had radial engines, and in this case the Army gunners shot first and identified later.

Out of a strike force that totaled 354 fighters, high-level bombers, torpedo bombers, and dive bombers, 325 returned to the carriers of *Kido Butai*—the Japanese had lost, to anti-aircraft fire and fighters, a total of 29 aircraft. Eleven of them were shot down by the Hawaiian Air Force, at the cost of four pilots: Lieutenants Sterling and Dains, along with Lieutenants George Whiteman, who was shot down just as his P-40 was taking off, and Lieutenant Hans Christiansen, who was cut down by a strafing Zero as he was climbing into the cockpit of his P-40 at Bellows Field. No one yet knew the fate of the five midget submarines, but none of their 10 crewmen would ever return to Japan. Three days hence, on December 10, dive bombers from the carrier *Enterprise* would sink the fleet submarine *I-70*, one of the boats assigned to patrol the waters around Hawaii and sink any ships that might escape Pearl Harbor during the attack; she had remained behind to intercept and hopefully sink any warships sent to reinforce the American naval base at Pearl.

In return, behind them the Japanese left four battleships sunk, two of them so badly damaged that they were beyond salvage; four more battleships were damaged, some heavily, as were three cruisers; two destroyers were total losses and one suffered critical damage; a repair ship and a seaplane tender were damaged, and an elderly minelayer sank at her moorings. Of the 402 American aircraft stationed in Hawaii or on their way to the islands that morning, 188 were destroyed and 159 damaged, many of the latter beyond repair. Worst of all, 2,403 Americans were dead and 1,178 were wounded.

Little more than two hours after it had begun, the Japanese attack was over.

CHAPTER 10

Shock and Awe

Ambassador Nomura and Special Envoy Kurusu sat cooling their heels in the secretary of state's outer office, while behind the soundproof door that led to his private office, Cordell Hull finished what was one of the most devastating telephone conversations of his entire life. President Roosevelt confirmed for him that less than an hour previously the Imperial Navy had, without warning, launched a major air attack on the US Navy's base at Pearl Harbor. Just how extensive, how severe, the damage was wasn't yet known for certain, but ships had definitely been sunk, and hundreds—possibly thousands—of American lives lost. Whatever it was that Nomura and Kurusu had to say at 1:00 PM, at 2:00 PM it was clearly irrelevant. Roosevelt's advice to Hull was to formally receive the Japanese diplomats, be as brief as possible, and then coolly excuse them from his office. The secretary agreed, replaced the telephone handset in its cradle, took a few moments to collect himself, then asked his secretary to send in Nomura and Kurusu.

For Cordell Hull, this was the most professionally demanding and emotionally trying diplomatic meeting of his career. He respected Nomura, had come to like the Japanese ambassador, and something very near a genuine friendship had developed between the two men. He was also reasonably certain—having been privy to so much of the traffic between the Washington Embassy and Tokyo—that Nomura truly had no foreknowledge of the attack that had just taken place; for that matter, it was possible that even now he didn't fully know the details of what had just transpired in Hawaii. Still, none of that could wholly mitigate Hull's anger: if Nomura had been used as Tokyo's unwitting dupe, the secretary knew he had been used as one as well.

The two men exchanged the usual social pleasantries, then Nomura presented Tokyo's formal response to Hull's November 26 note. Hull, of course, had already read the MAGIC decryption of the note, but, as it was now more important than ever to maintain the security surrounding MAGIC, he made a pretense of reading the note for the first time.

It was an odd document, peculiar as much for what it didn't say as for what it did. Reduced to its essence, the note informed the American government that in the considered opinion of the Imperial Government nothing further could be accomplished by negotiation in the effort to resolve the diplomatic differences between Japan and the United States; as further talking would be futile, Japan would seek other means of resolving the crisis. The implication, of course, was that Japan would resort to military action to resolve the issue, but because the note never quite said as much, that uncertainty might serve to keep the American armed forces from going to full alert before the attack on Pearl Harbor actually began.

It was not an actual declaration of war, then—though it would come to be regarded as such in light of what had just happened at Pearl Harbor. For that matter it didn't even explicitly break off diplomatic relations between America and Japan, although it was worded in such a way that could have been argued to make the case. It was, in fact, little more than a recapitulation of Japan's grievances against the United States, Great Britain, and the Netherlands, nothing that hadn't been presented multiple times before. Standing alone, there was no real point to the message—but had it been delivered as scheduled, it would have been Japan's diplomatic fig leaf, as it were, allowing the Emperor along with his ministers, admirals, and generals, to claim that the Empire had observed all of the diplomatic customs and formalities before going to war with America. Instead, arriving as it did over an hour too late, it appeared to be the quintessential act of treachery, of the sort which was part and parcel of so many Japanese stereotypes.

Placing the hastily typed pages on his desk, then carefully, neatly, squaring them, Hull finally spoke. The self-righteous posturing of the note, coupled with what he had just learned about the attack in Hawaii, was too much for the courtly old Southern gentleman, and there was cold steel in his voice when he addressed Nomura:

"I must say that in all my conversations with you during the last nine months I never uttered one work of untruth. This is borne out absolutely by the record. In all my 50 years of public service I have never seen a document that was more crowded with infamous falsehoods and distortions—infamous falsehoods and distortions on a scale so huge that I never imagined until today that any government on this planet was capable of uttering them."

Nomura, taken aback by Hull's evident if carefully controlled anger, made to reply, but Hull would have none of it. Without saying another word, he gestured toward the door, and the embarrassed diplomats bowed themselves out. As they left, Hull's secretary pulled the inner office door closed, and heard the secretary of state mutter, "Scoundrels and piss-ants."[1]

Hull would never see Nomura or Kurusu again.

* * *

Secretary Hull's shock and anger effectively mirrored the initial reaction in the White House, the State Department, and the War and Navy Departments. Secretary of the Navy Frank Knox had just returned to his office after meeting with Henry Stimson, the secretary of war, and Cordell Hull, when Commander Ramsey's FLASH message arrived: "AIR RAID PEARL HARBOR X THIS IS NOT DRILL." Knox took one look at it and blurted out, "My God, this can't be true! This must mean the Philippines!" Admiral Stark, who had joined the secretary only minutes earlier, took one look at the originating address—CINCPAC—and said heavily, "No, sir, this is Pearl." Knox gave himself a few moments to collect his thoughts, then telephoned the White House.[2]

Roosevelt was surprised that the Japanese had what he regarded as the audacity to strike Pearl Harbor, although he was not exactly shocked by the news of the Empire's naked aggression: after reading the report that Japanese troop transports heading for Malaysia even as Tojo's government was offering to withdraw from French Indochina, he'd remarked, "This means war." He realized that the hard line he insisted be taken by the secretary of state with the "Hull Note" had, in effect, forced the Imperial Government to choose between acting and talking. The Japanese had been caught with their hand in the cookie jar, so to speak: they could no longer maintain the pretense that they were negotiating in good faith rather than merely buying time to complete the preparations for their attacks.

As the afternoon wore on, the shock and anger in Washington began to morph into something closer to shock and awe as information began to trickle in from all across the Far East. An hour before the first bombs fell in Hawaii, the troops carried by those transports that had so worried Colonel Bratton and so provoked Roosevelt and Hull began wading ashore at Kota Bharu in Malaya; a few hours later Singapore experienced its first Japanese air raid. Japanese soldiers were landing on Guam at almost the same time the last of the attacking aircraft left Pearl Harbor. In Manila, which was west of the International Date Line, at 40 minutes past noon on December 8 the air raid sirens sounded and Japanese bombs began falling on US Army airfields across the Philippines; an attack on Hong Kong began an hour later. The 16-day battle for Wake Island began when 36 Imperial Navy bombers cratered the runway and destroyed two-thirds of the Marine fighters defending the island. And in what would become little more than a footnote in the day's carnage, the S.S. *Cynthia Olson*, a small American freighter, was torpedoed and sunk by a Japanese submarine somewhere between Hawaii and the West Coast; her wireless operator was able to get off a distress call before the *Olson* went down, but none of her 33 crewmen were ever found, alive or dead.

As the reports, official and unofficial, accumulated, a much larger picture of aggressive Japanese actions revealed itself than just the attack on Pearl Harbor. The Hawaii Operation had been only a part of what in scope was the single largest offensive ever attempted, one that dwarfed even Operation Barbarossa, Nazi Germany's invasion of the Soviet Union: the Japanese were carrying out near-simultaneous attacks across an arc that spanned over 6,700 miles, the furthest, the Pearl Harbor strike, being 4,000 miles from Tokyo. It was the most audacious military campaign in history.

* * *

By 10:00 AM in Hawaii, as Washington was just beginning to grasp the scale of Japan's Pacific offensive, the skies over Oahu were once again clear of Japanese aircraft, but this time no one was assuming the attack was actually over—for all the Americans knew, a third wave could be on its way. Everyone was on edge, and for the next several days there would be seemingly endless succession of false alarms and incidents as jumpy civilians and trigger-happy sentries were seeing Japanese invaders, saboteurs, and spies behind every bush and in every shadow. That night, around 9:00 PM, six Grumman Wildcat fighter planes from the carrier *Enterprise* would be shot down by Navy anti-aircraft guns when they tried to land on Ford Island, killing three of the pilots—the gunners in Pearl thought the Japanese were returning for another attack, this one under the cover of darkness.

One by one, the ships in Pearl Harbor stood down from General Quarters, though they remained at a heightened level of alert and kept most of their anti-aircraft guns manned and ready. Damage control and firefighting were now the priorities, though, and the work begun between the first and second waves of the Japanese attack was hastily resumed, as hundreds of sailors, soldiers, and Marines continued their fight for survival. The hospital ship *Solace* became the focal point for those efforts in the first hours after the air strike; that effort was underway even as the first bombs were falling.

When the signal "AIR RAID PEARL HARBOR X THIS IS NOT DRILL" went out, *Solace*'s captain, Benjamin Pearlman, immediately ordered all watertight doors and scuttles closed, alerted the medical staff to stand by to receive casualties, and called away two rescue parties, one for each of the ship's motor launches. When *Arizona* blew up, the launches were dispatched to Battleship Row, along with several smaller boats. They were most certainly going into harm's way; the crews knew this and refused to be daunted at the prospect. Once alongside the burning battleship, they began taking wounded and burned sailors from *Arizona*'s afterdeck, pulling others out of the water, some of the men from *Solace* going aboard *Arizona* to help evacuate the worst of the wounded, braving the flames from her burning superstructure as well as the aviation fuel fire on the quarterdeck.

By 8:20 the heavily laden launches were on their way back to *Solace*, where the injured sailors and marines were quickly but carefully taken off; the launches then turned around and went back to Battleship Row, where they once again pulled close alongside *Arizona*, *West Virginia*, and *Oklahoma* to take off still more survivors. The fires around the sunken, broken warships were even worse this time: when a crewman on one of the launches threw makeshift lifelines to Ensign Edmond Jacoby and a sailor nearby who was struggling to keep his head above water, the paint on the boat's bow ignited in the heat.

In the meantime, Captain Pearlman, his crew, and medical staff made *Solace* ready to receive patients in numbers that far exceeded anything for which the ship had been designed to provide care and comfort. Some orderlies and corpsmen pulled extra beds out of stowage and set them up in the wards, then struck up cots on all the decks anywhere there was sufficient room. Others began prepping hundreds of glass flasks of plasma and whole blood, while nurses inventoried drugs, syringes, bandages, and dressings; surgical nurses laid out scores of instrument trays in *Solace's* operating theater. Her quarterdeck, where the launches and boats unloaded the wounded, was soon slick with blood as burned and injured men were sorted by priority and sent forward for surgery or treatment; there was a growing number of men who remained on the deck, covered by a single sheet or blanket, for whom time had run out before they reached *Solace*.

The oil gushing from *Arizona's* ruptured bunkers, ignited by her blazing super-structure, swirled around *Tennessee's* stern and flowed along the narrow strip of open water between her and *West Virginia*, pushed forward by the wind and the outgoing tide. Still more bunker fuel flowing from the mangled sides of *Wee Vee* and *Oklahoma* was soon alight and added to the conflagration. Even so, the motor launches nosed into the flames, paintwork blistering, and their crews hauled oil-covered sailors out of the water, lifted crippled or burned seamen from the battleships' decks, and took on as many survivors as the boats could carry; the heat from the burning ships and oil was so intense that at one point the coxswain of launch #1 had to seek out a patch of clear water so that he could momentarily jump into it—his uniform had begun to smolder. After four trips back to *Solace*, the boats returned to Battleship Row where they stayed until well past midnight, supporting the desperate effort to free crewmen trapped in *Oklahoma's* upturned hull.

On the other side of Ford Island, a similar rescue effort, though on a much smaller scale, began almost as soon as the Japanese departed and the guns fell silent. Crewmen who had been taking cover on the island after being forced to abandon the capsized target ship *Utah* began to hear a loud, metallic rapping coming from somewhere in her hull. The sound was steady and regular, a sure sign that it wasn't being caused by loose equipment or machinery—obviously someone trapped inside *Utah* was signaling for help. Sure enough, inside the old battleship's starboard bilge, Fireman Second Class Jack Vaessen was fighting to stay alive in a slowly shrinking pocket of stale air, using what dwindling strength he had to beat against *Utah's* shell plating with a wrench.

When *Utah* was torpedoed and began to list, Vaessen began shutting down draft fans and switching on emergency lighting. The ship rolled over so quickly that Vaessen had no chance to evacuate his compartment—he was too busy trying to keep clear of tools and equipment that were tumbling about as the ship capsized.

When she finally stopped moving, Vaessen found himself trapped—the distance between his compartment and any access to the outside of the ship was farther than he could swim underwater. There was only one way out, through the ship's bilges: the harbor was shallow enough, he knew, that if *Utah* was upside down, or nearly so, at least part of her keel was exposed. He was fortunate enough to have a flashlight with him, so he wasn't forced to work in the dark as he undid the bolts on one of the bilge hatches; as he crawled through it, he saw the water behind him rising slowly but steadily. Swinging the wrench he'd used to undo the hatch bolts, he started pounding on the hull plates overhead.

On Ford Island, two of *Utah*'s surviving crew, Machinist Stanley Semanski and Chief Machinist Mate Terry Selwiney, who heard the pounding noise coming from the old ship's hull, borrowed a cutting torch from the cruiser *Raleigh* and went back out to *Utah*, searching for the sound's origin. Hoping they were right, they began cutting through the one-inch-thick steel shell plating. Inside the hull, Vaessen saw a faint reddish glow that grew steadily brighter form on one of the plates overhead; the red glow soon became a white-hot line as the acetylene torch cut through the steel, carving out a circular section that was large enough, when it fell free, to allow Semanski and Selwiney to pull Vaessen through it and into the fresh air. It had been a close run, as the water was just three feet below the top of the bilge when they broke through. Vaessen's escape wasn't exactly easy, but it was far simpler compared to the effort that would have to be made to eventually free crewmen trapped inside *Oklahoma* and *West Virginia*.

* * *

About the same time that Jack Vaessen was freed from the depths of *Utah*'s hull, the last Japanese aircraft were landing on the carriers of *Kido Butai*. The aviators returned to a tumultuous welcome, as word had spread quickly among the ships' crews that not only had the strike force achieved total surprise over the Americans, but that it had done tremendous damage to the Pacific Fleet as well as the US Army Air Corps. Forgotten for the moment was the absence of any of the US Navy's aircraft carriers; surely this would be a victory to be celebrated as long and as proudly as Tsushima!

Not everyone was exulting, however. Fuchida landed on *Akagi* at noon; a yeoman was waiting for him, informing the mission commander that Admiral Nagumo wanted to see him immediately. Fuchida delayed reporting to the flagship's bridge, however—not as an act of disrespect to the admiral, but to be certain he had all the information he knew Nagumo would want. After a quick conversation with Genda, followed by an equally brief examination of the large chart where the damage reports had been tallied, Fuchida climbed up to *Akagi*'s bridge and came face to face with an anxious Admiral Nagumo, along with Admirals Kusaka and Oishi, and the rest of Nagumo's staff. Fuchida began to give a formal report but was interrupted by

Nagumo, who immediately cut to the quick of the matter. "The results," the old admiral asked, "what are they?"

"Four battleships sunk," Fuchida replied. "I know this from personal observation. Four more are damaged."

Showing where his priorities lay, Nagumo then asked, "Do you think the American fleet could not come out from Pearl Harbor within six months?" Fuchida answered by saying that no, the Pacific Fleet would certainly not be able to leave Pearl Harbor for at least that span of time; at that Nagumo nodded, apparently satisfied.

Admiral Kusaka then took up the questioning, asking Fuchida for his opinion on what should be the target of the next air strike, and raising the possibility of an American counterattack. Fuchida didn't hesitate, saying that the docks, fuel reserves, and any surviving ships should be targeted; he was confident that given the damage done to the US Army Air Corps, Japanese air superiority over Oahu was assured. Oishi wanted a more precise answer: "Is the enemy in a position to counterattack *Kido Butai?*"

This put Commander Fuchida in an uncomfortable spot, in that a meaningful answer required knowledge which Fuchida did not possess—information which at that moment was unknown to anyone on *Akagi*'s bridge. Temporizing and evasion were not in Fuchida's nature, though, so he gave Admiral Kusaka the best—and most honest—answer he could. "I believe we have destroyed many enemy planes, but I do not know if we have destroyed all of them. The Americans probably could still attack *Kido Butai.*"

Nagumo spoke up once more, again going directly to the heart of the matter, asking, "Where do you think the missing American carriers are?" Fuchida responded by saying that they were almost certainly at sea, training their aircrews, and that by this time they had been made aware of the attack on Pearl Harbor. It would be reasonable to assume that they were looking for the Japanese strike force.

Turning to Genda, who had arrived on the bridge with Fuchida, Nagumo asked for his assessment of the situation. Almost breezily, Genda said, "Let the enemy come! If he does, we will shoot his planes down!" When pressed on the question of whether or not a follow-on strike against the naval installations at Pearl Harbor, and not simply the ships at anchor there, should be carried out, Genda wholeheartedly endorsed Fuchida's recommendation and choice of targets. Pearl, he opined, should be rendered useless to the US Navy as a fleet base.[3]

Admiral Nagumo found Genda's almost offhand response unsettling; the young aviator was, in the older man's eyes, overconfident and too dismissive of the American threat. Here Nagumo was being unfair to Genda: no sooner had they begun landing than the Kates and Vals were taken down to their hangar decks, where, on Genda's advice, they were rearmed with torpedoes and armor-piercing bombs, the weapons they would need to engage an enemy fleet at sea. The young commander knew that if a third strike was ordered, time would be of the essence, lest the shock of the first and second wave attacks begin to wear off the Americans at Pearl On a deeper level, though, Nagumo was correct—Genda *was* overconfident. He seemed to take for granted, as Nagumo did not, that the incredible run of good fortune which had so far characterized almost every aspect of the Hawaii Operation would continue. Nagumo refused to be so sanguine about the possibility. He offered Fuchida his heartfelt congratulations on carrying out the attack on Pearl Harbor with such remarkable success, but refused to confide in either Fuchida or Genda, for the moment, at least, whether or not he would agree to another attack on Oahu.

Nagumo, who would not survive the Second World War, left behind no account of how he arrived at what would become one of the most intensely debated command decisions of the conflict, but make up his mind he did. At 1:30 PM, a signal to all carriers ran up on *Akagi's* mast: "Preparations for attack cancelled." At the same time, Nagumo gave the order for *Kido Butai* to turn westward; First Air Fleet had accomplished its mission. Almost from the minute the decision was made, a debate began which would be argued for decades to come.

For all of the "what ifs," "yes, buts," and "might have beens" that would be heaped upon Nagumo, his reputation, and his decision, a perfect storm of circumstances came together that all but made the choice for him. The first was that the stated objective of the Hawaii Operation had been from the beginning to render the US Navy's Pacific Fleet ineffective for at least six months—it had never been part of the plan to deny the Americans the use of Pearl Harbor as a fleet base. Here the issue was determined, almost by default, by the Imperial Navy's own doctrine for exercising naval airpower. For all its potential, the Japanese had never regarded the First Air Fleet as a strategic force: its purpose was to win battles, not campaigns. It had just won the Battle of Pearl Harbor, and achieved the objective Yamamoto had set forth when he conceived of the operation. Genda had envisioned the attack as an integral part of a broad, aggressive strategy directed at the United States, one which included invading and occupying Oahu, an idea which Yamamoto firmly—and rightly—quashed as unrealistic, as it was beyond the resources available to Japan. Yet, at the same time, Genda was hoist on his own petard, as for all of the contingency planning he had done in preparing for the attack as it was carried out, he never made allowance for the sort of success *Kido Butai* had just experienced, and so had no follow-on plan drawn up to properly exploit it.

Had the Japanese launched another attack on Pearl Harbor, then, it would have been a hastily improvised affair, "drawn up in the dirt," as it were, and nothing at all like the carefully thought-out action of that morning. This time there would be no element of surprise, and the potential losses among aircraft and aircrew could well be severe. A total of 29 planes did not return to their carriers—five torpedo bombers, 15 dive bombers, and nine fighters—only eight percent of the total attack force. But of the 325 aircraft that did return, 73 were damaged to one degree or another and rendered at least temporarily unflyable, meaning that over a quarter of the attack force had been shot down or damaged and put out of action. Those losses had been inflicted with the defenders totally surprised and stunned; how high would the losses be if the Americans were ready for the Japanese?

And finally, there was the question of the American carriers. *Saratoga* was known to be well on her way to San Diego and could be discounted—it would have been impossible for her to get within range to launch a strike against the Japanese carrier force for at least three days. *Lexington* and *Enterprise* could not be so easily dismissed, however: their whereabouts were completely unknown, and to Nagumo the worst possible scenario was an American airstrike on *Kido Butai* while its own aircraft were away yet again raiding Pearl Harbor. The Japanese would be faced with an unpalatable choice: keep enough fighters aboard the carriers to defend them against an attack, and leave the air strike with inadequate fighter protection, or send the fighters off with the bombers and risk leaving *Kido Butai* uncovered. Fuchida was confident that the Japanese would have air superiority over Oahu, but superiority was not supremacy, and an inadequately defended air strike invited decimation if the Americans still had a respectable fighter force of their own—something Fuchida could not guarantee was not so.

Nagumo would be characterized as thinking like "a gambler who has staked his life savings on the turn of a card and won. His only idea was to cash in and go home as quickly as possible," but this is an easy, almost simplistic depiction of his actual situation, readily put forward by those not burdened with the actual command responsibility for *Kido Butai*. Those who criticized Admiral Nagumo, then, are guilty of the besetting sin of being wise after the event; at the time, there was no other decision he could have made—or should have made. He had won the victory he had been sent out to win; in light of the strategy that Japan had chosen for the war in the Pacific, striving for even greater results would have been a case of dangerous overreach.[4]

Legend and mythmaking would eventually create a scene where a debate, variously described as "spirited" or even "heated," took place on Akagi's bridge as Genda and Fuchida strove to change Nomura's mind. In reality, nothing of the sort took place: this was the Imperial Navy, Fuchida and Genda might—and did—respectfully protest, but they did not argue with Nagumo. The commanding officer had made his decision and issued his orders, and that was the end of it. *Kido Butai* would withdraw to the west, its passage as uneventful as the eastbound voyage. On December 16 *Hiryu* and *Soryu* would be diverted to support the attack on Wake Island, while the remaining carriers of First Air Fleet would arrive in their home waters off Kyushu on December 23. The Hawaii Operation was complete.

* * *

Back on Oahu, Nagumo's decision to turn west without launching another airstrike would have been greeted with universal—and universally weary—sighs of relief. The situation at all four hospitals—the Army facilities at Wheeler and Hickam Fields, Tripler Hospital at Fort Shafter, and Naval Hospital Pearl Harbor—was just barely short of chaotic. Doctors, nurses, medics, and corpsmen were quickly forced to resort to simply performing first aid—administering morphine and quickly applying bandages, splints, or tourniquets as needed—in an effort to get the wounded stabilized so that they could eventually be treated according to the severity of their wounds and injuries. The dreadful hierarchy of "triage"—deciding which victims would survive but who had wounds that urgently required attention, which were those whose treatment could be delayed, and which were those who were mostly likely to die no matter what care they were given—quickly imposed itself.

The problem was numbers—or lack of them: there were fewer than 1,000 nurses in the entire Army, and just 82 of them were stationed in Hawaii on December 7, 1941; when the attack began, only two nurses and one physician were on duty at Hickam—Wheeler, Tripler, and the Navy Hospital were no better off. As soon as the first bombs fell the off-duty medical personnel began rushing to their respective posts, and did their best to be prepared and waiting when the first casualties arrived, but soon the sheer scale of the carnage became nigh-on overwhelming. Working non-stop, surgeons performed countless emergency operations to remove bomb fragments, tie off severed arteries, save torn and lacerated viscera, and salvage mangled limbs. They succeeded most of the time, but not always; those were the truly trying moments, when they did their best to offer what comfort they could to their stricken patients. At Tripler Hospital, Colonel John Moorehead, who had been a combat surgeon in France in 1918, found himself explaining to a frightened 19-year-old private that the young man was going to lose his foot: "Son, you've been through a lot of hell, and you're going into some more. That foot has to come off. But there's been many a good pirate with only one leg!"[5]

Tripler was the destination for those most severely wounded once they were stabilized; the staff at Wheeler and Hickam both knew that an already critical situation would turn disastrous if they filled all of their beds and then were suddenly caught up in a surge of casualties with no place to put them, even temporarily. The swift imposition of the triage process was the result. Soldiers and airmen who could be immediately sent back to their units were treated and released, while nearly all the rest went on to Tripler—the surgeons at Wheeler and Hickam would operate only on those casualties who wouldn't survive being transferred to Tripler, but who might live if they went into surgery immediately.

What no one foresaw was that it was Tripler which might be overwhelmed. There, medical supplies—surgical instruments, syringes, gloves and face masks, suturing thread, whole blood and plasma—quickly ran short, then ran out as more and more injured sailors and soldiers arrived; doctors, nurses, and medics made do using sterile cleaning cloths as makeshift masks; surgeons were forced to operate without gloves, reusing scalpels, clamps, and needles as quickly as they could be run through the autoclaves. Peacetime regulations and protocols which just hours before were stringently enforced went out the window as both Army and Navy medical corps were suddenly and ruthlessly introduced to the realities of combat medical care. "Meatball surgery"—operations hastily performed to stabilize critically wounded patients long enough to allow them to be transported elsewhere for more comprehensive procedures—became the order of the day. The staff at Tripler managed to stay ahead of the rising influx of badly wounded and burned servicemen just long enough for civilian doctors and nurses to converge on the hospital from all over Honolulu and shift some of the burden off the shoulders of the Army personnel.

Civilians responding to the emergency wasn't limited to just medical professionals arriving to assist at Tripler. When word got out that all of the government hospitals were running short of blood and plasma, Dr. Forrest Pinkerton personally went to the Honolulu blood bank, gathered 253 flasks of plasma there, stowed them in his car and delivered them to Tripler, Hickam, and the Navy Hospital. At a hastily improvised blood donor station at Tripler, over 500 civilians lined up to give blood, so many that the hospital staff ran out of standard flasks and resorted to using sterilized Coca-Cola bottles.

Complaints from the wounded men were, perhaps inevitably, the least of the problems the medical staffs had to face. Time and again seriously wounded men would tell a doctor or nurse to go attend to someone who "really needed help." Flight Surgeon William Schick, who had been hit by a strafing Zero as he scrambled from one of the B-17s that landed at Hickam, repeatedly brushed off attempts to treat his wounds, pointing out other wounded men and saying, "Take care of them." Eventually he was put on an ambulance bound for Tripler, but bled to death before he arrived. Dr. Pinkerton never forgot the soldier who, when he was told that other, more critically injured men would have to be treated first, simply replied, "Just do what you can, I know there are other people waiting." It was also at Hickam that a young soldier, his arm blown off just below the shoulder, calmly walked through the front door, waving hello to the nurses.[6]

The steps of its front entrance red with fresh blood, Tripler resembled an abattoir—in an echo reminiscent of far too many Civil War and Great War hospitals, for a time the bodies of dead servicemen were being stacked outside the hospital's back entrance—but at least it was spared the ordeal of coming under enemy fire. Not so the hospitals at Wheeler and Hickam. While the Japanese never deliberately bombed either building—or the hospital ship *Solace*—there were more than a few heart-stopping and dangerous near-misses. Monica Conter was one of two nurses on duty at Hickam when the attack began—the other was Second Lieutenant Irene Boyd—when she suddenly realized that this Sunday morning was going to be unlike any she had ever known, before or since. She later described the moment, recalling that, "We heard this plane. It was losing altitude. We both just stopped suddenly and stared at each other. Then 'bang!'" Conter promptly dived under one of the hospital beds, clutching a galvanized steel trash can lid over her head for cover. Aiming for the enormous barracks complex on the opposite side of the road, one of the Vals released its bomb a fraction of a second too soon, and the 550-pound projectile landed 20 yards in front of the hospital; cries of "Gas!" went up as the unfamiliar smell of explosives began spreading. One of the medics was killed on the flightline, trying to bring in wounded men, and from time to time bullets would "thud" into the hospital's walls as one of the Japanese planes made a strafing pass, but no one was killed or injured inside the building.

The nurses, who, like thousands of soldiers, sailors, and Marines had been given quite a fright at the beginning of the attack, quickly regained their composure and went to work; no one later had anything but praise for how calm and determined they were. First Lieutenant Annie Gayton Fox, the charge nurse at Hickam Field Hospital that morning, would become the first woman to be awarded the Purple Heart; the medal had been reinstated by President Hoover in 1932 for what the Army termed "singularly meritorious act of extraordinary fidelity or essential service," as well as being wounded in action. Later when the Purple Heart was reserved solely for wounded personnel, Lieutenant Fox was awarded the Bronze Star in its place.

Even though the bomb that landed in front of the hospital wasn't aimed at the building, there were still deaths among non-combatants and civilians for which the Japanese were responsible. Probably the first Americans to die that morning were three men in a pair of Piper Cubs, one of them flying solo, who were shot down as the first wave was sweeping into Pearl Harbor from the west; the Japanese were worried that the pilots might get off a last-minute warning to Pearl Harbor about the approaching air strike. Seven civilians were wounded and one was killed when, for reasons that are still unknown, Japanese fighters fired on the Waipahu sugar mill; the same planes attacked the sugar mill at Wahiawa leaving nine people wounded and two dead. Two more civilians were killed and another seven wounded when Zeroes machine-gunned the sugar mill near Ewa; one of the Japanese fighters, swooping down a bit too low, crashed into a house, killing the pilot. Evidently, though no one can say for certain, the Japanese pilots mistook the sugar mills for some sort of military installation; ironically, at least half the victims were Japanese immigrants. A single Zero made a long strafing run down the runway of Honolulu's John Rodgers Airport, killing a civilian flight instructor who was standing on the flightline.

While none of the Japanese bombers deliberately attacked civilian targets, the Zero pilots, absent any significant opposition by the Army Air Corps, seemed inclined to shoot at whatever took their fancy. Linemen on telephone poles, civilian cars on highways, family housing at Wheeler and Hickam, civilians running for cover on the roadside. It could have been worse: a Hawaiian Airlines DC-3 bound for Maui took off from John Rodgers Airport only minutes before the first Japanese aircraft arrived over Pearl Harbor, and Pan American's *Anzac Clipper*, with 36 passengers aboard, was scheduled to arrive at 8:30 AM. A big, lumbering Boeing 314 flying boat, the *Clipper* would have been a sitting duck for the Zeroes, but a late departure from San Francisco had left the flight running almost an hour late. When her pilot, Captain Lanier Turner, was handed a radio message warning him that Pearl Harbor was under attack, he was able to divert his plane to the island of Hilo and safety.

Tragically, more civilians had been killed this morning by the US Navy than by the Japanese. At least forty 3-, 4-, and 5-inch anti-aircraft shells fired by the ships in Pearl Harbor landed in and around Honolulu and Pearl City and exploded on impact; several more were later found that were duds. In their haste to get into action against the Japanese bombers, some of the gun crews forgot to set the fuzes on their shells to self-destruct, others set the fuzes to go off only on contact—which meant, of course, that unless the shells actually struck one of the enemy aircraft, they wouldn't explode until they eventually hit the ground. Thirty-two people were killed in Honolulu, including a 7-month-old baby and a 2-year-old girl; all told, including workers at the Navy Yard, 68 civilians died during the attack.

Many of the buildings and most of the homes in Honolulu were of wood frame-and-siding construction, and several of those that were hit caught fire when the errant anti-aircraft shells exploded. Local residents had to make do with whatever was at hand to contain the flames, as most of the civilian firemen and their equipment were at Hickam and Wheeler Fields—they had rushed down to help the Army personnel struggling to gain control of the fires in the hangars and among the aircraft on the flightlines. Exploding bombs shattered water mains at both airfields, which only made the situation worse, and the firefighting equipment was all too conspicuous: the Vals and Zeroes pounced on them, wrecking the engines, pumps, and extinguishers, and taking a toll of the soldiers and civilians working them. Sergeant Joseph Chagnon, one of the crew chiefs, had just enough time to shout a warning to his men as one of the dive bombers roared down toward the engine they were manning. Private First Class Howard King dropped prone a split-second before the bomb hit; the engine was torn apart, as was Sergeant Chagnon—King's left leg was broken in the blast.

At Hickam, Fire Chief William Benedict put on a remarkable display of *sang froid*, calmly gnawing away on an apple as he supervised his crews. Twice wounded by shrapnel, he ignored the injuries and continued to work away at the apple and issue orders—that is, until he was thrown across the runway when a bomb exploded nearby; as the Val responsible zoomed past, its rear gunner blazed away at Benedict, but missed. Even so, the chief was in a bad way: he'd been hit by over 20 bomb fragments, and soon passed out from loss of blood. Initially he was reported as missing and presumed dead, and it wasn't until more than two hours after the last Japanese plane left Pearl Harbor that he was found and packed off to Tripler. It took a while for word to spread that the news of his demise had been greatly exaggerated, and a few days later Benedict had the dubious privilege of being able to read his own obituary in the local newspapers.

* * *

With the Japanese showing no sign of returning, and the hospitals tending the wounded while firefighters beat back the flames at Wheeler and Hickam, the officers and men down on Battleship Row were doing what they could to and with their burning, broken ships. *Arizona* and *Oklahoma* were total losses, of course, while *California* and *West Virginia* were badly damaged—both had sunk but were sitting upright on the bottom of Pearl Harbor. They could—and would—be raised and returned to service, but only after months of salvage work, repairs, and rebuilding. Even though *Maryland* and *Tennessee* had taken comparatively light damage, for the time being they weren't able to move, pinned as they were, if only temporarily, between Ford Island and the hulls of *West Virginia* and *Oklahoma*. Repairs to *Pennsylvania* would take at least four months, but before she could be moved her missing propeller shafts would have to be replaced.

Nevada was something of a special case: while she could hardly be described as fully seaworthy or combat-ready, at the moment she was the only battleship in the Pacific fleet that could move under her own power. Once she was safely aground on Waipio Point, her entire complement set to fighting fires and making what stop-gap repairs they could; Lieutenant Commander Thomas took charge of the damage control effort. Lieutenant Ruff began a tour of the ship, taking note of the exact nature and extent of the damage done to her. When Captain Scanland finally caught up to *Nevada*, Ruff met him on the quarterdeck with a full report. Scanland, who had spent the night ashore with his family, had commandeered a launch and set out in pursuit of his ship as she made her epic sortie down Battleship Row and into the entrance channel to Pearl Harbor. Once aboard, and thanks to Ruff's timely report, the captain immediately took hold of the situation. One of his first actions was to send Ruff ashore to CINCPAC headquarters, where the lieutenant would repeat his report for the benefit of Admiral Kimmel.

It would be far wide of the mark to say that CINCPAC welcomed Ruff's report, but the lieutenant's effort was appreciated: Kimmel needed to obtain as complete a picture of the situation as he could. There was no "good face" to be put on it, yet the admiral was still in command of the Pacific Fleet—what was left of it—and he and his staff were still professionals. It was up to them to come up with the Navy's response to the Japanese attack, contain and mitigate the damage as far as possible, and retaliate in some way if the opportunity presented itself. For the latter to happen, Kimmel needed to know where to find the Japanese carrier force, and here the last failure by Navy intelligence in the Pearl Harbor drama came into play, although this time no one in Washington had a hand in it.

Several reports had already come to CINCPAC, confirming that the Japanese planes were headed north when they flew away from Pearl Harbor, but no one on Kimmel's staff was prepared to take it on faith that the Japanese carriers could indeed be found north of Oahu. Both the first and seconds waves of the attack had struck from multiple directions, and for all Kimmel or his staff knew, the Japanese had simply established a rally point somewhere north of Pearl where the attacking aircraft rendezvoused before turning onto the actual heading that would take them back to their ships. What reports Kimmel did have lacked details and many were contradictory; HYPO had picked up some brief wireless transmissions from *Kido Butai*, but could only get a reciprocal bearing off them: the best advice that Commander Layton could give CINCPAC was that the Japanese fleet lay either directly to the north—on a bearing of 003—or directly to the south, on 183. Without a cross-cut bearing from another station, there was no way to be certain which was correct: adding what must have seemed insult to injury, the direction-finding station at Lualualei, which would have provided the answer, couldn't be reached—the station's communications lines ran through an Army telephone exchange which had stopped working.

For a moment, Kimmel's temper flared and he snapped at Layton, "Goddammit! We're under attack here and you don't even know whether they're north or south!" Regaining his composure, Kimmel put together what scant information he had, and concluded that the Japanese carrier force was somewhere south of Oahu. Orders went out to the *Lexington* and *Enterprise* task forces—*Saratoga* was too far away to be able to support them—to begin searching the waters south of the Hawaiian Islands. It was the wrong call, of course, as the two American carriers found nothing but open water, and yet it was fortunate, too: had either—or both—*Enterprise* or *Lexington* gone north and encountered *Kido Butai*, they would have been decisively outnumbered and almost certainly sunk, taking most if not all of their crew to the bottom with them.[7]

Perhaps the most galling moment of the day for Kimmel, short of the attack itself, of course, came at 3:00 PM, when an Army courier from Fort Shafter arrived at CINCPAC and reported directly to Kimmel, handing him a message from General Short's headquarters. The admiral glanced at it, called his staff to attention, then read the message aloud.

> The Japanese are presenting at 1 P.M. Eastern Standard Time, today, what amounts to an ultimatum. Also they are under orders to destroy their code machine immediately. Just what significance the hour set may have we do not know, but be on alert accordingly. Inform naval authorities of this communication. Marshall.

It was the warning the army chief of staff had sent out almost nine hours earlier.

Lieutenant Colonel French, in Washington, had hoped that Western Union, using RCA's 40-kilowatt transmitters, would be able to get the warning through to Short and Kimmel before the 1:00 PM (Washington time) deadline, and the message almost made it, arriving at Western Union's Honolulu office at 7:33 AM—three minutes past the deadline but still in plenty of time for Short and Kimmel to put their respective commands on full alert had it been delivered immediately via the Western Union teletype link to Short's headquarters at Fort Shafter. But inexplicably, French failed to mark it as priority traffic, so that when the message arrived in Honolulu, it was treated as a routine communication. As it was, the teletype link was down, so the signal was handed to an ordinary messenger for routine delivery by hand. He was still en route when the Japanese attack began, and in the confusion and chaos couldn't reach Fort Shafter's signals office until the raid was over. Distracted by the Japanese attack, the signals staff took almost three hours to decrypt the message, so that it was nearly 3:00 PM when Marshall's warning reached General Short, who immediately forwarded it to CINCPAC. Kimmel, torn between anger and despair, dismissed the courier with the remark that the message was no longer of any use or interest, and threw the paper into a waste basket.[8]

Meanwhile, Lieutenant Ruff was making repeated trips between *Nevada* and the naval facilities shore. Just as officers from all of the sunken or damaged ships in the harbor were doing for their crews, his first priority was making certain that *Nevada's* wounded were properly transferred to either *Solace* or the Navy Hospital; he then set to finding billets ashore for *Nevada's* sailors, many of whom had their berths on the ship burned or blasted into oblivion, and make messing arrangements for them all. When his men left the ship, Captain Scanland went with them, leaving behind a skeleton crew to man *Nevada's* anti-aircraft guns and keep a fire watch. He could do more for his men and his ship ashore than he could had he remained on board: there were always foot-dragging Navy yard bureaucrats to be chivvied along and tight-fisted storekeepers who would need to be "encouraged" to provide their carefully hoarded equipment and spares without first completing reams of paperwork. Commander Thomas did stay on board *Nevada*, though: Scanland had placed him in charge of directly overseeing the most urgent repair work. It would be more than two solid days before a thoroughly exhausted Thomas allowed himself the luxury of a few hours' sleep.

The crew who remained on *Nevada* worked just as hard as Commander Thomas, no one more so than one Warrant Machinist who had been carried, unconscious, from below decks just after the ship had grounded on Hospital Point. This was Donald Ross. When he was revived he refused to be evacuated, insisting that the ship needed him more than he needed a hospital, and parked himself in a chair next to a telephone box on the quarterdeck. Still blind—it would be months before his eyesight returned— he sat in that chair for two and one-half days as he worked entirely from memory, using his encyclopedic knowledge of the battleship's internal layout to direct the work details assigned to clean-up and repairs. It was only after he collapsed from exhaustion that Ross finally gave in and allowed himself to be moved ashore to the Navy Hospital—and it took a direct order from Commander Thomas to accomplish that.

Fighting fires—*Arizona* would be wrapped in flames for three days before the fires finally burnt themselves out—containing and controlling damage, and making basic repairs were the order of the day all across Pearl Harbor, but the single most important and intense operation being carried out was the effort to rescue crewmen trapped inside the upturned hull of *Oklahoma*. Even as the last of the Japanese planes were winging away from Pearl, hollow, metallic "thuds" and "clangs" could be heard echoing along the bottom of the capsized battleship, and a quick muster of *Oklahoma*'s crew showed that well over 500 of them were unaccounted for—killed, wounded, or otherwise missing. Some were already aboard or on their way to *Solace* or the base hospital, and there were bound to be stragglers who hadn't yet reported or whose information was still on its way to Captain Bode or Commander Kenworthy; even so, the fate or whereabouts of hundreds of sailors remained unknown, and some of them were definitely alive but trapped inside their ship.

By mid-afternoon, work crews—"yard dogs" in Navy parlance—from the salvage ship *Widgeon*, along with teams from the Navy Yard including 20 civilians from Yard Shop 11, equipped with air-hammers and oxy-acetylene cutting torches, were crawling along *Oklahoma*'s keel, trying to figure out where to begin cutting. Experienced shipwrights listened carefully, knowing that sounds could reverberate long distances inside a ship's hull and seem as if they were coming from places far distant from where they actually originated. It was, they knew, a race against time, as the men inside had limited air and were likely caught in spaces and voids where the water was still rising—but cutting in the wrong place would be just as wasteful as taking too long to begin.

For the crewmen inside *Oklahoma*, their experience was the stuff of nightmares: plunged in a darkness that could only be described as stygian when the power was knocked out, many of them hadn't realized that the ship had turned turtle. Others knew full well what had happened, but had no idea of how to escape—or if escape was even possible. After a few hours, Seaman Stephen Young, one of about 30 men trapped in the trunk of Number 4 gun turret, with the air growing increasingly foul and the water slowly but steadily rising, had resigned himself to his fate and made a wager with his best friend, Seaman William Hinsperger, that they would suffocate before they drowned. The enthusiasm with which the men in the turret trunk had been banging a wrench against bulkhead plates was diminishing, becoming almost desultory.

Not everyone in the compartment shared Young's fatalism, and from time to time one of them would dive into the water, down to the escape hatch 30 feet below, hoping to be able to make their way through the hatch to what had once been the open quarterdeck, and pull themselves hand-over-hand along the deck to open water—and fresh air and daylight. One by one they disappeared, and none of them returned: convinced that all of them had died in the attempt, the dozen or so men who remained in the trunk did what they could to make themselves comfortable while they awaited the end. What they didn't know was that at least one man did reach open water, a seaman by the name of Weisman; he was able to use the hull drawings the Navy Yard workers had with them to show the right places to start cutting.

It was almost 1:00 AM on December 8 before the work gang from Shop 11 were able to cut through to the base of the Turret Number 4 trunk. They had stopped using their oxy-acetylene torches for the time being: the risk of cutting into a pocket of combustible or even explosive gasses, or igniting the fuel oil bunkered in *Oklahoma*'s double bottom, was simply too great. Lead Man Julio DeCastro, a civilian and a Honolulu native, was in charge, and when they finally reached the deck plates separating them from the turret trunk, he took over the air-hammer himself. For the men inside the trunking—which was in fact, a huge cylinder—the noise was unnerving, beyond deafening, and yet at the same time nothing had ever sounded so sweet. By the time DeCastro had cut away enough of the deck plating to make a hole large enough for a man to pass through, only Young, Hinsperger, and eight others were left alive.

Astern of where DeCastro's men were cutting through *Oklahoma*'s hull, George DeLong and his bunkmates in Steering Aft could hear the air-hammers reverberating along the hull, and, whenever the hammers fell silent, resumed banging out their "S O S." After a quick look at the ship's drawings to be certain of where they would be cutting, a rescue team moved into position above the compartment. This time, with little danger of a fire or an explosion—the bunkers were all forward of the steering position—a cutting torch began slicing into the one-inch-thick shell plating. It was slow work, even though the yard dogs were cutting as small a hole as possible—just barely large enough for a man to pass through. They were worried that too large a hole might let the air in the compartment rush out and allow the water rising from below to overwhelm the men they were trying to save. Once the hole was cut, yard dogs quickly grabbed onto outstretched arms and pulled: all eight men in Steering Aft got out alive—they had been trapped for 32 hours.

Altogether, 32 sailors were extricated from *Oklahoma*'s hull by day's end on December 8. There were others still trapped—sporadic tapping and banging came from the battleship's hull for several more days—but wherever those men were, they couldn't be located in time, or else they were trapped so deeply inside the ship that they were unreachable. When *Oklahoma*'s hulk was righted in 1943, the remains of another 388 sailors and Marines were found—evidence indicated that at least some of them survived for several days after the ship capsized, waiting for a rescue that never came.. Most were never positively identified and were buried in mass graves in the Nu'uanu and Halawa cemeteries; in 1950 they were all reinterred at the National Memorial Cemetery of the Pacific, situated on the inner slopes of an old volcanic crater known locally as the "Punchbowl".

An even more heartbreaking situation was revealed when *West Virginia* was raised from the bottom of Pearl Harbor in February 1942. The bodies of 66 sailors were found inside her hull, but the discovery which shook everyone was when Ronald Endicott, Clifford Olds, and Louis Costin were found. In the opening minute of the attack, along with the call to General Quarters the order was passed throughout *WeeVee* to "set Condition Zed," that is, establish complete watertight integrity throughout the ship. What that bit of dry phrasing meant was that every watertight door, hatch, and scuttle from bow to stern would be slammed shut and dogged down—and would not be opened again *under any circumstances* until the ship secured from General Quarters. Sailors who were assigned to battle stations below their ship's waterline knew that there was always a chance they could be caught in a compartment suddenly blown open to the sea, and that the only door or hatch that would lead to safety would remain irrevocably closed, leaving them to either suffocate or drown. It was always thought of, though, as the sort of thing that would happen to "the other guy." Endicott, Olds, and Costin had the misfortune to be three of those "other guys."

Certainly they knew that *West Virginia* had settled to the bottom of Pearl Harbor, as the motion of the ship would have been unmistakable. So there they were, sealed in an utterly dry compartment that was completely surrounded by water, 40 feet down. They took refuge in compartment A-111, a pumping station that was known to be thoroughly watertight, located on the very bottom deck of the ship. They seemed to be well-situated at first: they had a good supply of fresh water, tinned rations, and foodstuffs, and plenty of flashlights—the compartment served as a storage area as well as a pump room. They also had a calendar and an eight-day Seth Thomas clock to help them keep track of the passage of time. Their circumstances were far from pleasant, but the three men had felt *West Virginia* shudder and shake repeatedly as the Japanese torpedoes exploded against and then inside her hull, and they knew that many of their shipmates had suffered agonizing deaths; they could be patient and wait for rescue.

It never came. From time to time one of the men would bang on one of the bulkheads with a heavy wrench, to remind the work crews who might be nearby that the three of them were still trapped, but also still alive. The workers indeed heard the signals, but were helpless—there were hundreds of tons of wreckage inside *West Virginia*'s hull that had to be cut, lifted, and cleared away before anyone could begin searching for the source of those signals: torn and twisted deck and hull plating, bent and buckled slabs of armor, collapsed bulkheads and displaced machinery, tons of live ammunition, plus the deritus of tens of thousands of bits and pieces of everyday items that accumulated inside a ship as it functioned.

The efforts expended in freeing trapped sailors on *Oklahoma* had taught the Navy a lot in a very short time: when cleared away, once-blocked hatches and doors could be blown out by the air pressure behind them as soon as they were undogged, usually with lethal consequences for those inside the opened compartment; cutting torches could ignite explosive gasses at any moment; the water pressure inside a ship's hull could collapse an air pocket in minutes: some sailors had drowned in front of their would-be rescuers eyes, overtaken by rising water before a hole large enough to pull them through could be made. The work doggedly continued, but there was no purpose in senselessly rushing to reach the trapped men, only to kill even more sailors than would be saved in the process. So the air in the isolated pump station grew steadily fouler, the three men increasingly weaker, with each passing day. Finally, on December 24, the banging was heard for the last time.

When A-111 was finally opened up in February, Commander Paul Dice, who was directing the salvage operation, was the first to step inside. The compartment was bone-dry, and one of the first things he saw was an open manhole cover on a freshwater tank. On the deck he found candy wrappers, empty ration tins, worn-out flashlight batteries—and the bodies of Endicott, Olds, and Costin. He also found the clock, long since having wound down, along with the calendar; the last day marked off on it was December 23—at least one of the three men had held out one more day before succumbing to the foul air.

The fate of the three sailors became something of a dark legend, especially among dockyard workers and salvage crews. The Navy took great care to not let the families of the three men know the details of their fate—they were told that their sons died during the attack on December 7; it was deemed to be too cruel to tell them otherwise. And in truth, there was little the Navy could have done: the nation was at war, and the procedures of peacetime had given way to a new, more ruthless set of priorities. Getting *West Virginia* back into service was, in the cold calculus of wartime, far more important than the fate of three sailors. But the three sailors would not be forgotten, nor be consigned to being merely the stuff of legend. Commander Dice took both the calendar and the clock, but not to keep for himself: the calendar was sent by mail to the chief of naval personnel in Washington DC, where, sadly, it was lost; some researchers spent decades trying to track it down, but the trail quickly grew hopelessly cold. Not so the Seth Thomas clock: originally donated to the USS *West Virginia* Museum in the town of Parkersburg in the battleship's name state, it is now the property of the West Virginia Division of Culture and History.

* * *

All over Pearl Harbor, launches were moving slowly around and between sunken and damaged ships, retrieving bodies—and body parts—from the water. It was not a job for the faint of heart, and for the most part, this duty went to the more experienced and senior enlisted men; a handful of officers, supernumerary to their ships for the time being, also took on the task. One of these enlisted men was Bosun's Mate Second Class Nick Kouretas of the cruiser *Raleigh*, who later recalled how it was done: "We would lasso a leg, an arm, a head, and maybe tow four or five or six bodies behind us slowly in the launch over to the landing." Once the bodies reached the shoreline, they could be gathered by corpsmen who would wade into the water with sheets, then lay them out on docks and landings at various points ashore on the Naval Base. By unspoken agreement among the work details, they paused momentarily in their labors whenever another body was carried past them, a silent, final salute to lost shipmates.[9]

The routine, quickly established, was always the same: the bodies would be laid out in two rows, heads facing inward to allow for easier identification, with space for a walkway between the rows. Bosun's Mate Kouretas, after being released from the retrieval detail, spent hours searching in vain for his brother. "I would run along the aisle…and look for him. He chewed his nails. I knew where he had a wart… I would get so far and say, 'Well, this guy looks like him,' but I couldn't see his face. I'd pick up the hand and say, 'No, that's not him,' and go on." Kouretas was lucky—his brother, James, survived the attack; for some reason he had been aboard the destroyer *Blue* that morning, and while Nick was searching for him among the dead, James was very much alive and well out to sea.[10]

Eventually the dead were placed on flatbed trucks and carried to the Naval Hospital, where corpsmen did their best to formally identify them. All too often, dogtags were missing and facial features had been so badly damaged they were unrecognizable. All told, 2,403 American sailors, soldiers, and airmen died that morning, or succumbed to their wounds shortly thereafter; 1,178 more were missing—immolated, disintegrated, carried to the bottom of the harbor and never found. By the third day after the attack, the number of bodies and body parts grew so large that a temporary morgue had to be set up at Aiea Landing in the far east end of Pearl Harbor. Above the landing rose the Aiea Heights, atop which sat the tea house from which Lieutenant Yoshikawa had spent many relaxing hours, watching the comings and goings of the United States Navy's Pacific Fleet.

The burials began on December 8. The dead were watched over by a six-man honor guard as the graves were being dug, some of them mass graves because it had been impossible to tell where the pieces of one body ended and another began. Marine Private Leslie Le Fan was assigned to one such honor guard, and the memory of that morning's detail remained vivid in his mind for the rest of his life. "We had our rifles, and were given three rounds of blank ammo to fire the salute. The chaplain, who was a captain in the Navy, gave a prayer. His words came, at the end, with tears in his eyes. Believe me, these were grown sailors and Marines standing there, unashamedly crying. They had lost buddies; they had lost friends; they had lost ships.

"The chaplain said, when he wound up, that 'we are beaten to our knees, but we shoot pretty good from that position. With God's help, we will win this war.' Foremost in my mind, right then, was: 'these Japs aren't going to get away with this!'"[11]

* * *

Unnoticed at the time by anyone in the United States, one final diplomatic curlicue was dispensed with by the Japanese Government. In Tokyo, at 6:10 AM on December 8, 1941, the Imperial Rescript declaring war on the United States and the British Empire was formally issued. There is no record of what Emperor Hirohito, in whose name the rescript was promulgated, thought or felt at the time. It was not his place to share such thoughts with his subjects, nor was it the place of mere mortals to be privy to them. With a sole exception, his military advisors hailed the attack on Pearl Harbor as a great victory: the war had not been ended in a single masterstroke to be sure, but Japan's chances of victory were suddenly seen to be immeasurably enhanced.

The lone voice of dissent in the chorus of celebration was, perhaps inevitably, Yamamoto Isoroku. Now was his chance to, as he predicted, "run wild across the Pacific," yet he saw something deeper in the events of December 7, 1941, than did any of his colleagues who had not studied in America, not lived among its peculiar, aggravating, exasperating, sometimes contradictory but always fascinating people, not witnessed first-hand the nation's immense industrial potential. Flawed though his understanding of America's national character might be, he knew enough to understand one fundamental truth about them: they would never accept that the strike on Pearl Harbor had been a legitimate stratagem of war. Because the delivery of the Imperial Government's final note to the American State Department—in which it was made clear that the Japanese would seek resolution to the diplomatic crisis between America and Japan outside of diplomatic means, that is, through war—had been delayed, so that it was handed to Secretary of State Hull while bombs were already falling in Hawaii, the strike would be seen by the American people as a sneak attack. It was, in fact, worse than that, he knew—the Americans even had a name for how they would perceive the raid on Pearl Harbor: it was a "sucker punch," a blow landed on an unprepared and passive victim. At Pearl Harbor, the Americans would tell themselves, the United States had been "sucker punched" by the Japanese Empire. And Americans, Yamamoto knew, despised people who threw sucker punches.

Yamamoto felt dishonored by the fact that the attack began before that last diplomatic note had been delivered. In January 1942, replying to a question from Taketora Ogata, one of Japan's leading journalists and one of the Empire's most influential political figures, as to the long-term consequences of the attack, Yamamoto said, "A military man can scarcely pride himself on having 'smitten a sleeping enemy'; it is more a matter of shame, simply, for the one smitten. I would rather you made your appraisal after seeing what the enemy does, since it is certain that, angered and outraged, he will soon launch a determined counterattack." Though he would never say that all Japan had done was awaken a sleeping giant and fill him with a terrible resolve, once America's "determined counterattack" began, the effect and consequences would be the same.[12]

Retribution...

"Mr. Vice President, Mr. Speaker, members of the Senate and the House of Representatives:

"Yesterday, December 7th, 1941—a date which will live in infamy—the United States of America was suddenly and deliberately attacked by naval and air forces of the Empire of Japan.

"The United States was at peace with that nation, and, at the solicitation of Japan, was still in conversation with its government and its Emperor looking toward the maintenance of peace in the Pacific.

"Indeed, one hour after Japanese air squadrons had commenced bombing in the American island of Oahu, the Japanese Ambassador to the United States and his colleague delivered to our Secretary of State a formal reply to a recent American message. And, while this reply stated that it seemed useless to continue the existing diplomatic negotiations, it contained no threat or hint of war or of armed attack.

"It will be recorded that the distance of Hawaii from Japan makes it obvious that the attack was deliberately planned many days or even weeks ago. During the intervening time the Japanese Government has deliberately sought to deceive the United States by false statements and expressions of hope for continued peace."

The sonorous voice, with its measured yet slightly staccato phrasing, filled every nook and cranny of the Congressional chamber; the silence into which it projected was so profound that nothing interfered with even a single syllable. This address to Congress by President Franklin Roosevelt, in which he would ask for a declaration of war on the Empire of Japan, was one of the most momentous Presidential speeches in the entire history of the American Republic. Roosevelt was determined to be realistic and direct: there was no way to sugar-coat the disaster, and he refused to try, saying bluntly that,

"The attack yesterday on the Hawaiian Islands has caused severe damage to American naval and military forces. I regret to tell you that very many American lives have been lost. In addition, American ships have been reported torpedoed on the high seas between San Francisco and Honolulu.

"Yesterday the Japanese Government also launched an attack against Malaya.

"Last night Japanese forces attacked Hong Kong.

"Last night Japanese forces attacked Guam.

"Last night Japanese forces attacked the Philippine Islands.

"Last night the Japanese attacked Wake Island.

"And this morning the Japanese attacked Midway Island.

"Japan has therefore undertaken a surprise offensive extending throughout the Pacific area. The facts of yesterday and today speak for themselves. The people of the United States have already formed their opinions and well understand the implications to the very life and safety of our nation…"

President Roosevelt had worked on this speech far into Sunday night, grimly determined to make a case not just to Congress but to the American people that the time for bickering and division over the role the United States would play in what was already being called the Second World War was irrevocably past: Japan had made that decision for America. Now, he declared, "our people, our territory and our interests are in grave danger."

Yet there was no note of defeat in his address, however dire the news might be. For weal or woe, Franklin Roosevelt was arguably the most accomplished politician ever to sit in the Oval Office, and he now bent all of his formidable skills to the task of projecting an air of steely resolve, first to the Representatives and Senators seated before him, then to the American people as a whole. Thus his voice was iron-hard when he affirmed that "No matter how long it may take us to overcome this premeditated invasion, the American people in their righteous might will win through to absolute victory. I believe that I interpret the will of the Congress and of the people when I assert that we will not only defend ourselves to the uttermost but will make it very certain that this form of treachery shall never again endanger us."

Then came his masterstroke, as he laid the onus of victory on the shoulders of the average American, framing the challenge in such terms that no true patriot could possibly resist: "With confidence in our armed forces—with the unbounding determination of our people—we will gain the inevitable triumph—so help us God."[1]

Roosevelt closed his address with a formal request to Congress for a declaration of war on the Empire of Japan; the joint resolution formalizing the state of war passing in both houses in less than an hour, with only a single dissenting vote. Across the country, apart from a few fanatical holdouts who had been hopelessly discredited by events but refused to recognize the new reality, isolationism collapsed like a sandcastle in the incoming tide. America was united in its desire to bring retribution upon the Japanese Empire as it had never before been nor would ever again be united in a single cause.

* * *

"Remember Pearl Harbor" became America's shibboleth and the title of the country's most popular war song. Enlistment posters emblazoned with those words—along with "Remember the *Arizona!*", "Avenge Pearl Harbor!", and "Remember December 7th!" encouraged young American men to enlist in the Navy, Army, Air Corps, or Marines, and hundreds of thousands did so, even among those who had been fortunate enough to have had high draft numbers and who would otherwise have been able to avoid conscription.

That is not to say that once war was declared, it was all over but the shouting—far from it. Within hours of the attack on Pearl Harbor, the Japanese struck at the Philippines, Wake Island, Guam, and Malaya, and by the end of April, Bataan, Corregidor, Wake, Singapore, Thailand, and the whole of the Malay Peninsula had been overrun and occupied; Japanese columns were driving deep into Burma, threatening India with invasion, while the Allied defenders in New Guinea had their backs to the wall. Everywhere in the Far East, the Japanese outfought, out-thought, and out-endured their enemies. During the six months which Yamamoto assured would be theirs following the Pearl Harbor attack, the Japanese did indeed "run wild" in the Pacific.

And yet, the successes were not unalloyed. What would later be known as "victory disease" began to creep into the thinking of many senior officers in both the Imperial Army and Navy. It was a peculiar world view where the thought and the deed were deemed to be as one: Japanese officers, especially senior officers who should have known better, began to believe they only had to plan and then initiate an operation and victory would be inevitable. Their *Bushido* was supreme, Japanese soldiers, sailors, and airmen were indeed superior in all respects to their *gaijin* foes. The years of rampant militarism had inculcated a mindset that was beginning to divorce the Japanese leadership from a genuine appreciation of reality.

That sense of superiority was shaken—though not shattered—on Saturday, April 18, 1942, when 16 B-25B Mitchell medium bombers were launched from the US Navy's aircraft carrier *Hornet* at a point roughly 650 nautical miles east of the Japanese home islands. Taking aim at military targets in Tokyo and other major cities on the island of Honshu, the operation was more of a hit-and-run raid than a strategic strike, and it caused little material damage. At the same time, though, it threw into stark relief the fact that the Home Islands were more vulnerable to American air attack than the emperor's generals and admirals had believed possible.

So it was that, as April eased into May in 1942, while almost all of the objectives of Japan's pre-war strategy seemed to have been attained and the Japanese hold on the western half of the Pacific Ocean appeared unshakable, Japan's most senior officers were uneasy. The sheer audacity of the American airstrike, immortalized among Americans as the "Doolittle Raid" after James Doolittle, the Army Air Corps Lieutenant Colonel who led the mission, had caused considerable consternation in Tokyo and compelled the Naval General Staff to completely reassess its ability to defend the Home Islands. In particular, Admiral Nagano Osami, chief of the Navy's General Staff, had been stunned by the attack, muttering over and over as he heard bombs exploding in the middle distance, "This shouldn't happen, this just should not happen!"[2]

Admiral Yamamoto, who himself suffered a not insignificant loss of face as a consequence of the Doolittle Raid, swore to make certain that it would not—could not—happen again. To make it so, the Empire's defensive perimeter must be pushed as far east as possible. There would be only one way to accomplish this: seize Midway Island, the largest of a long chain of coral islands in the northern part of the Central Pacific positioned some 1,400 miles west-northwest of Oahu.

Strictly speaking, Midway consisted of two islands, Sand and Eastern, that were part of a central coral atoll. Eastern Island was large enough to support an airfield capable of handling the heaviest aircraft in service with the US Army or Navy—including B-17 bombers. That airfield was the key to Yamamoto's strategy of using Midway as the Empire's eastern outpost, guarding Japan's left flank: it could handle the very-long-range Mitsubishi G4M bombers—the type the Allies called a "Betty"—that would be able to patrol the broad reaches of the Northern Pacific and ensure that the US Navy could never again slip a carrier task force close enough to the Home Islands to once again launch another attack as it did in April. Once captured, Midway would be so heavily fortified and manned by such a large garrison that the Americans would regard the cost in men and material necessary to retake the atoll as utterly prohibitive.

He also foresaw an opportunity to complete the unfinished business of the Pearl Harbor attack. Midway's strategic position was too vital to the Americans for them to allow the garrison there to be abandoned and overrun as they had done at Wake Island six months earlier: whoever possessed Midway could dominate the northern Pacific. From there the Japanese could threaten and indeed strike at the Hawaiian Islands or even the West Coast of the United States; conversely, if the Americans retained their hold on Midway, they would be poised to strike deep into the Central Pacific, at the heart of Japan's newly acquired empire of island chains. Either alternative meant that the Americans *had* to defend Midway if they were to win their war with Japan. To do so meant that they would have to commit their remaining aircraft carriers to a showdown with those of the *Kido Butai*; Yamamoto was confident that, facing at least two-to-one odds in carrier strength alone, what was left of the Pacific Fleet would be annihilated. Still, the security of the Home Islands was paramount, therefore the first priority was neutralizing and occupying Midway. Once the atoll was secure, then the Imperial Navy would have free rein in dealing with what was left of the US Navy's Pacific Fleet.

Unfortunately for Yamamoto, the Imperial Navy, and Japan, this was one of the moments when the worst effects of the "victory disease" made themselves manifest. At the same time they wanted to move eastward and occupy Midway Island, the

Japanese also wanted to take Port Moresby, on New Guinea's southern coast. An airfield at Moresby would allow squadrons of G4M bombers to cut the shipping lanes between the United States and Australia, effectively isolating the Land Down Under—the western approaches to Australia were already under interdiction from Imperial Army airfields in Malaya and Borneo. Both operations were viable, both were strategically necessary; the problem was that they couldn't—and shouldn't—be carried out simultaneously, which is essentially what the Imperial Navy planned to do nonetheless, with the attack on Port Moresby going in just three weeks before the Midway operation began. The axes of advance for the two operations were widely divergent, so that the forces committed to the attacks would be moving away from each other, with no possibility of any mutual support between them. Critically for the Imperial Navy, it wouldn't be possible for Japan's already over-worked dockyards to repair any ships damaged in the Moresby attack in time for the advance on Midway, and worst of all, from the Japanese perspective, the Imperial Navy lacked sufficient aircraft carriers to guarantee that *both* attack forces would have an overwhelming superiority in airpower in any likely encounter with the United States Navy.

The strike southward toward Port Moresby ended in the Battle of the Coral Sea, which lasted from May 4 to May 8. It was the first naval battle ever fought entirely by aircraft, with the opposing fleets never coming within sight of each other; more importantly, it was the Imperial Navy's first strategic setback in the war. Three Japanese aircraft carriers, *Shokaku*, *Zuikaku*, and the light carrier *Shoho* squared off against the Americans' *Lexington* and *Yorktown*. In a see-saw exchange of airstrikes, *Shoho* was sunk while *Shokaku* took very heavy damage and *Zuikaku's* air group suffered crippling losses; *Lexington* and *Yorktown* in turn were both damaged, *Lexington* severely so. What would have been a marginal tactical victory for the US Navy, though, instead went to the Japanese when, on May 8, a flaw in *"Lady Lex's"* damage control measures caused three huge internal explosions that crippled the ship. The damage was so extensive the American task force commander, Rear Admiral Frank Fletcher, had no choice but to order the *Lexington* to be scuttled. A fleet carrier for a light carrier was hardly an equal exchange, which is what gave the tactical victory, such as it was and what margin there was to it, to the Japanese.

But on the much larger stage of strategy, the Coral Sea battle was decisive in ways not immediately discernable. While the attack on Port Moresby was thwarted, the Japanese did manage to occupy several islands in the Solomons chain—yet they would be the Empire's last Pacific conquests of the war; the Battle of the Coral Sea marked the high tide of Imperial Japan. The loss of *Shoho*, while an inconvenience to Yamamoto's planning for the capture of Midway at the beginning of June, wasn't critical—what would prove to be devastating for the Imperial Navy would be the absence of *Shokaku* and *Zuikaku*. *Shokaku* would actually come close to sinking on the return voyage to Japan; her repairs wouldn't be completed until six weeks after the Battle of Midway ended. *Zuikaku's* problems were of an entirely different nature: she had taken no damage at Coral Sea, but lost one Zero, eight Vals, and 14 Kates, which accounted for a third of her dive bombers and over half of her torpedo bombers. She had to return to Japan to take on new aircraft along with replacement aircrews, which meant that she would be unable to sail with the rest of the Midway strike force when it left Japanese waters on May 27.

Yet, so confident had the Japanese become that victory was theirs by right, the absence of *Shokaku* and *Zuikaku* was regarded as little more than a nuisance. In fact, as the planning and preparations for the Midway operation progressed, that confidence began morphing into a dangerous arrogance. The extent and effect of this arrogance was made manifest—or would have been to an objective observer—in the wargames conducted aboard Yamamoto's flagship, *Yamato*, in late April and early May.

Unlike the highly analytical and ruthlessly self-critical exercises that preceded the attack on Pearl Harbor, where no interference with their progress and outcome was tolerated and umpires rulings were inviolate, the usefulness of the wargames staged before the Midway operation was utterly undermined by Rear Admiral Ugaki Matome, Yamamoto's chief of staff. Arrogantly refusing to accept any outcome of events in these wargames that did not favor the Imperial Navy, he repeatedly interfered to shade and shift the results, despite having no authority to do so. At one point, when the games' umpire ruled that a surprise airstrike by American dive bombers had sunk both *Kaga* and *Akagi*, Ugaki stepped forward and announced that only *Kaga* had been sunk, while *Akagi* suffered no more than minor damage. Later, when an additional flight deck was needed to carry out a specific attack, Ugaki blithely raised *Kaga* from the bottom of the Pacific and included her in the operation. Incredibly, none of the officers present, not even Yamamoto, questioned Ugaki's actions, and whatever lessons might have been learned had the games been allowed to continue unhindered were lost. Worse, those same officers repeatedly underestimated the US Navy's determination and willingness to fight. The Japanese had begun to believe their own propaganda, for which they would pay dearly.

As the month of May progressed, Yamamoto assembled an armada of 46 destroyers, 16 cruisers, 11 battleships, and four fleet carriers, as well as a dozen support and supply ships, along with 14 transports carrying Imperial Marines and construction crews to occupy Midway itself. Yamamoto would take personal command of the operation; the First Air Fleet, once more designated the *Kido Butai*, would again be led by Vice Admiral Nagumo. Acting as a screen and scouting force for this enormous concentration of naval power, tasked with spotting any American aircraft carriers before they could get within range of the Japanese carrier force, were 21 fleet submarines that would be picketed around the Hawaiian Islands and along the approaches to Midway.

Supremely confident of victory, the Japanese were nonetheless operating under one severe, decisive handicap, which Yamamoto had no idea existed. In January 1942, OP-20-G finally began to crack the JN-25b code. Four days before the attack on Pearl Harbor, the Japanese replaced JN-25a, which was beginning to yield useful intelligence to ONI, with a new variant, which, because it was recognizable as a variant on the original JN-25 and not an entirely new code, the US Navy cryptographers dubbed JN-25b. The Navy's cipher and codebreaking efforts had expanded rapidly after Pearl Harbor, so that more man-hours of labor could be dedicated to breaking into JN-25b than had been possible with the earlier variants: by March the US Navy was able to listen in on the most critical—and highly classified—Imperial Navy communications. Moreover, Station HYPO in Hawaii at last had access to the raw information it needed to properly interpret the decryptions, as the obstructive and obstreperous Rear Admiral Turner was no longer in a position to ration out intelligence as he saw fit: he had been bundled out of the War Plans Division and ONI with almost obscene haste after the attack on December 7. By mid-May, Commander Layton and Lieutenant Commander Rochefort assembled a reasonably complete picture of the Imperial Navy's overall plan, and, after a clever radio-intercept ploy, positively identified Midway as the objective. Admiral Chester Nimitz, who was Husband Kimmel's permanent replacement as CINCPAC, listened closely when Layton and Rochefort spoke: if they were correct, there could be an opportunity for the Pacific Fleet to spring a trap on the Japanese.

"If," of course, is a perilous word when applied to operational planning, but in this case Layton and Rochefort were able to speak with near-certitude. They had correctly deduced, for example, that Yamamoto had organized his fleet into four distinct components: the *Kido Butai,* which included the four fleet carriers *Kaga, Akagi, Soryu,* and *Hiryu* as the advance strike force; a "main body" of mostly surface warships, under Yamamoto's direct and personal command; an invasion force of battleships and cruisers tasked with shelling Midway's defenses into submission or oblivion—either would do; and an occupation force made up of troop transports and their escorts.

The staff at Station HYPO had even established a nearly exact schedule for the movements of the four fleets headed eastward toward Midway. This allowed Layton and Rochefort to present Nimitz with a surprisingly accurate projection of what was Yamamoto's overall operational plan, including where and when the Japanese were going to strike, and in what strength. From this information CINCPAC immediately saw that the Japanese plan was overly elaborate, and that its complexity created a situation where Yamamoto's various forces would be too widely separated to be able to provide mutual support should any one of them be attacked.

This intelligence was a godsend to Nimitz, who was determined to exploit it as thoroughly as possible in springing his own trap for the Japanese. Layton would later recall how, at a Pacific Fleet staff conference on May 27, Nimitz put Station HYPO and its analysts on the spot: "'I want you to be specific,' Nimitz said, fixing me with his cool blue eyes. 'After all, this is the job I have given you—to be the admiral commanding the Japanese forces, and tell me what is going on.' ... Summarizing all my data, I told Nimitz that the carriers would probably attack on the morning of 4 June, from the northwest on a bearing of 325 degrees. They could be sighted at about 175 miles from Midway at around 0700 local time."[3]

Yamamoto, by contrast, had very little reliable information about the strength and location of American naval forces around Midway and Hawaii, or the defenses on Midway itself. Imperial Naval Intelligence had never placed as high a priority on cryptography as had the US Navy's ONI, nor were the Japanese signals analysts in Tokyo as skillful as their American opposites in Washington DC. This time, too, there was no industrious Lieutenant Yoshikawa to provide precise details about the Pacific Fleet's coming and goings at Pearl Harbor. The Japanese admiral would be taught the hard way that Imperial Naval Intelligence assessments of the US Navy's capabilities and intentions were badly flawed and baselessly optimistic.

Nimitz knew yet another critical detail of which the Japanese were also blissfully ignorant: he would be able to send not just two carriers—*Enterprise* and *Hornet*—out to face Yamamoto at Midway, as the Japanese admiral believed, but *three*. Imperial Naval Intelligence had reported that not only was *Lexington* lost at the Battle of the Coral Sea, but that *Yorktown* had gone down as well. Rumors of *Yorktown*'s demise were, however, greatly exaggerated: she took damage to her hull and flight deck at Coral Sea, to be sure, and when she arrived at Pearl Harbor on May 27, the surveyors at the Navy Yard estimated that repairs would take three months to complete. Nimitz flatly told the repair crews they had three *days* to make the ship combat-capable—the yard dogs, almost all of them working around the clock, did the job in two. The repairs were rough-and-ready at best, and far from complete, but they were good enough: Nimitz needed a working carrier *now*, not a pristine ship sometime later; the work done would be sufficient for *Yorktown* to carry out air operations for two or three weeks, long enough for the issue at Midway Island to be decided one way or another.

Nimitz appeared to be gambling when he ordered the three carriers set out on a high-speed dash to a position—optimistically named "Point Luck"—about 300 miles north of Midway. The escorting elements of Task Force 16 and Task Force 17 were composed entirely of cruisers and destroyers—Nimitz chose to leave all of the Pacific Fleet's surviving battleships on the West Coast, where they would be a final line of defense if worse came to worst. He was determined to fight a carrier battle at Midway, not engage in a slugfest, and if the situation began to turn against the American fleet, he wanted his ships to be able to withdraw fast enough to evade Yamamoto; in such a scenario, having battleships attached to the task forces would have only slowed down the carriers and allowed the Japanese to overtake them.

Still, there was a huge disparity in the firepower that Yamamoto commanded and what Spruance and Fletcher would have at their disposal, so that if there *was* a surface battle—a nighttime engagement, for example, the sort of action at which the Imperial Navy excelled—things would go very badly for the Americans. Such was the element of risk in Nimitz's decision that in Washington, Admiral Earnest King, now the US Navy Commander-in-Chief, and his entire staff openly expressed serious reservations about it, although King, respecting the principle that "the man on the spot knows best," refused to go so far as to overrule CINCPAC.

But Nimitz made the right decision: the US Navy had always regarded its aircraft carriers as strategic assets, unlike the Imperial Navy, where the carriers' utility was seen as primarily tactical. In the often curious, sometimes seemingly inverted calculus of war, *Enterprise*, *Hornet*, and *Yorktown* together were ultimately more valuable than Midway Island: the US Navy was loathe to lose Midway but it simply could not afford to lose the carriers. Yet, if Nimitz was gambling—and he was, however carefully calculated the gamble might be—he was also playing with a deck stacked in his favor. The air groups normally deployed on Japanese carriers were roughly three quarters the size of those aboard their American counterparts, and all four of Nagumo's carrier air groups were significantly under-strength, so that with three carriers rather than just the two Yamamoto would be expecting, the US Navy, instead of being heavily outnumbered in carrier planes, would be meeting the Japanese at something close to parity in airpower. If reading Yamamoto's "mail," so to speak, was the joker in the deck being played, the third American carrier at Midway would be Nimitz's ace in the hole.

* * *

The curtain went up on the Battle of Midway in a rather desultory manner on the morning of June 3, and as opening acts went, it was hardly a rousing affair. Nagumo's First Air Fleet and Yamamoto's Main Body remained undetected as of yet, but a US Navy PBY flying an early-morning reconnaissance patrol spotted the Occupation Force 500 miles to the west of Midway. Nine B-17s based on the island were sent out to attack the transports but failed to score a single hit; there were no casualties on either side. That single, ineffectual air strike was the only fighting to take place that day.

June 4 would prove to be very different, however—it would, in fact, be witness to the most intense carrier battle of the entire Pacific War. At 4:30 AM, the four carriers of the *Kido Butai* sent out an air strike against Midway, 36 Val dive bombers and the same number of Kates armed as level bombers, with 36 Zero fighters flying escort. Absent from the ranks of the Japanese fliers was Commander Fuchida, who had led the attack on Pearl Harbor. In the planning for the Midway operation, he had been the designated leader of the attack, but was in no condition to fly this morning: on May 27, he was stricken with acute appendicitis which required emergency surgery, and he was still recuperating in *Akagi's* sickbay. Lieutenant Tomonaga Joichi stepped into his shoes and was leading the aerial attack on Midway.

Meanwhile, the cruisers screening *Kido Butai* were launching aircraft of their own, patrol planes scouting for the American carriers Admiral Nagumo suspected might be lurking somewhere near Midway. Meticulously following Yamamoto's specific orders, he'd held back half of his available aircraft in anticipation of the moment when the American fleet was discovered. Those planes were armed with torpedoes and semi-armor-piercing bombs—the latter ideal for penetrating the decks of American carriers. If there *was* an American fleet out there somewhere, Nagumo would be ready for them.

About the same time the Japanese strike force was taking off, a dozen PBY Catalinas stationed on Midway lumbered into the air to search the quadrant northwest to southwest of the islands for the enemy carriers. A quick analysis of the previous day's B-17 air strike had shown that only transport ships and their escorts made up the fleet those bombers had attacked. The *Kido Butai* remained undetected; it would be up to the big, awkward-looking PBY's to find it.

At 5:30 AM, one of those Catalinas sighted the enemy carrier force. Through the scattered cloud cover the PBY's pilot, Lieutenant Howard Ady, saw an array of aircraft carriers, battleships, cruisers, and destroyers appear below him. It was, he later recalled, as if he were "watching a curtain rise on the biggest show in our lives." His radio operator hurriedly tapped out a sighting report, "Two carriers and main body ships, carriers in front, course 135, speed 35," as the Catalina hastily banked behind a rain squall just as the Japanese anti-aircraft guns were finding the range. Ten minutes later another PBY spotted the Japanese aerial strike force headed for Midway and transmitted a terse warning: "Many planes headed Midway bearing 320 degrees, distance 150."[4]

The response by Midway's aviators—a mixed bag of Navy, Marine, and Army Air Corps pilots and aircrew—to the two reports was immediate but ragged. A detachment of six fresh-from-the-factory Grumman TBF torpedo bombers, originally assigned to *Hornet*'s Squadron TB-8, was the first to take off. A new torpedo bomber design, the TBF Avenger was about to receive its baptism of fire, as these six planes had been sent to Midway for combat evaluation. The fat, somewhat ungainly looking Grummans were followed into the air minutes later by a half-dozen Air Corps B-26 bombers armed with torpedoes. Next came a gaggle of torpedo bombers and dive bombers—11 SBC-3 Vindicators and 16 SBD Dauntlesses from Marine Squadron 241. Last into the air were 15 Army Air Corps B-17's. On paper, this was a formidable assembly of aircraft, but in the various units' haste to get airborne there had been no chance to plan a coordinated attack. Worse, there was no fighter escort: all the Marine fighters on Midway—20 Brewster Buffalos and seven Grumman Wildcats—remained behind to defend the island from the Japanese attack everyone now knew was coming.

The TBF's were the first to engage the Japanese fleet—they began their torpedo runs at 7:10—and for the next two hours the American flyers pressed home a succession of incredibly brave but piecemeal attacks, the Avengers followed by the bombers of Marine Squadron 241, with the Army Air Corps B-26's attacking last. Carefully arrayed so that the fire from their anti-aircraft guns would be mutually supporting, the carriers opened up a furious barrage against the oncoming American planes, while the Zeroes flying top cover for the carriers swooped down. The result was so one-sided an engagement as to be a near-massacre. The American pilots and gunners did their best, bringing down three of the defending Zeroes, but at the cost of two B-26's, 10 of Squadron 241's dive- and torpedo-bombers, and all but one of the new TBF's. The high-flying B-17's got away unscathed, as the Zero pilots focused their attention on the Avengers, Vindicators, and Dauntlesses. Not a single bomb or torpedo from any of the American planes hit the Japanese carriers or any of their escorts.[5]

The American attacks on the *Kido Butai* hadn't yet begun when the Japanese strike force appeared over Midway at 6:30 AM, and what befell the Marine fighters defending the atoll *was* a massacre. The incoming air strike was located by the radar unit on Eastern Island while the Japanese planes were still 20 minutes away, sufficient time for the Marine pilots to get airborne and climb to a fighting altitude. But not only were the American fliers outnumbered four-to-one, most of their machines were hopelessly out-classed. While the sturdy Wildcat could, in the hands of a capable pilot, hold its own against a Zero, the already-obsolete Buffalo, slow, clumsy, underpowered and under-gunned, was easy prey for the veteran fliers of the Imperial Navy. Within minutes, two of the Wildcats and 13 Buffaloes were shot down, and nearly all the remaining American fighters were heavily damaged, in exchange for five Kates and one Zero shot down. When the enemy strike force turned away from Midway, only two Wildcats could still fly; 14 American pilots were killed in the fighting.

The Japanese didn't have it entirely their way, though. The defensive fire put up by Midway's anti-aircraft batteries was intense and accurate, bringing down three more Kates and damaging 43 others—including 14 that, when they returned to their carriers, were so badly shot up they were declared unserviceable: one way or another, close to one-quarter of the strike force aircraft had been put out of action. Worse, from the Imperial Navy's perspective, while some of Midway's facilities had been damaged or destroyed, the defensive positions on both Sand and Eastern Islands were largely untouched.

This was more than just problematic for the Japanese, as they wanted no part of another such debacle as the one they had experienced at Wake Island six months earlier. In the two weeks following the attack on Pearl Harbor, the garrison on Wake, some 600 strong, mostly Marines but with a smattering of Army and Navy personnel, put up such a fierce defense of their island that the Imperial Navy had been compelled to eventually deploy two fleet carriers, two heavy cruisers, eight destroyers, and 2,500 troops to eventually take the island. It was hardly surprising, then, that Lieutenant Tomonaga, whose carrier *Hiryu* had been part of the assault on Wake, sent out an urgent message to Admiral Nagumo: "There is need for a second attack wave."[6]

On *Akagi's* bridge, Nagumo carefully weighed his options, likely wondering if the aftermath of the December 7 attack was again being played out, though with one crucial difference: the first strike on Pearl Harbor had achieved the Imperial Navy's primary objective, crippling the US Navy's Pacific Fleet. To Nagumo, there had been no compelling reason to continue risking the *Kido Butai* to a sudden counter-attack by American carriers, whose location was a complete mystery at the time, while his own planes had flown off on what in his eyes would have been a pointless attack. Here, now, however, his carriers' first mission—destroying Midway's defenses—had yet to be accomplished. At 7:15 AM the admiral gave his assent for another attack on Midway. Plane handlers, mechanics, and armorers on *Kaga, Akagi, Soryu*, and *Hiryu* immediately set to work on the Kates waiting in the hangar decks, removing the torpedoes and replacing them with bombs. It was a time-consuming process, as limitations on manpower and equipment meant that on each carrier only six of the bombers could be rearmed simultaneously.

Nagumo hadn't forgotten that a pair of American aircraft carriers *might* be lurking about somewhere near Midway, but he was far from certain of it—Naval Intelligence couldn't confirm that *Enterprise* and *Hornet* had yet left Pearl Harbor. No sighting reports had come from any of the submarines screening Oahu, tasked with spotting the carriers if they sailed. Even if, by some evil mischance, the Americans had eluded the subs and were closing on Midway, as a precaution he could hold back most of the Zeroes to protect his own carriers and still feel confident of sending out another attack with only minimal fighter cover, knowing that Midway's fighters had been all but annihilated. And in truth, had the American carriers sailed out of Pearl bound for Midway, Nagumo had no reason to believe the enemy was within range of his own ships: by 7:00 AM all the patrol planes sent out at dawn by the cruisers and battleships escorting his carriers had reported finding nothing within 250 miles of *Kido Butai*.

All save for of the aircraft sent out from *Tone*, that is. Along with her sister, *Chikuma*, the cruiser *Tone* had been designed to carry six long-range scout planes, the better to act as the "eyes" of the Imperial Navy's carriers, which had no reconnaissance planes of their own. On this particular morning, mechanical problems had delayed the launch of *Tone's* scout plane 4 by nearly an hour. Ordinarily this sort of malfunction would have been no more than a minor inconvenience, but on this morning, that particular aircraft's assigned patrol sector was precisely where three American carriers were located. Though Nagumo couldn't know it, at that moment Fortune was turning her back on the Imperial Navy.

* * *

Enterprise and *Hornet* had indeed departed Pearl, sailing together on May 28 as Task Force 16, escorted by the heavy cruisers *Pensacola, New Orleans, Vincennes, Northampton,* and *Minneapolis,* the light cruiser *Atlanta,* and nine destroyers, under the command of Rear Admiral Raymond Spruance. Two days later, Task Force 17—*Yorktown,* the cruisers *Portland* and *Astoria,* along with a screen of six destroyers—followed, with Rear Admiral Frank Fletcher flying his flag from *Yorktown's* bridge. Both task forces went undetected by the Japanese picket line of submarines, having sailed before the enemy subs arrived on station. The task forces rendezvoused north of the Hawaiian Islands on June 1 and pressed on to a position north-northeast of Midway that Admiral Nimitz had christened "Point Luck."

Trusting the intelligence collected by the cryptographers and codebreakers at OP-20-G in Washington and Station HYPO at Pearl, along with the conclusions drawn by Rochefort and Layton, Nimitz intended "Point Luck" to be the spot from where Fletcher and Spruance could mousetrap the Imperial Navy's carrier force. Now, on June 4, the trap was about to be sprung. Just after sunrise, plane handlers began positioning—"spotting"—aircraft on the flight decks of *Enterprise* and *Hornet,* where they were fueled and armed. One of *Yorktown's* SBD squadrons had already taken off in the predawn darkness to locate the exact position of the Japanese carriers that Spruance and Fletcher knew were approaching Midway from somewhere northwest of the island.

The situation began to clarify itself for the two American admirals when the PBY report that the Japanese carrier force had been sighted was relayed to Task Force 16 and Task Force 17, followed seconds later with the warning of the air strike bearing down on Midway. At 6:07, while *Yorktown* waited for her scouting squadron to return, Fletcher signaled to Spruance: "Proceed southwesterly and attack enemy carriers when definitely located. I will follow as soon as planes recovered."[7] Spruance wasn't given over to waiting, though: a brief conference with his staff and a quick study of the charts, using the bearing and distance from Midway reported by the PBY to establish a baseline position for the Japanese carriers, convinced him that the enemy fleet was in range of his aircraft—just barely—and that any delay in attacking them would give those ships an opportunity to escape. Turning to his chief of staff, Spruance said simply, "Launch everything you have at the earliest possible moment and strike the Japanese carriers." Moments later, the first planes were taking off from *Enterprise* and *Hornet*; all told, 65 SBD Dauntless dive-bombers, 29 TBD Devastator torpedo bombers, and 20 F4F Wildcats were airborne by 7:50. As each squadron settled into formation, it turned and flew westward to seek out the enemy.[8]

* * *

It was at 7:28 AM that the first reports from *Tone's* scout plane 4 reached Admiral Nagumo: "Sighted what appears to be ten enemy surface ships, in position 10 degrees distance 240 miles from Midway. Course 150 degrees, speed over 20 knots."

So now the admiral knew for certain that American warships were present, but the signal didn't resolve the question to which Nagumo vitally needed an answer: were any of those ships aircraft carriers? Despite whatever frustration this oversight may have caused him, the admiral's phlegmatic nature asserted itself and he refused to be panicked into an unwise decision by what might be no more than a handful of cruisers and destroyers. The orders he'd been given by Yamamoto hadn't changed: Midway was still the priority for the *Kido Butai*. Nagumo refused to entirely ignore the American warships, though, and he chose a course of action that seemed an elegant compromise. At 7:45 he issued instructions for those planes which had already been rearmed to carry on with their preparations for the second strike on Midway. Those aircraft which still retained their torpedoes and semi-armor-piercing bombs would be sent out to attack the enemy ships. As if to confirm the soundness of his decision, another message arrived from *Tone's* scout plane 4 at 8:09, this one announcing that, "Enemy ships are five cruisers and five destroyers."[9]

Nagumo's assurance was to be short-lived, however. At 8:20, as *Akagi* was maneuvering furiously to avoid the bomb and torpedo attacks of Midway's Marine Squadron 241, yet another message from the tardy scout plane was passed to the admiral: "The enemy is accompanied by what appears to be a carrier...." Nagumo's staff was stunned by the news. How had an American carrier been able to get past the Japanese submarine force posted around Hawaii with the specific mission of reporting if and when any American carriers left Pearl Harbor? Those officers had no way of knowing, of course, that the work of Stafford, Lawton, and the cryptographers at Station HYPO had allowed Admiral Nimitz to dispatch Task Force 16 and Task Force 17 in time to arrive at Point Luck before the Japanese submarines were ever in position to spot them.[10]

Nagumo's stoic exterior never cracked, however, even though for him the operational picture had changed drastically, as that American carrier presented both a threat and an opportunity. The threat was obvious, and as such had to be honored and met. The opportunity was the chance to destroy that carrier—and likely another, as even the Americans wouldn't be so foolish as to send only a single carrier to defend Midway. The change in the operational picture dictated a change in operational requirements. This was a moment to be seized with both hands: that American carrier was to be sunk as quickly as possible, lest it elude the Japanese and escape; Midway, on the other hand, wasn't going anywhere, it could be neutralized later. The only decision to be made was whether to immediately launch the planes that had been held in reserve aboard *Soryu* and *Hiryu*—36 Vals and an equal number of Kates—or wait for the Midway air strike to be recovered and rearmed and attack with a force twice as large. Rear Admiral Yamaguchi Tamon, aboard *Hiryu*, pressed Nagumo to attack immediately, but the deliberate, methodical old admiral refused to be goaded into anything impetuous. Nagumo concluded that this was no time for half-measures: the wisest course of action would be to hit the Americans with as powerful an airstrike as the *Kido Butai* could muster. At 8:40 he reversed his earlier order: all of *Kaga*'s and *Akagi*'s Kates and Vals were now to be rearmed for an attack against the American carriers.

To save time, the ordnance crews aboard the four carriers, already tired and harried from having armed and then rearmed the Vals and Kates, once more unloaded the fragmentation bombs, this time simply setting them aside for the moment, rather than sending them below to the magazines. Meanwhile, semi-armor-piercing bombs were once again brought up and trundled over to the waiting Vals, while the torpedoes that had been removed and stowed in waiting racks in the hanger decks were hoisted back into place underneath the Kates. Fueling hoses snaked back and forth across the hangar decks, topping off the tanks of each aircraft. Overhead, plane handlers on the flight decks overhead began preparing for the aircraft returning from the Midway air strike. As those planes landed, they would be quickly manhandled to the flight-deck elevators and sent below; those that were still airworthy would likewise be readied for the attack on the American carrier. But until the last of those planes was recovered, none of the armed and fueled bombers waiting in the hangars could be sent to the flight-deck and spotted for launching.

* * *

Rather than form up into a single large attack formation, as the Japanese would have done, and which was, in fact, standard US Navy doctrine, the squadrons of dive- and torpedo-bombers from *Enterprise* and *Hornet*, soon to be joined by two squadrons of SBD's from *Yorktown*, more-or-less followed their own leads toward the enemy carriers. Lieutenant Commander John Waldron actually took the 15 Devastators of Torpedo Squadron 8, or "Torpedo 8", on a diverging course from the rest of the American planes, veering off almost due west with the Wildcats of Fighting 6 trailing above and behind, the fighters from *Enterprise* having mistaken *Hornet*'s aircraft for their own.

Meanwhile, the SBD's of Bombing 6 and Scouting 6, under the command of Lieutenant Commander Wade McClusky, set out to the southwest. Why Waldron and McClusky chose different courses remains a mystery to this day, but the result was that the two formations of aircraft soon lost sight of each other, while *Enterprise*'s Torpedo 6 eventually lost contact with McClusky's SBD's. This didn't bode well for the American attack, as it meant that, rather than suddenly appearing in one massive, overwhelming, coordinated strike, with dive bombers screaming down from above and torpedo bombers racing just above the wave tops, the individual elements would arrive piecemeal, much as had the attacks from Midway, with likely the same results.

It was Torpedo 8 that first found the Japanese carriers. Approaching from the northeast, Waldron's 15 TBD's sighted the *Kido Butai* at 9:20, and dove low to begin their attack on the nearest carrier, *Akagi*. Waldron split his squadron into two sections, hoping to execute a "hammerhead" attack, that is, attack *Akagi* from ahead and starboard simultaneously: no matter how the Japanese carrier turned, she would be presenting her broadside to one of the two groups of planes. But the TBD's settled into their attack runs, barely 20 feet above the water, the gunners aboard *Akagi* and *Soryu* quickly found the range and began taking a fearsome toll on the Devastators, forcing Waldron's group to turn away and attempt an attack on *Soryu*. Then the Zeroes came swooping down as they did on the earlier attack from Midway, and "bounced" the vulnerable torpedo planes.

One by one the American aircraft began to pitch into the sea, many of them on fire. Waldron himself was last seen standing in the cockpit of his burning TBD, trying desperately to get close enough to *Soryu* to guarantee his torpedo would hit; his plane nosed into the water and sank before he reached his release point. All 15 of the Torpedo 8's Devastators were shot down, and only one crewman, pilot Ensign George Gay, survived, clinging desperately to a rubber seat cushion as he thrashed about in the water. He didn't know it, but Gay would soon have a front-row seat for what would be the most devastating 20 minutes of naval history.

The last of Torpedo 8's planes were cartwheeling into the water when *Enterprise*'s Torpedo 6 found the Japanese carriers; the time was 9:38 AM. Much as Waldron had done with his squadron, Torpedo 6's commander, Lieutenant Commander Gene Lindsey, split his force into two sections to set up a hammerhead attack, this time against *Kaga*. And much the same fate that befell Torpedo 8 was visited on Torpedo 6: lookouts aboard *Kaga* spotted Torpedo 6 even before the American aircraft began setting up their attack, and the anti-aircraft guns were waiting. After a few minutes the gunfire lifted, but that was only because the Zeroes were closing in on the Devastators. The Japanese fighters tore apart Lindsey's section, shooting him down along with three other TBD's; the surviving trio of Devastators pressed their attack hard, but despite launching their torpedoes, scored no hits on *Kaga*. Somehow, the three planes, each of them damaged by anti-aircraft fire or the Zeroes had escaped; two eventually returned to *Enterprise*, but somewhere on the way back, the third ran out of fuel and dropped into the sea. The second section of Torpedo 6 fared even worse: five of the seven planes in it were brought down before they could launch their torpedoes. The two survivors made clean drops but again there were no hits; both planes were heavily damaged, but somehow held together long enough to bring their crews back to their carrier.

Torpedo 3, one of the squadrons from *Yorktown*, was mauled when it tried to attack *Hiryu*. Once more carefully coordinated anti-aircraft fire combined with the waiting Zero fighters proved deadly: of the 12 planes of Torpedo 3 that took off from *Yorktown*, only one made it back to the ship. Five of the TBD's survived long enough to launch their torpedoes, but for the moment *Hiryu* led a charmed life, as her captain, Kaku Tomeo, skillfully maneuvered his command to avoid all of them. Of the 41 TBD's sent out by *Enterprise*, *Hornet*, and *Yorktown*, only six returned.

But the sacrifice of the torpedo bombers and their crews hadn't been an empty one, as they created the circumstances that allowed the devastation that was about to come. It wasn't just, as legend would eventually have it, that the torpedo attacks had drawn the Japanese fighters down to sea level, unable to climb back to their assigned patrol altitudes before the American dive bombers appeared. It was less obvious than that: by the time the last surviving Devastator withdrew, the Zeroes flying top cover for the *Kido Butai* were now critically low on fuel and ammunition. Though they had already fought off two determined American attacks, their success would be their undoing, as they were be too exhausted to drive off a third. At the same time, the four carriers, along with their escorting destroyers and cruisers, as they twisted and turned to avoid the TBD's torpedo attacks, gradually drew out of effective range of one another, breaking up the overlapping fields of fire which initially had allowed their anti-aircraft guns to be so effective. Even more subtly, as if to make the point that Fortune, Fate, or simply Lady Luck had abandoned the Japanese, as everyone aboard the carriers was looking out to sea for more oncoming torpedo planes. For a critical few moments, no one was looking high overhead.

* * *

The convalescent Commander Fuchida had climbed out of his bed in *Akagi's* sickbay to take in the sight of the planes returning from the strike on Midway, then waited for the next wave to be spotted on the flight deck and launched. But before that could happen, the American torpedo bombers appeared, and with the detachment of one professional observing another at work, he watched as the TBD's began their attack runs, running the gantlet of anti-aircraft fire and Zero fighters. As did probably every other officer and crewman aboard the four carriers, Fuchida heaved a sigh of relief when the last of the Devastators were either shot down or departed and their torpedoes evaded. He also found himself admiring the determination and courage of the American naval aviators; they were, he saw, every bit as brave as any pilot or airman in the Imperial Navy. He was contemplating this in the relative quiet that followed the last torpedo attack, but the watchful calm—along with Fuchida's moment of reflection—was shattered by near-panicked shouts from the *Akagi's* bridge.

> At that instant a lookout screamed: "Hell-divers!" [Fuchida later remembered.]I looked up to see three black enemy planes plummeting toward our ship. Some of our machine guns managed to fire a few frantic bursts at them, but it was too late. The plump silhouettes of the American "Dauntless" dive bombers quickly grew larger, and then a number of black objects suddenly floated eerily from their wings. Bombs! Down they came straight toward me! I fell intuitively to the deck and crawled behind a command post mantelet.
> The terrifying scream of the dive bombers reached me first, followed by the crashing explosion of a direct hit. There was a blinding flash and then a second explosion, much louder than the first. I was shaken by a weird blast of warm air. There was still another shock, but less severe, apparently a near-miss. Then followed a startling quiet as the barking of guns suddenly ceased. I got up and looked at the sky. The enemy planes were already gone from sight.[11]

In that handful of minutes while Fuchida was taking shelter from the gunfire and bomb blasts, dive bombers from *Enterprise* and *Yorktown* had gutted the *Kido Butai*.

* * *

In their search for the Japanese carriers, Lieutenant Commander McClusky's two-squadron flock of SBD's had actually edged past the safe limit of their fuel supply, the point where there was enough aviation gas in their tanks to bring them safely back to *Enterprise*. McClusky had been confident of his navigation and, flying at 20,000 feet, was certain that one of his pilots or rear-gunners would have seen *something* by now, but no matter how keenly the 64 pairs of eyes peered through the scattered cloud cover below, all they saw was empty ocean. However reluctantly, McClusky had to admit to having failed, and at 9:47 was about to order his two squadrons to return to *Enterprise*.

It was then that, far below, he saw the unmistakable white feather created by the wake of a ship heading north at high speed. It was the destroyer *Arashi*, steaming at top speed to catch up with the *Kido Butai* after an unsuccessful hunt for a prowling American submarine. Given her position, the ship could only be Japanese, and McClusky realized that she was pointing the way to the enemy carriers. Not wanting to give away the show by breaking radio silence, McClusky used hand signals to indicate to his pilots the new heading they should take. The dive bombers swiftly overtook the Japanese carriers, and at 10:02, the time for radio silence was over. McClusky sent off a contact report to Task Force 16 as he and his pilots sorted themselves out into their attack formations. Choosing one of the two largest carriers as his target—it was *Kaga*—McClusky nosed over into a 70-degree dive and his two squadrons followed him.

The Imperial Navy hadn't yet deployed a reliable search radar system for its ships, relying instead on lookouts specially selected for their keen eyesight. But because the Japanese regarded torpedoes rather than bombs as the greatest threat to their ships, most of those lookouts were scanning the horizon in anticipation of another wave of Devastators. They never saw the SBD's stooping down like hawks on the four carriers until it was too late to evade them. The Japanese communication network for directing combat air patrols onto approaching enemy aircraft was rudimentary at best and worked poorly, leaving the Zeroes still flying top cover for the *Kido Butai* to be taken by surprise, caught out of position, still climbing back to their assigned patrol altitudes. *Kaga's* anti-aircraft guns opened up on the SBD's as the planes plummeted downward, but they were too few to turn aside the American attack, and the other three Japanese carriers were now too far distant to bring their own batteries to bear.

Fifteen hundred feet above the carrier's flight deck, McClusky released his bomb, and one by one the pilots following him did the same. One SBD, its pilot either killed by anti-aircraft fire or else having lost control of his plane, plunged straight into the sea. The first three bombs missed *Kaga*, but Lieutenant Wilmer Gallaher saw his 500-pounder hit almost exactly amidships and detonate in a huge fireball. A second bomb landed on the ship's forward elevator, then four, possibly five, more walked their way down the flight deck. One bomb exploded among a collection of fuel bowsers sitting abreast of the carrier's island, showering the bridge with flaming gasoline which killed *Kaga*'s captain and most of the rest of her senior officers. The exploding bombs tore through the flight deck and into the hangar deck immediately below, rupturing fuel lines and water mains, destroying the fire-suppression system, and setting off the bombs and torpedoes on the waiting Kates and Vals in sympathetic detonation. Crewmen on the other three carriers watched in horror as *Kaga*'s sides blew out and the whole of the ship from the island aft was wrapped in a shroud of flames, one that rivaled the inferno which had engulfed *Arizona* at Pearl Harbor. Indeed, Lieutenant Gallaher, who six months earlier had been witness to the battleship's immolation, regarded the destruction he and his fellow pilots had wrought as he pulled out of his dive and felt a savage satisfaction and said to himself, "Arizona, *I remember you!*"[12]

Just as he was about to nose over into his attack on *Kaga*, Lieutenant Richard Best, leading a three-plane section of SBD's, saw the chain of explosions shattering the hapless carrier, and corrected the direction of his dive to drop down on the so-far untouched *Akagi* instead. Two bombs fell in near-misses, one exploding so close to the carrier's stern that it jammed her rudder and damaged the steering gear; the third bomb struck the midships elevator and exploded in the hanger deck. As happened on *Kaga*, torpedoes on *Akagi*'s Vals were set off by the blast, which ruptured the fuel tanks on the waiting Kates and Vals, and shattered the hangar's fuel lines. Flaming aviation gasoline washed across the deck, and those bombs and torpedoes that the carrier's ordnance crews hadn't bothered to send below to the magazines began to cook off. Within minutes the fire spread through the entire after half of the hangar deck and ignited the wooden flight deck above it; even if she could ultimately be saved, for the time being *Akagi* was finished as a fighting ship. Admiral Nagumo, after crawling through the shattered windows of the bridge and climbing down a rope to the flight deck—the flames had cut off any other escape route—transferred his flag to the light cruiser *Nagara*.

Hiryu's good luck continued, as Captain Kaku altered course sharply to the east and tucked her inside a nearby rain squall, where the American dive bombers couldn't see her. *Soryu* wasn't so fortunate. The SBD's of *Yorktown*'s Bombing 3 had taken off a half hour after *Enterprise*'s two Dauntless squadrons set out to find the enemy, but rather than follow Lieutenant Commander McClusky's formation, they took roughly the same course as had Torpedo 8. This brought them over the *Kido Butai* just as McCluskey's dive bombers began their attack, and Lieutenant Commander Max Leslie led his squadron straight toward *Soryu*.

A trio of 1,000-pound bombs landed at almost equidistant intervals on her flight deck, two exploding in the upper hangar deck, the third plunging even deeper, into the lower hangar, before detonating. As on *Kaga* and *Akagi*, catastrophic fires erupted, spawned and spread by the bombs, torpedoes, and gasoline stored on those decks, but it was the third bomb that truly spelled *Soryu*'s doom, as it ruptured the main steam lines to the engine rooms and cut off all electrical power throughout the ship. With the pumps inoperable there was no water to fight the fires, leaving the crew helpless to contain them. *Soryu* slowed, then stopped, and at 10:45 the order was passed to abandon ship.

In the space of less than 20 minutes, three Japanese fleet carriers had been reduced to flaming wrecks.

* * *

From his vantage point of *Hiryu*'s bridge, Rear Admiral Yamaguchi grimly watched as disaster overtook *Kaga*, *Akagi*, and *Soryu*. Bombastic, often abrasive, but a gifted naval aviation officer who didn't know how to back away from a fight, if anyone could salvage a victory from this debacle, it was he. When Rear Admiral Abe Hiraoki, aboard *Tone*, signaled "Attack the enemy carriers," Yamaguchi needed no encouragement, replying, "All our planes are taking off now for the purpose of destroying the enemy carriers." To his staff he bluntly stated his intention: "We, with *Hiryu* alone, are going to sacrifice ourselves to kill the damned enemy force."[13]

Crewmen were already spotting 18 Vals and a half-dozen Zeroes on the flight deck—the planes that had been rearmed for Nagumo's abortive attack on the American carriers. In the hangar deck, torpedoes were being hoisted into place underneath 10 Kates, while another six Zeroes had their fuel tanks topped off and their ammunition replenished; these would be the second wave of *Hiryu*'s attack. Takeoff for the Vals and their fighter escorts began at 11:00 AM; to find the American carriers they would follow the radio beacon of a scout plane from the cruiser *Chikuma* that continued to shadow Task Force 16 and Task Force 17.

It was at 11:50 that the advantage radar gave the American fleet first manifested itself. *Yorktown* picked up a formation of unidentified aircraft approaching while it was still 32 miles distant, and the three squadrons of Wildcats flying the combat air patrol overhead, one from each American carrier, were directed to positions where they could meet the oncoming enemy attack. This time it was the Japanese fighters who were hopelessly outnumbered, and the six Zeroes escorting *Hiryu*'s 18 Vals were quickly overwhelmed. The Wildcats then pressed home their defense, and in minutes 11 of the Vals were brought down. The remaining seven concentrated on the nearest carrier, *Yorktown*, and dove to the attack.

Yorktown's anti-aircraft destroyed three of the Vals, but not before the three were able to release their bombs, all of which struck the carrier. The first exploded just aft of the number two elevator on the starboard side, blowing a 30-foot hole in the flight deck, killing the crewmen working two of the ship's anti-aircraft guns and igniting a handful of small fires on the hangar deck. The second bomb crashed through the flight deck and detonated at the base of *Yorktown*'s funnel, while the third plunged through three decks and exploded, starting a fire in a storeroom. This could have been a crippling, even fatal, blow to *Yorktown*, as the compartment was situated between an aviation gas bunker and one of the magazines.

It was now that a critical difference between operations aboard Japanese and American carriers came into play: planes were fueled and armed on the open flight decks of American carriers, unlike the Japanese ships where that work was done in the closed confines of the hangars. The radar warning had given *Yorktown*'s crew sufficient time to clear the ship for action—closing fire curtains on the hangar deck, jettisoning exposed ordnance and damaged aircraft over the side, clearing away fire hazards on the flight deck, shutting down and draining the refueling system. There would be no repeat of the sort of catastrophe that had overtaken the Japanese carriers. Hard work by damage control parties kept the stubborn lower deck fire confined to the one compartment, and gradually extinguished it.

That second bomb *did* cripple the carrier, however: it struck *Yorktown* at one of the most vulnerable points on any ship—the funnel uptakes. The blast blew out the fires in five of the ship's six boilers, wrecking two of them completely, and with the loss of steam, *Yorktown*'s turbines couldn't turn her screws nor could her generators produce electricity. Twenty minutes after the Japanese attack, the carrier stopped dead in the water.

* * *

Only five Vals and three Zeroes survived to return to *Hiryu*, where they would report having sunk the carrier that had been their target, but long before they arrived the second wave, such as it was and what there was of it, of Yamaguchi's counterattack had taken off. Ten torpedo bombers and six fighters was a pitifully small force compared to the aerial armada that had attacked Pearl Harbor, yet it was all that remained left to the *Kido Butai*, itself now a shadow of what it had been only hours before. Led by a grimly determined Lieutenant Tomonaga, they set out for the position of the American fleet reported by the returning Vals, who also sent along an assurance that an American carrier had been heavily damaged and possibly sunk. For Tomonaga, no matter what the outcome of this attack, it would be a one-way trip: one of the fuel tanks on his aircraft had been damaged, and there hadn't been time to repair it; the plane could carry only half its usual load of gasoline. This knowledge, rather than discouraging the young pilot, only strengthened his resolve to make this attack successful.

Tomonaga's squadron found the American fleet within a few miles of the position the Val pilots had given, but the Japanese aviators were startled to find no trace of the smoking, crippled carrier they expected to see. Could it be true, they wondered, that the carrier the dive bombers attacked had actually sunk? Very well, then, the torpedo bombers would sink another. Tomonaga divided his small command into two elements of five planes each, while the accompanying Zeroes did their best to ward off the swarming Wildcat fighters long enough for the Kates to make their attack.

* * *

The approaching Japanese planes appeared on the USS *Pensacola*'s radar at 2:30 PM. The cruiser was one of nine ships that formed a protective screen around *Yorktown* while the carrier's crew worked feverishly to bring their ship back to life. Rear Admiral Fletcher, meanwhile, had already shifted his flag to the cruiser *Astoria*: a ship without power, dead in the water, was no place for an admiral with a task force to command. Captain Elliot Buckmaster, *Yorktown*'s commanding officer, had his crew set to work immediately, patching the flight deck, putting out fires, clearing away debris and wreckage. Down below, the engineers brought the auxiliary power system on line, which allowed the "black gang" in Boiler Room Number One to bleed steam into the other three undamaged boilers and relight them. By the time *Pensacola* warned the task force of the approaching enemy formation, *Yorktown* was underway again, making 19 knots.

Wildcats of *Enterprise*'s Fighting 6 along with those of *Yorktown*'s own Fighting 3 dove down on the approaching Kates and Zeroes, and "splashed" half the attacking force, including Lieutenant Tomonaga's aircraft, but three of the five surviving Kates were able to launch their torpedoes at *Yorktown*. Two struck the carrier's port side and exploded, blowing huge holes in her hull below the waterline; the ship took on a heavy list and once again all steam and electrical power was lost. This time the damage was beyond repair short of a stint in a dockyard, and there was a very real danger that the ship could roll over and sink at any moment. Both the damage control officer and the chief engineer reported as much to Captain Buckmaster, who gave the order to abandon ship at 2:55. Four of the screening destroyers took up positions alongside *Yorktown* to pick up her crew.

Twenty miles to the south, Admiral Spruance and his Task Force 16 hadn't been idle while *Hiryu*'s planes attacked *Yorktown*. The first order of business, as it were, was to recover the planes returning from the airstrike on the Japanese carriers. There was, of course, only a handful of TBD's that survived the massacre of Torpedo 3, 6, and 8, but while all the SBD's of Bombing 8 returned to *Hornet*, having never found the Japanese carriers, 10 dive-bombers from *Yorktown* and 14 from *Enterprise* had been lost. Some were brought down by Japanese fighters and anti-aircraft guns, but most of the missing planes, having used up their reserves searching for the *Kido Butai*, simply ran out of fuel while returning to their carriers, flew as close as they could to Task Force 16 and Task Force 17, and ditched in the sea. Many of the crews were rescued within minutes or hours of ditching, but not all—some broke apart on impact with the water and sank in seconds, taking their pilots and gunners with them. A handful of SBD's never relocated the American fleet at all and vanished into the empty reaches of the Pacific when their fuel finally ran out and they fell into the sea.

When *Hiryu*'s first strike was picked up on radar, the surviving American planes were already circling their carriers. When it was clear that *Yorktown* was the target, her aircraft were frantically waved off; they landed aboard *Enterprise*. Nearly an hour had passed before the last of the SBD's touched down, at which point Spruance ordered every serviceable dive bomber on *Enterprise* and *Hornet* readied for another attack on the Japanese. Regardless of whether or not *Yorktown* somehow remained afloat, she was unquestionably out of the fight: rather than having a three-to-one superiority in flight decks, the Carrier Strike Force's margin was now only two-to-one, and the grim determination with which *Hiryu*'s pilots had pressed home their attacks on *Yorktown* left no doubt that the Japanese believed this battle was far from over—and could still be won. What Spruance needed was *Hiryu*'s precise position; he was determined that there would be no repeat of the first attack's wild goose chase. At 2:45 PM he got it: just before noon 10 SBD's had taken off from *Yorktown* to search for the last Japanese carrier, and through good navigation combined with good fortune they found her. A signal went out to *Enterprise*: "1 CV, 2 BB, 4 CA, 4 DD"—one carrier, two battleships, four heavy cruisers, and four destroyers— "31E15'N, 179E05'W, course 000, speed 15". Spruance immediately saw that this information was given to the crews of the waiting dive-bombers, then ordered the airstrike launch. Within minutes 24 SBD's—10 from *Enterprise*, the rest the foundlings from *Yorktown*—began taking off. Communications errors and an inexperienced crew delayed *Hornet*'s launch by nearly an hour, but eventually 15 of her dive-bombers were following those sent off by *Enterprise*.[14]

* * *

Admiral Yamaguchi and his staff were elated. When the five Val torpedo planes and three Zero fighters returned to *Hiryu*, their crews excitedly reported that the burning, lumbering hulk the dive bombers had left behind was gone, and that their own attack had sunk a *second* American carrier. By this time, Yamaguchi knew that the US Navy had somehow managed to deploy three carriers to defend Midway, not just the two Imperial Naval Intelligence had assured him would be all that the Americans could muster. But if two of those three had been sent to the bottom, then it was now just *Hiryu* versus the sole surviving American carrier.

To be sure, Yamaguchi had very little left with which to continue the fight—five Vals, five Kates, and 10 Zeroes were all that remained of the *Kido Butai*'s once fearsome air arm. But the Japanese admiral had no doubts that the skill and courage of his aviators were superior to that of their American counterparts, and if the US Navy's carriers were as fragile as they seemed to be—as indeed the Imperial Navy's own carriers had proven to be—then even this comparative handful of planes would be sufficient to sink *Hiryu*'s remaining adversary. The order was given to prepare for one final attack on the American fleet.

That attack would never take place. Instead, at 5:05 PM, the SBD's from *Enterprise* arrived over *Hiryu*, diving out of the sun. Once again betrayed by a lack of any search radar system, the Japanese lookouts were effectively blinded until the last moment. Yamaguchi had committed a quartet of his remaining Zeroes to flying top cover for Hiryu, but they could only bring down three of the American planes before the bombs started to fall.

At least four, probably five, and possibly even six hits tore apart *Hiryu*'s flight deck, causing the bow section to collapse in on itself—one explosion hurled the carrier's forward elevator against the face of her island. Though she was spared the sort of inferno that had engulfed each of the other three Japanese carriers, *Hiryu* still found herself ablaze as several medium-size fires broke out on her hangar deck and slowly merged into a single blaze. Her boilers and turbines were undamaged, though, and for the time being it seemed that, while she was unquestionably out of action, she might be saved. At the same time, the fires were sufficiently severe that when *Hornet*'s 15 SBD's arrived overhead, it was quite evident that further attacks on of *Hiryu* would be a waste of ordnance, so they targeted the battleship *Haruna* and the cruisers *Tone* and *Chikuma* instead. As it was, they still wasted their bombs, failing to achieve a single hit on any of the three ships.

That futile attack by Bombing 8 proved to be the anti-climactic full stop on the day's fighting. The American dive-bombers returned to *Enterprise* and *Hornet*, the last of them landing at 6:08 PM, as the sun was setting; by 7:20 all of the Wildcats flying top cover were back aboard their carriers.

* * *

Soryu was the first of the Japanese carriers to sink. She'd continued to burn throughout the morning and afternoon of June 4; as sunset approached the fires began to die down, and there was a flicker of hope among her surviving crew that she might be saved, but the ship had suffered far too much damage, and the destroyer *Isokaze* was ordered to scuttle her with torpedoes. But at 7:00 PM, before *Isokaze* could move into a firing position, a gigantic explosion tore apart *Soryu*'s stern. Ten minutes later, what was left of the carrier disappeared below the surface, taking with her 703 of her 1,100-man crew, including Captain Yanagimoto Ryusaku, her commander, who chose to go down with his ship.

Even though they were still afloat, and despite heroic efforts by their crews, fires continued to burn furiously aboard *Kaga* and *Akagi*. At 5:00 PM *Kaga*'s situation was finally deemed hopeless and the order given to abandon ship. Despite a heavy list to starboard, the carrier stubbornly refused to sink, however, and at 9:30 PM, just minutes after *Soryu* went down, the destroyer *Hagikaze* fired two torpedoes into

Kaga's side; moments later, with a dignity befitting the grand old lady of the *Kido Butai*, she settled back onto an even keel and finally sank.

Akagi's crew fought a valiant rear-guard action against the fires but ultimately couldn't contain them, and shortly after *Kaga* went under the order to abandon ship was given. *Akagi* proved to be just as obstinate as *Kaga*, however, and as dawn approached on June 5, though she was a smoldering wreck clearly beyond any hope of being salvaged, she was still afloat. None of the senior officers of the *Kido Butai*, from Nagumo down, wanted to give the inevitable order that she be scuttled—for 15 years, even more than *Kaga*, *Akagi* had been regarded as the embodiment of Imperial Naval airpower. It was unthinkable that she should be destroyed by ships of her own fleet.

Finally, at 3:50 AM, a saddened Admiral Yamamoto told his staff aboard the battleship *Yamato*, "I was once the captain of *Akagi*, and it is with heartfelt regret that I must now order that she be sunk." The signal to scuttle her was sent to the ships standing by the shattered carrier, and a quartet of destroyers fired one torpedo each into the still-burning hulk. At 5:20 AM, she sank bow first in 18,000 feet of water, her wreck coming to rest on the bottom only a few miles to the east-northeast of *Kaga*.[15]

For a time it seemed that, despite the heavy damage she'd suffered, *Hiryu* might still be saved. At 9:00 PM, Admiral Nagumo received a report from one of the destroyers standing by the carrier that *Hiryu* was still capable of making 28 knots, but sometime during the night her steering gear failed, leaving her un-maneuverable, and at midnight a huge explosion—a magazine or a gasoline bunker, no would ever know which—shook the entire ship. That was her death-knell: at 2:30 AM on June 5, Captain Kaku ordered *Hiryu* abandoned—he remained behind, observing the Japanese tradition of the captain dying with his ship; Admiral Yamaguchi chose to join him. The two men were last seen standing on a catwalk aft of the carrier's island, the remnants of the flight deck burning behind them, calmly exchanging remarks on the beauty of the rising moon. At 5:10 AM, the destroyer *Makigumo* torpedoed *Hiryu*, which finally sank at 9:10.

As the Japanese carriers were in their death throes throughout the night of June 4 and the morning of June 5, Admiral Spruance withdrew the Carrier Strike Force and its escorts eastward from Point Luck, moving to stay well clear of Yamamoto's battleship force, which was advancing steadily from the southwest. But the Japanese movement was an empty threat: once he learned that all four carriers were put out of action, Yamamoto knew the battle was lost. Further fighting was pointless: without airpower to protect Midway while the islands' defenses were being built, the Japanese marines and engineers holding the islands would be vulnerable to destruction in detail by American carrier strikes. The aircraft initially committed to the garrison's defense for the first six months after Midway was taken had been stowed aboard the four carriers of the First Air Fleet. To scrape together a sufficient number of planes to replace those aircraft lost and the transports to bring them to Midway would take weeks, and the Imperial Navy simply couldn't defend the islands for that span of time with surface ships alone: the effort to properly support those ships while they remained on station, serving as floating anti-aircraft batteries, would have strained Japan's maritime logistic capacity beyond its breaking point. At 2:55 AM on June 5, Yamamoto acknowledged reality and issued the orders cancelling the Midway operation. The surviving elements of the Combined Fleet dutifully turned westward; Spruance cautiously followed suit and the Carrier Strike Force returned to the waters around Point Luck.

The fighting wasn't quite over yet, however. The afternoon of June 6 saw *Hornet*'s dive bombers draw blood at last, battering the heavy cruiser *Mikuma* so severely that she sank some time after nightfall; at almost the same time *Mikuma* was being mauled, the submarine *I-168* was stalking *Yorktown*, which had somehow remained afloat and was now the center of a determined salvage effort. The destroyer *Hammann* had drawn up close alongside the carrier, providing power for Captain Buckmaster and his salvage crew, who had reboarded *Yorktown* late on June 5. *I-168* fired four torpedoes; one missed both ships, passing under *Yorktown*'s stern, but one struck *Hammann* squarely amidships and broke the destroyer's back. She sank in three minutes, taking 80 of her crew with her. The other two torpedoes exploded deep against *Yorktown*'s hull, tearing two more huge holes in the carrier's side. This time the flooding was too extensive to be contained, and she was well and truly done for: the salvage crew abandoned the carrier, and she sank at 4:58 AM on June 7.

The Battle of Midway was over. The price paid by the Imperial Navy was steep: not only were four nigh-irreplaceable aircraft carriers lost, along with a heavy cruiser, but 3,057 Japanese officers and ratings were killed or went missing in action, among them hundreds of experienced pilots and skilled aircraft technicians, losses that Japan's training programs would be hard pressed to make up. As for the US Navy, the only ships lost were *Yorktown* and *Hammann*, while the number of dead and missing was only a tithe of the Japanese losses, totaling 307.

Just as he'd predicted when planning the attack on Pearl Harbor, for six months Yamamoto had "run wild" in the Pacific, but now the myth of the Imperial Navy's invincibility was shown to be precisely that—a myth, and one that was now irreparably shattered, taken to the bottom of the Pacific in the wrecks of four Japanese aircraft carriers. The tide of the war had turned against the Empire in the span of a single day, as a few hundred American naval aviators tore the strategic initiative from the hands of the Japanese and gave it to the Allies, who never lost it. And in those same hours, the United States Navy exacted a fearsome retribution on its Japanese counterpart, for while Pearl Harbor had been a disaster for the American fleet, Midway was a catastrophe for the Imperial Navy, a situation the Japanese tacitly acknowledged when the First Air Fleet—the *Kido Butai*—was formally disbanded five weeks after the battle. Pearl Harbor had been avenged.

...and Reckoning

Even when the tide turned against them, the Japanese were not about to roll over and play dead, and in places with exotic-sounding names like Guadalcanal, New Guinea, Peleliu, Tarawa, Kwajalein, Luzon, Leyte, Okinawa, Saipan, and many others, Japanese soldiers and marines proved time and again that they were fighting men rightly to be respected, and indeed feared. In a dozen cut-and-thrust naval battles, in the air and on the surface, the Imperial Navy often gave as good as—and sometimes better than—it got, and even while the quality of their aircraft and their skills as pilots were declining, Japanese aviators never lacked for courage.

When Japan's military and political leaders gave their approval to the attack on Pearl Harbor, they had, at least privately, acknowledged that in the war against the United States which they were about to trigger, the Empire could not win outright. They knew the best that could be achieved was a draw, and after Midway, even that possibility became increasingly remote with each passing month. Yet those same leaders, and the soldiers, sailors, marines, and airmen of all ranks who followed them, would not—could not—allow the Empire to go down without the most tenacious fight they could muster; it was part of their national identity, their personal identity, it was in their blood: they might individually die but *Dai Nippon* would continue. And so, hoping against hope that some miracle might deliver a victory to the emperor and his subjects, they fought on, and they *did* die, often in appalling numbers.

The War in the Pacific which began on December 7, 1941, would span three years, eight months, and eight days; on August 8, 1945, the Empire of Japan formally communicated that it was prepared to surrender unconditionally to the Allied Powers. Between those two dates, some 20,000,000 human beings—a conservative estimate—uniformed and civilian, lost their lives either in combat, as a result of wounds or injuries, by aerial bombing, through famine and disease brought on by the war, or executed by their enemies. An accurate total will never be known—some chroniclers maintain that the true number may be half again as large—since many records, especially those of the Japanese, in particular in regard to Japan's conduct of its war in China, were lost during the course of the war, and in some cases those responsible simply couldn't be bothered to keep an accurate tally of the slaughter they carried out.

Candidly, this was inevitable, given that the Japanese were never so obsessively compulsive as, say, the Germans at the bureaucratic crossing of t's and dotting of i's. The dead—especially foreigners and civilians in conquered territories—were simply the dead, and as such no further attention need be paid to them, unless those deaths in some way impinged on Japan's war effort. This was a perspective—an attitude—that the Allies mistook for callousness; to the Japanese, it was a pragmatism, however dark and grim, that was a consequence of the rampant militarism that had gripped *Dai Nippon* for almost two generations.

The *Bushido*—the Japanese "way of the warrior"—as it was taught in the 1920s and 1930s, bore little resemblance to the western way of war. The seemingly fanatical determination to defend their positions to literally the last man and last round, and so give their lives for the emperor and *Dai Nippon*; the indifference, often mingled with capricious cruelty, to the welfare and fate of prisoners of war who were captured or who believed they had surrendered honorably; the methodical ruthlessness toward conquered civilians—none of these had any real counterpart in the Allies' means, methods, or ideologies. Conduct which to the Japanese required no explanation was incomprehensible to westerners, particularly Americans.

The result was predictable: the Pacific War would be fought without quarter. The Japanese, already poorly understood as a people by most Americans, and now the object of deep-seated hostility for the "sneak attack" at Pearl Harbor, became thoroughly demonized by the government, the military, and the media. The war in the Pacific would know little of the straightforward, simple antagonism Americans felt toward the Germans, one that only began to approach genuine hatred in the closing months of the war in Europe, when the true scale and nature of Nazi barbarity was finally revealed and confirmed. Rather, America's hostility coalesced early on into outright loathing of the Japanese, so much so that Japanese culture was eventually turned into a weapon to be used against the emperor's soldiers, sailors, and airmen: if they were so willing to die for him, then American soldiers, sailors, and airmen would do their best to accommodate. When, in 1943, Admiral Halsey ordered a huge billboard constructed on a hillside on the island of Tulagi, visible well out to sea, that read, "KILL JAPS. KILL JAPS. KILL MORE JAPS. You will help to kill the yellow bastards if you do your job well," he was only expressing the near-unanimous attitude of the United States armed forces and the American people. Ultimately, the decision to drop atomic bombs on the cities of Hiroshima and Nagasaki would be made in the hope that the scale of the destruction wrought would compel the Japanese to surrender, relieving the Allies of the need to invade the Home Islands in order to secure Japan's capitulation, and thus saving hundreds of thousands of Allied lives. That millions of Japanese lives might also be spared was not a major consideration.

To be sure, Japanese attitudes also hardened as the war continued, so that by 1944, Japan's state-run radio and newspapers, as well as the propaganda organs of the Imperial Army and Navy, were routinely assuring the emperor's subjects that Americans were "white devils," little more than semi-sentient beasts given over to the wanton murder and rape of civilians, mindless destruction, and any imaginable atrocity. By the summer of 1945, when everyone knew that the invasion of the Home Islands was imminent—it was only a question of "when," not "if"—and the Allies having declared at the Potsdam Conference that nothing less than Japan's unconditional surrender would be acceptable, that depiction had morphed into the cornerstone of "The Glorious Death of One Hundred Million," Japan's ultimate plan of defense. It was little more than a mass-suicide pact: rather than face the dishonor of surrender to and enslavement by the *gaijin*, every man, woman, and child was expected to sacrifice themselves for the glory of the emperor, if possible taking one of the "foreign devils" with them however they could. There would be no surrender; the only glimmer of hope Fate might offer the Japanese would be for the Allies to become so sickened by the slaughter that they would offer a negotiated peace. Thankfully for both sides—and the adverb, however guarded its use, is appropriate—the Hiroshima and Nagasaki bombs forestalled such a ghastly undertaking.

Japan's formal surrender on September 2, 1945, finally brought an end to the killing. As General Douglas MacArthur declaimed from the deck of the battleship Missouri, where the documents certifying the Empire's capitulation were signed, "Today the guns are silent. A great tragedy has ended. A great victory has been won. The skies no longer rain death. The seas bear only commerce. Men everywhere walk upright in the sunlight. The entire world is quietly at peace…" MacArthur went on to say that, "Men since the beginning of time have sought peace… Military alliances, balances of power, leagues of nations, all in turn failed, leaving the only path to be by way of the crucible of war." He could well have been speaking directly to the failed efforts by the United States and Japan to settle their disputes and back away from the confrontation that culminated in the attack on December 7, 1941.[1]

* * *

Could it all—Pearl Harbor, the war and its death and destruction, Hiroshima and Nagasaki—have been avoided? Was there truly ever a solution which somehow eluded the politicians and diplomats, admirals and generals in Tokyo and Washington DC? Was there a moment when the Japanese and American governments could have arrived at a compromise which would have been sufficient to the dictates of national honor, national conscience, and national survival without resorting to what MacArthur aptly deemed "the crucible of war"? Bluntly, the answer is "No."

The irreducible truth is that, much like the National Socialist regime in Germany, though driven by far different motives, Japan's Imperial Government *wanted* to go to war: it was an act of national destiny, not the bastard by-product of a half-baked political "ideology" cobbled together by a charismatic madman. In what has become the West's *de facto* definition of war, Carl von Clausewitz's dictum holds that "War is the continuation of national policy by other, non-political means." But for the Japanese, war was not a method of extending national policy to achieve national objectives, war *was* a national policy.[2]

War—or at the very least the threat of it—had throughout Japan's history been the catalyst which had propelled Japan forward; it had united Japan as a nation under the shogunate, then created a genuine empire in the decades that followed the Meiji Restoration, and ultimately produced one of the world's Great Powers in the first years of the 20th century. War, then, was not something Japan feared, nor shied away from, nor regarded as a last resort when the duplicities of the diplomats in striped trousers failed to resolve quarrels between nations. To Japan's leaders, and indeed, her people, the war to conquer the western Pacific was the continuation of a millennium of tradition and perceived destiny. To them, war was, if not righteous, at least right: in short, war was honorable.

But from its opening act at Pearl Harbor, this war brought no honor to Japan; even as the attack on the Pacific Fleet was being hailed as a great victory, there was a loss of face among those responsible for its execution. Trying to be too clever by half, the Japanese blundered out of the starting gate in attempting to coordinate diplomacy with military planning, enraging the American people, who perceived only treachery in the attack being delivered while Japan and the United States were still ostensibly at peace. It could be said that the missteps of the Hawaii Operation became the template for Japanese operations in the war with America. Throughout the Pacific War, the Japanese repeatedly embraced over-complicated battle plans that, when they went awry, as all plans must do to some degree, fell into a disarray that virtually guaranteed defeat, usually accompanied by heavy losses. Once Yamamoto's six months of "running wild" were brought to a screeching halt at Midway, victories came few and far between, the final two years of the war yielding only an unbroken string of defeats. The emperor's soldiers, sailors, marines, and airmen fought with fanatical courage and tenacity, to be sure, yet in the end, all honor was lost, replaced with the disgrace of total capitulation.

* * *

American concepts of honor were very unlike those of the Japanese: rather than as a strict code of conduct, the word "honor" was most commonly employed in the sense of commemorating men and women whose acts and actions set them apart, in a way deserving to be remembered, from their peers and contemporaries. At Pearl Harbor on December 7, 1941, there were scores of such individuals.

Citations for 15 Medals of Honor were issued to officers and enlisted men of the US Navy. The awards to Rear Admiral Isaac Kidd and Captain Franklin van Valkenburgh, both aboard *Arizona*, were, of course, posthumous, as was that of Captain Mervyn Bennion, *West Virginia*'s skipper. Ensign Francis Flaherty and Seaman First Class James Richard Ward, earned their medals when they chose to stay behind in their gun turrets when *Oklahoma* capsized, holding battle lanterns that guided other crewmen to safety—at the cost of their own lives. Chief Peter Tomich remained aboard *Utah* long enough to secure the ship's boilers and prevent a massive internal explosion—but "long enough" proved to be just that bit too long, and Tomich died at his post. Ensign Herbert Jones organized a human chain to carry ammunition to *California*'s anti-aircraft guns, and when mortally wounded by a bomb fragment, insisted that his men continue passing shells rather than tend to him.

Two other men of *California*'s crew were awarded the Medal of Honor, as well. Radioman Thomas Reeves was part of one of the ammunition chains; working in a burning passageway, he continued to hand off the 70-pound 5-inch shells until he was overcome by heat and toxic fumes. Not far from where Reeves was laboring, Machinist's Mate Robert Scott deliberately chose to remain behind in a flooding compartment, determined to keep feeding the compressed air that powered the guns as long as possible.

The outright heroism of Bosun Edwin Hill aboard *Nevada*, had it not been so well attested to by so many witnesses, would likely have been quickly relegated to the status of a "sea story." The US Navy had few opportunities for glory that December morning, but *Nevada*'s sortie was one, and Hill's actions made that moment possible. It was pure chance that put Hill on the battleship's foredeck at just the wrong time to ensure that his Medal of Honor award would be posthumous.

Machinist Donald Ross, Hill's shipmate on *Nevada*, Jackson Pharris, a Gunner aboard *California*, *Arizona*'s Lieutenant Commander Samuel Fuqua, Commander Cassin Young, *Vestal*'s captain, and Lieutenant John Finn at Kaneohe Bay seaplane base, all survived the attack to personally receive their medals. Ross eventually regained his eyesight, was given a commission, and finished the war as a lieutenant commander; retiring from the Navy seven years later, he passed away in 1992. Fuqua retired from the US Navy in 1953 as a rear admiral; he died in 1985. Finn was commissioned a lieutenant during the war, and lived to the age of 100. Young, promoted to captain, took command of the heavy cruiser USS *San Francisco* on November 9, 1942. Four days later, off Guadalcanal, his ship was engaged in a furious gunnery duel with the battleship *Hiei*; *San Francisco*'s bridge took a direct hit, and Young was killed instantly.

No medals or decorations were awarded to Ensign John England, who, as *Oklahoma* was capsizing, kept going back into the ship to lead crewmen to safety until he made the trip one too many times and didn't return. But the Navy didn't forget him: the destroyer escort *England* became his namesake; the ship made her distinctive mark during the war by sinking six Japanese submarines in the span of just 12 days in May 1944. Later, a guided missile cruiser would carry on the name USS *England*, spending the whole of her 30 years of service, appropriately enough, in the US Navy's Pacific Fleet. Four more destroyer escorts were launched wearing the names of men lost on *Oklahoma*: the USS *Austin*, named for the ship's Chief Carpenter, John Austin; the USS *Stern* took her name from Ensign Charles M. Stern, Jr.; the USS *Schmitt*, in honor of *Oklahoma*'s Catholic chaplain, Aloysius Schmitt; and the USS *J. Richard Ward*, the namesake of the 20-year-old seaman who had earned a Medal of Honor. Another four destroyer escorts would be christened with the names *Tomich*, *Reed*, *Scott*, and *Hill*. A *Fletcher*-class destroyer, the USS *Cassin Young*, carried on the fighting legacy of *Vestal*'s skipper; likewise, destroyers were christened in honor of Admiral Kidd and Captains Bennion and van Valkenburgh.

They were among the hundreds of other ships of every size and description, that were all built and launched after the Pearl Harbor attack, the products of America's awesome industrial strength which Yamamoto had openly feared. He had been right, of course: the United States' wartime output didn't merely dwarf that of Japan, it grew so vast that America was able to not only supply and equip her own navy, army, and air corps to fight in two distinct theaters of war, but at the same time produce ships, aircraft, tanks, vehicles, and munitions to the British, the Chinese, the Free French, and the Soviets—while the Japanese strained every logistic sinew they possessed to merely sustain the forces they already deployed. Japan's hope of fighting to a draw with the United States would prove singularly forlon when finally confronted by the full might of American manpower and industry.

The Battle of Midway put a stamp of certitude on that outcome. Vicious and costly naval battles would be fought thelength of the Solomon Islands chain later in 1942 and for much of 1943—at one point the Japanese and Americans were each reduced to having only a single operational fleet carrier in the Pacific—but the issue was never really in doubt. In the aftermath of Midway, the Imperial Navy couldn't even fully replace the ships it lost—Japanese shipyards would launch only three new fleet carriers by the time the Empire surrendered—while the US Navy commissioned 16 new carriers in the same span of time. More critical still for Japan were the hundreds of veteran aircrew who were killed or went missing at Midway; while there were over 2,000 qualified aviators in the Imperial Navy's air service in June 1942, the pilots, bombardiers, and aerial gunners aboard the four carriers of the *Kido Butai* were the most experienced of all, and with their deaths went the opportunity for them to pass on the hard-learned lessons of combat to their colleagues as well as to subsequent classes of aviators. Most critical of all, though, were the hundreds of engine and airframe mechanics, riggers, and armorers killed aboard *Kaga*, *Akagi*, *Soryu*, and *Hiryu*: they were a priceless asset, as Japan in the early 1940s had achieved only a fraction of the mechanization that had permeated American society. It took years for those men to acquire the training and achieve the levels of skill they had attained, something that the few months of training for their replacements could never hope equal. After at Midway, even when sufficient numbers of aircraft and aircrews were available, the Imperial Navy struggled to keep its airplanes flying.

The militarists who had hijacked the Imperial Government had driven Japan across a national Rubicon when in November 1941 the decision was made to attack Pearl Harbor, exclaiming, in essence, *"Iacta alea est!"* When the dice landed at Midway, they came up snake eyes.

* * *

The dice rolled badly for Yamamoto as well. In early April 1943, US Navy code-breakers at Station HYPO in Hawaii were working on intercepted Imperial Navy communications transmitted in the JN-25b code, the same code that had baffled American analysts and cryptographers in the critical days leading up to the Pearl Harbor attack, but which just months later offered up the crucial intelligence which allowed Admiral Nimitz to spring his trap at Midway. Once again they struck gold, as one of the intercepts contained the itinerary for a series of unit inspections in the Solomon Islands and New Guinea by Yamamoto that were scheduled for the middle of the month. The critical part of the messsage revealed that on April 18, the Japanese admiral would be flying from Rabaul to a small airfield in the Solomons. It was just possible that US Army Air Corps P-38s based on Guadalcanal, the only American fighters with sufficient range, could, with painstaking planning and careful flying, intercept Yamamoto's flight and shoot it down.

The execution and timing was almost perfect: on the morning of April 18, the pair of Mitsubishi G4M "Betty" bombers carrying Yamamoto and his staff, along with an escort of six Zeroes, were spotted just off the island of Buin by a flight of 16 P-38s less than a minute ahead of the interception time worked out for the mission plan. Four of the P-38s attacked the two Japanese bombers while the others tangled with the escort. In quick succession one Betty went down in flames and crashed in the Buin jungle, the other made a crash landing just off the island's shoreline. Yamamoto had been a passenger in the first Betty; struck by two bullets, he died instantly.

* * *

The dice also did not roll well for Admiral Kimmel nor for General Short, although they didn't come up as badly as they had for Yamamoto. Hardly had the final words of President Roosevelt's address to Congress on December 8 left his lips than the American press and public began clamoring for Washington DC to give them answers. *How could the attack on Pearl Harbor have even happened?* was the question that was on everyone's lips in the days and months that followed the attack. How did the Japanese do it, and how did they get away with it? Why didn't the Army or—especially—the Navy see it coming? Who was asleep at the switch? Who was to blame?

Answers would be slow in coming, and when they did, they were neither straightforward nor always particularly honest. In part this was because America was at war, and answering those questions honestly could reveal to the Japanese secrets that otherwise could give the Army and Navy significant, even decisive, strategic and tactical advantages—especially the existence of MAGIC and OP-20-G's work at breaking the Japanese naval codes. But it was also because some of those answers might prove to be embarrassing to the president and his subordinates, which, wartime be damned, would be the equivalent of blood in the water to sharks for Roosevelt's political opponents. So the politicians did what politicians have always done when the truth is inconvenient and outright falsehoods were too dangerous—they looked for scapegoats.

In the aftermath of Pearl Harbor, the scapegoats were easily to hand: Husband E. Kimmel and Walter Short. Neither man was immediately singled out to be sacrificed on the altar of political expedience, as in keeping with the old adage that "first impressions are usually correct," if the "blame game" was going to be played, there was more than enough blame to go around between the Army, the Navy, the State Department, and the White House. True, both men were quickly relieved of their commands, but, as Kimmel so dramatically made clear on December 7, it was not an unexpected consequence of the attack: both the Navy and the Army had long traditions of holding responsible the man on the spot for whatever occurred, good or bad, on his watch. In this case, the practice particularly suited the political leadership in Washington, notably the president. If all the blame could be laid on the shoulders of Kimmel and Short, the disaster at Pearl Harbor could be easily explained to the public: Washington had done its job properly—the failure was totally the fault of the local commanders.

The process began when, two days after the attack, Secretary of the Navy Frank Knox, with the president's blessing, left Washington bound for Hawaii; he arrived on December 11 and immediately set about spending two days asking questions and getting answers. He arrived back in Washington on December 14, and produced two reports, one to be released to the public and one for Roosevelt's eyes only. The public report can be fairly described as propaganda: however angry the American public might be, its morale was still shaky, and by focusing as it did on the courage and heroism of American sailors and airmen during the attack, Knox's public report was meant to be reassuring.

His report to Roosevelt was another matter. He bluntly stated that "Neither the Army or the Navy Commandant in Oahu regarded an air attack on the Army air fields or the Navy Stations as at all likely," but also pointed out that "The Army and Naval Commands had received a general war warning on November 27th, but a special war warning sent out by the War Department at midnight December 7th to the Army was not received until some hours after the attack on that date." Here Knox was slightly in error, as the "special war warning" to which he made reference was actually sent between 11:00 AM and noon on December 7. In either case, however, Knox left no doubt that somewhere along the line, someone in Washington had dropped the ball.[3]

He also stated, "This attack has emphasized the completeness of the Naval and military information in the hands of the Japanese, the meticulous detail of their plans of attack, and their courage, ability and resourcefulness in executing and pressing home their operation." No small detail this, as it pointed a sharp finger at an institutional shortcoming shared by both the Navy and the Army: the attitude of "Not invented here" disdain which has always plagued the American armed services. It was widely—and firmly—believed that such an operation as the Pearl Harbor strike was beyond the intellectual and technical capabilities of the Japanese—in short, "If we can't do it, the Japs certainly can't"—a belief, Knox was coming to realize, that was utterly false.[4]

Once he'd digested Knox's report, Roosevelt empaneled a special commission to further investigate the findings the secretary of the navy had presented. Supreme Court Justice Owen Roberts was assigned to lead the inquiry, which inevitably became known as the Roberts Commission. It was here that the scapegoating began: a fact-finding commission, and not a formal legal forum nor a court-martial, the five-member panel of two generals and two admirals, plus Justice Roberts, concluded that Kimmel and Short were both guilty of dereliction of duty. Despite the fact that they were under investigation, neither Short nor Kimmel were allowed to call witnesses, present evidence, or conduct an organized defense of themselves or their actions. Once the Commission presented its findings on January 28, 1942, because four of the five members were senior officers, much of Congress believed that the Commission's conclusions were a formal verdict—an opinion that quickly came to be shared by most of the American people.

The finding of the Roberts Commission had immediate personal consequences for both Short and Kimmel, as both men now stood condemned in the court of public opinion. Short, whose narrow-minded interpretation of his orders were far more at fault for leaving Pearl Harbor vulnerable to air attack than any of Kimmel's mistakes, a responsibility both Knox's report and the Roberts Commission heavily emphasized—became despondent, and because he loved the Army, he convinced himself that if it were necessary for the good of the service, he would resign his commission and retire, which he ultimately did on February 28, 1942. Kimmel soon followed suit, even though he was more inclined to fight for his exoneration than was Short, trusting that in time enough facts would come to light to restore his reputation and good name.

And in truth Kimmel could make a much stronger case for his exoneration than Short could make for his own. While both men could reasonably claim to have been denied critical intelligence by Washington, Kimmel's mistakes weren't the product of a fixation on a single part of his orders to the exclusion of all others, unlike Short's obsession with preventing the sabotage of Army aircraft, which blinded him to his larger mission, namely that the defense of the fleet when it was in port was the responsibility of the Army Air Corps. Had Short devoted a fraction of the time he gave over to protecting his airplanes and training Air Corps personnel in ground tactics, he might have come to see that, for the purpose of defending Oahu, the Army's fighters and bombers were more important than all of his infantry. It was as if he never fully realized that because Oahu was an island, preventing the Japanese from from executing a successful air attack on the Pacific Fleet took precedence over trying to contain an enemy landing force—it would then be up to the Navy to forestall any Japanese invasion force. In a nutshell, Short had his priorities backwards.

Kimmel, on the other hand, was betrayed—and that is scarcely too strong a word—by Admiral Turner's inept handling of the Office of Naval Intelligence, as well as Admiral Stark's passive approach to command as chief of naval operations. Both men, the one consumed with empire-building, the other more focused on the intricacies of Washington politics than overseeing the actions of the fleet, made certain, through ineptitude and lethargy, that Kimmel was never granted access to the "big picture," access that he needed to properly lead a fleet tasked with defending American interests and possessions that spanned the Pacific Ocean.

For a time, the whole issue of who was truly responsible for the Pearl Harbor disaster was pushed to the back burner, so to speak, while the nation was grimly focused on first stopping, then turning back, Japan's advance across the Pacific. But by early 1944, when it was clear that the Japanese were on the defensive and the initiative had well and truly passed to the Allies, the question was reopened, and to answer it a series of inquiries and investigations began. The first was the Hart Inquiry, ordered by Secretary Knox in mid-February 1944. Strictly speaking, it was yet another fact-finding mission rather than a formal inquiry: Knox was concerned that "certain members of the naval forces, who have knowledge pertinent [to the Pearl Harbor attack], are now or soon may be on dangerous assignments at great distances from the United States" and might be killed or go missing in action without ever having given any form of sworn statement. Admiral Thomas Hart, the commanding officer of the Asiatic Fleet at the beginning of the war who now sat on the Navy's Advisory Board, was given the task of locating as many of these individuals as possible and collecting their testimony; at the same time, he wasn't authorized to assign responsibility or blame to anyone involved. The assignment took four months to complete, Hart delivering his report to Knox on June 15, 1944.[5]

A month after the Hart Inquiry concluded, two investigative boards were convened, one by the Army, the other by the Navy, both in response to an act of

Congress passed on July 13. Lieutenant General George Grunert and Major Generals Henry Russell and Walter Frank were assigned to the Army Pearl Harbor Board; the Navy Board was formed by Admirals Orin Murfin and Edward Kalbfus, and Vice Admiral Adolphus Andrews. The two inquires ran for three months and concluded almost simultaneously, the Navy inquiry on October 19, the Army inquiry on the following day.

Surprisingly, neither board attempted to whitewash its parent service, as might have been expected; equally surprising were the names singled out for censure. While Kimmel was fully exonerated, the Navy Board bluntly stated that "Admiral Harold R. Stark, U.S.N., Chief of Naval Operations and responsible for the operations of the Fleet, failed to display the sound judgment expected of him in that he did not transmit to Admiral Kimmel, Commander-in-Chief, Pacific fleet, during the very critical period 26 November to 7 December, important information which he had regarding the Japanese situation and, especially, in that, on the morning of 7 December, 1941, he did not transmit immediately the fact that a message had been received which appeared to indicate that a break in diplomatic relations was imminent, and that an attack in the Hawaiian area might be expected soon."[6]

General Short didn't fare as well at the hands of the Army Board as Kimmel did with the Navy Board. In its final report, the Army Board repeatedly chastised Short for his intense focus on potential Japanese saboteurs and fifth-columnists, as well as his preoccupation with training, to the near-exclusion of other defensive measures. At the same time, the board criticized both General Marshall and then-Brigadier General Gerow, Chief of the War Plans Division, for failing to ensure that Short was carrying out all of the directives assigned to him when he was given command of the Hawaiian Military Department in February 1941, as well as not providing Short with all of the relevant intelligence collected in Washington regarding Japanese activity in the Pacific.

Of course, nothing in Washington DC is final until Congress delivers its considered opinion on the matter, so despite the fact that the findings and conclusions of the Army and Navy Pearl Harbor boards should have been the last words of each service on the subject, everyone knew that the show wasn't over. In anticipation of the inevitable Congressional investigation, three more fact-finding inquiries were carried out between September 14, 1944 and September 12, 1945. The Clausen Investigation, the Hewitt Inquiry, and the Clarke Investigation individually set about to obtain testimony to supplement the investigations already done by the Navy and Army Boards, as well as to provide a somewhat clearer picture of how the intelligence divisions of both services communicated with each other prior to Pearl Harbor. As with Admiral Hart's earlier inquiry, none of the three were empowered to assess responsibility or assign blame to anyone involved in the events leading up to or on the day of the Japanese attack. That was reserved for the career politicians appointed to the Joint Congressional Hearings, which convened on November 15, 1945.

Established by a Joint Congressional Resolution, this investigation promised, publicly at least, to be the most thorough and impartial investigation yet conducted into how the Pearl Harbor attack happened, and who was responsible; its conclusions were intended to be the final word on the subject. At the specific direction of President Harry Truman, the congressional committee was to be given unrestricted access to *all* relevant documents—classified and unclassified—as well as the authority to call any witnesses whose testimony the committee might deem necessary.

But appearances were deceiving. Given that these were politicians being asked to, in some cases, pass judgement on other politicians, party affiliations and loyalties inevitably came into play. The membership of the committee was strongly tilted in favor of the Democratic Party, which at the time held the majority in both the Senate and the House. The chairmanship was accorded to the senior of the three senators appointed to the committee, Alben Barkley, a Democrat from Kentucky; the other members from the Upper House of Congress were Walter George, a Georgia Democrat, and Homer Ferguson, the senior senator from Michigan and the lone senatorial Republican. Congressmen sitting on the committee were Jere Cooper of Tennessee, J. Bayard Clark of North Carolina, and John Murphy of Pennsylvania, all Democrats; they were joined by two Republican congressmen, Bertrand Gearhart of California, and Frank Keefe of Wisconsin.

The Congressional investigation ran from November 15, 1945 to May 31, 1946, its findings eventually being published in a total of 40 volumes, with an additional volume containing the Committee's conclusions and recommendations. Separate majority and minority "final" reports were issued, the former endorsed by all of the Democratic members of the investigation, the latter by the Republicans. In both the lion's share of the blame was dropped squarely on the shoulders of Admiral Kimmel and General Short, while Secretary of War Stimson, Secretary of the Navy Knox, Generals Marshall and Gerow, and Admiral Stark, were subjected to various degrees of censure. Curiously, the closer to the White House any individual happened to be, the more muted was the criticism; the Democratic majority report shied away from any statements or findings that might reflect unfavorably on President Roosevelt, whose memory within the party was in the process of near-apotheosis at the time, while the Republican report sniped at the now-deceased chief executive, but, being the minority report, was unable to attach any significant degree of blame for the Pearl Harbor debacle on him.

Once the Congressional Hearings were concluded, General Short appeared to have resigned himself to being remembered as one of the two men most responsible for the greatest military disaster in American history. His health was already failing, and he made no effort to publicly defend himself after the findings of the Congressional Committee were published. He died at the age of 69 on September 3, 1949.

Husband Kimmel, by way of contrast, never accepted the judgements of the Roberts Commission or the Congressional Investigation, and for the remaining

22 years of his life he was vigorous in his defense of his actions as CINCPAC in 1941. Kimmel was firm in his belief that, unlike General Short, whose failures were of his own making, he had been betrayed, through acts of both commission or omission, by Harold Stark and Richmond Turner. He held unwaveringly to the contention—and insisted that the factual record backed his contention—that Stark and Turner, for petty, personal reasons, deliberately withheld critical intelligence from him, information that, if he had it to hand, Kimmel would have had the Pacific Fleet fully alert and ready to defend itself against the Japanese attack. His animosity toward Stark in particular grew so bitter that, in 1968, not long before his death at the age of 86, he wrote a personal letter to the former chief of naval operations in which he declared,

> You betrayed the officers and men of the Fleet by not giving them a fighting chance for their lives and you betrayed the Navy by not taking responsibility for your actions; you betrayed me by not giving me information you knew I was entitled to and in your acquiescence in the action taken on the request for my retirement; and you betrayed yourself by misleading the Roberts Commission as to what information had been sent to me and by your statements made under oath before the Court of Inquiry that you knew were false.
>
> I hope that you never communicate with me again and that I never see you or your name again that my memory may not be refreshed by one so despicable as you.[7]

Even after Kimmel himself departed this mortal coil, his family continued to have the findings of the Roberts Commission and the Congressional Investigation reversed, and so restore his good name and reputation. Three times they petitioned the sitting United States President to posthumously restore Kimmel's four-star rank, although no action was taken on any of the requests, while in 1999 a non-binding resolution to exonerate both Kimmel and Short was passed in the United States Senate by a 57 to 43 vote. The resolution was purely symbolic, however, and the nation's official reckoning against Admiral Kimmel and General Short, whether just and deserved or not, still stands.

* * *

If there was to be no resurrection of the reputations of Admiral Kimmel and General Short, the same wasn't true of the battered warships at Pearl Harbor. Only five ships were written off by the US Navy in the wake of the attack, although the fleet actually fudged on two of them. All eight of the battleships in Pearl on December 7, 1941, were damaged, of course, and five of them technically sank as a result. "Technically" because only two of them were sent to the bottom of the harbor damaged beyond any hope of repair—*Arizona* and *Oklahoma*.

Arizona, of course, had been devastated by the explosion of her forward powder magazine; her back was broken, most of her internal bulkheads ruptured by the blast, she was structurally unsound—any effort to raise the wreck, let alone repair it, was pointless. Instead, whatever fittings and equipment that were still serviceable were salvaged—including most of her 14-inch guns, which were converted into shore batteries and sited at critical points on Oahu's coastline. Her superstructure and tripod masts were cut away, and the hull was left resting on the harbor bottom. During the salvage work, the bodies of 105 of *Arizona*'s crew were recovered, but when the final determination was made in December 1942 that raising the wreck was an impossibility, the Navy designated the battleship's hulk a war grave and declared that the officers and men still entombed in the wreck were officially "buried at sea."

Oklahoma was a different story. Because the navigable channel between Ford Island and the Navy Yard was so narrow, the capsized warship was a hazard to navigation. Being at the time the US Navy's largest permanent forward base in the Pacific, Pearl Harbor was busier than ever, with a constant influx and outflow of ships that made clearing the channel a priority. In early 1942 a survey of the ship determined that raising *Oklahoma* was preferable to scrapping her in place, as scrapping would have blocked the channel indefinitely. In a massive engineering project that took the better part of 18 months, the old battleship was turned upright, and after a huge cofferdam was built around her, the damage to her port side was patched, and on November 3, 1943, *Oklahoma* was refloated. She was eventually moved to a slip in the Southwest Loch, where she sat for the next three years; sold for scrap at the end of 1946, she was towed out of Pearl Harbor on May 16, 1947, on her way to a San Francisco breakers yard. The next day, 500 miles northeast of Oahu, a storm came up and *Oklahoma* began shipping water, then broke her tow lines and sank in a matter of minutes. The exact position of her wreck remains unknown.

As had happened on *Arizona*, salvage divers and repair workers found remains of sailors and Marines who died aboard *Oklahoma*. A total of 388 were discovered, all of them badly decomposed and thus impossible to identify, and were initially buried in the Nu'uanu and Halawa cemeteries; in 1950 all were moved to the National Memorial Cemetery of the Pacific. They lay there undisturbed for 55 years, until April 2015, when the Navy, embracing the latest advances in genetic science, announced that the remains would be disinterred and DNA-matching tests carried out to confirm as many identities of *Oklahoma*'s unknown dead as possible. By the end of 2019, 238 positive identifications have been made.

An attempt similar to the effort to raise *Oklahoma* was undertaken with *Utah*, but failed. The all but submerged hull, lying on its port side, was left in place and a small memorial was eventually raised at the wreck site in 1972. As with *Arizona*, *Utah* is a designated war grave, the final resting place for 52 men entombed inside her.

When the fires were finally quenched on the destroyers *Cassin* and *Downes* in the 1010 Dock, naval surveyors found that, while their hulls were damaged beyond repair, the machinery on both ships—boilers, condensers, engines, and main generators—was still serviceable. The Navy, not willing to let a pair of perfectly good powerplants go to waste, built new hulls, installed the machinery from the original *Cassin* and *Downes* inside them, then commissioned the new ships with the same names and pennant numbers, DD-372 and DD-375 respectively, as the originals. Both ships went on to have very active combat careers in the Pacific.[8]

Despite the spectacular explosion of her forward magazine, the destroyer *Shaw* was left more or less intact and serviceable from her bridge aft. The damaged bow was cut away and replaced by a stubby temporary bow, sufficient to allow *Shaw* to sail for San Francisco on February 9, 1942. A new bow was built and at the end of August *Shaw*, once more fighting trim, was back in Pearl Harbor on her way to the Central Pacific, where she would earn 11 battle stars over the next three years. Worn out by such heavy use, she was decommissioned at the end of the war and scrapped a year later. The handful of other ships damaged in the Japanese attack were repaired and returned to service within a few weeks to a few months, including the minesweeper *Oglala*, which suffered the indignity of being sunk, then raised, only to sink again when her pumps failed before she could be moved into drydock. Raised a second time, she was converted into a repair ship and was sent to support Admiral Thomas Kincaid's 7th Fleet in the spring of 1944.

But the most dramatic chapter in the aftermath of December 7, 1941, was the fate of the other six battleships in Pearl Harbor that morning. The damage done to *Pennsylvania, Tennessee*, and *Maryland* had been minor—"minor" being a very relative adjective in this case—and while *Nevada* had undeniably taken a beating and "technically" sank when she grounded on Hospital Point, her boilers, engines and main armament remained intact. After repairs sufficient to guarantee they were seaworthy, *Pennsylvania, Tennessee*, and *Maryland* left Pearl Harbor together on December 20, 1941, the former bound for San Francisco, the latter two for Puget Sound. *Nevada*, with temporary steel patches welded to her hull, followed in April 1942. Once in the hands of the yard dogs, all four ships were modernized with new radars, fire-control, and new anti-aircraft batteries of 16 5-inch guns in eight twin turrets. Some of the new equipment required modifications to the ships' superstructures, and all had their after masts—a "cage" mast on *Maryland*, tripods on *Pennsylvania* and *Nevada*—cut down or removed to improve the arcs of fire for the new anti-aircraft guns. By mid-October, three of the four ships were back with the fleet, *Maryland* and *Pennsylvania* initially assigned to protecting the West Coast, while *Nevada* was sent to the Atlantic Fleet, where she escorted convoys to Great Britain.

Tennessee, meanwhile, was taken in hand for what the Navy deemed was "modernization"; in practice the ship was completely rebuilt. Both of her cage masts were cut away and her superstructure razed to the upper deck, replaced by an entirely different construct that was visually very similar to that of the new *South Dakota*-class battleships. With it came new radar and fire-control systems, fire control, and a new twin-gun eight-turret anti-aircraft battery. Her hull was widened by the addition of anti-torpedo bulges, and her internal protection was improved with added deck and side armor and reinforced bulkheads. By the time the work was completed in

May 1943, *Tennessee* was all but unrecognizable as the ship that was moored in Pearl Harbor 18 months earlier.

Compared to the first four battleships returned to service, salvaging *California* and *West Virginia* was more problematic. While *Nevada* had "sunk" in the sense that she settled on the bottom at Hospital Point, it had been a calculated action: with just a few feet of water under her keel, her upper decks remained above water, with just a handful of compartments flooded. Repairing her hull wasn't particularly easy, but it had been a fairly straightforward job. *California*, though, had two gigantic holes torn in her side by Japanese torpedoes, and despite the heroics of her crew, when the ship lost power the inrush of water became uncontrollable and her hull was completely flooded; she settled to the bottom in 40 feet of water, her upper decks awash. Patching *California's* hull and refloating her took five months; another seven months passed before her boilers and engines were repaired—her complex turbo-electric motors had to be completely rebuilt—and she was able to make for the Puget Sound Navy Yard at the beginning of October 1942. Once there, she underwent the same modernization that had been carried out on her sister, *Tennessee*. The experience gained in rebuilding *Tennessee* allowed four months to be shaved off the time needed to reconstruct *California*, and she was ready for sea once more in January 1944.

West Virginia had been almost as badly mauled by Japanese torpedoes as had been *Oklahoma*, and came close to capsizing just as the older battleship had done. But because her crew had the time—just—to begin counterflooding, time that the men on *Oklahoma* never had, *WeeVee* settled in the water on something close to an even keel. Not only did that spare her superstructure from being crushed against the harbor bottom, it also prevented all the internal damage a ship suffers when she turns turtle. Still, once the decision was made to raise her, it took seven months to build the 300-foot cofferdam that temporarily patched *West Virginia's* hull, pump her dry, and refloat her. She was moved into Dry Dock No. 1 at Pearl, where repairs were made sufficient to allow her to steam to Puget Sound. She was rebuilt along the same lines as *Tennessee* and *California*, and sailed for the 7th Fleet anchorage at Manus Island, New Guinea; there she joined *Tennessee, California, Pennsylvania, Maryland*, and *Mississippi*, the core of Rear Admiral Jesse Oldendorf's Fire Support Group.

One week after *WeeVee's* arrival, 7th Fleet sailed out of Manus, heading north to Leyte Gulf, where General Douglas MacArthur would fulfill his famous pledge, "I shall return," and begin the campaign to liberate the Philippines. The Fire Support Group was at the tip of the spear, so to speak: before the US Sixth Army went ashore, Admiral Oldendorf's six battleships, four heavy cruisers, four light cruisers, and 29 destroyers bombarded Japanese defensive positions on and near the landing beaches, smothering them with carefully laid out fire plans, then stood by to bring their guns to bear on any pockets of heavy resistance the Army encountered. It was an operation the US Navy had all but perfected in more than a dozen invasions since November 1942.

For the Japanese, this was *the* decisive moment of the war. The Empire literally could not afford to allow the Americans to gain a foothold in the Philippines: as soon as the US Army Air Corps could base bombers in the islands, they could sever the sea lanes from Malaysia, cutting off Japan's only source of crude oil, starving the Imperial Navy and Army Air Service of fuel. There would be nothing to stop the Americans short of their ultimate goal: invading the Japanese Home Islands.

In what was an all-or-nothing throw of the dice, the Imperial General Staff concocted an ambitious but overly complex plan to destroy the fleet of transports and supply ships supporting the landing on Leyte. First, the "Northern Force," formed around Japan's four remaining aircraft carriers—which had very few aircraft embarked, as the Japanese were critically short of trained naval aviators by this point—would act as bait to draw the carriers of Admiral Halsey's 3rd Fleet, which providing air cover for 7th Fleet, far to the north of Samar Island, where it would be out of range of Leyte Gulf. After that, the "Center Force," a powerful collection of battleships, cruisers, and destroyers was to sail around the north end of Samar, down the island's east coast, and into Leyte Gulf, where it would fall upon the hapless transports and destroy them in detail.

Meanwhile, a "Southern Force" would steam up from the south into Surigao Strait, to act as the "cork in the bottle," as it were, blocking the escape of any American ships trying to escape southward. If it worked—and like far too many of the Imperial Navy's plans from Midway on, its success was dependent on every phase being carried out flawlessly and the US Navy reacting and responding exactly as needed—the entire landing force, 200,000 officers and men, would be cut off, unable to withdraw, and compelled to surrender. It would be the greatest military defeat in American history; Tokyo was hoping that the shock of such a catastrophe would cause the American public to demand a negotiated settlement to the war in the Pacific.

The plan began to unravel almost from the beginning, though. The Northern Force succeeded beyond all expectations, luring the American carriers far out of range of the Center and Southern Forces, but poor communications left the commander of the Center Force completely unaware of this. Off Samar Island, the Center Force stumbled upon a handful of destroyers and destroyer escorts screening a motley collection of small escort carriers, which the Japanese could have—should have—swatted aside with ease. Instead, in what would go down in history as the Battle of Samar Island, the American's light warships opened fire on opponents 20 times their size and launched near-suicidal torpedo attacks, while aircraft from the escort carriers swarmed over the Japanese battleships and cruisers, attacking with whatever ordnance they were carrying at the moment. The admiral commanding the Center Force convinced himself that he was facing Halsey's fleet carriers, and fearing that his ships would be overwhelmed and annihilated, withdrew in confusion. There would be no massive battle fleet falling on near-defenseless transports and supply ships in Leyte Gulf.

But before the Battle of Samar Island was joined, the Southern Force, led by Vice Admiral Nishimura Shoji had entered Surigao Strait. His command included two battleships, *Fuso* and *Yamashiro*, the heavy cruiser *Mogami*, and four destroyers; coming up behind him were two more heavy cruisers, *Nachi* and *Ashigara*, the light cruiser *Abukuma*, and another four destroyers, under the command of Vice Admiral Shima Kiyohide. US Navy patrol planes had already located the Southern Force, and as night fell on October 24, 1944, Rear Admiral Oldendorf laid a deadly trap for Nishimura's ships. Sitting astride the northern entrance to Surigao Straight, where it was the narrowest, leaving little room for the Japanese ships to maneuver, his battleships took up a position to cross the Japanese admiral's "T", the classic naval tactic where one force can bring its full broadside to bear on the enemy, which can only reply with its ships' forward guns. Then they waited.

As the Southern Force approached the entrance to the Strait, it was spotted by one of the American PT boats, the first sighting report being sent to Admiral Oldendorf at 10:36 PM. For the next four hours, the small, fast attack craft, some 35 in all, began shadowing the Japanese ships, repeatedly darting close to make torpedo attacks. Though none of their torpedoes found a target, the PTs kept Oldendorf informed in detail of Nishimura's progress northward, which allowed the American admiral to choose to a nicety the moment to send in his destroyers to make torpedo attacks of their own, the first beginning at 2:58 AM. They succeeded spectacularly, sinking two Japanese destroyers and damaging a third, while both of the battleships were hit. Two torpedoes struck *Yamashiro*, which was slowed but not stopped by the damage. Only one struck *Fuso*, but it started a fire in her fuel bunkers that within minutes flared up out of control. Listing heavily to port, *Fuso* struggled on briefly, then fell out of line when her engines stopped, and drifted off to the northwest, burning for much of her length.

Nishimura pressed ahead despite these losses, but by now, the American battleships were following what remained of the Southern Force—one battleship, one heavy cruiser, and one destroyer—on their tracking radars, while their fire-control radars were dialing in the range to a fare-thee-well. At 3:51, when the Japanese ships were 20,000 yards—10 miles—distant, Admiral Oldendorf gave the order to fire. One minute later, *West Virginia*'s eight 16-inch guns opened up with a roar, followed by the 14-inch guns of *Tennessee* and *California*, along with all of the cruisers; *Maryland*, *Mississippi*, and *Pennsylvania* were slower off the mark, hindered by their older fire-control units.

The American battleships concentrated on *Yamashiro* at first, then shifted their fire to the other two Japanese ships. For 18 minutes the trio of Japanese warships were the target of six battleships and eight cruisers, all firing as rapidly as possible. For once the old cliché "a hail of fire" held true, as the Americans hurled 265 14- and 16-inch shells, and 1,185 6- and 8- inch shells at their targets. The Japanese did their best to shoot back at their tormenters, but Admiral Nishimura quickly lost tactical control of the battle, and his ships frantically fired at any target, real or imagined, that presented itself. Halfway through the bombardment, the Japanese admiral gave the order to reverse course, hoping to save his command. It was too late. Fires sprang up all along *Yamashiro*'s decks, and one of her midships gun turrets exploded, while *Mogami* and the destroyer accompanying her were pummeled as well. Another torpedo attack by American destroyers produced two more hits on the stricken battleship, which began listing heavily.

Seeing the enemy turn away, Admiral Oldendorf ordered a course change for his own battleships, but *California*'s captain misunderstood the order, so that when she turned, she masked the Japanese force for a time, and other American battleships stopped firing in order to avoid hitting her. When she had worked clear, *Yamashiro* and her consorts were drawing out of range. *Mississippi* got off one final salvo—the last time any battleship would fire her guns in a ship-to-ship engagement. A report that Japanese torpedoes were in the water reached Oldendorf, who ordered his ships to make an evasive turn to the north. With that, the Battle of the Surigao Strait ended, and the curtain of naval history fell on the Age of the Big Gun.

Fuso capsized and sank somewhere in the darkness at about the same time the American battleships opened fire on *Yamashiro*. Precisely how *Fuso* met her end remains a mystery: she went down so suddenly that only 10 of her crewmen survived. *Yamashiro* followed her to the bottom shortly thereafter, her list increasing until she lost all stability and abruptly turned turtle; as with *Fuso*, only 10 of her crew escaped the sinking ship. When Rear Admiral Shima, still doggedly steaming north, encountered the survivors of Nishimura's command—*Mogami* and a single destroyer—limping southward, with neither Japanese battleship in sight, he knew the battle was lost and immediately reversed course. US Navy TBF Avengers finished off *Mogami* the next day, putting the last exclamation point to the Battle of Surigao Strait.

"The Battle of Leyte Gulf" would be how history remembered the quartet of engagements—the battles of the Sibuyan Sea, Surigao Strait, Samar Island, and Cape Engano—fought between October 23 and 26, 1944. Leyte Gulf was the "Great Decisive Battle," the Kanto Kantai, that the Imperial Navy had been seeking since the beginning of the Pacific War; it was also Japan's last throw of the dice to bring the war to an end with a positive balance on the Imperial ledger.

It failed.

The losses suffered at Leyte Gulf—Japan's last fleet carrier, three light carriers, three battleships, 10 cruisers, and nine destroyers, plus roughly 300 aircraft, along with 12,500 crewmen and naval fliers—crippled the already badly outnumbered Imperial Navy to the point that it was reduced to near-impotence. Never again would the

Japanese be able to assemble a fleet with anything approaching the strength needed to seriously threaten the US Navy. Within months, the Empire's army and navy starved of fuel, Japanese strategy and tactics would be reduced to those of despair: denied even the prospect of a draw, Japan could now only make its defeat as costly and painful as possible for the United States.

The war the Japanese had so doggedly sought, and hoped could be ended even as it began with the attack on the US Navy's Pacific fleet at Pearl Harbor, the war that Yamamoto Isoroku had worked desperately to avert, then died trying to win, the war that the American government and public never imagined could happen, culminated in the destruction of the Imperial Navy, crushing forever Japan's dreams of empire. In a symbolism lost on no one present on September 2, 1945, *West Virginia*, sunk at Pearl Harbor and resurrected to fight again, would be among the fleet of Allied warships anchored in Tokyo Bay when the Japanese government signed the instrument of its surrender.

The Ship that Weeps for her Dead

At sunset on December 7, 2019, the USS *Arizona* Memorial in Pearl Harbor was witness once more to a ceremony that had been carried out 43 times since its inception in 1982. Naturally, this day's observance would be conducted with the same dignity and reverence that had marked its predecessors, but with one key difference: this was the last time this particular service would be held—ever.

The memorial, a low, graceful, structure, much like a shallow, inverted arch, is almost stark in its simplicity, an unspoken reminder that the event it commemorates, and not the memorial itself, is the focus here. Dedicated in 1962, the *Arizona* memorial sits athwart the shattered wreck of the battleship, but at no place does it ever touch it. One and one-half million people pass through it every year; visitors are quiet, subdued, almost reverent—it's as if some echo of the raw power of the disaster which overwhelmed the ship at 8:06 that December morning still clings to the wreck.

Though not crystal-clear, the water around *Arizona* allows those visitors to view the entire length of the wreck, and view the awful damage done to her hull when the forward powder magazine blew up. Often noted by those visitors is the trace of black oil rising gently from *Arizona*'s quarterdeck, forming a rainbow-hued slick that spreads slowly across the water. A bit more than two quarts of fuel seeps from the ship's bunkers daily; they've become known as "the tears of the *Arizona*," the ship still figuratively mourning the 1,177 officers and men who died aboard her.

On this particular December 7, the service being held was the interment of the ashes of Lauren Bruner, who had been a fire controlman for *Arizona*'s anti-aircraft guns when the Japanese attacked. Barely escaping immolation when the ship exploded—his post had been high in the superstructure, just on the edge of the fireball that destroyed *Arizona*'s forward half—he was burned over three-fifths of his body, and hit twice by machine-gun fire from strafing Japanese planes. Acknowledged to be the second-to-last man to leave the ship—Commander Fuqua was the last—he reached safety by hauling himself hand-over-hand along a lifeline to the repair ship *Vestal*. After a year of mentally and physically recovering from his ordeal, he was once more at sea, aboard a destroyer, taking the war back to the Japanese.

Bruner passed away in his sleep on September 10, 2019, at the age of 98. He'd already made arrangements to have his ashes placed inside *Arizona*'s wreck, rejoining his shipmates, a privilege first allowed in 1982 to those crewmen who survived the attack. Since then, 43 of *Arizona*'s former officers and enlisted men had asked that the old ship serve as their final resting place. Bruner would be the 44th, and last: though four other *Arizona* crewmen were still alive at the time of his passing, they had all arranged to be buried with their families when their time came to leave this life.

So, with the sun low on the horizon, the speeches given, the eulogy delivered, and the Lord's Prayer recited, a small procession of family members and friends, escorted by two US Navy admirals, walked through the assembled guests, down the length of the *Arizona* Memorial, and out onto the dock at its south end. There, they passed the urn containing Lauren Bruner's ashes to a quartet of divers who carried it down into the barbette of Turret Number 4, and placed it beside the 43 identical urns already resting there. "Taps" was sounded, the elaborate ritual of folding the memorial flag flawlessly executed, and the newest addition to the roll call of *Arizona*'s crew who had returned to their ship was unveiled.

Forty feet below the now-tranquil surface of Pearl Harbor, Lauren Bruner rests in peace aboard the ship that weeps for her dead.

Imperial Japanese Navy "Hawaii Operation" Order of Battle, December 7, 1941

First Air Fleet—Vice Admiral Chuichi Nagumo
  1st Carrier Division—Vice Admiral Nagumo
    Akagi
      Level Bombing *Sentai* (Group)
        3 *Chutai* (Squadrons/Flights)—15 x Nakajima B5N2 ("Kate")
      Torpedo Bombing *Sentai*
        4 *Chutai*—12 x B5N
      Dive Bombing *Sentai*
        6 *Chutai*—18 x Aichi D3A1 ("Val")
      Fighter *Sentai*
        3 *Chutai*—27 x Mitsubishi A6M2 ("Zero")
    Kaga
      Level Bombing *Sentai*
        3 *Chutai*—15 x Nakajima B5N ("Kate")
      Torpedo Bombing *Sentai*
        4 *Chutai*—12 x B5N
      Dive Bombing *Sentai*
        9 *Chutai*—27 x Aichi D3A1 ("Val")
      Fighter *Sentai*
        3 *Chutai*—27 x Mitsubishi A6M2 ("Zero")
  2nd Carrier Division—Rear Admiral Yamaguchi Tamon
    Soryu
      Level Bombing *Sentai*
        2 *Chutai*—10 x Nakajima B5N ("Kate")
      Torpedo Bombing *Sentai*
        4 *Chutai*—8 x B5N
      Dive Bombing *Sentai*
        6 *Chutai*—18 x Aichi D3A1 ("Val")
      Fighter *Sentai*
        3 *Chutai*—27 x Mitsubishi A6M2 ("Zero")
    Hiryu
      Level Bombing *Sentai*
        2 *Chutai*—10 x Nakajima B5N ("Kate")
      Torpedo Bombing *Sentai*
        4 *Chutai*—8 x B5N

Dive Bombing *Sentai*
    6 *Chutai*—18 x Aichi D3A1 ("Val")
Fighter *Sentai*
    3 *Chutai*—27 x Mitsubishi A6M2 ("Zero")

5th Carrier Division—Rear Admiral Hara Chuichi
Shokaku
  Level Bombing Sentai
    3 *Chutai*—27 x Nakajima B5N ("Kate")
  Dive Bombing *Sentai*
    3 *Chutai*—27 x Aichi D3A1 ("Val")
  Fighter *Sentai*
    2 *Chutai*—15 x Mitsubishi A6M2 ("Zero")
Zuikaku
  Level Bombing *Sentai*
    3 *Chutai*—27 x Nakajima B5N ("Kate")
  Dive Bombing *Sentai*
    3 *Chutai*—27 x Aichi D3A1 ("Val")
  Fighter *Sentai*
    2 *Chutai*—15 x Mitsubishi A6M2 ("Zero")
Akigumo (destroyer)

3rd Battleship Division—Vice Admiral Mikawa Gunichi
Hiei
Kirishima

8th Cruiser Division—Rear Admiral Abe Hiroaki
Tone
Chikuma

1st Destroyer Squadron—Rear Admiral Omori Sentaro
CL Abukuma

17th Destroyer Division
Urakaze
Isokaze
Tanikaze
Hamakaze

18th Destroyer Division
Kagero
Shiranuhi
Arare
Kasumi

Submarines
I-19
I-21
I-23

1st Supply Train
Kyokuto Maru (tanker)
Kenyo Maru (tanker)
Kokuyo Maru (tanker)
Shinkoku Maru (tanker)
Akebono Maru (tanker)

2nd Supply Train
Toho Maru (tanker)
Toei Maru (tanker)
Nippon Maru (tanker)
6th Fleet—Vice Admiral Shimizu Mitsumi
1st Submarine Squadron—Rear Admiral Sato Tsutomu
I-9
I-15
I-17
I-25
2nd Submarine Squadron—Rear Admiral Yamazaki Shigeaki
I-7
I-1
I-2
I-3
I-4
I-5
I-6
3rd Submarine Squadron—Rear Admiral Miwa Shigeyoshi
I-8
I-68
I-69
I-70
I-71
I-72
I-73
I-74
I-75
Special Attack Unit—Captain Sasaki Hankyu
I-22 w/ *I-22tou* (midget submarine)
I-16 w/ *I-16tou* (midget submarine)
I-18 w/ *I-18tou* (midget submarine)
I-20 w/ *I-20tou* (midget submarine)
I-24 w/ *I-24tou* (midget submarine)
Submarine Reconnaissance Unit—Commander Kashihara Yasuchika
I-10
I-26

United States Armed Forces Order of Battle Pearl Harbor and Oahu, December 7, 1941

United States Navy
  14th Naval District—Rear Admiral Claude Bloch
  Pacific Fleet—Admiral Husband Kimmel
    Battle Force (Task Force 1)—Vice Admiral William Pye
      Battleships, Battle Force—Rear Admiral Walter Anderson
      Battleship Division 1— Rear Admiral Isaac Kidd
        Arizona (BB-39)
        Nevada (BB-36)
        Oklahoma (BB-37)
      Battleship Division 2—Rear Admiral D. W. Bagley
        California (BB-44)
        Pennsylvania (BB-38)
        Tennessee (BB-43)
      Battleship Division 4—Rear Admiral Walter Anderson
        Maryland (BB-46)
        West Virginia (BB-48)
      Cruisers, Battle Force—Rear Admiral Herbert Leary
      Cruiser Division 6
        New Orleans (CA-32)
        San Francisco (CA-38)
      Cruiser Division 9—Rear Admiral Herbert Leary
        Phoenix (CL-46)
        Honolulu (CL-48)
        St. Louis (CL-49)
        Helena (CL-50)
      Destroyers, Battle Force—Rear Admiral Milo Draemel
      Destroyer Flotilla 1
        Raleigh (CL-7)
      Destroyer Squadron 1
        Phelps (DD-360)
      Destroyer Division 1
        Dewey (DD-349)
        Hull (DD-350)
        Macdonough (DD-351)
        Worden (DD-352)

Destroyer Division 2
Farragut (DD-348)
Dale (DD-353)
Monaghan (DD-354)
Aylwin (DD-355)
Destroyer Squadron 3
Selfridge (DD-357)
Destroyer Division 5
Reid (DD-369)
Conyngham (DD-371)
Cassin (DD-372)
Downes (DD-375)
Destroyer Division 6
Cummings (DD-365)
Case (DD-370)
Shaw (DD-373)
Tucker (DD-374)
Destroyer Flotilla 2
Detroit (CL-8)
Bagley (DD-386)
Blue (DD-387)
Helm (DD-388)
Mugford (DD-389)
Ralph Talbot (DD-390)
Henley (DD-391)
Patterson (DD-392)
Jarvis (DD-393)
Other Destroyers
Allen (DD-66)
Schley (DD-103)
Chew (DD-106)
Ward (DD-139)
Submarine Warfare
Submarine Tender
Pelias (AS-14)
Submarine Rescue Ship
Widgeon (ASR-1)
Submarines
Narwhal (SS-167)
Dolphin (SS-169)
Cachalot (SS-170)
Tautog (SS-199)
Mine Warfare—Rear Admiral William Furlong
Oglala (CM-4)
10 x Minesweepers
6 x Destroyer Minesweepers
9 x Destroyer Minelayers

Support Ships and Auxiliaries
Oilers
Ramapo (AO-12)
Neosho (AO-23)
Ammunition Ship
Pyro (AE-1)
Repair Ships
Medusa (AR-1)
Vestal (AR-4)
Rigel (AR-11)
Hospital Ship
Solace (AH-5)
1 x Patrol Gunboat
2 x Destroyer Tenders
6 x Seaplane Tenders
12 x Miscellaneous Auxiliaries, including *Utah* (AG-16)
US Navy Aviation—Pacific Fleet
Patrol Wings
Kaneohe NAS
Patrol Wing 1 (VPW-1)
Patrol Squadron 11 (VP-11)
2 x PBY-5
Patrol Squadron (VP-12)
12 x PBY-5
Patrol Squadron 14 (VP-14)
12 x PBY-5
Other aircraft
1 x OS2U
Pearl Harbor NAS (Ford Island)
Patrol Wing 2 (VPW-2)
Patrol Squadron 21 (VP-21)
1 x PBY-3
Patrol Squadron 22 (VP-22)
14 x PBY-3
Patrol Squadron 23 (VP-23)
12 x PBY-5
Patrol Squadron 24 (VP-24)
6 x PBY-5

United States Marine Corps
14th Naval District Marine Officer—Colonel Harry Pickett
Marine Barracks Pearl Harbor— Colonel Gilder Jackson Jr.
Marine Barracks, Naval Ammunition Depot, Oahu
1st Defense Battalion
3rd Defense Battalion
4th Defense Battalion
2nd Engineer Battalion

Marine Corps Air Station (MCAS) (Ewa)
  Marine Aircraft Group (MAG-21)
    Marine Scout Bomber Squadron 232 (VMSB-232)
      19 x SBD-1, 3 x SBD-2
    Marine Utility Squadron 252 (VMJ-252)
      2 x R3D-2, 2 x J2F-4, 1 x SBD-1, 1 x JO-2, 1 x JRS-1, 1 x SB2U-3
    Marine Fighting Squadron 211 (VMF-211)
      11 x F4F-3, 1 x SNJ-3

United States Army
  Hawaiian Military Department—Lieutenant General Walter Short
  Schofield Barracks
    24th Infantry Division—Brigadier General Durward Wilson
      19th Infantry Regiment
      21st Infantry Regiment
      299th Infantry Regiment, Hawaiian Territorial Guard
    25th Infantry Division—Major General Maxwell Murray
      27th Infantry Regiment
      35th Infantry Regiment
      298th Infantry Regiment, Hawaiian Territorial Guard
  Hawaiian Coast Artillery Command—Major General Henry Bargin
    Hawaiian Separate Coast Artillery Brigade
      15th Coast Artillery Regiment
      16th Coast Artillery Regiment
      41st Coast Artillery Regiment
      55th Coast Artillery Regiment
    53rd Coast Artillery Brigade
      64th Coast Artillery Regiment
      97th Coast Artillery Regiment
      98th Coast Artillery Regiment
      251st Coast Artillery Regiment, California Army National Guard
  US Army Air Corps
  Hawaiian Air Force (7th Air Force)—Major General Frederick Martin
  Hickam Field
    18th Bombardment Wing—Brigadier General Jacob Rudolph
    5th Bombardment Group (Heavy)
      23rd Bombardment Squadron (Heavy)
      31st Bombardment Squadron (Heavy)
      72nd Bombardment Squadron (Heavy)
      11th Bombardment Group (Heavy)
      26th Bombardment Squadron (Heavy)
      42nd Bombardment Squadron (Heavy)
    Other Units
      4th Reconnaissance Squadron (Heavy)
      50th Reconnaissance Squadron (Heavy)
        Total of 33 x B-18 and 12 x B-17D

Wheeler Field
  14th Pursuit Wing—Brigadier General Howard Davidson
  15th Pursuit Group
    45th Pursuit Squadron
      15 x P-36A, 2 x B-12, 2 x P-40B, 1 x BT-2BI
    46th Pursuit Squadron
      21 x P-36A, 5 x P-40B, 1 x AT-12A, 1 x BT-2BI, 1 x P-26A
    47th Pursuit Squadron
      11 x P-40B, 2 x P-26B, 2 x P-36A, 2 x P-40C, 1 x B-12
    72nd Pursuit Squadron
      Awaiting aircraft
    Other aircraft
      2 x P-36A, 1 x OA-9
  18th Pursuit Group
    6th Pursuit Squadron
      16 x P-40B, 1 x P-26A, 1 x P-26B
    19th Pursuit Squadron
      15 x P-40B, 2 x P-40C
    44th Pursuit Squadron
      9 x P-40B, 7 x P-40C, 2 x P-26A, 2 x P-26B
    73rd Pursuit Squadron
      13 x P-40B, 1 x P-26B
    Other aircraft
      2 x AT-6, 2 x OA-9

Endnotes

Prologue: Dawn at Pearl

1   Bergamini, *Japan's Imperial Conspiracy*, p. 843.

Chapter 1: The Rising Sun

1   The bulletin was read at approximately 2:25 PM Eastern Standard Time during radio station WOR's broadcast of an NFL football game between the New York Giants and the Brooklyn Dodgers at the Polo Grounds. The bulletin itself came from the CBS radio network.

2   *"Dai Nippon"*—literally "Great Japan," used in much the same way that the British Isles have been known as "Great Britain."

3   This narrative follows the traditional structure for Japanese personal names, that is, the first name recorded is the family name, the second is the person's given name.

4   Geoffrey Regan, "The Battle of Tsushima 1905," *The Guinness Book of Decisive Battles*, p. 178.

5   Howarth, *Fighting Ships of the Rising Sun*, p. 152.

6   Bergamini, pp. 725–727.

7   Prange, *December 7, 1941*, p. 209.

Chapter 2: The Sleeping Giant

1   Fromkin, "Entangling Alliances."

2   "The Monroe Doctrine," The Avalon Project.

3   Borah quoted in John Milton Cooper, *Breaking the Heart of the World: Woodrow Wilson and the Fight for the League of Nations* (Cambridge: Cambridge University Press, Reprint 2010), p. 357.

4   "The Immigration Act of 1924 [The Johnson-Reed Act]," US Department of State, Office of the Historian.

5   The sheer scale and complexity of the Great Depression encourages oversimplification, which usually does more harm than good; with that in mind, the author wishes to direct the reader's attention to the fact that the Depression *per se* is, obviously, outside the scope of this work, aside from its immediate and direct effects of Japanese–American diplomacy and each nation's respective foreign and military policies. A reader seeking to learn more about the Depression, especially how it came about, will find the following two works of inestimable value in unraveling the tangled threads of causes and effects: Ben Shalom Bernanke, *Essays on the Great Depression* (Princeton, NJ: Princeton University Press, 2004); and Milton Friedman and Anna J. Schwartz, *A Monetary History of the United States, 1867–1960* (Princeton, NJ: Princeton University Press, 1963).

6   United States Department of State, *Papers Relating to the Foreign Relations of the United States, Japan: 1931–1941*, Volume I, p. 76.

7   Stimson and Bundy, *On Active Service in Peace and War*, pp. 277–278.

8   Despite sharing the same surname, Smedley Butler and the author are not related.

9   Folsom and Folsom, *FDR Goes to War*, p. 17.

10 "Proclamation 2348—Neutrality of the United States," The American Presidency Project.

11 "Fireside Chat, September 3, 1939," The American Presidency Project.

12 George W. Baer, *One Hundred Years of Sea Power*, p. 167.

Chapter 3: Men, Ships, Planes, and Plans

1   Bergamini, pp. 774–775.

2   Hoyt, *Yamamoto*, p. 30.

3   *Banzai* was a verbal shorthand for "Long live His Majesty the Emperor!" that was the Army and Navy's battle cry.

4   Smith, *The Great Ships,* pp. 37–38.

5   Ibid, p. 37.

6   Craig Nelson, p. 55.

7   University of Wyoming, Admiral Husband E. Kimmel Collection, Microfilm Roll 4.

8   Hoyt, *Yamamoto*, p. 101.

9   Hiroyuki Agawa, p. 189.

10 In 1901, the six senior military academies were: The United States Military Academy (West Point); Norwich College; Virginia Military Academy; The Citadel; Texas Agricultural and Mechanical College (now Texas A&M University); and North Georgia Agricultural College (now the University of North Georgia).

11 Congressional Investigation, Part 33, pp. 926–985. The full text of the War Department's Operations Plan RAINBOW 5 was entered into Investigation's record as Exhibit 4.

12 Prange et al, *At Dawn We Slept*, p. 122.

13 George C. Marshall, pp. 411–414.

14 John D. Correll, "Rendezvous with the *Rex*," *Air Force Magazine*, December 2016, p. 57.

15 Wesley Frank Craven and James Lea Cate, *Army Air Forces in World War II: Volume 1—Plans and Early Operations, January 1939 to August 1942* (Washington, DC: Air Historical Group, Office of Air Force History, United States Air Force, 1948), p. 292.

16 Yamamoto quoted in Prange, *At Dawn We Slept*, pp. 11–12.

17 After the war, the chief of staff of the Combined Fleet, Vice Admiral Fukudome Shigeru, stated that Yamamoto first discussed an attack on Pearl Harbor as early as March or April 1940.

18 Reynolds, p. 232.

19 Nofi, pp. 166–167.

Chapter 4: MAGIC and the Color Purple

1   Kahn, *The Reader of Gentlemen's Mail*, p. 98. Some historians maintain that Stimson's remark—and subsequent reaction—were triggered by the revelation that the Black Chamber was routinely reading the diplomatic signals sent to and from the Vatican: Stimson made his comment and then stalked from the room immediately after being told of this.

2   Kahn, *The Reader of Gentlemen's Mail*, p. 62.

3   What could rightly be considered MAGIC's finest moments came in 1943 and 1944, when the Japanese envoy to Berlin, Baron Oshima Hiroshi, used his PURPLE machine to make regular reports to Tokyo about the state of the German war effort. Highly regarded by Adolf Hitler, Oshima

was made privy to some incredibly sensitive information, particularly the details of the Atlantic War defenses in France and the Low Countries, intelligence that, as soon as Oshima's messages were decrypted, was immediately forwarded to the officers planning Operation OVERLORD, the amphibious invasion of western Europe. Even after the Allies had successfully landed in Normandy, Oshima still performed a valuable service: the Allies had conducted an incredibly complex cover and deception operation, called FORTITUDE, designed to lead the Germans into believing that the Normandy landings were a feint and that the "real" invasion would take place further up the coast, at the Pas de Calais. Oshima's reports to Tokyo, when read by Allied cryptographers, established conclusively that the deception had succeeded and that the Germans were giving priority to the defenses on the wrong beaches. It can be said that MAGIC redeemed itself by helping make possible the Allied success on June 6, 1944.

4 One of the core arguments in the myth that the United States government, and President Roosevelt in particular, had foreknowledge of Japan's planned attack on Pearl Harbor has always been the claim that the Americans were "reading the Japanese codes." The rationalization is that if one Japanese encryption system was broken, all of them must have been broken. Unfortunately those who subscribe to this belief fail to make the distinction between a code and a cipher, and do not understand that PURPLE was a cipher and JN-25 (and its revisions) was a code, which meant that the two were completely unrelated —access to one did not grant or even aid in gaining access to the other. As a rule, those who cling, limpet-like, to the foreknowledge theory also fail—or worse, simply refuse—to recognize the significance of the fact that before the attack on December 7, 1941, only 10 percent of the traffic transmitted in JN-25a was readable. The 10 percent figure is often rejected by revisionists, most vocally by Robert Stinnett in *Day of Deceit* (The Free Press, 1997), who allege that there is evidence indicating that some OP-20-G documents were altered during or after the war and are thus unreliable, and the entire body of documentary evidence must be regarded as unreliable. The perceptive reader will immediately recognize the logical fallacy of the hasty generalization—along with the intellectual laziness that produced it—and react accordingly.

5 Safford quoted in Carlson, p. 131.

6 Zacharias quoted in Farago, p. 45.

7 *Joint Congressional Committee on the Investigation of the Pearl Harbor Attack*, referenced hereafter as "Congressional Investigation," Part 8, p. 3395.

8 Layton characterized in a speech given by Captain Forrest Biard USN (Ret) to the National Cryptologic Museum Foundation.

9 Congressional Investigation, Part 26, p. 235.

10 Prange *et al*, *At Dawn We Slept*, 329.

11 Congressional Investigation, Part 35, p. 355.

12 Prange *et al*, *At Dawn We Slept*, p. 75.

13 Congressional Investigation, Part 35, p. 531.

14 Samuel Eliot Morison, *The Rising Sun in the Pacific, 1931–April 1942,* p. 63.

15 Congressional Investigation, Part 10, pp. 4845–4846.

16 Ibid, Part 4, p. 1861.

17 Ibid, Part 4, p. 1862.

Chapter 5: "Climb Mount Niitaka"

1 Robert Goralski, *World War II Almanac 1931–1945*, p. 135.

2 Prange *et al.*, *At Dawn We Slept*, p. 24.

3 Ibid, pp. 20, 22.

4 Excellent, concise overviews and assessments of the planning for the Pearl Harbor attack can be found in a pair of papers prepared for the United States Air Force Air Command and Staff College: Major Robert Isaman's "Pearl Harbor: Strategy and Principles of War" (Report No. 85-1305, April 1985); and Major William Walters' "Pearl Harbor—A Study in the Application of the Principles of War" (Report No. 84-2705, April 1984).

5 Prange *et al.*, *At Dawn We Slept*, p. 16.

6 Ibid, p. 11.

7 Ibid, p. 340.

8 Department of State Bulletin, December 20, 1941. Initially put forward by Hull on April 16, 1941, these four principles would be reiterated by Roosevelt himself on September 6.

9 Cordell Hull, *The Memoirs of Cordell Hull*. vol 2, p. 1000; Yagami Kazuo, *Konoe Fumimaro*, p. 111.

10 Congressional Investigation, Part 29, p. 2309.

11 The American Presidency Project https://www.presidency.ucsb.edu/node/209779

12 University of Virginia Law Library, The Tavenner Papers & IMTFE Official Records, Box 26, Miscellaneous Documents on Japanese Nationalism and Militarism, Box 26, "Miscellaneous" Folder.

13 "Memorandum on Armaments", Yamamoto, 7 January 1941, quoted in James William Morley, ed., *The Final Confrontation: Japan's Negotiations with the United States 1941* (New York, NY: W. W. Norton, 1996), p. 273.

14 Congressional Investigation, Part 12, p. 261.

15 Ibid, Part 6, pp. 2542–2543.

16 Department of State Bulletin, Vol. V, No. 129, December 13, 1941.

17 Ibid.

18 Ibid.

19 Congressional Investigation, Part 11, p. 5424.

20 Ibid, Part 14, p. 1406.

21 Gannon, *Pearl Harbor Betrayed*, p. 189.

Chapter 6: *"To-ra! To-ra! To-ra!"*

1 Prange *et al.*, *At Dawn We Slept*, p. 487.

2 Fuchida, "I Led the Air Attack on Pearl Harbor," US Naval Institute Proceedings, p. 945.

3 Ibid, p. 944.

4 John W. Dower, *Cultures of War: Pearl Harbor / Hiroshima / 9-11 / Iraq* (New York, NY: W. W. Norton & Company, Reprint edition 2011), p. 53.

5 Prange *et al.*, *At Dawn We* Slept, p. 488.

6 Walter Lord, *Day of Infamy* (New York, NY: Henry Holt, 1957), p. 33.

7 Department of State Bulletin, Vol. V, No. 129, December 13, 1941.

8 Congressional Investigation, Part 8, pp. 3392–3393, 3907; Part 33, p. 858

9 Ibid, Part 2, p. 933.

10 Ibid, Part 29, p. 2309; Part 9, p. 4518.

11 Ibid, Part 5, pp. 2132–2133.

12 Ibid, Part 13, p. 1334.

13 For more than 60 years, *Ward*'s attack on the midget submarine, known variously as the *Type A No. 20*, *HA-20*, and *I-20tou* ("*tou*" is "tube" in Japanese, one of the code names for the midget subs which the crews adopted as the type's nickname), that sank the submersible was regarded

only as "unconfirmed," "possible," or "probable." Absolute confirmation finally came on August 28, 2002, when a research team from the University of Hawaii found the almost intact *I-20tou* in 1,300 feet of water just a few miles from the position where the action with *Ward* had taken place. The only significant damage found apart from some minor hull deformation caused by settling on the bottom was a shell hole found in the starboard side of the conning tower and a corresponding hole on the bottom of the submersible; there was no evidence of depth charge damage, which was not surprising, as *Ward*'s depth charges had been set to go off at 35 feet and the midget sub was on the surface when the charges were rolled. Flooding caused by the shell holes slowly filled *I-20tou* until she sank to the bottom, while drifting away from the site where the engagement with *Ward* took place. The bodies of Ensign Hiroo Akira and Petty Officer Katayama Yoshio are still inside *I-20tou*'s hull.

14 Log of USS *Ward* for December 7, 1941; Congressional Investigation, Part 36, pp. 56–57; Part 37, p. 704.

15 Wilfred D. Burke, "Remembering Pearl Harbor," *Saga*, December 1981, pp. 14–15.

16 Meg Jones, *World War II Milwaukee* (Mt. Pleasant, SC: The History Press, 2015), p. 30.

17 Congressional Investigation, Part 22, p. 499.

18 Ibid, Part 32, p. 444; Prange *et al.*, *At Dawn We Slept*, p. 497.

19 Ibid, Part 23, p. 1193.

20 Stephen Young, *Trapped at Pearl Harbor: Escape from Battleship Oklahoma*, pp. 128–129.

21 Prange *et al.*, *At Dawn We Slept*, pp. 501–502.

22 Congressional Investigation, Part 22, p. 223; Part 27, pp. 531–532, 568, 569

23 It is widely if erroneously believed that what the wireless operator was sending was "Tiger! Tiger! Tiger!" as the word *tora* means "tiger" in Japanese, but in this case what was being sent was the first syllables of the words *totsugeki raigeki*, which together mean "lightning attack."

Chapter 7: "THIS IS NOT DRILL!"

1 Somewhere between December 7, 1941, and the present day, someone decided that the phrase "Not drill" was a typographical error, and revised it to "No drill." "Not drill" is the correct wording, and is also the correct naval terminology for the time.

2 Lord, *Day of Infamy*, p. 63

3 Ibid, p. 65.

4 Bill McWilliams, *Sunday in Hell: Pearl Harbor Minute by Minute*, p. 561.

5 Morrison, *The Two Ocean War*, p. 58.

6 Michael Gannon, *Pearl Harbor Betrayed: The True Story of a Man and a Nation Under Attack*, pp. 238–239.

7 Prange *et al.*, *At Dawn We Slept*, p. 508.

8 "Eyewitnesses to Pearl Harbor," *WWII History Magazine*, December 6, 2016.

9 Prange *et al.*, *At Dawn We Slept*, p. 509; Lord, *Day of Infamy*, p. 68.

10 Commander Roscoe Hillenkoetter, Action Report for 7 December 1941.

11 Ricketts, his Action Report for 7 December 1941.

12 "Eyewitnesses to Pearl Harbor."

13 Lieutenant Commander John Adams, Action Report for 7 December 1941.

14 Prange, *At Dawn We Slept*, p. 470.

15 Lord, *Day of Infamy*, p. 91.

16 Congressional Investigation, part 23, pp. 723–724.

17 Fuchida, "I Led the Air Attack on Pearl Harbor," *Proceedings*, pp. 948–949.

18 Henry C. Woodrum, "Cloak of Darkness," *Aerospace Historian*, December 1988, p. 282.

19 Burke, "Remembering Pearl Harbor," pp. 17–19.

20 W. Hoover, "This Pilot was Caught on the Ground," *The Sunday Star-Bulletin & Advertiser*, December 7, 1986, p. A-18.

21 Nelson, *Pearl Harbor*, pp. 223–224.

22 Prange *et al.*, *December 7, 1941: The Day the Japanese Attacked Pearl Harbor*, pp. 188, 193, 293; Michael Slackman, *Target: Pearl Harbor*, p. 130.

23 Blake Clark, *Remember Pearl Harbor!*, p. 40.

Chapter 8: "A Devastating Sight…"

1   James Bounds, in an interview with Parks Stephenson, *I-16tou.com*; Young, *Trapped At Pearl Harbor*, p. 49.

2   Hobby in *Eyewitness to Infamy*, p. 170.

3   For more than a half-century, it was believed that four bombs directly hit *Arizona*. John De Virgilio conducted a series of underwater examinations of the wreck in the 1990s, specifically to measure the dimensions of holes punched in *Arizona*'s upper decks, and found that only two were large enough to have been created by the impact of a Type 99 bomb—the others were exit holes created by debris and wreckage, along with fragments of 5-inch shells set off in sympathetic detonation, blown out of the ship by the powder magazine explosion. Re-examination of what were believed to be the other two hits has shown that they were, in fact, very close misses. Given what was happening at the time, and that less than a minute separated the hit aft from the hit forward that destroyed the ship, it's understandable that witnesses' memories would be imperfect and people would make errors in what they believed they saw happen.

4   Artis Teer, interview, January 10, 1977, University of North Texas.

5   Donald Stratton and Ken Gire, *All the Gallant Men*, p. 128.

6   James Cory, interview, December 21,1976, University of North Texas.

7   Joy Waldron Jasper *et al.*, *The USS* Arizona, pp. 106–109.

8   Fuchida quoted in Stillwell, p. 13.

9   Lord, *Day of Infamy*, pp. 73, 92.

10 It is often recounted that *Oklahoma* capsized before *Arizona* exploded, but this is incorrect. On board the hospital ship *Solace*, an army physician, Dr. Eric Haakenson, who was visiting Navy colleagues at the time, used a hand-held 8mm movie camera to film the attack. Purely by chance he happened to be filming *Arizona* when her magazine exploded. A frame-by-frame examination of the footage clearly shows that when the explosion took place, *Oklahoma* is listing at roughly a 30-degree angle to port. Her tripod mainmast is clearly visible: of the battleships moored along Battleship Row that morning, only *Oklahoma*, *Nevada*, and *Arizona* carried tripod masts. *Nevada* was astern of *Arizona*, meaning that there can be no mistake that the mast visible in the movie film belongs to *Oklahoma*.

11 Keith Rogers, "Looking Back on 1941." *Las Vegas Review-Journal*, December 7, 2008.

12 Ibid.

13 *Pittsburgh Courier*, March 14, 1942.

14 Diary of Ensign George Hunter, USS *West Virginia* website.

15 "Eyewitnesses to Pearl Harbor."

16 Ibid.

17 Prange *et al*, *At Dawn We Slept*, p. 514.

18 Lord, *Day of Infamy*, p. 87.

Chapter 9: Inferno

1 John Craddock, *First Shot*, pp. 188–189.
2 Peter Collier, *Medal of Honor: Portraits of Valor Beyond the Call of Duty* (New York, NY: Workman Publishing Company, 2006), p. 83.
3 "George Walters—Pearl Harbor Crane Operator" (Obituary), *Honolulu Star-Bulletin*, March 2, 1999.
4 Lord, *Day of Infamy*, p. 138.
5 Gannon, *Pearl Harbor Betrayed*, p. 245.
6 Prange *et al*, *At Dawn We Slept*, p. 546.
7 John Toland, *Infamy: Pearl Harbor and Its Aftermath* (New York, NY: Doubleday, 1983), p. 22; Prange, *At Dawn We Slept*, p. 516.

Chapter 10: Shock and Awe

1 Edwin T. Layton *et al*. *And I was There*, p. 314.
2 Congressional Investigation, Part 8, pp. 3835–38.
3 Prange *et al*, *At Dawn We Slept*, pp. 541–543.
4 Ibid, p. 543.
5 Lord, *Day of Infamy*, p. 186.
6 Robert F. Dorr, *Air Combat: An Oral History of Fighter Pilots*, p. 11; Lord, *Day of Infamy*, p. 186.
7 Layton *et al.*, *And I Was There*, p. 317.
8 Congressional Investigation, Part 13, p. 1334.
9 Nelson, *Pearl Harbor*, p. 330.
10 Ian W. Toll, *Pacific Crucible: War at Sea in the Pacific 1941–1942* (New York, NY: W. W. Norton and Company, 2012), p. 18.
11 Hixon, *The American Experience in World War II: Pearl Harbor in History and Memory*, p. 268.
12 Agawa, *The Reluctant Admiral*, p. 259.

Chapter 11: Retribution…

1 http://www.presidency.ucsb.edu.
2 Jonathan Parshall and Anthony Tully, *Shattered Sword: The Untold Story of the Battle of Midway* (Sterling, VA: Potomac Books, 2011), p. 62.
3 Layton, *et al.*, *And I Was There*, pg. 430.
4 Prange *et al.*, *Miracle at Midway* (New York, NY: Penguin Books, 1982), p. 190.
5 The commanding officer of VMSB-241 was Marine Major Lofton R. Henderson. He would be immortalized in military history, and especially the lore of the United States Marine Corps, in August 1942, when the Marines on Guadalcanal named the island's vital airstrip "Henderson Field" in his honor.
6 Prange *et al.*, *Miracle at Midway*, p. 206.
7 Ibid, p. 239.
8 Ibid, p. 238.
9 Craig L. Symonds, *The Battle of Midway*, p. 240.
10 Ibid, p. 243.
11 Fuchida Mitsuo, *Midway: The Battle that Doomed Japan*, p. 176–177.
12 William Manchester, *Goodbye*, p. 42.

13 Prange *et al.*, *Miracle*, p. 276.
14 Ibid., p. 288.
15 Parshall and Tully, *Shattered Sword*, p. 353.

Chapter 12: …and Reckoning

1 Quoted in the *Asahi Shimbun* (*"Morning Sun Newspaper"*), Tokyo, August 18, 1945.
2 Clausewitz, *On War*, p. 79.
3 Congressional Investigation, Part 25, p. 1756.
4 Ibid.
5 Congressional Investigation, Exhibit Number 144, p. 4.
6 Congressional Investigation, Exhibit Number 157, p. 321.
7 Gannon, *Pearl Harbor Betrayed*, p. 282.
8 It's worth pointing out that for many, if not most, seamen a ship's boilers and engines are considered its heart and soul, so what at first blush may seem to have been a bit of bureaucratic sleight-of-hand by the US Navy in giving the names *Cassin* and *Downes* along with their pennant numbers to a pair of newly built hulls was in fact a reflection of the truth that they were the same ships.

Bibliography and Sources

Books

Agawa, Hiroyuki. *The Reluctant Admiral: Yamamoto and the Imperial Navy*, trans. John Bester. Japan: Kodansha International, 2000.

Anderson, Charles Robert. *Day of Lightning, Years of Scorn: Walter C. Short and the Attack on Pearl Harbor*. Annapolis, MD: Naval Institute Press, 2005.

Arakaki, Leatrice R. and John R. Kuborn. *7 December 1941: The Air Force Story*. Honolulu, HI: University Press of the Pacific, 1991.

Baer, George W. *One Hundred Years of Sea Power: The U.S. Navy, 1890–1990*. Palo Alto, CA: Stanford University Press, 1996.

Barnhart, Michael A. *Japan Prepares for Total War: The Search for Economic Security, 1919–1941*. Ithaca, NY: Cornell University Press, 1987.

Beach, Edward L. *Scapegoats: A Defense of Kimmel and Short*. Annapolis, MD: Naval Institute Press, 1995.

Bergamini, David. *Japan's Imperial Conspiracy*. New York, NY: William Morrow and Co., 1971.

Bix, Herbert P. *Hirohito and the Making of Modern Japan*. New York, NY: Harper Collins, 2000.

Borch, Frederic L. and Daniel Martinez. *Kimmel, Short, and Pearl Harbor: The Final Report Revealed*. Annapolis, MD: Naval Institute Press, 2005.

Brown, Robert J. *Manipulating the Ether: The Power of Broadcast Radio in Thirties America*. Jefferson, NC: McFarland, 1998.

Burlingame, Burl. *Advance Force Pearl Harbor*. Annapolis, MD: Naval Institute Press, 1992.

Carlson, Elliot. *Joe Rochefort's War: The Odyssey of the Codebreaker Who Outwitted Yamamoto*. Annapolis, MD: Naval Institute Press, Reprint edition 2013.

Chang, Iris. *The Rape of Nanking: The Forgotten Holocaust of World War II*. New York, NY: Penguin Books, 1998.

Clark, Blake. *Remember Pearl Harbor!* New York, NY: Harper Brothers, 1942.

Clausen, Henry C. and Bruce Lee. *Pearl Harbor: Final Judgment*. New York, NY: HarperCollins, 2001.

Clausewitz, Karl von. *On War*. Edited and translated by Michael Howard and Peter Paret. Princeton, NJ: Princeton University Press, 1989.

Collier, Peter. *Medal of Honor: Portraits of Valor Beyond the Call of Duty*. New York, NY: Workman Publishing Company, 2006.

Connaughton, R. M. *The War of the Rising Sun and the Tumbling Bear—A Military History of the Russo-Japanese War 1904–5*. London: Cassell, 1988.

Cooper, John Milton. *Breaking the Heart of the World: Woodrow Wilson and the Fight for the League of Nations*. Cambridge: Cambridge University Press, Reprint 2010.

Craddock, John. *First Shot: The Untold Story of the Japanese Minisubs That Attacked Pearl Harbor*. Camden, ME: International Marine—Ragged Mountain Press, 2006.

Craven, Wesley Frank and James Lea Cate. *Army Air Forces in World War II: Volume 1—Plans and Early Operations, January 1939 to August 1942*. Washington, DC: Air Historical Group, Office of Air Force History, United States Air Force, 1948.

Dorr, Robert F. *Air Combat: An Oral History of Fighter Pilots*. New York, NY: Berkley/Penguin, 2006.

Dower, John W. *Cultures of War: Pearl Harbor / Hiroshima / 9-11 / Iraq*. New York, NY: W. W. Norton & Company, Reprint edition 2011.

Drea, Edward. *MacArthur's Ultra: Codebreaking and the War Against Japan, 1942–1945*. Lawrence, KS: University Press of Kansas, 1993.

Ericson, Steven and Allen Hockley, eds. *The Treaty of Portsmouth and Its Legacies*. Lebanon, NH: Dartmouth College Press, 2008.

Farago, Ladislas. *The Broken Seal*. New York, NY: Random House, 1968.

Feis, Herbert. *The Road to Pearl Harbor*. Princeton, NJ: Princeton University Press, 1950.

Felker, Craig C. *Testing American Sea Power: U.S. Navy Strategic Exercises, 1923–1940*. College Station, TX: Texas A&M University Press, 2007.

Fish, Hamilton III. *Tragic Deception: FDR and America's Involvement in World War II*. Old Greenwich, CT: Devin-Adair Publishing, 1983.

Folsom, Burton W. and Anita Folsom. *FDR Goes to War: How Expanded Executive Power, Spiraling National Debt, and Restricted Civil Liberties Shaped Wartime America*. New York, NY: Simon and Schuster, 2011.

Friedman, George and Meredith Lebard. *The Coming War with Japan*. New York, NY: St Martin's Press, 1991.

Fuchida, Mitsuo. *Midway: The Battle that Doomed Japan* (revised edition). Annapolis, MD: Naval Institute Press, 2001.

Gailey, Harry A. *War in the Pacific: From Pearl Harbor to Tokyo Bay*. Novato, CA: Presidio Press, 1997.

Gannon, Michael. *Pearl Harbor Betrayed: The True Story of a Man and a Nation Under Attack*. New York, NY: Henry Holt, 2001.

Goldstein, Donald M. and Katherine V. Dillon., eds. *The Pearl Harbor Papers: Inside the Japanese Plans*. Dulles, VA: Brassey's, 2000.

Goralski, Robert. *World War II Almanac 1931–1945: A Political and Military Record*. New York, NY: Perigee Books, 1981.

Haufler, Herve. *Codebreaker's Victory: How the Allied Cryptographers Won World War II*. New York, NY: New American Library, 2003.

Higham, Robin and Stephen Harris. *Why Air Forces Fail: The Anatomy of Defeat*. Lexington, KY: The University Press of Kentucky, 2006.

Hixson, Walter L., ed. *The American Experience in World War II: Pearl Harbor in History and Memory*. London: Taylor & Francis, 2003.

_____. *The American Experience in World War II: The United States and the Road to War in Europe*. London: Taylor & Francis, 2003.

Holmes, W. J. *Double-Edged Secrets: U.S. Naval Intelligence Operations in the Pacific During World War II*. Annapolis, MD: Naval Institute Press, 1979.

Howarth, Stephen. *The Fighting Ships of the Rising Sun*. New York, NY: Atheneum Books, 1983.

Hoyt, Edwin P. *Yamamoto: The Man who Planned Pearl Harbor*. New York, NY: McGraw-Hill, 1990.

_____. *Pearl Harbor*. New York, NY: G. K. Hall, 2000.

Hughes-Wilson, John. *Military Intelligence Blunders and Cover-Ups*. New York, NY: Robinson Publishing, 1999 (revised 2004).

Hull, Cordell. *The Memoirs of Cordell Hull*, (2 vols.). Andrew Henry Thomas Berding, editor. London: Hodder & Stoughton, 1948.

Jansen, Marius. *The Making of Modern Japan*. Harvard, MA: Harvard University Press, 2002.

Jasper, Joy Waldron, James P. Delgado, and Jim Adams. *The USS Arizona: The Ship, the Men, the Pearl Harbor Attack, and the Symbol*. New York, NY: St. Martin's Paperbacks, 2003.

Jones, Meg. *World War II Milwaukee*. Mt. Pleasant, SC: The History Press, 2015.

Kahn, David. *The Codebreakers*. London: Sphere Books, 1973.

_____. *The Reader of Gentlemen's Mail: Herbert O. Yardley and the Birth of American Codebreaking.* New Haven, CT: Yale University Press, 2004.

Kimmett, Larry and Margaret Regis. *The Attack on Pearl Harbor: An Illustrated History.* Bellingham, WA: NavPublishing, 2004.

Kotani, Ken. *Japanese Intelligence in World War II*, trans. Chirharu Kotani. Oxford: Osprey Publishing, 2009.

Lambert, Jack and Norman Polmar. *Defenseless, Command Failure at Pearl Harbor.* Minneapolis, MN: MBI Publishing, 2003.

Layton, Edwin T., Roger Pineau, and John Costello. *And I Was There: Pearl Harbor and Midway— Breaking the Secrets.* New York, NY: William Morrow and Co., 1985.

Lord, Walter. *Day of Infamy.* New York, NY: Henry Holt, 1957.

Madsen, Daniel. *Resurrection-Salvaging the Battle Fleet at Pearl Harbor.* Annapolis, MD: Naval Institute Press, 2003.

Manchester, William. *Goodbye, Darkness.* Boston, MA: Little, Brown and Company, 1980.

Marshall, George C. *The Papers of George Catlett Marshall, Volume 2, "We Cannot Delay," July 1, 1939–December 6, 1941.* Baltimore, MD and London: The Johns Hopkins University Press, 1986.

McWilliams, Bill. *Sunday in Hell: Pearl Harbor Minute by Minute.* New York, NY: Open Road Media, 2014.

Morison, Samuel Eliot. *The Rising Sun in the Pacific, 1931–April 1942: History of United States Naval Operations in World War II, Volume 3 (History of United States Naval Operations in World War II).* Annapolis, MD: Naval Institute Press, Reprint edition 2010.

_____. *The Two Ocean War—A Short History of the United States Navy in the Second World War.* New York, NY: Little, Brown, 1989.

Morley, James William, ed. *The Final Confrontation: Japan's Negotiations with the United States 1941.* New York, NY: W. W. Norton, 1996.

Nelson, Craig. *Pearl Harbor: From Infamy to Greatness.* New York, NY: Simon and Schuster, 2017.

Nofi, Albert. *To Train the Fleet for War: The U.S. Navy Fleet Problems, 1923–1940.* Newport, RI: Naval War College Press, 2010.

Paine, S. C. M. *The Sino-Japanese War of 1894–1895: Perceptions, Power, and Primacy.* Cambridge: Cambridge University Press, 2003.

Parker, Frederick D. *Pearl Harbor Revisited: United States Navy Communications Intelligence 1924–1941.* Ft. George G. Meade, MD: Center for Cryptologic History, 1994.

Parshall, Jonathan and Anthony Tully. *Shattered Sword: The Untold Story of the Battle of Midway.* Sterling, VA: Potomac Books, 2011.

Peattie, Mark. *Sunburst: The Rise of Japanese Naval Air Power, 1909–1941.* Annapolis, MD: Naval Institute Press, 2001.

Peattie, Mark R. and David C. Evans. *Kaigun: Strategy, Tactics, and Technology in the Imperial Japanese Navy.* Annapolis, MD: Naval Institute Press, 1997.

Pérez, Louis A. *Cuba in the American Imagination: Metaphor and the Imperial Ethos.* Chapel Hill, NC: UNC Press Books, 2008.

Prange, Gordon W. with Donald M. Goldstein and Katherine V. Dillon. *At Dawn We Slept: The Untold Story of Pearl Harbor.* New York, NY: McGraw-Hill, 1981.

_____. *Miracle at Midway.* New York, NY: Penguin Books, 1982.

_____. *Pearl Harbor: The Verdict of History.* New York, NY: McGraw-Hill, 1986.

_____. *December 7, 1941: The Day the Japanese Attacked Pearl Harbor.* New York, NY: McGraw-Hill, 1988.

Regan, Geoffrey. "The Battle of Tsushima 1905," *The Guinness Book of Decisive Battles*, edited by Geoffrey Regan. London, UJ: Guinness Publishing, 1992.

Reynolds, Clark G. *Admiral John H. Towers: The Struggle for Naval Air Supremacy.* Annapolis, MD: Naval Institute Press, 1991.

Schencking, J. Charles. *Making Waves: Politics, Propaganda, and the Emergence of the Imperial Japanese Navy, 1868–1922.* Palo Alto, CA: Stanford University Press, 2005.

Slackman, Michael. *Target: Pearl Harbor.* Honolulu, HI: University of Hawaii Press, 1990.

Smith, Carl. *Pearl Harbor 1941: The Day of Infamy,* Osprey Campaign Series #62. Oxford: Osprey Publishing, 1999.

Smith, Peter C. *The Great Ships: British Battleships in World War II.* Mechanicsburg, PA: Stackpole Books, 2008.

Stille, Mark E. *Tora! Tora! Tora!: Pearl Harbor 1941,* Osprey Raid Series #26, Oxford: Osprey Publishing, 1999.

Stillwell, Paul, ed. *Air Raid, Pearl Harbor!: Recollections of a Day of Infamy.* Annapolis, MD: Naval Institute Press, 1981.

Stimson, Henry L. and McGeorge Bundy. *On Active Services In Peace And War.* New York, NY: Harper and Brothers, 1948.

Stratton, Donald and Ken Gire. *All the Gallant Men: An American Sailor's Firsthand Account of Pearl Harbor.* New York, NY: William Morrow, 2016.

Symonds, Craig L. *The Battle of Midway.* Oxford: Oxford University Press, 2018.

Takeo, Iguchi. *Demystifying Pearl Harbor: A New Perspective From Japan.* Tokyo: I-House Press, 2010.

Thomas, Evan. *Sea of Thunder: Four Commanders and the Last Great Naval Campaign 1941–1945.* New York, NY: Simon and Schuster, 2007.

Toland, John. *Infamy: Pearl Harbor and Its Aftermath.* New York, NY: Doubleday, 1983.

Toll, Ian W. *Pacific Crucible: War at Sea in the Pacific 1941–1942.* New York, NY: W. W. Norton and Company, 2012.

Travers, Paul Joseph. Eyewitness to *Infamy: An Oral History of Pearl Harbor, December 7, 1941.* Guilford, CT: Lyons Press, 2016.

van der Wat, Dan. *Pacific Campaign: The U.S.-Japanese Naval War 1941–1945.* New York, NY: Simon and Schuster, 1992.

Walder, David. *The Short Victorious War: The Russo-Japanese Conflict, 1904–5.* New York, NY: Harper & Row, 1974.

Warner, Denis and Peggy Warner. *The Tide at Sunrise, A History of the Russo-Japanese War 1904–1905.* London: Routledge, 1975.

Wetzler, Peter. *Hirohito and War: Imperial Tradition and Military Decision Making in Prewar Japan.* Honolulu, HI: University of Hawaii Press, 1998.

Willmott, H. P. *The Barrier and the Javelin: Japanese and Allied Pacific Strategies, February to June 1942.* Annapolis, MD: Naval Institute Press 1983.

Wohlstetter, Roberta. *Pearl Harbor: Warning and Decision.* Palo Alto, CA: Stanford University Press, 1962.

Yagami Kazuo. *Konoe Fumimaro and the Failure of Peace in Japan, 1937–1941: A Critical Appraisal of the Three-time Prime Minister.* Jefferson, NC: McFarland and Company, 2006.

Young, Stephen. *Trapped at Pearl Harbor: Escape from Battleship Oklahoma.* New York, NY: North River Press, 1991.

Zimm, Alan D. *Attack on Pearl Harbor: Strategy, Combat, Myths, Deceptions.* Havertown, PA: Casemate Publishing, 2011.

Periodicals

Asahi Shimbun (*"Morning Sun Newspaper"*), Tokyo, August 18, 1945.

Altimari, Daniela. "He Didn't Expect To Make It Home." *The Hartford Courant,* May 27, 2002.

Burke, Wilfred D. "Remembering Pearl Harbor." *Saga,* December 1981.

Correll, John D. "Rendezvous with the *Rex*." *Air Force Magazine*, December 2016.

Condon-Rall, Mary Ellen. "The U.S. Army Medical Department and the Attack on Pearl Harbor." *The Journal of Medical History*, January 1989.

Fromkin, David. "Entangling Alliances." *Foreign Affairs*, July 1970.

Fuchida Mitsuo. "I Led the Air Attack on Pearl Harbor." *US Naval Institute Proceedings*, September 1952.

Hoover, W. "This Pilot was Caught on the Ground." *The Sunday Star-Bulletin & Advertiser*, December 7, 1986.

Rodgaard, John, Peter Hsu, Carroll Lucas, and Captain Andrew Biach. "Pearl Harbor—Attack from Below." *Naval History*, United States Naval Institute, December 1999.

Rogers, Keith. "Looking Back on 1941." *Las Vegas Review-Journal*, December 7, 2008.

Woodrum, Henry C. "Cloak of Darkness." *Aerospace Historian*, December 1988.

"Eyewitnesses to Pearl Harbor." *WWII History Magazine*, December 6, 2016.

"George Walters—Pearl Harbor Crane Operator." (Obituary) *Honolulu Star-Bulletin*, March 2, 1999.

"Mess Attendant Turned Machine Gun on Japanese." *Pittsburgh Courier*, March 14, 1942.

United States Government Documents

United States Air Force Air Command and Staff College: Major Robert Isaman. "Pearl Harbor: Strategy and Principles of War." Report No. 85-1305, April 1985.

United States Air Force Air Command and Staff College: Major William Walters' "Pearl Harbor—A Study in the Application of the Principles of War." Report No. 84-2705, April 1984.

United States Congress. *Joint Congressional Committee on the Investigation of the Pearl Harbor Attack*. 79th Congress, 40 parts. Washington DC: United States Government Printing Office, 1946.

United States Department of State. *Department of State Bulletin*, Vol. V, No. 129, December 13, 1941. Washington DC: Government Printing Office, 1945.

United States Department of State. *Department of State Bulletin*, Vol. V, No. 129, December 20, 1941. Washington DC: Government Printing Office, 1945.

United States Department of State, *The Immigration Act of 1924* [The Johnson-Reed Act], Washington DC: Government Printing Office, 1924.

United States Department of State. *Papers Relating to the Foreign Relations of the United States, Japan: 1931–1941*. Volume I. Washington DC: United States Government Printing Office, 1931–1941.

United States Department of State. *U.S. Department of State, Publication 1983, Peace and War, United States Foreign Policy 1931–1941*. Washington, DC: Government Printing Office, 1943.

United States Navy. *U.S. Navy Report of Japanese Raid on Pearl Harbor*. Washington, DC: United States National Archives, Modern Military Branch, 1942, archived from the original on January 13, 2008.

Miscellaneous Sources

Naval History and Heritage Command

Adams, John. "Action Report, USS *Tennessee*, 7 December 1941." http://www.ibiblio.org/hyperwar, retrieved April 2, 2016.

Hillenkoetter, Roscoe. "Action Report, USS *West Virginia*, 7 December 1941." http://www.ibiblio.org/hyperwar, retrieved March 22, 2016.

NavSource Naval History. "Organization of the Japanese Air Attack Units December 7, 1941," http://www.navsource.org, retrieved December 8, 2019.

Ricketts, Claude. "Action Report, USS *West Virginia*, 7 December 1941." http://www.ibiblio.org/hyperwar, retrieved March 22, 2016.

The American Presidency Project. "Address to Congress Requesting a Declaration of War with Japan," https://www.presidency.ucsb.edu, retrieved June 28, 2016.

_____. "Executive Order 8832—Freezing Japanese and Chinese Assets in the United States," http://www.presidency.ucsb.edu, retrieved May 30, 2016.

_____. "Fireside Chat, September 3, 1939," http://www.presidency.ucsb.edu, retrieved April 20, 2016.

_____. "Proclamation 2348—Neutrality of the United States," http://www.presidency.ucsb.edu, retrieved May 7, 2016.

The Avalon Project. "The Monroe Doctrine,", http://avalon.law.yale.edu/19th_century/monroe.asp, retrieved July 12, 2016.

University of North Texas Oral History Collection. Number 355: "Interview with Artis Teer, January 10, 1977."

_____. Number 356: "Interview with James Cory, December 21, 1976."

USS *Shaw*, destroyerhistory.org, archived from the original on June 17, 2011, retrieved January 5, 2016.

Wallin, Homer N. "Pearl Harbor: Why, How, Fleet Salvage and Final Appraisal", http://www.ibiblio.org/hyperwar

retrieved October 15, 2017.

University of Virginia Law Library, The Tavenner Papers & IMTFE Official Records, Box 26, Miscellaneous Documents on Japanese Nationalism and Militarism.

University of Wyoming. Admiral Husband E. Kimmel Collection, Roll 4.

USS *West Virginia* Website. Diary of Ensign George Hunter, usswestvirgini.org/stories/, retrieved January 24, 2016.

Index